Dyslexia, Dyspraxia and Mathematics

Dorian Y

Emerson F

W
WHURR PUBLISHERS
LONDON AND PHILADELPHIA

© 2003 Whurr Publishers

First published 2003 by
Whurr Publishers Ltd
19b Compton Terrace, London N1 2UN, England
325 Chestnut Street, Philadelphia PA19106, USA
Reprinted 2003

British Library Cataloguing in Publication Data

A catalogue record for this book is available from the British
Library.

ISBN 1 86156 323 X

Printed and bound in the UK by CPI Antony Rowe, Eastbourne

Contents

Part IV More Addition and Subtraction: Working with Larger Numbers

Part V Multiplication and Division

Foreword

Education is never still. There are constant changes and developments. Some of these enhance our knowledge of how children learn and thus how they can be taught most effectively. Some are merely cosmetic where the only increase in output is in administration. This book takes a proud place in the first category.

Our awareness of the diversity of special needs has increased greatly over the past thirty years. For example the term 'specific learning difficulties' was once promoted as the preferred term for 'dyslexia'. Now we are aware of a cluster of specific learning difficulties, including dyspraxia.

Awareness of a learning difficulty is a good start, but it can result in stereotypical concepts and inadequate and inappropriate interventions. What Dorian Yeo has done in this book is to extend awareness to understanding and has then set the understanding of the *individual* within sound, clearly and thoroughly explained underlying principles.

Before the publication of this book there was a great need for material for the younger learner and for the dyspraxic learner. It is fascinating to see the comparisons between the problems experienced by dyslexic learners and dyspraxic learners. There seem to be more similarities than differences, which will not come as a surprise to those who work in special education. As important as this observation is, the realisation that good intervention for special needs is good intervention for all learners is even more important. Few learners (if any) are perfect, so this too should not be a surprise.

This book is about good practice. To paraphrase Professor Tim Miles, this good practice will help all learners, but it is an essential for dyspraxic and dyslexic learners.

Dorian Yeo's book is written from deep personal understanding and knowledge, but not from knowledge built on a sample of one, but of many similar yet diverse pupils. It combines a comprehensive explanation of the difficulties young children experience when learning numeracy with many practical, structured and developmental ideas for teaching. It has been a privilege to see Dorian's vision become reality.

Steve Chinn
August 2002

Preface

Emerson House is a small and intensive specialist teaching and learning centre which caters for the core learning needs of dyslexic and dyspraxic primary school children. When I established the maths department at the rapidly growing Emerson House some years ago, I already knew that many dyslexic children did not learn maths as easily as the majority of 'ordinary' children did. I had also discovered, through experience, that access to concrete materials could make a difference to the performance of dyslexic children. In the early days, however, I assumed that children with specific learning difficulties simply needed more practice – with concrete support – in order to make progress in learning the aspects of maths which they found hard. From working with our children and our teachers in a questioning way, I discovered that 'overlearning', however patiently orchestrated, was often not enough. Inspired by Steve Chinn and Richard Ashcroft's work with secondary school pupils, I realized that we needed to know more about how young children make sense of numbers and why some children – and dyslexic and dyspraxic children, in particular – can find the early stages of working with numbers so difficult. As we began to change aspects of how we taught maths at Emerson House, we realized that our most important task was to set out to make the foundations of number-work as simple, clear and easily understood as possible. In this book I have set out to describe the teaching ideas which have made a difference to the happiness, confidence, progress and attitude towards maths of the children whom we have taught.

I would like to thank Jane Emerson for the support and encouragement which she has always given me.

Dedication

For my husband, Dudley, and for my children, Lisa, Claire and Russell. Also for my sister, Kay, who, like me, survived; and for my brother, mother and father who did not.

PART I

Definitions and Premises

CHAPTER 1

Background information

Introduction

This is a book which sets out to explore how primary school dyslexic and dyspraxic children with varying degrees of maths learning difficulties understand and learn maths. It discusses a number of important ideas about some of the cognitive features which seem to underlie general maths learning difficulties or which may underlie difficulties learning specific aspects of maths, such as the *times tables* facts. It outlines the ways in which children usually learn the foundation aspects of maths and considers the special cognitive needs of dyslexic and dyspraxic children in this context. It aims to offer practical support and detailed teaching suggestions to teachers, tutors and parents who wish to help dyslexic or dyspraxic children make real and sustained progress in learning maths.

The book has grown out of the experience of teaching maths to primary school dyslexic and dyspraxic children, aged from about 6½ years upwards. From the outset the shape of this experience has been profoundly influenced by the work of Steve Chinn and by Steve Chinn and Richard Ashcroft's seminal and forward-looking book, *Mathematics for Dyslexics: A Teaching Handbook* (1998). Above all, the experience has been driven by the conviction, based on experience, and directly expressed in *Mathematics for Dyslexics*, that to teach maths well to children with specific learning difficulties, 'a different attitude and approach is needed' (Chinn and Ashcroft, 1998, p. 1).

In the challenging and ongoing process of further developing and refining 'a different attitude and approach' which aims to meet the needs of younger primary school dyslexic and dyspraxic children, there have been a number of other important sources and influences. It has, of course, been possible to draw on the available research into 'dyslexia specific' maths difficulties and, in particular, into their difficulties with memorized *times tables* facts. There are also valuable teaching-based accounts of the ways in which many of the underlying cognitive difficulties associated with dyslexia seem to affect the maths learning abilities of dyslexic children. Such accounts include those of Chinn and Ashcroft (1998), Henderson (1989; 1998), Henderson and Miles (2001) and Miles and Miles (1992). However, as Steve Chinn frequently points out, there is a disappointingly limited body of research and a relatively limited range of literature exploring themes related to dyslexia and maths learning. In particular, there is very little consideration of the typical learning profiles and particular learning needs of young primary school dyslexic and dyspraxic children.

In recent years, on the other hand, there has been an explosion of research into how 'ordinary' young children make sense of numbers. Many studies set out to explore the ways in which children come to learn about, and make progress in, the crucial foundation stages of number-work. These studies have practical implications for how these 'building block' areas of maths are best taught. Furthermore, a number of contemporary researchers are interested in understanding the maths behaviours of the small numbers of children who can be found in any maths classroom who have difficulty making sense of numbers and who fail to make progress in number-work from the very earliest stages of mathematics. This contemporary research provides many illuminating insights into the maths learning profiles of primary school dyslexic and dyspraxic children. In particular, as we will see, the work of Karen Fuson and her colleagues in the US, Ian Thompson, Eddie Gray and Judith Anghileri, in the UK, and the work of the contemporary generation of Realistic Education proponents in The Netherlands have shaped many aspects of the 'attitude and approach' to teaching maths which are described in the book.

More general but illuminating books by Brian Butterworth (1999) and Stanislas Dehaene (1997) – both of which set out to explore the anthropological and biological bases of our knowledge of numbers – have also influenced some of the key discussions. In particular, I am indebted to Brian Butterworth's very clear account of the structure of the number system and to Dehaene's suggestive ideas about the *times tables*. I have also tried to make a layperson's sense of their neuroscientific contribution towards understanding why and how we know about numbers in the first place and make some brief and tentative suggestions about what their studies and accounts of 'maths in the brain' seems to suggest about maths learning difficulties.

Which pupils does the book cater for?

Dyslexia, Dyspraxia and Mathematics explores ways of helping primary school dyslexic and dyspraxic children acquire a sound foundation in all of the key numeracy aspects of maths. Although many dyspraxic children also have difficulty with the non-number, spatial aspects of maths, these difficulties have not been addressed in this book.

In the last decade, or so, it has been increasingly widely accepted that a substantial proportion of dyslexic children have at least some difficulties learning the basic number aspects of maths. In recent years, as more children are diagnosed as belonging to the dyspraxic side of the specific learning difficulties spectrum, many teachers, educational psychologists and parents are finding that a very substantial proportion of young dyspraxic children have difficulties with number-work, too.

It is often noted that it is hard to generalize about the maths learning abilities and difficulties of dyslexic children. As Chinn and Ashcroft write,

> many dyslexics have difficulty in at least some aspects of mathematics, but this is not necessarily in all aspects of mathematics. Indeed, some dyslexics are gifted problem solvers, despite persisting difficulties in, for example, rote learning of facts. (1998, p. 14)

Some researchers, for example Steeves (1983) and Miles and Miles (1992) have found that a number of dyslexics are broadly gifted in most aspects of maths and informal reports from teachers and parents seem to confirm Steeves's and Miles and Miles's finding.

Unfortunately there appears to be no detailed published research on the maths abilities of children who have been formally diagnosed as dyspraxic. Standard ability measures used by educational psychologists show that dyspraxic children are often weak at maths. Teachers report that a great many of the dyspraxic children in their classrooms have difficulties with the numeracy aspects of maths. Diagnostic assessments and teaching experience show that dyspraxic children with high verbal scores and with long-term and working-memory strengths frequently do well in the routine, procedural aspects of maths. However teachers report that a great many of the dyspraxic children whom they teach have severe problems in the very earliest stages of maths and that most dyspraxic children have serious word-problem-solving, 'number-puzzle'-solving, and pattern-solving weaknesses which persist throughout their primary school careers.

Although it is hard to generalize about the maths abilities of dyslexic children, as we have noted, it is well documented and widely acknowledged that dyslexic children who show some ability in the numeracy aspects of maths nevertheless often have marked difficulty with two of the foundation aspects of number-work: dyslexic children typically have difficulty remembering exact maths facts, such as the *times tables* facts, and (like many dyspraxic children) dyslexic children also have difficulty with the *place value* conventions of the written number system. This book addresses these seemingly 'dyslexia-typical' and 'dyspraxia-typical' weaknesses and offers practical teaching suggestions which will help children in these areas.

While the available literature has offered a fairly clear picture of the number-related 'gaps' which can be described as 'dyslexia-typical' behaviours, it has been less widely acknowledged that some dyslexic children, and many dyspraxic children, have difficulties with number-work which are really very deep-seated and profound and which seem to go back to the very earliest stages of making sense of numbers. In fact, classroom teachers report that a sizeable proportion of dyslexic and dyspraxic children have quite severe all-round (global) maths learning difficulties. It is this group of children – the children who fail to make progress from the earliest stages of learning about numbers onwards – whom classroom teachers and parents are often most concerned about. It is also quite typically this group of children who do not seem to respond to 'ordinary' additional maths tuition and who seem to require 'specialist' understanding and help. This book sets out to examine the better understood 'typical' dyslexic and dyspraxic maths learning difficulties. It also sets out to begin charting the maths-learning profiles and apparent learning needs of the hitherto rather neglected group of dyslexic primary school maths learners who appear to have longstanding difficulties with all aspects of number-work and who can be described as children with very significant maths learning difficulties. As we will see later, these are also the children who are sometimes labelled *dyscalculic*.

Recent changes in maths teaching and a consideration of present-day maths learning situations

In broad maths educational terms this is an exciting but also potentially confusing time to be thinking about maths teaching and learning. In the wake of the explosion of research into how young children understand and learn about numbers, which was briefly mentioned above, far-reaching educational reforms have been introduced into primary school maths classrooms in many parts of the Western European world, including in the UK. The radical National Numeracy Strategy Framework was implemented in English state school classrooms in September 1999.

In general terms, many of the recent maths education reforms have been largely positive ones for dyslexic and dyspraxic maths learners. Influential contemporary maths educationalists, including Chinn and Ashcroft, have campaigned for a long time for some of the changes which have been enshrined in the Numeracy Strategy Report and in the Numeracy Strategy Framework. For instance, in reaction to the understood shortcomings of traditional maths teaching, the Numeracy Strategy, like most other newer maths teaching approaches, sets out to try and help children make genuine sense of mathematics. Instead of expecting that children simply learn facts and procedures solely *by heart*, or through rote 'drill', there is an emphasis on helping children understand logical principles, important concepts, and underlying patterns and structures. In keeping with this, there is a far greater emphasis on 'mental' mathematics, in general, and on logic-based and numeracy-friendly, informal ways of calculating.

The contemporary ideas about maths learning, together with the reforms they have inspired, have not, however, affected all primary school children in the UK in the same measure. The maths educational 'map' of what actually happens on the ground in maths classrooms is quite complex at present. While state-sector classrooms in England follow the Numeracy Strategy guidelines, the Numeracy Strategy has not been implemented in Scotland, Wales or Northern Ireland; and although Scotland and Wales have instituted their own maths teaching reforms, maths continues to be taught in quite traditional ways in Northern Ireland. Furthermore, private-sector schools in England are not bound to implement the National Numeracy Strategy.

In fact, the maths educational picture in private-sector schools in England is particularly complex and would seem to be in a state of flux at present. On one hand, it is evident that the Numeracy Strategy has had ripple effects on maths teaching in a number of private schools: for example, the teaching ideals, goals and recommendations of the Numeracy Strategy have shaped the ways that recent maths textbooks and schemes have been designed, and the Numeracy Strategy has also informed the content of the standardized maths National Curriculum Tests. Some head teachers and heads of maths departments in private schools have actively welcomed changes in maths teaching practices, and have looked favourably on the impetus towards reform – in particular, on the greater weight accorded in newer maths teaching approaches to *mental maths*. On the other hand, it is also evident that a considerable number of private schools have continued to teach maths in largely unchanged, traditional ways. Many private schools continue to use older teaching methods, textbooks and materials, and many private schools also place greater weight on the results of hitherto more traditional 'Common Entrance' maths papers (or similar papers) than they do on the reform-based goals of the National Curriculum tests.

In the context of this book, it is of course the learning needs – and therefore the teaching requirements – of dyslexic and dyspraxic children which is the paramount consideration. Although the teaching issues are extremely complex (and some of the complexities will be explored, later on) it is also important to give an overview perspective on the ways in which different approaches to maths teaching and learning can affect the ability of dyslexic and dyspraxic children to make progress in learning maths.

On one hand, as we will see, and as Steve Chinn has frequently demonstrated, the memory requirements of traditional maths approaches create broadly *unfavourable* maths learning environments for dyslexic and dyspraxic maths learners and contribute to the severe difficulties that most dyslexic and dyspraxic children experience in the majority of traditional maths classrooms. The complex memory difficulties, which are commonly associated with dyslexia and dyspraxia, and which affect maths learning, will be explored in greater detail later on. In brief, however, traditional maths approaches require that maths facts are acquired through rote learning with little emphasis on the inter-relationships between facts. A good proportion of maths learning time is devoted to memorizing standard calculation procedures in columns. Learning the standard procedures depends on a good visual memory and a very good memory for sequential sets of instructions.

On the other hand, institutionalized, progressive approaches to teaching maths, such as that embodied in the Numeracy Strategy, create potentially *favourable* environments for dyslexic and dyspraxic children to learn maths. As suggested above, most of the principles and goals which lie behind recent maths reforms are principles and goals which apply, in essence, to dyslexic and dyspraxic maths learners, too. However, the cognitive weaknesses associated with dyslexia and dyspraxia, and the severity of the weaknesses affecting individual children, also influence the degree to which dyslexic and dyspraxic children are able to make progress in mainstream maths teaching approaches – approaches which are, in the main, designed to cater for the learning needs of 'ordinary' young children. It is perhaps not surprising that the progress of dyslexic and dyspraxic children in, for example, Numeracy Strategy classrooms has been somewhat mixed to date. On the one hand teachers report that although maths fact acquisition continues to be an area of difficulty for most dyslexic children, more mathematically able dyslexic and dyspraxic are generally enjoying maths and are making good progress within the framework of the relatively flexible, pattern and logic-based approach to learning maths which characterizes the Numeracy Strategy. On the other hand, there have been more worrying reports that some children with specific learning difficulties – generally children who are found to have moderate to severe maths learning difficulties – are not faring particularly well in classrooms which are guided by the Numeracy Strategy approach. Indeed, since 1999 it has become increasingly clear that a significant number of dyslexic and dyspraxic children – together with other children who find maths learning difficult – are not making expected progress in otherwise successful state school classrooms. Many educationalists, teachers, and support teachers have recognized that if all dyslexic and dyspraxic children are to be helped to make the best possible progress in learning mathematics some teaching practices will have to be modified to take account of the number-related learning needs which dyslexic and dyspraxic children may have.

To sum up: Steve Chinn, and Steve Chinn and Richard Ashcroft, have convincingly shown that traditional maths teaching approaches do not suit the learning needs of the vast majority of dyslexic children. They have pioneered the argument, in the UK, that children with specific learning difficulties need to be taught in such as way that they are able to understand all aspects of the maths they are learning and that they need to be taught to reason effectively instead of being expected to rote learn facts and procedures. They have passionately fought for open-minded and flexible maths classroom environments. Contemporary progressive maths approaches, such as that of the Numeracy Strategy, share many of the maths teaching and learning ideals and principles for which Chinn and Ashcroft have campaigned. However overview assessments of children's progress at the primary school level shows that the particular maths learning needs of a great many dyslexic and dyspraxic children seem to require a degree of special consideration. This book is inspired by the aim of describing an understanding-based approach to teaching the numeracy aspects of primary school maths which also takes into account the special cognitive features of dyslexic and dyspraxic primary school children.

Basic definitions and important features associated with dyslexia and dyspraxia

While there can be marked cognitive and behavioural differences between *classic dyslexic* and *classic dyspraxic* learners, the distinctions are often harder to make in practice. As Madeline Portwood (2000) clearly explains, there is a very significant degree of overlap or comorbidity between different specific learning difficulties, such as dyslexia and dyspraxia. Madeline Portwood explains further that dyslexia and dyspraxia can also be comorbid with attention deficit disorders (ADD and ADHD) and Asperger's syndrome. From the point of view of this book this means that many children will have both dyslexic and dyspraxic cognitive and learning features. Dyslexia and dyspraxia also share a number of important learning-related characteristics, as we will see. This partly explains why so many classic dyspraxic learners have been diagnosed as dyslexic in the past.

Nevertheless it is important to acknowledge that *classic dyslexia* and *classic dyspraxia* are associated with some widely divergent weaknesses and strengths. The brief descriptions of dyslexia and dyspraxia, which follow, draw attention to some key differences and some of the key similarities in the cognitive profiles of dyslexic and dyspraxic children.

'Classic dyslexia'

Basic definitions of dyslexia usually centre on the difficulties which dyslexics experience in processing the symbolic aspects of language. Dyslexic children have difficulty learning to read and spell in large part because they have difficulty mapping segments of sound (phonemes) on to written symbols (graphemes). Some dyslexics have difficulties with phoneme awareness or the initial discrimination of sounds. Many dyslexic children have language acquisition, word finding or semantic (meaning-related) difficulties. Underlying cognitive weaknesses associated with dyslexia include: poor long-term verbal memory; poor working memory; poor sequencing skills and sequential memory; difficulties with auditory and/or visual perception and memory; and poor left/right discrimination. Because dyslexia is so strongly associated with difficulties to do with processing symbols, *standardized assessment profiles* which are administered by educational psychologists – for example, the Wechsler Intelligence Scales or WISC – tend to show depressed *verbal* scores in relation to overall *intelligence* and *performance* (non-verbal) stores. In terms of very broad brain function, dyslexia is often broadly characterized as a tendency towards general left-hemispheric weakness. On the other hand, the *performance* scores of many dyslexic individuals show strengths in spatial or visuo-spatial areas. Such strengths, 'which may contribute to outstanding creative skills' (L. Peer in Smythe, 2000, p. 67), are sometimes said to be the 'compensatory gift' of dyslexia. Although some *classic dyslexics* do not have exceptionally strong *performance* skills, dyslexia is associated, generally speaking, with a tendency towards relative right hemispheric strengths in the brain (Portwood, 2000).

'Classic dyspraxia'

In essence, dyspraxia is associated with motor co-ordination difficulties – often with gross and fine motor co-ordination difficulties – and with percep-tual and spatial-perceptual weaknesses. According to Portwood (2000, p. 26) all dyspraxics have 'co-ordination difficulties' and the vast majority 'show significant perceptual problems' (p. 26). Additional weaknesses associated with dyspraxia include: left/right confusion; poor tactile percep-tual skills; poor hand–eye co-ordination; poor working memory; poor visual memory; poor sequencing skills; poor short-term visual or auditory memory; poor verbal memory; poor memory for verbal instructions; and finger agnosia (loss of 'finger sense' or an intuitive knowledge of the fingers). Standardized assessments of dyspraxics classically show depressed *perfor-mance* scores. They also show that 'on average verbal scores are higher than performance.' (Portwood, 2000, p. 47). In terms of hemispheric dominance this means that dyspraxia can be associated with a tendency towards right hemispheric weakness or 'immaturity' and with relative left hemispheric strength. In this regard it is worth noting that classic dyspraxia is not always associated with significant difficulties with learning to read although it is often associated with significant spelling difficulties.

Some cognitive weaknesses which dyslexic and dyspraxic children commonly share and which can affect maths learning

It is, of course, vital to acknowledge that each individual dyslexic or dyspraxic child will bring 'different combinations of strengths and weaknesses' to maths and that, as we have seen, there are 'enormous varia-tions' in maths abilities among individual children with specific learning difficulties (Chinn and Ashcroft, 1998, p. 5). However, it is also vital to be aware of what one might call 'the big picture' in the relationship between specific learning difficulties and maths learning difficulties. Before we go on to explore some of the significant ways in which dyslexic and dyspraxic learners can diverge in terms of how they process number tasks, it is important to start out by outlining some of the significant underlying learning constraints which a great many dyslexic and dyspraxic children have in common.

Poor long-term memory in maths learning

It is widely documented that dyslexic and dyspraxic children have difficulty automatizing maths facts and maths procedures – in other words, dyslexic and dyspraxic children have difficulty recalling number facts (such as subtraction facts, or multiplication facts) or the way to 'do sums'. As we will see, working memory weaknesses and sequencing difficulties contribute to many of the long-term memory difficulties which dyslexic and dyspraxic children experience in maths. In addition to this, as Miles and Miles (1992) and Chinn and Ashcroft (1998) have shown, the majority of dyslexic children find it a 'frustrating exercise' to learn verbally encoded facts (Chinn and Ashcroft, 1998, p. 68) and find it almost impossible to recall many of them 'in one'. Over and over again it is commented on that dyslexic children, and many dyspraxic children, fail to learn facts easily in the form of pure verbal associations. This has a disastrous impact on *times tables* learning, as we will see.

Poor working memory

Working memory weaknesses impact on maths learning in at least two key ways. First of all, most aspects of working with numbers, from basic counting onwards, are linear or step-by-step processes which involve holding several pieces of information in working memory at the same time. Children with learning difficulties often lose track of what they are doing, forget what the initial task was or forget the teacher's instructions. 'What was the sum again?' is a classic 'dyslexic' or 'dyspraxic' question. As Chinn and Ashcroft (1998, p. 8) explain,

> The pupil may not be able to 'hold' the visual image of the sum he is trying to solve. He may not be able to hold the sum in visual or auditory memory while he searches for a necessary number fact.

As number-work becomes more demanding, a greater number of elements need to be held in working memory at once. At the most obvious level, poor working memory affects the child's speed of thinking and calculating and, indeed, working in general in maths.

Secondly, memory weaknesses contribute to long-term memory difficulties and vice versa. The relationship between working memory and long-term memory is obviously complex, but, generally speaking, it would appear that in order for number information to enter long-term memory, working memory processes need to be relatively efficient. According to Ashcraft et al, the working memory has a limited capacity. In Eddie Gray's (1997) useful and succinct formulation, for information to enter long-term memory, in maths, it is important that the *input*, or question, and the *output*, or the answer to the question, are close together. In simple terms, poor working memory, or lengthy working memory processes, mean that number information is less likely to enter long-term memory. As we will see, sequencing difficulties contribute significantly to working memory difficulties in number-work, and ultimately – in a vicious cycle of cause and effect – to long-term memory difficulties. On the other hand, Ashcraft et al. (1996, p. 195) argue that long-term memory weaknesses (poor fact and procedure retrieval) contribute to working memory problems: long-term memory weaknesses drain processing resources or capacity from the 'executive' or managing component of the working memory in another complex cycle in which it is hard to disentangle cause and effect. In simple terms, limited working memory resources are 'drained' when children have to spend time trying to work out facts or trying to remember procedures and, once again, the ultimate outcome, or the steps of the procedure, are not remembered in the long-term.

Ashcraft et al. also maintain that maths anxiety affects the efficient functioning of working memory. We will touch on the theme of anxiety towards the end of this chapter, but one of Ashcraft et al.'s (1996, p. 193) significant suggestions is that anxiety causes 'intrusive thoughts and worry' to drain working memory resources. Hence Ashcraft et al. believe that maths anxiety affects cognitive functioning in maths tasks and therefore affects overall maths learning in a direct way. Chinn and Ashcroft (1998) and Henderson (1989, 1998) have noted that dyslexic children are often anxious about specific aspects of maths, such as the *tables* facts or division, and that some dyslexic children are anxious about maths in general. They show that many dyslexic and dyspraxic children are not confident enough to 'have a go' at answering 'challenging' maths questions: 'no attempt' errors contribute significantly to the poor scores which are commonly attained by dyslexic and dyspraxic pupils in maths assessments. Many parents of dyslexic and dyspraxic children volunteer that their children are anxious about maths. In diagnostic assessments of primary school dyslexic and dyspraxic children more than 70 per cent of the children assessed stated that they 'hated' maths.

Sequencing problems

The broad label *sequencing problems* covers a number of complexly interrelated areas:

1. *Counting and the number system* Very early on, from the beginning stages of learning how to count, children have to make sense of, and have to learn to use, complex sequences of number words. As we will see, the ability to count also involves mapping words on to sequences of objects. Remembering sequences of words and seeing patterns within these sequences is a crucial aspect of learning to understand the complex structures of the number system. Many dyslexic and dyspraxic children learn to count later than their peers and fail to understand the structures of the number system. In consequence they have difficulty *decoding* large numbers and have problems solving mental and written large number calculations.

2. *Counting in number-work* As we will also see, much of early number-work is bound up with quite lengthy sequences of counting, for example, in *counting on* in addition, and in *counting back* in subtraction. Difficulty managing counting sequences, and especially 'backwards' sequences, impacts on working memory efficiency and on the automatization of facts.

3. *Sequences of instructions* It is widely noted that many dyslexic and dyspraxic children have difficulty remembering sequences of verbal instructions. All larger number calculations involve completing a sequence of steps. The familiar standard calculation methods are usually taught 'procedurally' or as a series of verbal instructions – 'first, you do this, next you do this, next you do this, then you ...' Standard methods are consequently particularly difficult for dyslexic and dyspraxic children to learn. The newer mental calculation methods are generally relatively easy to understand and do not require to be taught in 'recipe-like' ways. However, a number of teachers do, in fact, resort to teaching mental methods as rote-learned verbal routines: this happens, in particular, when teachers wish children to learn a number of different mental methods for specific operations.

Directional confusion

Although *directional confusion* can simply mean that young children muddle written digits, for example '2' and '6', directional difficulties usually become particularly significant when two-digit numbers need to be read, or decoded, and written or encoded. As we will see, the fact that the number system is structurally different in the crucial second decade between 10 and 20 means that many children become confused about which digit in a two-digit number to say or write first. These 'normal' difficulties are compounded if children confuse direction or 'position.' Directional confusion can mean that children who know that the larger value is usually read or written first may sometimes still be confused about what 'first' means in positional terms – in 'left/right' terminology a child may suddenly flounder as to whether 'first' means left or right.

Directional confusion can have particularly devastating consequences if children are taught column-based methods of multi-digit calculation from the outset. As we will see, column-based methods of addition and subtraction begin from the right whereas numbers, words and sentences are read from the left. As Chinn and Ashcroft point out, the starting point for the standard division algorithm, which is on the left, can upset children's hard-won and overlearned 'right-to-left in calculation' response. In 'borrowing' in standard subtraction procedures, children have to move left and right and left in extremely taxing ways. Finally, the 'crossover' directional demands of formal long multiplication and the across-and-step-down demands of formal long division methods contribute to the difficulties which many dyslexic and dyspraxic children experience in trying to reproduce the standard ways of executing calculations.

Speed of working in oral and written work

Madeline Portwood (2000) suggests that the neurological immaturities ('wiring immaturities'), which may contribute to dyslexia and dyspraxia, mean that children with learning difficulties tend to be slow to process incoming information. Even when maths information has been lodged in long-term memory, many dyslexic and dyspraxic children take longer to access this stored information. It is often noted that an over-emphasis on requiring dyslexic or dyspraxic children to give quick answers to maths facts questions, or to figure out mental calculations rapidly, has the effect of undermining the dyslexic or dyspraxic child's ability to think. Of course working memory difficulties, attention deficits and anxiety all compound delays in processing and retrieving information. As Chinn and Ashcroft argue, this often has the further result that children with learning difficulties complete written work more slowly and complete less work than their peers. This, in turn, can mean that children may not reach more challenging examples in written exercises or may fail to reach, and therefore have the opportunity to work through, certain exercises altogether.

Poor ability to generalize in mathematics: a weak basic number-concept

In an early analysis of the maths profiles of dyslexic learners, Joffe (1983b) observed that many dyslexic pupils do not easily generalize the knowledge they have acquired in number-work. In supporting this statement, Chinn and Ashcroft (1992, p. 98) say, 'in our experience of teaching dyslexics we have observed another handicapping factor: a poor ability to generalize and classify facts and rules in mathematics'. They go on to say that, in their experience, many of their secondary school students view maths 'as an amorphous, disjointed mixture of facts, rules and methods. Although they can understand these parts in isolation, they frequently have difficulty in mastering the interrelationships and cross generalizations.' These broad generalizations apply to many dyslexic and dyspraxic primary school children, too. It is often observed that primary school dyslexic and dyspraxic children can be particularly rigid and inflexible in their thinking and that they tend to see numbers and calculations in *linear*, action based, and rather tunnel-like ways.

As we will see, inflexibility in working with numbers at a primary school level usually springs from what is increasingly called poor *number sense* and a related weak basic *number concept*. In essence this means that children view numbers and calculations in primitive ones-based ways. Fuson, Wearne, Hiebert et al. (1997) call a ones-based number concept a *unitary* concept of numbers. An over-reliance on counting in *ones* and an inability to see patterns and connections means that it is hard for children to develop the broader, flexible understandings in number-work which underpin the ability to make links with other aspects of number-work. As Ashcraft et al. (1996) and Gray (1997) suggest, this is in large part because children who are weak at maths use calculation methods (mainly counting) which place very big demands on working memory. Instead of developing increasingly complex webs of understanding, many dyslexic and dyspraxic children tend to think along isolated calculation tracks. An impoverished understanding of numbers and number relationships (which underpins a poor generalizing ability) has enormous repercussions, the most important of which have been well documented:

1. A large number of number of dyslexic and dyspraxic children can complete calculations presented in familiar, easily recognizable, standard ways, but cannot cope with unfamiliar presentations, or challenging tasks.
2. Dyslexic and dyspraxic children often have difficulty understanding which operation is involved in mixed word-problem work.
3. In mental calculation work, dyslexic and dyspraxic children often fail to select an appropriate 'figuring out' fact derived strategy or mental calculation method. In many instances, some dyslexic and dyspraxic children 'may be so confused us to have no clues as to where to start' (Chinn and Ashcroft, 1998, p. 8).

Diverging strengths and weaknesses

An interesting dyslexic maths learning personality

Although a large proportion of dyslexics have poor fact recall it has long been noted – by, for example, Tim Miles, Chinn and Ashcroft, and Anne Henderson – that a significant number of dyslexic children are good at the 'thinking', conceptual, or problem-solving aspects of mathematics. Teaching experience confirms that some dyslexic children solve certain maths tasks spectacularly quickly and without appearing to do much calculation. While fact-retrieval difficulties can slow down their calculation some dyslexic children quickly grasp the principles of logico-mathematical (or 'thinking') calculation strategies. With the right support, some dyslexic children are able to invent ways of figuring out difficult calculations for themselves. On the other hand, it is also commonly noted that the innate mathematical 'flair' of these dyslexic children can be difficult for them to harness, particularly in more traditional maths classrooms. Typically, dyslexic children who are able 'thinkers' are not able to explain the methods that they used to solve calculations or word problems. Since they appear to be working intuitively, they often seem genuinely unable to record their methods in written 'workings' or recording. In part because their exact fact knowledge is limited, their answers are often inaccurate, too.

A consideration of the numeracy profiles of dyspraxic children

Unfortunately there is very little available detail about the 'typical' numeracy profiles of dyspraxic children and general comments and teachers' responses tend to be somewhat gloomy. As we have already seen, Portwood notes that the majority of dyspraxic children have significant difficulties learning maths. Studies of children with 'spatial weaknesses' indicate that poor spatial ability correlates with weaknesses in the very earliest stages of number-work. One interpretation of this is that very early number-work depends on physical counting activities, and objects are often hard for children with spatial difficulties to manipulate; concrete work is also hard for children with poor spatial ability to process and visualize (Carter, Crawley and Lewis, 1999a). As we have already noted, too, teachers consistently report that the majority of dyspraxic children struggle to understand concepts, logico-mathematical ways of reasoning (such as fact-derived strategies, or mental calculation methods), word problems and number puzzles. It is often commented on that dyspraxic children seem to be particularly rigid maths thinkers. While there are no references in the available literature on dyspraxia or in 'mainstream' maths learning literature to surprising areas of *ability* among dyspraxic maths learners, some dyspraxic children are able to do reasonably well in certain areas of maths. As we have suggested, this is largely because some dyspraxic children have strong verbal memory abilities. While it is not the case that all dyspraxic children master *times tables* as verbal associations, it would seem that a small but significant proportion of dyspraxic children are able to do so. We have already commented on the fact that some dyspraxic children are able to learn the routine, procedural aspects of maths, and are able to perform well in familiar calculation situations.

Ways of interpreting the very different maths learning personality possibilities among dyslexic and dyspraxic maths learners

Very crudely speaking, able dyslexic maths learners and (relatively) able dyspraxic maths learners seem to have abilities at opposite ends of the broad spectrum of numeracy requirements. In simple terms, a small number of dyslexic children have 'thinking' abilities in maths whereas most dyspraxic children find the 'thinking' aspects of maths especially hard to manage. On the other hand, a small number of dyspraxic children have verbal memory abilities in maths whereas the vast majority of dyslexic children cannot remember verbally encoded facts and procedures.

There are two bodies of research and theoretical insights from within separate research paradigms which help cast some light on these opposing areas of strength. The first body of work, made very familiar by Steve Chinn, and explored by Chinn with different dyslexic maths learning *styles* in mind, is work which investigates the two very different maths personality types – the *grasshoppers*, at one end of the learning continuum, and the *inchworms*, at the other end of the continuum. The second body of work draws on the research into the 'maths areas' of the brain undertaken by the neuroscientists Brian Butterworth and Stanislas Dehaene. From the outset it should be made clear that neither Butterworth nor Dehaene have as yet directly studied the maths processing areas of the brains of dyslexic and dyspraxic individuals. However, Butterworth's and Dehaene's broader discoveries about the specialist maths processing regions of the brain, which they are busy mapping out, appear to offer some help with interpreting the dyslexic *grasshopper* strengths, on the one hand, as well as the rather extreme 'thinking' weaknesses of severely dyspraxic children and the very extreme verbal memory weaknesses of dyslexic children, on the other hand.

Maths learning personalities: different learning styles in mathematics

Although the American-based mathematician and maths learning specialist, Mahesh Sharma, has pursued broadly parallel investigations of maths learning personalities in the US, the work of Chinn and Ashcroft builds mainly on the research of Bath and Knox in the UK into how secondary school dyslexic children actually 'do' maths. To represent the two very different cognitive styles or maths learning extremes at opposite ends of a maths learning continuum Sharma uses the terms *qualitative* and *quantitative* maths learning personalities. Chinn and Ashcroft prefer Bath and Knox's suggestive terms, *grasshopper* and *inchworm*, to characterize the cognitive styles of dyslexic maths learners. Chinn and Ashcroft suggest that the learner's cognitive style is informed by his or her overall learning style.

Over time, many adults who are involved in thinking about dyslexia have found the *grasshopper–inchworm* distinction helpful. In particular, the description of *grasshopper* characteristics has helped parents and teachers better understand the learning needs – basically the need for informed and flexible, reasoning based teaching – of *grasshopper* children. Although

Bath and Knox, and Chinn and Ashcroft are careful to point out that many dyslexic children display both *grasshopper* and *inchworm* characteristics and that there are children at both 'extremes of the continuum' (Chinn and Ashcroft, 1998, p. 23) there has been a popular tendency to exaggerate somewhat the numbers of *grasshopper* dyslexic children. Involvement with some hundreds of dyslexic primary school children over the years has confirmed Chinn and Ashcroft's view that, among dyslexic children, 'there are more inchworms than grasshoppers' (Chinn and Ashcroft, 1998, p. 23).

More detailed accounts of 'grasshoppers' and 'inchworms' can be found in Chinn and Ashcroft (1992; 1998) and in Chinn et al. (2001). It is important, however, to give an overview description of the characteristics of *grasshoppers* and *inchworms*. The research of Bath and Knox, Chinn and Ashcroft, and Chinn, shows that dyslexics at the *grasshopper* end of the continuum approach maths in a 'holistic', global, conceptual, and intuitive way. *Grasshopper* dyslexics start from an appraisal – often a mental image, or picture – of the whole. In other words, *grasshopper* dyslexics usually solve tasks in what might be described as a top-down way. *Grasshoppers* are often the inventive and creative thinkers and good problem solvers whom we described a moment ago. However, research also shows that dyslexic *grasshoppers* have poor knowledge of maths facts and often pay poor attention to detail. Although some *grasshopper* children are able to use their thinking skills to circumvent their maths facts difficulties, dyslexic *grasshoppers* can be vulnerable in maths, as Chinn and Ashcroft stress, because their intuitive understanding can be undermined by poor facts knowledge and working memory difficulties. Chinn et al.'s (2001) three-year study of adolescent *grasshopper* and *inchworm* dyslexics in three different countries confirms that secondary school *grasshoppers* do particularly well in 'open' and reasoning-based learning environments, such as Realistic Education classrooms in The Netherlands, and Mark College.

Dyslexic children with *inchworm* styles solve tasks in a piecemeal or bit by bit way. *Inchworm* dyslexics cannot overview or visualize maths tasks. Instead, they approach tasks from what they believe is the first step and proceed in a linear step-by-step way until they reach the end of the task. Because *inchworms* work in a laborious 'bottom-up' way and cannot picture problems they have no sense of what the outcomes of maths tasks are likely to be. As Sharma (1989a) points out, traditional maths teaching approaches reinforce *quantitative* or *inchworm* maths learning styles. Although literature searches have not yielded any research into the 'maths learning personalities' of dyspraxic children, teaching experience bears out that dyspraxic maths learners have much in common with descriptions of dyslexics whose learning styles are situated towards the *inchworm* extreme of the maths personality continuum.

Maths 'in the brain': a neurophysical paradigm

As we have seen, the study of the learning behaviour of maths pupils and of the behaviour of dyslexic pupils as a special category of maths learner has led to the helpful idea that maths personalities (or learning styles) can be analysed and categorized along a continuum between maths personality extremes. In very general terms it may be said that the starting point for the new and very exciting work of those neuroscientists who are interested in exploring maths 'in the brain' is to ask the underlying and most fundamental *why?* questions. Neuroscientists set out to go behind observable maths behaviours to try and understand the brain-related aspects of maths considered as a special knowledge domain.

In very recent years, the neuroscientists Brian Butterworth (1999) and Stanislas Dehaene et al. (1999) have used various research techniques to begin the process of locating the parts of the brain which are used in thinking about numbers and in calculation. The research methods include testing the responses of stroke patients to various number-related maths tasks and using MRI scanning or functional magnetic resonance imaging. Although Brian Butterworth and Stanislas Dehaene have slightly different ideas about where and how numbers are represented in the brain their research also has important features in common. First of all, the new neuroscientific research seems to show that an understanding of numbers, and most processing involving numbers, takes place in a special brain site which is a non-language area of the brain. Neuroscience seems to show that an understanding of numbers is not, in the first instance, a 'special aspect of language' and does not derive in the first instance (as Piaget believed) from 'more primitive logical concepts,' either (Butterworth, 1999, p. 166). In other words, many aspects of number processing are specialized and are language independent, although both language and logic are thought to be implicated in the process of learning some of the more complex aspects of any culture's accumulated maths knowledge. Secondly, and broadly speaking, Butterworth's and Dehaene's work confirms that the key area for understanding and working with numbers is situated in the *parietal lobes* of the brain – a non-language area of the brain. Overall, the research suggests that the parietal lobes of the brain are activated or involved in most numerical processes, but Dehaene

et al.'s (1999) brain imaging research also points to the particular importance of the parietal lobes for intuitive, visuo-spatial, and non-verbal ways
of representing numbers. It should be noted that the broader functions of
the parietal lobes include visuo-spatial processing, visually guided
hand–eye coordination, finger control and attention orientation (Dehaene
et al., 1999). Thirdly, Butterworth and Dehaene both believe that we have
very specialist brain circuits, which are inborn, or are at least present very
early, which represent an 'inner core' of number ability, and which underlie
all subsequent numerical development. Brian Butterworth (1999) calls this
core number area an 'inner core start-up kit' and, more specifically, 'The
Number Module'. Butterworth's research leads him to believe that this
core number area is in the left parietal lobe of the brain.

From a teaching point of view, Dehaene's further studies of where and
how a very distinctive aspect of *institutionalized* arithmetical knowledge –
namely, immediately known maths facts – are represented, is also of
particular value. Dehaene et al. (1999) brain-imaging research shows that
the knowledge of immediately recalled 'exact facts' seem to involve a
'language dependent mode' of representation. According to Dehaene, the
site in the brain of the language dependent number mode is in the left
hemisphere of the brain, in the left inferior frontal lobe. The particular
significance of this location is that the left inferior lobe is a part of the brain
which is known to be responsible for verbal associations, such as generating verbs for given nouns. Dehaene has also measured the response
times of bilingual students to maths facts questions: the response times
seemed to demonstrate that exact facts are generally stored by the brain
as 'verbal associations', and probably as 'exact sequences of words'.
According to Dehaene, the responses of students seem to show that 'exact
fact arithmetic' is typically represented in a language specific format and,
that where a language format is used, this 'transfers poorly to a different
language or to novel facts, and recruits networks involved in word association processes' (Dehaene et al., 1999, p. 970).

An overview of the maths personality and neuroscientific paradigms: some speculative thoughts

Dyslexics and maths facts

As we have seen, it is a characteristic feature of dyslexics that they have
difficulty recalling exact maths facts. In general terms, dyslexic children

appear to demonstrate broad left-hemispheric weaknesses. It seems possible that many dyslexics may have weaknesses of the left inferior frontal lobe. As we will see in Part V, it is striking that it is precisely the 'exact sequences of words' or 'verbal associations' that so many dyslexics fail to remember. Miles in Miles and Miles (1992, p. 2) referred to the dyslexic pupils' difficulty with maths facts as a difficulty with 'paired associate learning'.

Grasshopper dyslexics

Thus far, we have concentrated in the main on those dyslexic children who have maths learning difficulties. However, as we have also suggested, a proportion of dyslexic children (estimates vary between quite a small percentage, to about 50 per cent, depending on how 'difficulty' is defined) do not have any significant degree of difficulty learning maths. The neuro-scientific finding that numbers are largely processed in a non-language area is clearly significant in this regard. In other words, dyslexic children may have 'impairments' in language areas only or – and this will mean that the child is likely to have more 'global' maths learning difficulties – they may have impairments in language areas *and* in number areas of the brain. As we have just seen, research and teaching experience and informal accounts indicate that some dyslexics who have poor maths facts knowledge nevertheless also have intuitive and seemingly visuo-spatial maths insights. Chinn often suggests that *grasshopper* dyslexics may become more *grasshopper-like* to compensate for poor 'in one' maths facts knowl-edge. As we have seen, dyslexia is generally associated with relative right-hemispheric strengths. From the general implications of 'maths-in-the-brain' studies it seems possible that *grasshoppers* may have relative parietal lobe strengths. In other words, brain studies seem to suggest that dyslexics are able to be 'gifted problem solvers' if they have 'spatial mode' or visuo-spatial strengths in the parietal lobes

Dyspraxia

Definitions of dyspraxia include visuo-spatial weaknesses as a character-istic feature of dyspraxia. We have seen that dyspraxia is associated with general *performance* weaknesses. The insights from brain studies into the different modes of representing numbers is highly suggestive for under-standing many of the number difficulties of moderately to severely dyspraxic children. In fact, the list of broader functions of the parietal lobes, or site of visuo-spatial representation of numbers, reads like a list of many of the 'typical' dyspraxic features. This suggests that many dyspraxics may have a degree of parietal lobe impairment. This would help explain why dyspraxics have 'poor intuitions' about maths tasks, and seem unable to visualize unfamiliar problems, challenging tasks, or maths puzzles. It would also help explain why dyspraxic children have difficulty understanding and remembering logico-mathematical ways of thinking in number-work. The inability to picture tasks would clearly underpin the tendency for dyspraxic children to display inflexible and 'bottom-up' *inchworm* maths processing characteristics.

Dyspraxia, and verbal strengths

We have seen that dyspraxia is associated with relative left-hemispheric strengths. Although most dyspraxic children are poor thinkers and problem solvers in maths and many dyspraxics share the verbal memory weaknesses of dyslexic children, a few dyspraxics have good verbal maths skills. This suggests that some dyspraxic children may prefer to represent numbers and maths facts whenever possible in the 'language dependent mode' and may have relative left inferior frontal lobe strengths. Such strengths, combined with visuo-spatial weaknesses, would probably confirm *inchworm*-like tendencies, even among relatively able dyspraxic maths learners.

Some teaching implications

In general terms it is important to bear in mind that dyslexia and dyspraxia are often comorbid and that dyslexic and dyspraxic children with difficulties in maths have many cognitive characteristics in common, as we saw earlier on. This means that the fundamental teaching principles for teaching maths to dyslexic and dyspraxic children are broadly the same. These principles are outlined in detail in Chapter 2. Nevertheless the considerations of the different cognitive, biological and learning personality strengths and weaknesses which can impact on individual children with specific learning difficulties do have some important teaching implications.

In brief, the strong visuo-spatial skills of *grasshopper* dyslexics lend themselves to visuo-spatial modes of representing numbers and number relationships. Mahesh Sharma (1989b) points out that *qualitative thinkers (grasshoppers)* identify with 'continuous' or spatially defined materials, such as Cuisinaire rods (these and other maths materials are described later on). Most dyslexic *grasshoppers* quickly make sense of spatial models of maths operations such as 2-D 'area models' of multiplication, for instance. Since *grasshoppers* reason in a 'top-down', holistic way they find the column-based standard models of calculation particularly difficult to make sense of. On the other hand, as we have noted, most dyslexic *grasshoppers* thrive on mental methods of calculating and, if encouraged, will often devise sophisticated methods of calculating for themselves. Since they work intuitively, most dyslexic *grasshoppers* have to be encouraged to record reasoning steps or partial calculations. Mental calculation methods allow *grasshopper* dyslexics to develop methods for recording their 'workings' which will support their ways of visualizing the tasks

On the other hand, the poor visualizing skills of severely dyspraxic children and dyslexic *inchworms* means that they can find spatially defined models of numbers and spatially defined materials – such as Cuisinaire rods – quite difficult to make sense of. As Sharma points out, *quantitative thinkers (inchworms)* seem to prefer discontinuous or discrete models and materials – such as small dots, or counters and cubes. Since most dyspraxic children and most dyslexic inchworms benefit from being helped to develop strongly defined and economical visual images for number relationships, it is generally important to encourage them to build and use visuo-spatial models. To ensure that dyspraxic children and dyslexic *inchworms* genuinely understand *qualitative* models and pictures it is often wise to use ones-based (discrete) models in order to introduce new concepts and relationships to them. When the ones-based models are understood, teachers can build up towards an understanding of spatially defined models. (It should be noted, however, that some severely dyspraxic children seem unable to make sense of predominantly spatial ways of representing relationships, even when they are carefully introduced.) The poor visualizing skills of dyspraxic children and dyslexic *inchworms* also affects their ability to understand certain logico-mathematical ways of reasoning. For example, children with poor visuo-spatial skills find it very difficult to understand 'holistic' *compensation* methods of reasoning, such as $38 - 19 = (38 - 20) + 1$. Finally, teaching experience has shown that the extremely poor visuo-spatial skills of very severely dyspraxic maths learners can seriously hamper the ability of these children to subtract or divide: it would appear that children with severe visuo-spatial weaknesses find it easier to visualize the processes of putting quantities or numbers together (addition and multiplication) than breaking quantities or numbers apart (subtraction and division).

A note on the term dyscalculia

The label dyscalculia is quite often used to describe an inherent and severe difficulty with acquiring numerical skills. From the start, the idea that there may be a specific mathematics difficulty has been controversial. Some respected figures in the dyslexia world, for example Tim Miles, believe that dyscalculia is really part of other specific learning difficulties, such as dyslexia, and that there is no need for yet another label.

In very general terms, there is a broad consensus among those experts who favour using the term dyscalculia about how it should be characterized:

1. Dyscalculia is described as a global arithmetic learning difficulty. It is understood to affect all aspects of basic numeracy. Dyscalculic learners have a poor intuitive sense or *feel* for numbers and for number relationships. They usually have difficulty learning facts and procedures. They have problems understanding concepts and logical principles. They have grave difficulties understanding the number system. Some dyscalculics are able to acquire facts and procedures but give answers or solve tasks mechanically and with little understanding.
2. Dyscalculia is described as a very severe number learning difficulty. The mathematical attainment levels of dyscalculic children are very significantly lower than their peers: at age 7, for example, dyscalculic children could be functioning at the level of an average 4–5 year old. By 11 years of age dyscalculic children are often 5 or 6 years behind their peers in number-work. Some dyscalculic adults are still functioning at the level of a young primary school child. It is often noted that the majority of dyscalculic children (and even adults) complete calculations by counting in *ones* and that they often use their fingers to do so.
3. The label dyscalculia is not usually used to apply to individuals with severe *general* intellectual impairment. It is generally reserved for individuals who otherwise function fairly normally. The term dyscalculia is understood to be meaningful when there is a discrepancy between overall intellectual ability and levels of attainment and the individual's arithmetical ability.

Many experts who value the term dyscalculia nevertheless disagree about whether it should be seen as an entirely separate learning difficulty (a specific and separate difficulty with numbers, only) or whether it should be understood as comorbid with, and sharing common underlying causes with, other specific learning difficulties. Although the arguments about whether dyscalculia is linked to, or entirely separate from, *language processing difficulties* are too complex to explore here, it is possible that some of the debates about dyscalculia have been limited by omitting considerations of dyspraxia from the debates; instead, many discussions focus on a *dyslexia-versus-dyscalculia* frame of reference, alone. Although the theoretical debates about dyscalculia will probably only begin to be resolved when we have a better understanding of 'the mathematical brain' – when scientists have begun to map out in detailed ways which parts of the brain are affected in a wide range of children and adults of different ages who are 'very poor at numbers' – it is also possible to make some comments from a pragmatic teaching point of view:

1. As Chinn and Ashcroft (1998, p. 3) argue, the percentage of children who have 'learning difficulties which are solely related to mathematics' seems to be small. Most children who experience severe difficulties in learning about numbers also seem to have another attributable specific learning difficulty, such as dyslexia or dyspraxia. As Chinn and Ashcroft suggest, children with number difficulties and with no other learning difficulty do exist and it is obviously valid to label such children dyscalculic but it seems unduly limiting to circumscribe the label 'dyscalculia' to such children, alone.
2. As we have seen, a significant proportion of children with language difficulties (dyslexic children) also have severe difficulties learning maths.
3. Dyspraxia seems to be highly correlated with severe and deep-seated maths learning difficulties. It should also be noted that many research definitions of the cognitive features of children with *maths learning difficulties* but with no significant language learning difficulties (for example, in Sharma, 1986) correlate very strongly with descriptions of dyspraxia. In particular, visuo-spatial difficulties are found by many researchers to be a key underlying feature of children with so-called *specific maths learning difficulties* (Sharma, 1986).
4. Teaching experience has shown that the vast majority of children with very severe maths learning difficulties – who are functioning many years behind their peers – can be helped to make reasonable and sustained progress. Sharma (1986) suggests that a key to enabling dyscalculic children to make progress in maths is to help them break with the habit of counting in *ones*. This idea is a key theme informing the learning approach described in this book. In contrast to a 'counting

habit', the teaching proposals contained in this book set out to foster a 'reasoning habit' – although it is also important to acknowledge that counting can persist in certain calculation situations and that counting responses also typically re-emerge under stress. Teaching experience has also shown, however, that there are also a very few children who seem to have such a disastrously poor intuitive grasp of numbers and who are so inflexible in their thinking about numbers that they seem unable to make significant progress in learning to work with numbers, at all. It is tempting to speculate that a very important and specialized core number processing part of the brain – possibly Butterworth's 'start up kit' or Number Module – is very significantly impaired in such children. At present there seems to be no available knowledge about how to teach maths successfully to such extremely severely impaired children.

CHAPTER 2

Teaching premises

Some considerations

Maths as a unique and difficult subject

Chapter 1 sets out to establish the important premise that many dyslexic and dyspraxic children come to maths learning with inherent cognitive features which will certainly shape and will often constrain their ability to learn maths. There is a great deal of evidence to show that learning maths is simply harder for considerable numbers of children with specific learning difficulties than it is for 'ordinary' children.

While a large part of dyslexic and dyspraxic children's maths-learning difficulties is cognitively based, it is also important to acknowledge that, for many learners, maths is an intrinsically difficult subject to make sense of. It is often said that maths by its very nature is abstract, uses very abstract and difficult language, and relies on an extremely compressed system of written symbols. In considering the difficulties which children face in learning about numbers, Karen Fuson (1992, p. 56) tellingly talks about 'the unreasonable power of mathematics'. She also points out that young children have a much more concrete understanding of numbers than most adults do. Fuson, Gray and others, show that the ability to begin thinking more and more abstractly about numbers underpins the ability of children to make progress in maths learning.

Maths is also intrinsically difficult in another very important regard. Even quite basic arithmetical skills are actually multi-layered and have to be acquired in a *building block* way. The *building block* aspect of maths has important repercussions. To make progress in mathematics, children have to acquire certain basic foundation understandings and they then have to go on to master subsequent layers of concepts and skills. Memory inevitably plays an important part in acquiring the essential building blocks – children who fail to acquire key concepts or skills, or who cannot remember facts or procedures, will obviously become 'stuck', or 'arrested' at 'lower' levels of functioning. Children who fail to acquire the very foundation skills and concepts become stuck at a very primitive level of functioning.

The conventional style of traditional maths teaching

Karen Fuson (1992) has argued that the main goal of maths educators in the past was to produce the efficient human 'calculators' which a society without mechanical calculating machines obviously needed. In essence, the emphasis on producing reliable human calculators meant that traditionalist maths educators believed it was important to teach the most efficient ways of calculating as early and as quickly as possible and that maths education was largely about good calculation skills. As Karen Fuson suggests, creative thinking and problem-solving do not tend to feature prominently in such ways of viewing mathematics. Many commentators have pointed out that traditional maths teaching practices were – and still are, in some instances – very restrictive. Concepts and skills are usually directly taught or *transmitted* in a top-down way. *Transmission* approaches to teaching rely heavily on the verbal explanations, or routine 'verbal patters', which accompany demonstrations of abstract written procedures. Children are obliged to learn the standard calculation procedures: these are considered to be the only correct and, indeed, the only possible way of proceeding in calculation. Methods other than the compact standard procedures are usually deemed 'wrong' and children are strongly dissuaded from using them. In the early maths years, some traditional maths teachers use concrete demonstrations or pictorial representations to demonstrate skills and concepts; however, it is only in the very first year of formal schooling that children may be given access to materials such as counters, or blocks, for use as learning supports.

To sum up: In traditional teaching approaches teachers are considered the active conduits of culturally arbitrated 'correct' ways of doing things. It is assumed that teachers have all the important knowledge about arithmetic which they have to directly impart to children. Children are the passive recipients of this knowledge. In traditional classrooms children have to listen, watch, comprehend, remember and reproduce what they are taught. As many commentators have pointed out, for this kind of approach to be successful, it is imperative that children have good memory resources.

The teacher–child relationship in contemporary maths teaching approaches

In contrast to traditional theories of maths teaching and learning, most contemporary theories pl..ce greater emphasis on the creativity of the child, or on the *child-as-learner*, in the teacher–child relationship. A central idea informing newer approaches to maths teaching is that for children to understand maths – and to make progress in maths through growing understanding rather than through parroting what they have learned – they need to be active in making sense of it. Most contemporary maths educationalists believe that children need to be encouraged to construct increasingly sophisticated meanings about numbers and number relationships and that children should be encouraged to think about, and find solutions to, the whole range of primary school numeracy tasks, including number calculations and word problems. It is also recognized, however, that constructing meanings in number-work and thinking mathematically is not an easy task for children. Teachers have to ensure that children are given the necessary cognitive support for meaning-making and mathematical reasoning to be made possible. In the sphere of thinking about dyslexia it was the very significant achievement of Steven Chinn and Richard Ashcroft to recognize that because memory weaknesses lie at the heart of many 'dyslexic' failings in maths, dyslexic children need to be helped to construct meanings for, and helped to learn to reason about, all of the key numeracy aspects of maths. Like many other maths educationalists, Chinn and Ashcroft drew on an intellectually powerful, alternative, tradition of maths learning and, in the debates about dyslexia and maths, pioneered the arguments that to help dyslexic children learn through growing understanding, certain teaching and learning conditions should be met. In essence they argued that:

1. Dyslexic children with maths learning difficulties should be given access to concrete materials and concrete materials should be used to help children makes sense of all of the conceptual and calculation aspects of maths. They made clear that many individual dyslexic children benefit from using concrete materials at critical points throughout their maths learning careers.
2. Care needs to be taken to ensure that dyslexic children understand the *language* aspects and the *symbolic* aspects of maths
3. Dyslexic children should preferably be taught in a carefully structured way. Teaching needs to ensure that the necessary foundation

understandings are in place within each 'topic' or area in maths; teaching methods also have to be compatible with understandings required in learning more advanced aspects of maths (for example, in fraction work); sufficient 'overlearning' and revision needs to be catered for and should be built into a *spiral programme* of learning maths.

It should be noted that these principles broadly inform many contemporary, progressive approaches to teaching numeracy. They also lie at the heart of the teaching approach described in this book. However, since primary school children, in general, and young dyslexic and dyspraxic children, in particular, have a number of rather unique learning needs which require to be met if teaching is to be successful, these broad teaching principles need to be elaborated on with the learning constraints and specific needs of young dyslexic and dyspraxic children in mind. Some further, related, teaching issues also need to be considered.

Conceptual tools

During the last two decades or so, many progressive maths educationalists have argued that primary school children need to be given good access to conceptual tools so that they are able to construct helpful and increasingly mature meanings, or understandings, in number-work. It is also argued that the *tools* which enable children to make sense of numbers and think mathematically include:

1. *Concrete objects, or concrete materials* (In the US, concrete materials are often called concrete manipulatives). Concrete materials are understood to include small objects such as: counters, cubes, cocktail sticks, 1p coins and so on. They are also usually understood to refer to specially designed materials, such as Cuisinaire rods and Base Ten materials.

2. *Abstract visual-spatial number models* Abstract number models are widely understood to refer to *number-line* and *100-square* formations. In addition to these newly fashionable models, the familiar TU, HTU column-based methods of visualizing larger numbers are also widely advocated. Finally, domino-like *number patterns* are recommended by many specialists in the field of dyslexia and maths.

In essence, the broad arguments for using conceptual tools in maths teaching include the following points: first, conceptual tools help children construct, experience and directly visualize or 'see' maths relationships, concepts, structures and problems. Secondly, conceptual tools help children sustain working memory processes in the early stages of thinking through problems in new maths domains. Conceptual tools also aid the ongoing development of meaning-making – in other words, they help children develop increasingly sophisticated 'webs of understanding'. Finally, as Richard Skemp (1971) famously argued some decades ago, the improved understanding and visualizing skills which conceptual tools can help bring about, also support the long-term memory of concepts, reasoning skills, and so on.

Concrete materials

The debate

Following the work of Chinn and Ashcroft, there is an overwhelming consensus in the literature on specific learning difficulties and maths that dyslexic and dyspraxic children require to be taught using concrete materials in order to make good progress in learning maths. Although concrete materials are advocated by a great many contemporary mainstream maths educationalists for the general reasons given above, there has also been some controversy in the mainstream maths-learning literature over whether the use of concrete materials can be said to genuinely work – or, in other words, whether using concrete materials can really be shown to lead to greater understanding on the part of children. Based on the ways in which concrete materials are often used in classrooms, the 'concrete learning sceptics' make the following important points. First it is argued that children often use materials in mechanical ways and simply count out or 'read off' answers. This does not encourage children to think and tends to foster dependence on the materials. Secondly, it is said that children may not necessarily understand particular ways that teachers are using concrete materials, especially where complex layouts of materials are involved. Teachers may assume that children see the same meanings 'in the materials' or 'in the layouts' as they do. Thirdly, it is claimed that children may not make the link between concrete work and more abstract maths calculation and problem-solving and especially between concrete materials and the use of symbols in maths. And finally, some sceptics say that concrete materials introduce too much clutter and distracting 'noise' which interferes with the task of thinking and learning.

In essence, however, while it is helpful for teachers to keep all potential teaching-related (pedagogical) limitations in mind, these criticisms should be understood to relate – primarily at least – to transmission-based, and rather simplistic uses of concrete materials. As Karen Fuson et al. (1997b) state, 'What is crucial in the use of objects is the theory with which the objects are used.' As Fuson et al. suggest, conceptual tools cannot, and do not, automatically bring about understanding – to the contrary, all tools should be used in carefully considered ways. In brief, then, what lies at the heart of successful concrete work is the key idea, or 'theory of learning' outlined briefly above, in which it is understood that the role of teachers is to ensure that the learners *actively construct* meanings in mathematics. With specific regard to the use of concrete materials this means that:

1. Teachers need to monitor the use of concrete materials in maths learning carefully and ensure that children are helped to use materials to foster thinking. *Conceptual tools* should never be used as pure mechanical supports. With the exception of very young children, primary school children should not be encouraged to *count out* number facts in purely mechanical ways.
2. Teachers should encourage children to use the concrete materials, themselves, and should assist children to build concrete models of problems, number structures and so on. As Chinn and Ashcroft suggest, dyslexic and dyspraxic children should use materials to *do* mathematics in a 'hands-on' way. In other words, children should not be made to watch passively while teachers use concrete materials to demonstrate concepts and calculation procedures. Teachers should ensure that the concrete models which children are assisted to build are appropriate to their level of understanding and to their overall cognitive style.
3. It is well established in the research literature that concrete work and abstract oral and written work should not be treated as entirely separate activities. From the outset, teachers should set out to help children forge links between concrete activities and abstract maths work. Teachers should ensure that children are able to use concrete models and activities, to 'figure out' oral and written tasks. Written methods of recording can be introduced by recording the abstract equivalents of concrete work immediately alongside the concrete activity. Alternatively, children can be asked to solve a few abstract tasks soon after the concrete model or activity is completed. While children are still in the relatively early stages of making sense of

concrete models, it is helpful to promote *thinking* responses towards concrete work by covering up the models soon after they are completed and challenging children to 'figure out' related but abstractly presented tasks. (Should children have difficulty with the challenge, the model can, of course, be uncovered and further explored and discussed). In a next phase, before purely abstract tasks are presented to children, teachers should introduce 'intermediate' activities in which children are asked to visualize materials or concrete models so that they are able to answer abstract questions. These suggestions complement Karen Fuson et al.'s (1997b) point that if concrete work is to be successful, the concrete-to-abstract transition has to be thoughtfully and sensitively managed by teachers. Fuson et al. argue that while children should certainly not remain dependent on concrete materials for longer than is necessary, working with concrete objects is hardly ever an instantaneous, 'insta-matic' flash-of insight kind of understanding. As Fuson et al. say, it can take time and many concrete experiences before children are able to build up the required degree of understanding.

4. In structured and concretely based learning activities, teachers should be very clear about the role which they intend concrete materials to play. In the main, whenever materials are used to solve tasks in a relatively contained way, they are not experienced by children as distracting. However, it is certainly helpful to limit the range and amount of materials immediately available when working with very young children or with particularly distractible dyslexic and dyspraxic children. The Montessori practice of requiring children to put away concrete materials as soon as they are not longer needed is a useful one. Furthermore, although periods of 'free', undirected exploration of materials – such as Cuisinaire rods, or Base Ten material – can be valuable, especially in the early stages of learning maths, it is usually best to organize designated sessions of 'free play', which are entirely separate from learning activities.

Recommended concrete tools

Small objects or 'ones'

Although the small *ones* mentioned above – the counters, cubes, 1p coins and so on – are perfectly acceptable learning tools, they can, in fact, all be difficult for young children, and especially for children with fine-motor and spatial difficulties, to manipulate. Widely available glass nuggets – decorating nuggets used in flower displays, and so on – or, small and relatively evenly shaped pebbles, are more rounded and are slightly heavier than many conventional small materials or *ones*. They are therefore somewhat easier for primary school dyslexic and dyspraxic children to manipulate and control. Glass nuggets come in a range of different colours. It is advisable to select a uniform colour (or sometimes two colours) for use in any one activity so that the colours do not distract from the learning point which is the focus of the task.

Special maths materials

Base Ten materials, or Dienes Blocks (named after Zoltan Dienes, who invented them) are particularly valuable tools for helping children make sense of the number system and for helping children learn two-digit calculation methods. In essence, Base Ten materials are proportional blocks which represent the number system values, *one*, *ten*, *one hundred* and *one thousand*. The *tens* blocks are often known as 'longs', the *hundreds* as 'flats', and the *thousands* as 'cubes'.

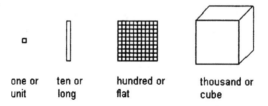

one or   ten or   hundred or   thousand or
unit   long   flat   cube

Since Base Ten blocks represent the relatively limited range of units-of-value to one thousand, most children – including children with poor visuo-spatial skills – quickly learn to identify and visualize them. Base Ten materials made from wood, or from plastic, are commercially available. Wooden Base Ten materials are slightly more expensive than the plastic coloured versions. However, in teaching situations in which Cuisinaire rods (which are now made from plastic) are also used, wooden Base Ten materials provide a usefully contrasting visual and tactile experience.

Cuisinaire rods are coloured, 1cm-based, proportional rods which are designed to represent the basic counting numbers from 1 to 10. In Cuisinaire rod sets the colours are entirely standardized for example a *five* rod is always yellow and a *ten* rod is orange.

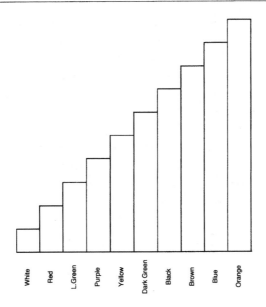

A 'staircase' of Cuisinaire rods, one to ten.

From a teaching and learning point of view, one important advantage of Cuisinaire rods is that they are relatively efficient materials to use. This is certainly true if one compares *rods* with small *ones*, such as counters, or nuggets. For example:

Rods | FIVE | FIVE | 5 + 5 = 10

Nuggets OOOOO   OOOOO   5 + 5 = 10

Cuisinaire rods are popular with many dyslexic and dyspraxic children. Visually able children are quickly able to identify the coloured rods and often volunteer, quite spontaneously, that the rods help them to 'think'. With proper support, less visuo-spatially able children are also able to benefit from the economical way in which Cuisinaire rods are able to express relative values, close relationships and simple operations. For example:

4 = 3 + 1   3 + 4 = 3 + 3 + 1   3 x 3

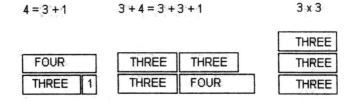

As we have seen, there are, however, some children with very severe visio-spatial difficulties who find it very difficult to identify with the primarily 'spatially defined' Cuisinaire rods and almost impossible to visualize them. Children who express a dislike of the rods should not be required to use them and teachers need to ensure that children with very severe visuo-spatial difficulties have genuinely understood the concept or relationship which Cuisinaire rod models are intended to signify. (It should be noted that less the widely available Stern blocks are similar to Cuisinaire rods and can certainly be substituted for Cuisinaire rods. In some instances, interlocking cubes, for instance, unifix cubes, may also be used as a substitute for Cuisinaire rods.)

More abstract visual-spatial number models

The debate

In general terms, the teaching principles which underlie successful use of concrete materials – namely that children should actively use all models in genuinely *thinking* (or logico-mathematical) ways – also apply to the successful use of visio-spatial models.

Institutionalized progressive maths teaching approaches, such as the Numeracy Strategy, often assume that the kinds of visual models which many adults actively use – such as the *number-line* or *100 square* – also help the majority of primary school children make sense of difficult aspects of maths. With regards to abstract visuo-spatial number models, two important challenges to this view need to be taken into consideration. First, representations of numbers such as the numbered *100 square* and conventional *number-line* are already quite abstract. As we will see in detail below, dyslexic and dyspraxic children frequently fail to make sense of *100 square* representations. They also do not readily understand the rather difficult, interval-based, nature of the conventional *number-line*.

Secondly, research shows that many children, including dyslexic and dyspraxic children, use abstract number models in entirely unthinking and purely mechanical ways. This is especially true of *number-line* representations. Dyslexic and dyspraxic children generally use *number-lines* to count in ones.

In essence, the teaching implications of these concerns are also far-reaching ones. If abstract number models are to be used to foster the dyslexic and dyspraxic child's ability to reason, two very important teaching conclusions follow. These are that teachers should assist dyslexic and dyspraxic children to build all of the visuo-spatial models in very accessible concrete forms before abstract models are introduced. This enables children to clearly understand the structure of the models. Teachers should also promote conceptual formats which have been shown to lend themselves to *thinking* responses.

Number models

The 100 square model

In recent years, and particularly since the advent of the Numeracy Strategy, the 100 square has become a very familiar model in classrooms and in newer maths textbooks. It is the abstract and numbered 100 square which has become the conventional learning model or classroom norm:

1	2	3	4	5	6	7	8	9	10
11	12	13	14	15	16	17	18	19	20
21	22	23	24	25	26	27	28	29	30
31	32	33	34	35	36	37	38	39	40
41	42	43	44	45	46	47	48	49	50
51	52	53	54	55	56	57	58	59	60
61	62	63	64	65	66	67	68	69	70
71	72	73	74	75	76	77	78	79	80
81	82	83	84	85	86	87	88	89	90
91	92	93	94	95	96	97	98	99	100

However, as contemporary Dutch Realistic Education maths educationalists, such as Treffers and Beishuizen (1999) have argued, there are a number of features which make the abstract *100 square* model hard to understand. First of all, the numbered *100 square* contains an enormous amount of information. For dyslexic and dyspraxic children this amount of information is often visually confusing and mentally overwhelming. Secondly, the difficult *tens* structures and *tens*-based patterns which teachers wish children to grasp from the *100 square* are not particularly transparent: for example, the pattern 2, 12, 22, 32 is also meant to be understood as 2-plus-10-plus-10-plus-10. Many children with visualizing weaknesses and problems with breaking down numbers fail to understand why *plus-10* 'leads to the number directly below' and end up feeling stupid and anxious. Thirdly, the widely demonstrated *plus-10* and *minus-10* (*plus-9, minus-9,* and so on) patterns can be very hard for children to visualize mentally: such patterns may be employed and enjoyed while children have the numbered *100 square* in front of them but may be harder to visualize in abstract mental calculation situations. Fourthly, there are reports that large numbers of children – and, in particular, children who are weak in maths – locate the many patterns on *100 squares* in purely pragmatic and often counting-based ways.

Of course it is important to acknowledge that the great advantage of the *100 square* as a model for two-digit numbers is that it is very neatly contained. For this reason some prominent teachers, for example Eva Grauberg (1998), rate the *100-square* very highly and use it extensively in their teaching. In her work with children with language difficulties, Eva Grauberg uses a version of the familiar concrete analogue of the *100-square*, namely the counting-frame or bead-frame abacus to 100. It is, however, important to note that Grauberg prefers a two-colour, wide and easy-to-'read' *Slavonic abacus*: she makes the point that it is difficult to 'read' quantities which have been 'built' from rows of beads on the ordinary and much narrower counting frames.

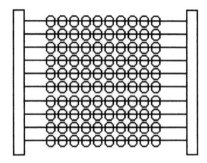

An ordinary counting-frame.

As well as recommending the Slavonic abacus, Grauberg makes the case for using empty – as opposed to numbered – *100 square* frames and she promotes the use of diagrammatic *frame-of-100* representations of numbers. For example, 36 =

For empty (un-numbered) *100 square* work, Grauberg has devised, and describes in some detail, a paper abacus model. Dutch educators, have also experimented with various concrete analogues of the numbered *100 square*. They acknowledge that the *100 square* form can be useful for highlighting the structure of two-digit numbers. However, Dutch researchers have founded the *100 square* form very limited in terms of how it can be used to support and develop addition and subtraction competence. Most critically they found that children who are weak at maths cannot mentally visualize the *100 square* form when they are required to perform mental calculations. They also found that the *100 square* form does not lend itself to supportive diagrammatic representations – mathematically weaker children who try to draw the *100 square* frame end up becoming confused and demoralized.

Using the 100 square model with dyslexic and dyspraxic children

In part because *100 squares* are used so widely in classrooms, it is important to ensure that dyslexic and dyspraxic children understand the structure of the *100 square* form. At present the Slavonic abacus, recommended by Eva Grauberg, is not available in the UK. Nevertheless, children can be guided to construct a very simple analogue of the tenframe structuring by counting glass nuggets or counters into *tens* lines. For example:

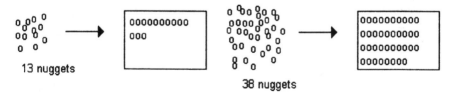

Cuisinaire rods, or Base Ten *tens* and *ones* can also be used on 'emptier' or 'empty' *hundred* frames, to build concrete representations of two-digit numbers which can be 'read', or processed 'in one go', within the containing *frame-of-one-hundred*.

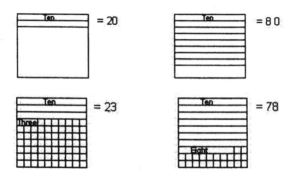

Grauberg's paper abacus suggestions are strongly recommended if teachers wish to pursue further *frame-of-one-hundred* work. Our own teaching experience, together with comments from classroom teachers, support teachers, and from primary school dyslexic and dyspraxic children themselves, confirm that the vast majority of dyslexic and dyspraxic children find the *100 square* form extremely difficult to use as a genuine support in calculation. On the other hand, it should be noted that some dyslexic grasshoppers with good visualizing skills, and with some experience of the *100 square* format, are able to use the *100 square* model to good effect in a range of addition and subtraction calculation situations.

The number-line model

Some writers believe that the *number-line* model is a fairly natural model to employ as a tool for visualizing numbers. For example, Stanislas Dehaene (1997) argues that many adults have an internal mental *number-line* which helps them to visualize numbers and to approximate mental calculations. (It should also be acknowledged that mental *number-lines* can take many forms – for example, some adults have an internal mental *number-line* which ascends vertically). Research by Resnick (1983) and later by Fuson (1992) shows that many primary school children also construct a form of internal mental '*number-line*'. Importantly, Fuson shows that young children's *number-lines* are much better described as mental *number-lists* or *tracks* of number:

Conventional number-line.

$$\boxed{1}\ \boxed{2}\ \boxed{3}\ \boxed{4}\ \boxed{5}\ \boxed{6}\ .\ .$$

Number-list.

$$\boxed{1\,|\,2\,|\,3\,|\,4\,|\,5\,|\,6}\ .\ .\ .$$

Number-tracks (1).

$$①②③④⑤⑥ ....$$

Number-tracks (2).

In mainstream maths educational writing, there has been a long-standing and strong tradition of promoting the conceptual power of the *number-line* model: for example, Haylock (1991), Haylock and Cockburn (1989) and Cockburn (1999) argue that *number-lines* help children understand the sequential and relational aspects of numbers and that using the *number-line* can pave the way for an understanding of negative numbers, as well.

Like the numbered conventional *hundred square*, the numbered and conventional *number-line* is very much in evidence in many contemporary accounts of how to help primary school children learn the numeracy aspects of maths. The ordinary *number-line* is also used extensively in most newer maths textbooks and is an extremely significant tool in Numeracy Strategy classrooms.

Nevertheless, as Karen Fuson has shown, there are very significant grounds for arguing that the conventional *number-line* is not a suitable model of numbers to use with younger maths learners. In essence, Fuson's extensive research shows that it is simply not correct to believe that 'the number-line teaching aid would be readily and fully understood by children' (Fuson, 1984, p. 219). In working with dyslexic and dyspraxic children there are two areas of concern about the conventional *number-line* model. First, as suggested above, many primary school children do not understand the interval, or length-based, structure of the conventional *number-line*. Fuson's (1984) research reveals that many primary school children and *teachers* are confused between discrete and quantity-based models of number and much more abstract, interval or 'gap' models of number. As Fuson shows, children often interpret the interval marks, or the numbers below the lines, as *ones*, or countable entities.

Correct:

2 = the interval between 0 and 2.

Incorrect:

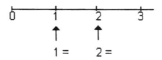

2 = the interval demarcations or 'lines'.

One consequence of the confusion between intervals and discrete *ones* is that it can lead to calculation errors: thus, in counting forwards or backwards to work out addition or subtraction facts, many children mistakenly treat the start-out number as an entity, or *one*, and begin counting before the first calculation 'jump' or hop. It should be acknowledged that many primary school children can be trained to use the conventional number-line as 'an answer-getting device' but often do so with little understanding (Fuson, 1984, p. 219). Dyslexic and dyspraxic children with visuo-spatial weaknesses, difficulties with sequences, and/or difficulties remembering instructions, typically fail to internalize 'where to start counting from' regardless of the amount of training they receive and are consequently 'out by one' in many calculation contexts.

Secondly, we have mentioned that dyslexic and dyspraxic children with *generalizing weaknesses* have a poor, ones-based or *unitary* concept of numbers. Most *number-lines* – and *number-tracks* – are fully numbered and most represent each and every number, one by one. Many conventional *number-lines* and *tracks* do not highlight the significant *tens* (or *hundreds*) structures in any way, or they designate them in such a way that the structures can be easily overlooked.

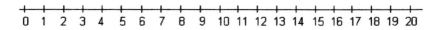

Number-track.

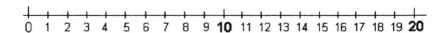

Number-line (1).

Number-line (2).

Work on ordinary *number-line* and *number-track* models can consequently end up reinforcing primitive ones-based models of numbers. Many dyslexic and dyspraxic children view the *number-line* or the *number-track* as an undifferentiated and never-ending series of *ones* – an ultimately rather indistinct or blurry line which is made up of one *one* after another. This view of numbers, in turn, reinforces the tendency of dyslexic and dyspraxic children to use number-lines as mechanical (if typically faulty) counting devices.

Using the number-line model with dyslexic and dyspraxic children

Despite these important concerns, contemporary Dutch maths educationalists have shown that the *number-line* model can prove to be an extremely useful and effective conceptual tool. For this to be possible, children have to be helped to understand the *number-line* in terms of its informing structures. In other words, successful *number-line* work foregrounds the structures rather than the individual *ones* which comprise the line or track. This enables all children, including dyslexic and dyspraxic children, to use the *number-line frame* as a model which genuinely and very effectively promotes and supports reasoning. Indeed, as Dutch writers like Beishuizen (1999) have convincingly shown, the *number-line* model can ultimately be reduced to a simple 'bare' stretch of line (the *empty number-line*), which can be used to support reasoning-based calculation methods. For example:

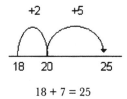

$$18 + 7 = 25$$

Although many contemporary maths-teaching guides, including the Numeracy Strategy Framework, suggest that primary school children should work with quantitatively based *number tracks*, before they are introduced to *number-lines*, in practice this advice is generally not heeded. To help dyslexic and dyspraxic children use the *number-line* model as effectively as possible, it is important to work with concrete quantity models, first, and to build children's understanding of the *line* concept in small incremental steps. To encourage relational thinking, *number-lines* should nearly always be as *empty* as possible. Detailed accounts of *number-track* and *number-line* activities can be found in specific learning contexts at various points throughout the book. In brief outline, however, *number-track* and *number-line* activities can be sequenced in the following way.

1. Children are introduced to the *tens* structures and to the relationship between two digit numbers and the *tens* structures through counting quantities of small *ones* into a tens-structured *number-track* formation:

   18 = OOOOOOOOOO OOOOOOO
   32 = OOOOOOOOOO OOOOOOOOOO OOOOOOOOOO OO

2. Simple tens-structured *tracks* are used to structure quantities of *ones* and are also used as tracks for simple games.

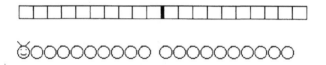

3. Quantities are 'read' in relation to *tens* structures; 1 less than 20 = 19:

4. Empty Cuisinaire rod tracks are used for rod number-building activities, and simple rod *track* games.

(Ten)			

5. As the Dutch educator, Meindert Beishuizen, suggests, children can engage in number-finding activities on *tens-structured* bead strings;

6. Emptier tens-structured *number-line* representations are introduced as analogues of concrete representations.

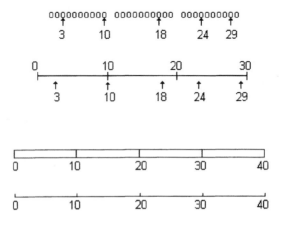

7. Children are introduced to a variety of different *tracks* and *lines*: two examples include:

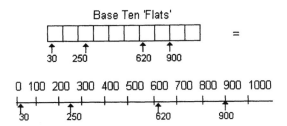

8. Children are introduced to the *empty number-line*:

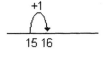

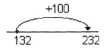

The place value column model

Many commentators point out that the *number system* conventions are arbitrary cultural inventions which simply have to be learned. As we have noted, the written number conventions and rules are very difficult for dyslexic and dyspraxic children to internalize. The written number aspects of the number system are best understood by dyslexic and dyspraxic children through constructing numbers from Base Ten materials on conventional *place value grids* or *place value mats*.

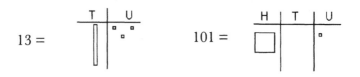

At a later stage, as Karen Fuson et al. (1997b) suggest, the column model and tens-structured materials can be used as the basis for quick sketches of numbers and calculations.

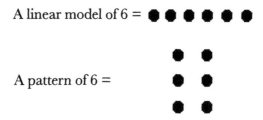

The number pattern model for the counting numbers to 10

We will see in Chapter 3 that some contemporary theorists (for instance Fuson, 1992) argue that all young children would benefit from working with easily visualized, pattern-based models of the basic counting numbers to 10.

A linear model of 6 = ● ● ● ● ● ●

A pattern of 6 =
● ●
● ●
● ●

While few institutionalized teaching approaches, primary school teaching guides, or textbooks build on this educational idea, it is recognized by all of the writers in the field of dyslexia and mathematics that *number patterns* provide useful tools for helping children with learning difficulties develop a basic *feel* for the numbers to 10. In the teaching approach which is outlined in this book, *number patterns* are used to help foster basic *number-sense,* to help children begin to acquire a more sophisticated components-based (rather than ones-based) concept of number and to help children visualize, and automatize, a set of key addition, subtraction and missing number (missing addend) facts. *Number patterns,* like all models for numbers, are introduced through concrete work.

Once children understand how the *number patterns* are constructed, familiarity with the *number patterns* is reinforced through drawn representations of the patterns on wall charts, home-made packs of *number pattern* playing cards, and so on.

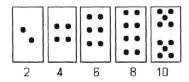

Language

The abstract language of mathematics

In traditional *transmission*-orientated classrooms, language is understood to be a key medium through which teachers (and textbooks) teach procedures and explain concepts to children. In the 'ideal' traditional classroom children listen to the teacher attentively and then work in silence to complete written examples of the procedures they have been taught. In traditional classrooms language is largely used by teachers and pupils in instrumental ways. 'First, you start in the units position, then you ... next you ...'

In contemporary, progressive maths-teaching approaches, language is understood to play a much more dynamic role in the process of learning about numbers. The natural language-related consequences of the principle that children make best progress in learning maths if they are actively involved in making sense of numbers are, first, that children need to be given access to vocabulary and maths-terms which they genuinely understand; secondly, children need to be encouraged to talk about their own thinking and describe their own reasoning processes. In other words, the process of acquiring the language of maths, and the process of acquiring appropriate language in which to describe mathematical procedures, is an interactive and two-way process of dialogue and communication between teachers and children.

The language of teachers

It is often pointed out that there are a range of different ways in which the language of maths can prove difficult for children to make sense of. Many basic mathematical terms are hard to visualize and to attribute meanings to (for example, *multiply* or *divide*), and many are ambiguous because they have ordinary language meanings which may interfere with specific mathematical meanings (for example, 'Find the *difference* between 5 and 8'). Research has also shown that young primary school children often fail to understand certain key words in very typical maths formulations – for example, research shows that many children are not sure of the meaning of the commonly used word 'each' which features in sentences, such as 'Four girls have three chocolates each ...' (Anghileri, 1997, p. 42).

Chinn and Ashcroft have noted that a number of dyslexic children have general symbolic understanding and language difficulties which impact on maths learning. Many dyslexic children have word-finding difficulties and difficulties memorizing difficult, abstract, or technical maths vocabulary. Portwood (2000), Grauberg (1998), and others, have shown that dyspraxia often correlates with language comprehension difficulties, and/or expressive language difficulties. In more general terms, Judith Anghileri's fine-grained classroom-based analyses of the ways in which primary school children understand – and misunderstand or fail to understand – the language of multiplication and division, show that adults need to examine constantly whether the mathematical language they use with young children is genuinely transparent to the children they are teaching. Language-related issues are discussed at a number of different points throughout the book. Nevertheless, in working with dyslexic and dyspraxic children, in particular, there are a number of broad language-related guidelines which are useful for teachers to follow:

1. In the early stages of working on each new area of maths, teachers should use 'colloquial' or 'everyday language' translations of difficult vocabulary (or written symbols) which children are genuinely able to make sense of. For example, the translation '3 times 5' for 3 × 5 is not as clear as the more easily visualized, and therefore transparent, trans-lations, '3 groups of '5' or '3 *fives*'.

2. Dyslexic and dyspraxic children with poor *number-sense* and a *unitary number concept* respond well to transparent language formulations which suggest well rehearsed and well understood concrete actions or activities. For example, 15 ÷ 5, or 15 divided by 5, can be translated as the action-based and unambiguous question 'How many *fives* would it take to build 15?' The very concrete language of 'building' or of 'making' specific examples of difficult number operations helps render otherwise opaque concepts much more accessible to dyslexic and dyspraxic children.

3. Teachers should gradually introduce more sophisticated terminology and the more abstract and formal language of mathematics. At first, the translations which children understand should be used alongside more difficult vocabulary and formulations. For example, teachers can ask, 'What is 30 divided by 5? – that means, how many *fives* are there in 30?'

4. Teachers should make sure that they do not limit maths vocabulary to 'everyday translations' which restrict or interfere with subsequent understandings in mathematics. As we will see, the colloquial translation of *subtract* as *take away* can have serious consequences in advanced subtraction work; in the same way, *divide* should not be limited to the colloquial language of *sharing*. From the earliest stages, harder but neutral vocabulary can be used alongside colloquial but limited associations. For example, children can be asked, 'What is 8 *minus* 5, that is, what is 8 *take away* 5'.

5. Many dyslexic children and some dyspraxic children have difficulty reading mathematical vocabulary. They consequently have particular difficulty with written maths work. Teachers should adopt a systematic approach to 'reading' in maths with children who have general 'reading difficulties'.

The language of children

Recent research overwhelmingly confirms that a key aspect of being able to engage with mathematics in a more active, positive and meaning-making way, is the ability to talk about maths (Whitebread, 1995) A fundamental principle of approaches which emphasize children's understanding in number-work is that children need to be encouraged to describe their thinking processes and explain concepts and principles in language which makes sense to them. Encouraging children to talk about number processes has five very important advantages. First, the process of articulating thought processes in language helps children clarify their thinking processes, and makes their thinking more coherent – in other words, talking about numbers contributes towards a deepening understanding of the ideas and processes which children are describing. Secondly, children who are asked to describe their thinking processes are given the important message that number-work is largely about thinking and that their thinking processes are valued. Because their thinking is sought and taken seriously, they become more thoughtful and reflective in number-work. They develop what is sometimes called *metacognitive awareness* – in other words, they begin to be able to think about their own thinking in number-work. Thirdly, children who are regularly asked to describe their thinking processes are more likely to listen to the reasoning processes of others. Fourthly, children who are regularly and respectfully asked to describe their thinking processes, regardless of whether they have given correct or incorrect answers, are more likely to discover flaws in their own thinking processes. Finally, teachers who regularly ask children to describe how they are thinking, gain important insights into children's present 'knowing state', or level of development in a particular area of maths, and also gain important information about children's understanding of the language of maths.

A number of important, practical teaching implications flow from these advantages.

1. From the very earliest stages in learning about numbers children should be asked simple questions such as 'What did you do?', 'How did you do it?', 'How did you get that answer?' Children who are working in groups need to be trained to listen respectfully to the thinking others.
2. In the early stages, children may need help with articulating their thought processes. For example, if children appear to count to work out a fact, teachers could ask the question, 'Did you *count on*?' Likewise, in the early stages of learning new ways of reasoning, such as fact-derived strategies, children could be asked, 'Did you use a *doubles* fact to help you?' From the outset it needs to be explained to dyslexic and dyspraxic children that they are going to be helped to reason as effectively (as quickly, and accurately) as possible, so that they can be helped to be 'really good', or 'even better than you are now', at thinking in number-work. As we will see in the next chapter, typical 'dyslexic' and 'dyspraxic' counting solutions are slow and lead to computational errors. In the first instance, counting solutions can be responded to by describing a different, reasoning-based response. 'Fine. You counted to

work out 9 plus 6. I did it a different way – the way we practised earlier on. I said, 9 needs one to make 10, so now I've got 10 plus 5; 10 plus 5 equals 15, so I got the answer of 15 by thinking.' As much as possible, teachers should aim to model thinking solutions (rather than automatized solutions) to problems. In other words, wherever appropriate, teachers should 'muse' thinking solutions 'out loud' – 'Hmm ... I need to work out 8 subtract 5 ... Well, 8 is made of 5 and 3, so 8 *subtract* 5 equals 3.' Children may need to be reassured that thinking is sometimes slower, at first, than counting, but that thinking becomes much faster with practice and that thinking is very much faster when 'sums' become harder. (Some readers may need reassuring, at this point, that it is extremely rare for children to resist describing their thinking processes. Karen Fuson (1992, p. 135) maintains that all children quickly 'become expert explainers if given appropriate opportunities to do so'. In our experience, the vast majority of children with specific learning difficulties – including children with very severe maths learning difficulties – also become 'expert explainers' of everything which they have understood in number-work.)

3. Many dyslexic and dyspraxic children have working memory difficulties, and/or auditory processing/memory difficulties. Too much 'talk' can quickly feel overwhelming. Teachers should avoid describing new, unfamiliar reasoning methods 'in words', only. Teachers should generally either affirm a useful reasoning method described by a child ('Well done! You used your knowledge of *ten* to subtract 6 from 30), or should describe one alternative reasoning solution only. Alternative reasoning solutions offered by other children may need to be 'translated' so that all children understand them. In group teaching situations it is usually best to limit the number of reasoning alternatives offered in response to each calculation, or problem: for example, children can 'take turns' to have a go at explaining how they thought. Of course, it is also true that *grasshopper* dyslexics are often stimulated by being exposed to many alternative ways of reasoning or by being challenged to devise more than one solution to problems for themselves.

4. In early work in each new area of maths it is best if teachers do not indicate too quickly whether a given answer is correct, or incorrect. Children who are encouraged to describe their reasoning processes before they are told whether they are 'right' or not are able to be more certain when a given answer is correct and also often realize for themselves when they have made a mistake. Children who have

frequently engaged in spoken self-monitoring processes are much better able to check, and self-correct, their written work.

5. Teachers should listen to children's explanations attentively and possibly jot down children's characteristic solutions and vocabulary. Teachers who have a detailed knowledge of how children are thinking are able to target, in a very precise way, the concepts, procedures and language which will constitute an appropriate 'next step' in learning.

A language-mediated aspect of maths: word problems

In most approaches to learning maths, word problems do not feature nearly as prominently as do abstract (or *bare*, to use the typical Dutch label) calculations. In traditional maths teaching approaches word problems are understood to test children's ability to apply their knowledge of already learned procedures. In other words, in traditional maths approaches, work which is aimed at helping children master abstract calculation procedures precedes related word-problem work. Research shows that a large number of traditionally taught primary school children particularly dislike word problems. It is also often mentioned in the literature on dyslexia and maths that although a few dyslexics are good problem-solvers, many others have particular difficulty knowing 'which operation' to apply in order to solve problems. It has been emphasized that dyspraxic children have particular difficulty with the 'thinking' aspects of maths, including word problems.

Many contemporary researchers and maths theorists have reconsidered and challenged the long-held conventional teaching views about word problems. Nowadays, two related arguments concerning word problems are frequently articulated. First of all, a number of influential maths educationalists claim that children understand many concepts and processes better if they are situated in meaningful, 'real-life' problem contexts. For example, the writer Martin Hughes (1986) argued that young children are able to grasp simple addition quite easily in contexts which are meaningful to them. For example, young children understand 'You have 4 sweets. I'll give you three more sweets. How many sweets do you have now?' much more readily than '3 plus 4 is?' or 3 + 4 = ? Recent research, exploring particular aspects of maths learning, confirms Hughes's view: research shows, for example, that concepts such as the concept of *difference* and the *sharing* concept of division are more easily grasped in carefully structured word-problem contexts than they are as abstract number concepts. Many educationalists argue, therefore, that word problems should play a central part in maths teaching. Secondly, many writers argue that primary school children are generally not given sufficient word-problem-solving experience and are usually presented with a very restricted range of word problems to solve. This state of affairs ends up limiting children's conceptual understanding in number-work and contributes to inflexible thinking patterns. On the other hand, research shows that children who are given varied and appropriately challenging word problems to solve within supportive teaching contexts usually develop deeper conceptual understandings and broader 'webs of understanding' in number-work, in general.

In challenging the traditional calculation-versus-word-problems (or skills-versus-concepts) balance, some theorists argue that word problems should always be presented to children first in all areas and at all levels of maths education. A number of very influential writers argue that children understand and learn maths in all areas best if they are given carefully selected and appropriately challenging word problems to solve. (These writers have usually been influenced by *constructivist* theories of learning maths.) On the surface, this view of word problems and of children learning easily through solving word problems does not match with the experience of most teachers who teach children in ordinary maths class-rooms and who have to teach with ordinary levels of support. It also does not match with the experience of many specialist teachers or parents who are trying to support the maths learning needs of dyslexic and dyspraxic children.

The contemporary researchers and writers, Verchaffel and Corte, directly address some of these difficulties and offer a number of very balanced and useful insights into the word-problem 'problem' and debate. They point out that a large number of children, including children in quite progressive classrooms, articulate a strong dislike of 'school' word problems. They also suggest that theorists and teachers are often unclear about how young children actually achieve 'understanding' and arrive at appropriate solutions when they attempt to solve word problems. Although their arguments cannot be explained in very great detail here, Verschaffel and Corte's closely argued articles are well worth reading in the original.

In essence, Verschaffel and Corte argue that able and experienced children and less able or inexperienced children solve 'school word problems' in two very different ways. On one hand, confident and able children in maths solve problems in fairly sophisticated 'top-down' ways, in which they are able to match an already attained good understanding or *schema* of a word-problem *type* to a given word problem. For example, children who have a good 'part-whole *schema*' of numbers are able to apply that *schema* to problems which contain part-whole situations. In situations in which children already have a good mathematical understanding of the *schema* which is embedded in the word problem, the children are generally able to cope with quite complex and condensed and abstract language usage. They are able to skim the problem, recognize the problem *type*, locate the key numbers, and use them to work out a solution.

On the other hand, less advanced and less confident thinkers, who are learning maths in supportive classrooms, begin the process of making sense of the problem and figuring out a solution by proceeding in a 'bottom-up' way. 'Bottom-up' thinkers have to actively construct the unfamiliar or not yet fully automatized mathematical situation or *schema*, which is contained in the word problem, for themselves. As Verschaffel and Corte explain, a crucial precondition for genuine 'bottom-up' understanding to be possible, in solving word problems, is that the situation of the word problem has to be clearly and unambiguously articulated – and articulated in very accessible and transparent language. Verschaffel and Corte argue that 'bottom-up' understanding is largely text driven or text dependent: their own research shows that condensed language forms may prevent children from understanding situations and may consequently prevent children from working out the solutions which more transparent language makes possible. As Verschaffel and Corte, Karen Fuson and others also argue, 'bottom-up' thinkers may need to be given access to appropriate concrete materials so that they can model the situation contained in the word problem. Modelling the situation may be an important intermediate step towards figuring out a solution.

Verschaffel and Corte's work has many implications for word-problem work with the majority of dyslexic children who seem to belong somewhere along the *inchworm* end of the maths learning personality spectrum, and with the vast majority of dyspraxic children. At a more general level, an implication of Verschaffel and Corte's work is that although familiar and frequently cited 'study-skills' types of approaches – which are often based on Polya's (1945; republished 1990) work on problem-solving – are appropriate when children have a good conceptual understanding of the areas which are targeted in specific word problems, they are not appropriate in situations where children have shaky conceptual foundations, or where children are still in the process of acquiring important conceptual understandings in the targeted area. As Verschaffel and Corte suggest, completely *inappropriate* responses to word-problem-solving – such as arbitrary guesses; the inappropriate application of one operation to all given word problems; or the more cunning ploy of ignoring the text altogether, and, instead, analysing the size and nature of the given numbers as a clue to the likely operation – are generally attributable to a poor conceptual understanding or to a poor grasp of difficult *schemas* which may underpin specific problems. A second general argument is that it is certainly important, as we will see in greater detail in subsequent chapters, that dyslexic and dyspraxic children – like 'ordinary' children – are given access to a broader range of word-problem types than are commonly found in most maths schemas, textbooks, or commercially available maths study guides.

On a more specific note, we have already seen that many dyslexic and dyspraxic children have complex combinations of working memory, general language-processing and specific reading difficulties. Many dyslexic and dyspraxic children do not have a good grasp of the maths concepts which they have encountered and have become extremely anxious about their perceived lack of word-problem-solving ability. Many dyslexic and dyspraxic children express a deep-seated fear, or 'hatred' of all word-problem forms. In working with dyslexic and dyspraxic children with general maths learning and word-problem-solving difficulties it is imperative that the schemas for word-problem forms are built up in the most accessible and appealing 'bottom-up' ways. Helpful ways of presenting the important types of word-problem forms for each of the four operations will be discussed in the relevant chapters in the book. (It is assumed that teachers will continue to present children with a broad range of word-problem types as time goes on – or, in other words, as the calculations which children are required to master in all of the operations become increasingly challenging.) In broad teaching terms, the following teaching suggestions can make a vast difference to dyslexic and dyspraxic children's overall attitude to word problems, and to their ability to solve appropriately presented word-problem examples. Because it is suggested that genuinely appealing 'un-school-like' problem situations are woven into maths sessions, the suggestions also help build children's general conceptual understanding in maths. However, it is not suggested that word problems should always precede calculation: in most maths sessions, it works well if there is a natural 'flow' between figuring out calculations and figuring out genuinely accessible word problems.

1. It is often assumed that word problems have to be presented to children in written form. Word problems should be presented orally at first,

'rooting' operations in vivid situations, using clear, colloquial and accessible language and simple *schemas* or situations. Teachers should be willing to continue 'translating' the situation until they are sure that children have grasped it. Very early word-problem situations should be built in an entirely 'natural' or informal and conversational way around attractive concrete materials – playing cards, plastic people/teddies, and so on. Mahesh Sharma points out that it is worth collecting attractive small materials. It is usually very successful to use real sweets or cakes or snacks when new concepts are being introduced. (A usual condition of 'nibble maths' is that food is 'banked,' along the way, and eaten at the end of the session). Situations can be presented very simply: 'On this pretend plate were going to put some of your favourite chocolates. You are allowed to have 8 chocolates. But look, I've only given you 3 chocolates. How many more chocolates do I need to give you?'

2. Dyslexic and dyspraxic children are particularly prone to relying on unsophisticated counting solutions to all tasks, including word problems. Like many conceptual tools, concrete ones lend themselves to mechanical counting solutions. As soon as possible, word problems which centre on materials should be described orally but the concrete materials should be held back (out of the child's reach) until the child has reasoned to find an attempted solution to the problem. Once a reasoned answer has been given, children can use the materials to model the problem and to check the given solution. (In the first instance, as suggested a moment ago, teachers should not indicate whether the given solution is correct, or not.)

3. As soon as possible, simple and clear problem situations should be presented purely orally (without visible concrete support). However, children should understand that concrete materials would be made available in any type of reasoning situation should the child become 'stuck' or unable to work the problem out. Informal spoken word problems should form an integral and natural part of all maths work – in other words, word problems should feature prominently at every level of work to understand and automatize the four maths operations. Thus, for example, oral questions can either be presented in skills-based, abstract ways, such as, 'You have 74, you need 100. 74 plus what is 100?' Alternatively, questions can be presented in situated ways, such as 'Your mum owes you £1.00. She gives you 65p. How much money does your mum still owe you?'

4. The written word problems which are found in most text books are stilted, dull and very predictable. So-called 'realistic' or 'real-life' problems are also often very dull. Spoken word problems should be designed to be as appropriate and engaging to the particular learner (or learners) as possible. The child's age and general personality should be taken into consideration. Children normally enjoy problems centred on themselves, their families, friends, pursuits and interests. The majority of children identify with problems centred on sweets and junk food. Children are usually very pleased when word problems are built around the latest widespread cultural 'fad' or 'craze'(often centring on a film release). Most children enjoy exaggeratedly vivid, humorous, bizarre, or fantastical (Roald Dahl-like) situations. Many boys – and some girls! – enjoy fairly gruesome situations. Some children enjoy word problems which build into an ongoing 'narrative' or 'soap fiction'. When word problems are lively or fun and fit 'organically' into maths sessions, most children will willingly make sense of 'the maths in them'. The vast majority of children have a very strong sense of what is *fair* or *just*, particularly where situations refer to them: rivalrous, competitive, or potentially unjust situations can be used to good effect in word-problem situations. Finally, Eva Grauberg makes the interesting point that word problems are made easier if only one name is used in word problems involving unknown protagonists. In Grauberg's words (1998, p. 98),

> do not use two names (e.g. Mary and Tom ...) but have one person described in a memorable special relation (e.g. Mary and her little brother). This will make the text livelier and it will also help the child to differentiate the two protagonists, visually as well as verbally. If this lessens the danger of mixing them up while trying to organize the problem.

5. Spoken word problems should be designed to become steadily more complex. Once simple *schemas* or word-problem *types* have been understood, more complex *schemas* should be introduced. For instance, as we will see in Part V, when children have automatized the *grouping schema* of division they are ready to make sense of the *sharing* concept of division. To support working memory difficulties teachers or pupils can record key facts or essential details.

6. Written word problems should be introduced into maths areas in which children have appropriate conceptual *schemas* and have shown that they are able to solve oral word problems with confidence. At first,

teachers should take great care to ensure that word problems are expressed in simple language and as clearly and concisely as possible. In time, the language of written word problems should be made more and more complex and school-like: in other words, children have to learn the 'game' and conventions of conventional 'school' word-problem-solving. It should be noted that dyslexic children have particular problems reading difficult or unusual names which have been given to word-problem protagonists (subjects) and can become side-tracked by this simple difficulty. Dyslexic children can be trained to label and identify word-problem subjects by their first letter: for example, in the problem 'Leonard had 7 apples ...' Leonard can be identified as 'L'.

7. In written solutions to more complex *schemas*, such as *missing number* problems or *difference* problems, children should be allowed to use informal, 'jotting'-like recording methods. For example, a computer-game based *missing number* problem such as 'You have to destroy 10 aliens. You have destroyed 6 aliens. How many aliens do you still have to destroy?' can be recorded as $6 + \_ = 10$; $6 + \underline{4} = 10$; Ans = 4. As Karen Fuson (1992) has shown, young children often become confused if they have to translate difficult schemas into their canonical (standard) forms, here $10 - 6 = 4$.

8. At all stages, and in working on all four operations, children should be encouraged to make up word problems to fit given *number sentences*. For example: (a) 'Can you tell me a short maths story about 3 *fours*?' (b) 'Make up a word problem to fit "$35 \div 5$".' As always, teachers can act as scribes when they work with children with writing and/or severe spelling difficulties.

In conclusion, it should be noted that although solving and creating a wide variety of word problems undoubtedly enriches the conceptual understanding of dyslexic and dyspraxic children, and does so in many subtle ways, the poor generalizing skills of many *inchworm* children with specific learning difficulties means that the ability to solve word problems in a given area does not necessarily transfer or generalize to an ability to solve the equivalent 'bare' calculation. For example, a dyslexic or dyspraxic child may be able to solve a difference word problem, but without the guiding context he or she may not be able to figure out the answer to the equivalent 'abstract' subtraction or *missing addend* problem. In sum, then, children need experience at solving word problems and number calculations.

The skills, or calculation aspects of maths

Maths facts

We have noted a number of times that traditional maths approaches assume that primary school children should learn maths facts *by heart* and that they should be able to instantly recall them. Timed mental tests and oral quizzes, in which children are expected to give immediate answers to maths facts questions, feature prominently in traditional classrooms. In most contemporary approaches to learning maths, a somewhat different approach to the acquisition of maths facts is adopted. Generally speaking, children are not expected to learn facts *by heart* right from the outset. Instead, they are encouraged to see underlying patterns and connections between maths facts and, following on from this, they are encouraged to understand and use reasoning methods for working out 'harder' facts. For example, 5 + 7, can be figured out as (5 + 5) + 2. Likewise, 4 x 6 can be figured out as 2 x 6, or double 6, and then the partial outcome, 12, can be doubled again. As we will see, it is argued by many contemporary theorists that competent fact-derived strategy usage ultimately leads to automatized or *by heart* knowledge of facts.

We have already noted that most dyslexic and many dyspraxic children have verbal association memory difficulties and consequently have severe problems with the immediate recall of maths facts. Because of their long-term verbal memory difficulties, Chinn and Ashcroft argue that it is imperative that dyslexic and dyspraxic children are taught to reason to work out facts, or, in other words, that they are taught to use fact-derived strategies to figure out 'unknown' facts. However, with regards to younger primary school dyslexic and dyspraxic children, three significant points need to be made. First of all, primary school dyslexic and dyspraxic children often have a very poor foundation of already known facts which they are able to use to reason from. Since it is not a good idea to overburden the long-term memory capacity of primary school dyslexic children, especially in the confidence-building stages, it is important to target the absolutely essential facts – *key facts*, or *big value facts* – for immediate recall. We have noted that many primary school dyslexic and dyspraxic children also have difficulty seeing patterns and connections between numbers and have difficulty remembering the steps of calculation processes. It is therefore important to ensure that easily understood and widely applicable fact-derived strategies are targeted and that they are very carefully taught. These targeted strategies can be called *key strategies* or *big value calculation strategies*.

Second of all, it should be noted that while dyslexic and dyspraxic children learn best if they understand the reasoning methods that they are taught, they also need to have efficient access to facts so that they are able to calculate as efficiently as possible. It is sometimes assumed that automatization of facts follows fairly naturally from conceptual understanding. While 'drill' or 'overlearning' is often associated with meaningless rote learning, it is, in fact, a key feature of all successful approaches to teaching and learning maths. Over time, most dyslexic and dyspraxic children will have to overlearn intensively the *big value* facts and the *big value* ways of working our facts, so that

1. they can work facts as quickly as possible;
2. they are able to automatize and immediately recall a growing number of facts;
3. they are able to apply their larger stock of known facts to an extending repertoire of advanced fact derivation.

A third and final point concerning 'knowledge' of maths facts is also a key theme of this book. One very big advantage of highly structured approaches to teaching maths facts is that most dyslexic and dyspraxic children are able to break the counting habit to automatize the most basic maths facts and then (ultimately) to automatize a fair proportion of the entire repertoire of addition, subtraction, multiplication and division maths facts. Nevertheless, the verbal memory difficulties which make immediate fact recall so difficult mean that many dyslexic and dyspraxic children are obliged to continue to reason to figure out certain facts – usually the least easily visualized and least accessible or 'harder' maths facts – for the duration of their primary school years. If dyslexic and dyspraxic children are to make confident progress in learning maths, their primary school teachers and parents should be aware of the number-related consequences of a poor memory for verbal associations. They should take account of the necessity of giving dyslexic and dyspraxic children time to 'figure out' facts which are 'hard' for them and should actively foster the development of increasingly efficient use of reasoning strategies.

Calculation

In traditional maths teaching approaches all children are taught the standard, column-based, pencil-and-paper methods for two-digit calculation from the outset.

$$
\begin{array}{r}
4\ 6 \\
+\ 5\ 7 \\
\hline
1\ 0\ 3 \\
1
\end{array}
\qquad
\begin{array}{r}
{}^{0}\!\!\not{1}{}^{9}\!\not{0}{}^{1}\!0 \\
-\ 3\ 7 \\
\hline
\not{6}\ .3
\end{array}
\qquad
\begin{array}{r}
3\ 7 \\
\times\ \ 5 \\
\hline
1\ 8\ 5 \\
3
\end{array}
\qquad
6\,\overline{)\,8\ {}^{2}3\ {}^{5}5}\ \ \begin{array}{r}1\ \ 3\ \ 9\ \ r1\end{array}
$$

In the majority of contemporary, progressive maths teaching approaches, such as the Numeracy Strategy approach, young children are introduced to so-called *mental* (or *informal*) methods of calculating. As we will see in detail later on, *mental* calculation methods have been found to be easier for young children to understand than traditional methods. *Mental* methods of calculation also allow children to apply their maths skills in 'real-life' situations – in other words, they enable young children to be broadly numerate in the 'wider world' outside of the classroom. For example, primary school children who learn informal subtraction methods are able to work out change in shopping situations.

Since most dyslexic and dyspraxic children have difficulty remembering complex sequences of steps, and many dyslexic and dyspraxic children have spatial and left/right orientation difficulties, children with specific learning difficulties usually make best progress in more advanced two-digit (and three-digit) number-work if they are taught the 'newer' *mental* calculation methods first. Nevertheless, substituting *mental* calculation methods for standard calculation methods cannot, on its own, iron out all of children's early two-digit calculation difficulties. As Karen Fuson (1992) and other writers show, the sequences of steps which make up many of the *mental* calculation methods can also be quite difficult to follow and to remember. As we will see, many dyslexic and dyspraxic children feel overburdened and can become confused if they are taught and are expected to remember a large number of alternative calculation methods.

Teaching experience shows that dyslexic and dyspraxic children with calculation difficulties respond to a consistent and very structured approach to learning calculation skills, which needs to be adopted from the earliest stages onwards. In practical teaching terms, this means that the *key strategy* approach to fact derivation, which was mentioned above, can be extended to learning more advanced calculation methods. As we will see in detail, *big value* mental two-digit calculation methods for each of the four operations can be selected to teach to primary school dyslexic and dyspraxic children. We will also see that such a highly structured approach often acts as a foundation-building first stage in calculation. In time, confident dyslexic and dyspraxic *mental 'calculators'* are able to develop more flexible and inventive responses and solutions to many calculation tasks. It should be noted that relatively recent (1990) curriculum changes in already progressive Dutch Realistic Education classrooms have introduced a similarly tightly structured approach towards the acquisition of basic calculation skills (to 100) for *all* younger primary school children. Beishuizen (1999), quoting Anita Straker from the English Numeracy Task Force, says, 'given the great variety of mental strategies it is important to decide on "exactly which methods should be taught and in what order"'. In contemporary Dutch Realistic Education maths classrooms young primary school children study computation to 100 in a very carefully sequenced way and spend time developing a 'knowledge base of memorized number facts'. Once children have a sound basic foundation knowledge, teachers focus on encouraging the children to be flexible and inventive thinkers (Treffers and Beishuizen, 1999).

The teacher–child relationship

An overview discussion

We have seen that compared with traditional *transmission methods* of teaching mathematics, most contemporary theories about maths teaching and learning place greater emphasis on the child – the *child as active meaning-maker* – in the teacher–child relationship. There is, however, a great deal of debate in contemporary discussions in maths education about the role of the *teacher* in the maths educational progress of children

To simplify a complex and many-faceted discussion, some theorists argue that teachers should play a very restricted and purely facilitative role in the child's maths learning process. In this view, young children learn best through devising solutions for themselves to appropriately challenging problems and it is also argued that they learn best at their own pace. On the other hand, many theorists – like Karen Fuson, Ian Thompson, contemporary Realistic Education theorists in Holland, Chinn and Ashcroft and Mahesh Sharma – remain mindful of the pitfalls of transmission-orientated approaches but argue that teachers, too, have to play a very active role in the process of helping children learn about numbers. Such theorists argue that what is often called a *guided discovery approach* to teaching maths helps children – especially children with any degree of difficulty in maths learning – make the best progress in acquiring the numeracy aspects of maths. Furthermore, as Fuson, Smith and LoCicero (1997) suggest, the relative degree of teacher *guidance* and of independent *discovery* can, in fact, vary at stages or even at moments throughout the primary school maths years. For example, in the very early foundation phases of learning maths and in the introductory stages of each new area of number-work teachers will usually need to give a substantial amount of direct guidance to children. On the other hand, once children have understood the essential logico-mathematical premises within a given area and are beginning to reason confidently they will usually be able to discover patterns and principles, and devise (invent) reasoning methods for themselves – at least if they are given appropriate support and encouragement.

In the field of maths and specific learning difficulties, Chinn and Ashcroft, Anne Henderson, and Mahesh Sharma all report that children with specific learning and maths difficulties make best overall progress in maths learning within the framework of structured *guided discovery* approaches. In working with dyslexic and dyspraxic children teachers need to *guide* children *actively* for the following reasons:

1. Many important aspects of maths are objectively hard for children to understand and often involve difficult and arbitrary cultural inventions – for example, the *place value* conventions of the written number system.
2. While children's solutions to problems should be sought, and children's thinking always needs to be valued, it is also important to acknowledge that many dyslexic and dyspraxic children become 'stuck' in unsophisticated and unproductive ways of thinking about numbers and number relationships. For instance, many dyslexic and dyspraxic children endemically *count* to solve number tasks. As Karen Fuson (1997b) argues, an extremely important role of the teacher is to help children acquire more sophisticated 'conceptual structures' and skills in number-work. Steve Chinn also points out that active guided discovery approaches may help dyslexic and dyspraxic children avoid internalizing incorrect ideas and information in maths
3. Since it is a characteristic of many dyslexic and dyspraxic learners that they do not make connections in maths for themselves, it is important that teachers help children with specific learning difficulties construct all the necessary layers and 'webs' of understanding which ordinary children may intuitively acquire. As Chinn and Ashcroft (1998) point out, too, teachers need to ensure that new knowledge builds on previously acquired knowledge. Mahesh Sharma often argues that an important role of specialist maths teaching is to see that key *pre-skills* or

essential aspects of 'foundation knowledge' in any one area are in place before new concepts and skills are taught.

4. As we have seen, and for all of the complex reasons touched on earlier, many dyslexic and dyspraxic children have problems learning and recalling maths facts. Many dyslexic and dyspraxic children also have difficulty remembering the sequences of steps which make up calculation procedures. The essential learning reviews which help children automatize facts, fact-derived strategies and procedures, and which spiral through the overall programme of maths learning, need to be very carefully orchestrated by teachers.

The face-to-face, interactive, aspects of the teacher–child relationship

As many experienced teachers acknowledge, it is seductively easy to slip into a *transmission*-dominated mode of teaching in which teacher-talk, and teacher-demonstration ends up swamping children's thinking processes and turns children into passive recipients of 'knowledge'. It is much harder to structure teaching sessions as productive dialogues between teacher and child. In *guided discovery* approaches to maths learning, the paramount teaching goal is to develop children's conceptual knowledge and thinking from a present 'knowing state', and as much as possible, focus the learning process on the acquisition of an appropriate 'next step'. This is sometimes described as teaching maths in 'the zone of proximal development'. General guidelines for the face-to-face aspects of teaching primary school number-work to dyslexic and dyspraxic children include the following suggestions, some of which have been touched on before:

1. Wherever appropriate, and as much as possible, it is vital to assess how children are thinking, as we have seen. Most children respond to questions such as 'How did you get your answer?'; 'Explain to me how you worked that out'; 'Show me what you did'; or, very simply, 'What did you do?' Of course it is also crucial to give children as much positive 'feedback' as possible. In the early stages, it is a good idea to praise any attempt on the child's part to think or to reason, although more appropriate solutions may also need to be modelled, at times. In later phases, attempts to reason economically, to devise creative solutions, or to make connections with other aspects of maths, should always be warmly acknowledged.

2. Concepts, skills and number-structures should be *demonstrated* by

teachers as little as possible. Instead, as much as possible, children should be guided to use concrete materials to build models and construct relationships, or to use abstract number models *for themselves*. Children should be encouraged, and possibly guided, to talk through the concepts or skills which the materials or models are intended to make explicit.

3. Maths-learning sessions should be designed to be both interactive and lively. Although *written recording* is important, at least one-third to one half of each maths session should be *oral*. (To compensate for children's working memory difficulties teachers can record key numbers, important reasoning steps, and so on. The role of scribe is particularly important when children have writing difficulties.) *Oral calculation work* is economical, allows a great deal of teaching ground to be covered, allows teachers to question how children are thinking and can enable teachers to intervene swiftly, where necessary. Intervention can either take place immediately or can be held back for a subsequent session. Oral word-problem-solving work is also very economical and allows teachers to introduce many cognitively complex structures in an accessible way, as we have seen.

4. Compared with traditional maths teaching approaches, teachers should radically reduce the amount of written work to be completed in maths sessions. Much of the *written work* aspect of number-work should be designed to help children record and support their reasoning processes in number-work. Carefully designed written exercises can help reinforce reasoning processes and can also help teachers assess children's ability to think independently. In the main, written exercises should be kept brief and to the point. It is now widely accepted that working through pages of repetitive written examples does not help children achieve further levels of understanding.

5. Especially in the foundation-building stages, maths sessions should be structured to be quite broadly varied or full of contrasts. Many dyslexic and dyspraxic children lack appropriate knowledge across a wide range of basic areas of number-work. Covering a fairly wide spectrum of different topics in maths sessions can help prevent children from feeling patronized or bored. In each subsequent session, the different topics can be further developed in sufficiently small learning steps (or, indeed, in the case of some dyslexic *grasshoppers*, some large, or even very large, steps). As soon as children have demonstrated greater understanding and greater proficiency at a targeted level, teachers can move on to a different topic.

6. Different teaching *modes* can also be used to good effect. Changing the teaching mode can be especially valuable in working with dyslexic and dyspraxic children with poor attention spans. Thus, for instance, oral work which is designed to check knowledge in one topic, can be followed by concrete work to build understanding in another topic, and this can be followed, in turn, by a short amount of written work to consolidate reasoning processes in yet another topic. One or two carefully selected maths games can be woven into the overall plan to help liven up proceedings; playing a game at the end usually helps 'round off' the session positively. As the confidence, proficiency and ability of children in number-work, develops, it is more likely that maths sessions will be structured around fewer themes. Nevertheless, it is nearly always a good idea to begin maths sessions with a quick mental review of basic facts, or reasoning skills, and to end sessions with a well-chosen game.

Some final practical matters

A brief note on the emotional component of maths learning

Nearly all primary schoolchildren want to be able to learn and do well in all subjects, including maths. Children who find maths hard and who begin to struggle, fail, and fall behind in maths usually begin to dislike and fear maths. It is evident that children who have difficulty learning maths feel powerless and ineffectual in maths lessons. To them maths feels like a huge, amorphous and difficult body of knowledge 'out there' and learning maths feels like a never-ending series of difficult demands which they are supposed, somehow, to meet. Many children view maths as a seemingly endless number of facts to remember and a seemingly endless list of procedures to learn to reproduce. When both of these areas prove difficult for children, many of them completely lose heart.

As Chinn and Ashcroft suggest, teaching maths in the 'different' and understanding-based way, which they have campaigned for, is the most effective way 'of reducing this problem' (Chinn and Ashcroft, 1998, p. 13). Ensuring that children are taught at a level which is right for them and taking care to ensure that children are able to make sense of what they are learning, helps the majority of children feel that they are back at the centre of learning maths. As Chinn and Ashcroft and many other maths teachers have found, the vast majority of children, who feel that they are beginning to make sense of numbers, quite quickly begin to enjoy learning maths and feel far more competent in maths lessons. Many primary school dyslexic and dyspraxic children volunteer that they 'love' concrete materials and that they 'love' understanding-based maths sessions, too. Most children are also visibly pleased when they begin to be able to reason in maths in simple ways. Most children intuitively know that their new-found ability to reason in maths means that they are learning to engage in maths in an entirely different way from the 'childish', slow, difficult and unreliable counting based ways that they have hitherto relied on. Children who are no longer anxious about their maths abilities and who are enjoying number-work are nearly always willing to 'have a go' at solving maths problems. Many primary school children quite quickly and proudly announce that they are now 'good' at maths.

A significant proportion of children with specific learning difficulties seem to 'take off' in quite a steady way when the foundations of maths begin to be 'unlocked' for them. These children enjoy the fact that maths is much easier for them and maths often becomes one of their 'favourite' subjects. Some children – usually dyslexic *grasshoppers* – 'take off' in number-work in a very rapid way and seem to grasp the foundation aspects of maths very quickly indeed. Many of these children go on to be very able mathematicians. However, it should be noted that children with severe maths learning difficulties can be a little slow to make initial progress, and children with specific learning difficulties do not always continue to make progress in maths at the same rate. Children who have become 'stuck' in maths often have a great deal of ground to make up and there are often periods or stages in understanding-based learning when children need time to consolidate what they have learned. It can feel disheartening to teachers when some young children seem very slow to 'take off', or when they seem to 'plateau' after having made very good progress. It is also important for teachers to understand that when primary school children with specific learning difficulties take on new and challenging areas in maths, they can sometimes 'fold back' (return) to more 'primitive' responses in areas of maths in which they had seemed to make good progress. In general, when children are learning slowly, it is vital that teachers continue to review knowledge and to reinforce skills in a positive way.

Sometimes it is important for teachers to return, temporarily, to an earlier level of work in areas which seem to be particularly challenging to the child. For example, children who have had undermining experiences trying to rote-learn the *times tables,* and are who having particular difficulty with early sequence-based *tables* work, might benefit from returning to work on a more basic understanding of 'groups' in maths. When children need time to master areas which are difficult for them, teachers often have to be particularly inventive in devising ancillary reinforcement activities. It is crucial that teachers enable children to continue to enjoy maths (and feel that they are 'good' at it) through 'slower' periods of learning. Very often, children who have been supported through 'plateau' periods are able to make surprisingly rapid progress soon afterwards.

A brief note on maths games

We have already touched on ways in which teachers can help make maths sessions more lively and fun. Games can play a very important role in maths learning sessions. As Richard Skemp (one of the most outstanding 'grandfathers' of understanding-based maths learning) argued, playing maths games with children can be made a key part of a positive learning process (Skemp, 1971). Like the games which Skemp devised, the games which are described in this book are intended to be played by a support teacher and child or by a small group of children; but like Skemp's games, many of the games can be adapted as activities for whole class use. In fact, many of the games are so simple that they can be sent home with a child for the child to play with a parent.

In working with dyslexic and dyspraxic children with maths learning difficulties, a key aim is to 'help the pupil to "catch up" with his peers' (Chinn and Ashcroft, 1998, p. 13). If games are to be a central part of the learning process – and not simply a somewhat time-consuming 'fun factor' – they need to fulfil a number of important criteria:

1. Games need to be simple to set up and quick to play. They also need to be easy to make. (With very few exceptions, widely available commercial games take too long to play to form a structural part of maths learning.)
2. Teachers need to be clear about the overall purpose of the games. In general terms, some games help children learn new maths skills. These are usually games which employ concrete materials. On the other hand, many games are designed to help children practise already learned reasoning 'routes'. This means that maths games can be carefully selected to do different 'jobs'. Certain games can be used to help consolidate conceptual understanding. 'Overlearning' games can be used in more immediate practice to consolidate newly learned skills or in longer term 'review' practice.

3. The purpose of all of the games is to help children to reason confidently. Many of the games help children derive maths facts very quickly and, where possible, to memorize them. In the early stages, some children may need to be reminded to think, rather than to count out facts. For this reason, games should always be at an appropriate level of difficulty. The outcome of all of the games described in this book is ultimately not determined by skill but by sheer luck – the outcome is determined, for example, by the throw of a dice or by where a spinner arrow 'lands'. This is a huge relief to many dyslexic and dyspraxic children. The role of the teacher is to play or supervise the game, to help children to reason to work out any fact they may have difficulty with, or to help them to remember a procedure. As always teachers should nearly always 'muse' their own solutions out loud, instead of giving 'in one' automatized answers. (When teachers 'muse' their solutions quite slowly children will often interrupt and finish the reasoning process for them!)

The concrete games which are described in this book use the key concrete teaching materials which are a central part of the teaching-for-meaning approach adopted throughout: in other words, nearly all of the concrete games require Cuisenaire rods or Base Ten materials. The 'overlearning' games are designed to be simple to make and simple to learn to play. A key principle behind most of the overlearning games described in the book is that they should be part of a generic and popular type of game which can be played in many different contexts and at many different levels. The generic games which feature in this book are:

- Lotto based games – often called 4-in-a-row games;
- Card wars
- Dice wars
- Track games
- Pairs – often called Pelmanism
- Bingo.

The basic principles and rules of these games are described in the Appendix. The details of where and how the generic games can be played are given in the appropriate chapter. For example, the key Lotto 'tables' game is described in detail in the chapter on multiplication and division, on page 362. All of the generic games require a relatively circumscribed amount of special equipment. Many games require one or more dice.

Special dice (for example a 0–9 dice) are often required. Many games require a spinner. A number of games require small blank cards – the cards usually have individual *number patterns* or digits drawn on them. Details of where these items can be bought are also given in the Appendix. It is usually best if games are played on a game 'base' of some description. Most bases and 'playing boards' can be A4 in size. A few games require larger A3 sized bases or 'boards'. Game bases and 'boards' can be 'consumed' or 'filed' as a record of work – in these instances the relevant details are very quickly drawn on to paper (for example, HTU headings) or photocopied from a 'master base' (this is how I prefer to work). Some teachers prefer to laminate more permanent bases and 'boards'. This has the advantage that teachers and students can write on the 'boards' with water-based felt-tip markers.

A brief note on assessing primary school dyslexic and dyspraxic children.

It is generally fairly obvious when primary school children need extra support in learning maths. As we will see in detail in Chapter 3, an over-reliance on counting to work out facts is a good indication that children may need targeted help in order to make reasonable progress in maths learning. From the point of view of support teaching, the most important information which teachers need to have is, first, what the key areas of difficulty of each individual child are and, secondly, what level the teacher will need to begin teaching at. To start with, teachers benefit from access to diagnostic information about each child's current and most pressing areas of weakness.

Chinn and Ashcroft's relatively detailed descriptions of appropriate protocols for diagnostic assessments are very helpful (Chinn and Ashcroft, 1992; 1998). There is also a section in Ian Thompson's Issues in Teaching Numeracy in Primary Schools (1999b), which is devoted to 'Assessment issues'. However many teachers feel more comfortable about 'assessing' children if they have a pre-structured 'test' which they can use. Steve Chinn has devised an informal assessment (The Informal Assessment of Numeracy Skills) which is designed to provide teachers with helpful diagnostic information. There are also a number of more formal, standardized maths assessment tests which are available from their publishers. (Details of assessment tests can be found in the Appendix.) Standardized tests can be used as a way of obtaining diagnostic information about individual children as well as providing an indication of how far 'behind' the child is at the time of the assessment, compared with his or her peers. It is generally best to use standardized tests in a fairly relaxed way: for example, for diagnostic purposes, it is usually best for teachers to interact with children as tests proceed and time constraints can be used as rough guidelines. Most of the widely available 'test' or 'extra practice' booklets, which are devised for parents, and which can be found in many large newsagents, children's bookshops, and even toyshops, are suitable to use for informal diagnostic assessment purposes.

When individual children are obviously working at a level which is quite far behind that of the majority of their peers, it is often advisable to select an assessment or booklet which is intended for a slightly younger child. In undertaking informal diagnostic assessments of the maths abilities of primary school dyslexic and dyspraxic children, some key principles to bear in mind include the following:

1. The 'assessment' should be as relaxed and friendly as possible. Before they begin, children should be asked to give their views about maths. They should be asked to say what they like and dislike about maths. They should be asked what they are 'good' at and what they are 'bad' at in maths. All of this information should be noted: most children are fully aware of their areas of weakness, in particular.
2. Children should be asked how they figured out most of their answers. It helps to preface assessments by explaining to children that the assessment is largely to see how they are thinking in maths – what it is they 'do' to give answers in maths. All of the answers which children give should be accepted. It is usually best to give no indication as to whether the answers which children give are 'right' or 'wrong'. On the other hand, it is important to be very encouraging. If children claim that they haven't learned something which features in the assessment, or if they claim that something is too difficult, this should be noted. If a good rapport has been established and children are receptive, an example at an 'easier' level may be given in the place of the 'hard' one: 'That one is hard ... Let's try this one.'
3. In supporting primary school children with maths learning difficulties, it is important to know how much they use counting-based techniques in maths and which specific forms of counting they rely on. The different forms of counting are described in the next chapter. Information about counting should be carefully noted. *By heart* knowledge of facts (for example, the *doubles* facts) should be noted. Likewise any use of fact-derived strategies (for example, the near-doubling

strategy which is described in the next chapter) should also be noted. With particular regards to *times tables* 'knowledge', it is important to understand that most dyslexic and dyspraxic children assume that they 'know' a *tables* sequence if they are able to step-count quickly through the sequence. Part V will make clear that it is important for teachers to know whether dyslexic and dyspraxic children have memorized and immediate knowledge of individual maths facts (when the *tables* are asked out of sequence) whether they are able to quickly access individual *tables* facts, or whether they always step-count from the beginning to work out a given *tables* fact.

4. It is often useful to gain information and background insights from other people, such as: classroom teachers, previous classroom teachers, support teachers and from parents. It is important to note that the implementation of reform measures in maths teaching, such as the National Numeracy Strategy in English State School classrooms, means that teachers (and educationalist psychologists) should not assume that primary school children will have learned 'column arithmetic'. Younger children may be learning *mental* methods of calculating and may not have encountered 'sums in columns' and older dyslexic children are generally more proficient at *mental* (and horizontally presented) methods of calculating. As a rule of thumb, primary school children should preferably be given two digit (or three-digit) calculations in a horizontal format (for example, 36 + 28 =). Teachers should explain to children that they can set the 'sum' out in the way which makes best sense to them – or in the way in which they have been taught to 'set it out and work it out' at school.

A note on the structure of the rest of the book and the structure of each of the following chapters

The structure of the book is intended to be very simple. The book covers the 'whole number' aspect of primary school numeracy. It starts from the very beginning, with counting. Subsequent chapters cover more advanced aspect of maths. For example, the final chapter, Chapter 12 covers *long multiplication* and *long division*.

All the chapters which follow this one are also structured in a simple way. The main parts of the book start with a theoretical section. The 'theory' is always followed by a practical chapter or section in which very detailed teaching ideas and suggestions are described. Although some ideas are woven into the practical sections, it is largely possible for teachers who do not like theory to skip straight to the relevant teaching sections. For readers who are interested in the 'ideas' side of teaching, the theoretical discussions are also structured in as clear a way as possible. At the beginning of each topic, the central 'mainstream' contemporary teaching debates concerning that particular area are briefly described. The maths learning needs of dyslexic and dyspraxic children in the particular area under discussion are set into this context. Modified teaching proposals, which take these needs into account, are outlined. The teaching suggestions which follow the 'theory' are designed to describe ways of putting the modified teaching proposals into practice. In large measure, the 'theory' which is contained in each part of the book is quite detailed because the majority of the teachers with whom I have worked over the years have wanted to know the background *whys* and *wherefores* of the specific teaching recommendations which I make.

As I said in the opening comments of this book, *Dyslexia, Dyspraxia and Mathematics* is intended to help parents, as well as teachers, support dyslexic or dyspraxic children make progress in learning the numeracy aspects of maths. Since parents are in a 'teaching' role when they are working with children, I do not usually make a distinction between parents and teachers in the text. Because many of the children whom I have taught – and am currently teaching – are girls, however, I have chosen to refer to individual children as 'he or she' rather than as 'he'.

PART II

Basic Counting and the Early Stages of Addition and Subtraction

CHAPTER 3

Counting

The importance of counting

Counting is often thought to be a very basic and simple foundation number skill. It is certainly a proficiency which children begin to acquire in the infancy years and which most children appear to have mastered some time before they go to school. Unlike many subsequent areas of maths, most school age children with specific learning difficulties also master basic counting skills in time and, indeed, many employ counting-based methods of solving problems throughout the primary maths years. It might therefore seem unnecessary to examine the counting development and abilities of primary school dyslexic and dyspraxic children.

In fact, it is precisely because counting plays such an important role in children's emerging understanding of number, and also because many children with maths difficulties rely on counting procedures so heavily, that it is an important aspect of children's mathematical development to examine in some detail. In recent years it has become clear to a number of psychologists and maths educationalists that children's counting development – their growing skills, and their difficulties – are a defining aspect of their ability to make progress in learning about numbers.

The overall role of counting in learning about numbers

At one relatively obvious level, informal and formal counting activities help children become increasingly proficient at quantifying objects and, of course, at quantifying other aspects of the world, too: in other words, it is through counting that most children become increasingly adept 'counters' of, for example, sweets, clock chimes, ball bounces and the number of items on their birthday present wish list. At a somewhat less obvious level, counting has a number of additional and very important functions. First of all, as we will see in greater detail as the chapter unfolds, counting enables children to develop an increasingly sophisticated understanding of numbers as concepts or 'mental' entities. Secondly, it is through counting that children build their most basic *number-sense* or intuitive *feel* for numbers. Thirdly, counting introduces children to the spoken number system and contributes to children's deepening *number-sense*, helping them to acquire a growing *feel* for larger numbers. Finally, counting helps children build a simple understanding of addition and subtraction and forms the earliest basis for working out addition and subtraction facts.

From the point of view of considering the ways in which specific learning difficulties can impede early maths progress it is important to note that when the early counting development and counting skills of many dyslexic and dyspraxic children are explored more closely, a number of important features often emerge. In brief:

1. dyslexic and dyspraxic children typically learn to say the string of counting words later than other children;
2 dyslexic and dyspraxic children often take longer than ordinary children to learn to count quantities accurately;
3. dyslexic and dyspraxic children frequently have a very poor basic *number-sense*, or intuitive *feel* for numbers; they frequently have a primitive, *ones-based* model of numbers;
4. dyslexic and dyspraxic children often 'miscount' number facts and therefore get many basic number facts wrong;
5. dyslexic and dyspraxic children often remain tied to *ones-based* counting procedures in calculation long after their peers have moved on to more advanced ways of calculating.

It is clearly important to explore all of the different and interrelated aspects of counting in more detail. It is the early foundation development of children's abstract *number-sense* and *concept of number*, as well as the early developmental calculation aspects of counting, which will form a central focus of this chapter. To situate and understand the difficulties which often typify the young dyslexic or dyspraxic learner, it is necessary to examine what we know in general about young children's early counting development. The role of counting in the child's developing understanding of the number system will be explored in Chapter 5.

Investigations of children's counting and counting development

The different counting and number contexts

In the last three decades, or so, a very large number of studies have investigated children's counting skills and have done so from a range of different perspectives. As a way of pointing to the complexity of the world of numbers it is frequently noted that numbers are used in many different contexts and that the very different ways we commonly use numbers may initially confuse young children.

As we have already seen, one key aspect of counting is that it introduces children to, and helps children become good at, 'quantifying' the world around them. However, children's earliest experiences of the extended counting sequences will, in fact, often not be linked to quantifying objects (or events) at all. We often simply recite the sequence of numbers to five, or ten, or twenty, especially in songs or games, such as hide-and-seek. We also often 'count' objects, such as the stairs or the paving blocks in the pavement without paying attention to the result or overall quantity (numerosity) of the count. This aspect of counting is often called the *enumeration* aspect of counting. The important point, here, is that many of the informal counting exercises which we naturally engage with young children very often do not have the goal of the establishing quantity or numerosity at all.

Numbers are used in yet other ways, too. For example, numbers are very important in measuring: in relation to measurement, it is often pointed out that the way we measure and define a child's age – a key number in the minds of many young children – can be very difficult to grasp, and to explain. This is because measurement rests on an interval-based understanding of the 'units' of measurement, which, in the instance of age, are, of course whole years. Numbers, too, are used in an ordinal or ordering way, as in 'first', 'second', 'third' and so on. And, finally, numbers are commonly used in non-numerical ways, as convenient ways of labelling or identifying people or things. For example, numbers 'identify' footballers, or prisoners, or even buses.

As well as emphasizing the complex nature of numbers, the second point which is usually made in relation to the different counting contexts, is that it is part of the remarkable achievement of young children that they are nearly always able to separate out and give appropriate meanings to, the variety of ways in which numbers are used. Although this is certainly true, we will also see that it seems to be the way in which young children explore, manage and integrate those aspects of counting which are to do with quantities or numerosities which most helps them to 'ground' their early mathematical understanding of numbers. In essence, many studies show that it is the quantity-related, numerosity, or cardinal aspect of counting, which is central to the early number development. This has very important implications for many dyslexic and dyspraxic children.

A note on some of the important 'counting debates'

In the last few decades one important maths educational debate has centred on the concern to evaluate the maths learning significance of engaging children in counting activities at all. Following Piaget's seminal work it is very broadly accepted that children's early grasp of counting, and certainly of counting quantities, is constrained by their 'different' and limited cognitive understanding. However, while Piaget's work to uncover the underlying cognitive principles which govern a sophisticated understanding of counting seemed to suggest that it was more important to work on underlying logical principles (such as sorting, classifying, and ordering) rather than practise counting itself, it is now accepted that practical counting experiences play an essential and vital role in helping children develop a sound understanding of numbers. In other words, it is accepted that while children need to mature cognitively in order to count in more sophisticated or sufficiently 'principled' ways, part of their maturation will depend on the counting experiences that they have.

Secondly, and again following on from Piaget's work, an important theoretical component of recent counting debates has been the concern to define and describe the features of 'proper' or sufficiently principled counting and to indicate how early or late children could be said to adequately 'understand' counting as a basis for understanding number-work. From a teaching point of view, there are two points arising from contemporary discussions about counting which are helpful to emphasize. First of all, most contemporary teaching-orientated accounts of children's development accept that although children do, indeed, begin counting and applying helpful counting principles from about two years of age onwards, progress towards genuine mastery of some of the most important counting principles (such as the cardinal rule, which will be discussed below) is nonetheless quite slow. It is often pointed out, for example, that learning to count properly is a much more laborious process for most children than the process of acquiring language. Again, the issue of the objective difficulty of learning how to count is very relevant to the number difficulties of children with specific learning difficulties.

The second point is that while it is true that most children's understanding of numbers will continue to develop and refine throughout their number-learning careers, it is also helpful to try and define the kinds of understandings about counting, and about numerosities, which allow very young children to develop a 'good' basic model or *concept* of numbers – a model which will enable them to engage in positive ways in learning about the world of numbers. In other words, it is important to try to make some sense of which aspects of counting development are central to the ability to learn productively in the early maths years. This will clearly have important teaching implications for children who have not managed to attain a helpful model of numbers.

An account of counting development

To grasp the complexity of what is involved in the process of learning how to count, it is useful to have a framework for understanding the counting stages which mark or define children's counting progress. The account offered here is in large part based on Schaeffer, Eggleston and Scott's very influential 1974 research study and on some of Karen Fuson's subsequent work on the development of children's counting skills. Schaeffer et al.'s study, and some of Karen Fuson's ideas, have been made more broadly available through the maths education writings of the contemporary English maths educationalist, Ian Thompson, as well as through the two very helpful books on primary school maths education which he has edited (Thompson, 1997d; 1999b). The development of counting is thought to occur in four stages:

Stage 1   Earliest responses to numbers: subitizing and recitation

1. *Subitizing* There is a great deal of research to show that young children (and adults) do not need to count very small quantities, at all, but rather that the brain instantly recognizes, or subitizes, small quantities of up to about four objects. Indeed, on the basis of infant studies conducted by the American researcher Karen Wynn, many theorists and scientists, including Brian Butterworth, believe that the brains of babies, too, are 'wired' to subitize small quantities (Butterworth, 1999). While these studies are somewhat controversial – some researchers believe the babies are responding to things like amount rather than numerosity *per se* – it is

certainly widely accepted that children who are between 18 months and two years old are able to subitize small quantities. Most toddlers are able to instantly recognize small quantity arrays such as *two* or *three* without needing to count. However this sensitivity to the overall numerosity of sets or arrays (which is possibly inbuilt) seems to be limited to processing very small arrays. In order to make sense of quantities larger than the upper subitizing limit of 4, all children have to learn to count.

2. *Recitation* In pure recitation (Karen Fuson calls this the sequence aspect of counting) children learn to produce the counting words in the conventional sequence order but without any attempt to count objects or quantities. Children usually start learning the counting sequence from before their second birthday. The counting words are 'recited' in many contexts. As Fuson and Hall (1983, p. 53) write, the recited counting words

> may be produced spontaneously or in response to a command and alone or as part of a group recitation. They may also be produced for various purposes – for sheer practice, for timekeeping (e.g. saying the words to 20 in Hide-and-Go-Seek), for showing-off (*I can count higher than you can*), as well as for the various numerical contexts ...

The names of the counting words to ten have to be learned *by heart*. Beyond ten, the counting words in *Base Ten* number systems, like our own, are *Base Ten* constructs and children should, ideally, be able to generate many of the counting words, rather than learn them all *by heart*. In the English counting system, however, as we will see in some detail, children do not grasp the structure of the number system for some time. As Fuson and Hall point out, this means that very young children have to try to acquire quite a lengthy unstructured and 'meaningless' list of counting words. Fuson and Hall also point out that it takes time for children to learn to produce the counting string accurately. In time, of course, the early stages of recitational counting are automatized by nearly all children and the counting sequence can then be used as 'a representational tool in various contexts' (Fuson and Hall, 1983, p. 50). By and large, maths educationalists seem to agree that the majority of children make ongoing progress in learning to count orally and can 'recite the number sequence to 100 by the time they are about 6 years of age' (Maclellan, 1997, p. 34).

Stage 2   The stage of enumeration (approximately 2–4 years old)

At the stage of *enumeration* children continue to subitize small quantities and to consolidate their recitational knowledge. The key advance at this stage is that children also begin to learn to map the sequence of counting words on to sets of more than four objects; in other words, they begin to be able to count numbers of objects as well as recite the counting string. In this initially difficult 'mapping' process, most children intuitively learn to apply what the researchers Gelman and Gallistel (1978) call *the one-to-one principle*, understanding that a single counting word needs to be applied to each item to be counted, in turn. Children also learn to use the last counting word to indicate the end or termination of the 'counting' or 'mapping' process.

However, although the stage of the *enumeration* is marked by important advances, children's grasp of the counting process is still limited in very important ways. As many researchers demonstrate, children who are at the stage of *enumeration* do not really understand the cardinal aspect of quantities and of number words – the abstract 'how-many-ness' of a quantity which is larger than four or *five*. Most significantly, it is a characteristic of this stage that when children are asked to clarify 'how many' objects there are in a group of objects which they have just *enumerated*, children will count the group of objects over again. Indeed they may even offer a different count outcome after the second 'count' is completed. It is believed that one explanation for this limitation is that children at the stage of *enumeration* may think that the last counting word labels or 'tags' the last object counted:

$$6 = \bigcirc \bigcirc \bigcirc \bigcirc \bigcirc \underset{\uparrow}{\bigcirc} \quad \text{or sixth object}$$

Similarly, children at the stage of *enumeration* believe that the order in when a count is undertaken will affect its outcome: thus research shows that children at this stage will count an array again if they are asked to count the same array from a different starting point.

In summary, the characteristic features of the stage of *enumeration* are that children are beginning to gain a more distinctive understanding of quantities and number words above 4 – moving away from a 'one, two, three, many...' conception of number – but they do not yet have a sense of the stability of individual quantities or the number words which refer to them.

Stage 3   Understanding the cardinal rule: the count – cardinal transition (about 4 years old)

By the time that they are about four years old, most children confidently subitize quantities up to 4 or so, can recite the basic counting sequence well beyond 20, and can count backwards from about 20. As the heading indicates, the particular achievement of children at the cardinal stage is that they come to understand the cardinal or quantitative aspect of counting, the cardinal use of number words and (increasingly) the cardinal use of written number symbols; in practical terms this means that they begin to understand that the last counting word used in the counting process indicates the total quantity of the objects counted – the fixed or stable numerosity of a specific group or 'set' of things. Because children now understand that counting tells us 'how many' there are in a group they do not count a group of objects again in response to further 'how many' questioning. Children who understand the cardinal principle also come to understand what Gelman and Gallistel call the order-irrelevance principle – that is they come to understand that the 'count outcome' or named total always remains the same no matter where the counting process begins. In contrast to children who are at the stage of *enumeration*, children who demonstrate an understanding of the cardinality principle have clearly achieved a much more stable understanding of quantities and number words and possibly of some of the written symbols which refer to them. In understanding that counting yields a constant 'how-many-ness' for individual quantities children are well on the way towards understanding, for instance, the constant *seven-ness* of 'seven'. The emerging understanding that a counted individual quantity, such as 'seven', *is* or remains 'seven' is, in fact, a key breakthrough understanding in the early stages of making sense of numbers.

Stage 4   The stage of quantity comparison: developing a relational understanding of numbers (about 4-5 years old)

As their understanding of the cardinal rule strengthens, children begin to be able to use number words to compare relatively large quantities with each other. Thus, in building on the key understanding that individual quantities remain constant, children begin to use cardinal words to determine the relative sizes of two or more quantities. First, children learn to understand the idea that if two quantities are counted and have the same cardinal outcome (for example, 'seven') then the two quantities are necessarily equivalent; in Fuson and Hall's words: 'the same count word means the same numerosity' (Fuson and Hall, 1983, p. 75). During this process children learn to disregard misleading perceptual cues such as length: for example, a counted 7 sweets which are presented in a tightly packed array will be understood to be equivalent to the same 7 sweets spread far apart. Using Piaget's famous terminology, children can be said to have learned to *conserve* quantities. Next, children embark on the difficult and lengthy process of learning to process non-equivalent quantities and number words in relation to each other. For example, they will understand that a counted '7' is always equivalent to another counted '7' but they will always select '7' as a greater numerosity than '6'. Thus children begin to be able to order quantities, number words and ultimately number symbols in terms of relative magnitude or size.

It is clear that children who are developing an increasingly relational understanding of numerosities and the cardinal number words and written symbols which refer to them are continuing to develop a more sophisticated general understanding of numbers. Children now understand that numbers can always be defined in relation to other numbers – that '7' is always '7', but that '7' is also always bigger than '6' and smaller than '8', and so on. In developing this increasingly stable and relational understanding of numbers, children are better able to process numbers as 'things-in-themselves', or nouns. In other words children are more likely to think of an abstract or disembodied 'seven' or '7', as well as 'seven sweets' or 'seven hugs'.

A crucial 'by-product' of counting development: the development of number-sense

It can be argued that children with a stable understanding of number words and the numerosities they refer to have a basic abstract model or concept of numbers: this is because they are able to begin thinking about numbers (for example, the number 'seven' or '7'), in abstract or 'mental' ways.

We will see in the next chapter that the development of a consistent and stable basic abstract number concept has important implications for the development of early calculation skills. However, as children's ability to count in more mature ways grows, a second, less tangible, but extremely important development usually takes place. As most children progress through the counting stages, they become more and more efficient and accurate at counting: in other words, the process of enumerating or mapping counting words on to objects becomes increasingly effortless and may ultimately be said to become automatic, or automatized. In this process, children usually become more confident about the accuracy of their counted outcomes. This means that in the process of understanding the stable numerosity of the groups of objects which they count – the *seven-ness* of '7', and so on – children also usually begin to develop a *feel* for the range of individual quantities (usually up to about 10) which they frequently count. As well as knowing that '7' is or remains '7' (unless something is done to it) most children develop an intuitive sense of the unique or special 'sevenness' of '7'. This *feel* for numerosities and the number words and written symbols which refer to them is usually described as *basic number-sense*.

Basic *number-sense* would seem to be relatively easily acquired for very small numerosities such as 3 or 4, probably because they are processed more immediately: thus the majority of children would have an intuitive sense of the *three-ness* of '3'. However, counting skill and counting confidence is a significant aspect of developing *number-sense* for the larger numerosities above the subitizing limit of 4. Although *number-sense* is hard to define in any very precise way (it is sometimes described as an 'at homeness with numbers') it is widely reported and acknowledged to play a significant role in children's general ability to feel at ease with numbers and to make confident progress in the early stages of primary school number-work. As a working definition, good basic *number-sense* may be described as an intuitive *feel* for numerosities and numbers, whereas poor basic *number-sense* may be described as a lack of an intuitive *feel* for numerosities and numbers.

Dyslexic and dyspraxic children: counting, concept of number and 'number-sense'

Unfortunately children with specific learning difficulties are often only formally assessed and diagnosed as dyslexic or dyspraxic from about seven years onwards: there is thus no research data on the counting abilities of two- to seven-year-old children with specific learning difficulties. Beyond seven years of age counting itself can still be difficult, particularly for severely dyspraxic children, but the majority of children with learning difficulties have successfully mastered the four stages of counting development. The broadly typical counting profile of children with specific learning difficulties and maths difficulties, which is presented here, has consequently been pieced together from the comments and descriptions of parents and teachers, from classroom observations and from diagnostic teaching assessments of a number of five- to seven-year-old dyslexic and dyspraxic children, who have been referred, and assessed, early on.

Recitation difficulties

Learning the conventional sequence of counting words is not particularly easy. 'As adults we have mastered the task and therefore may not appreciate how difficult its achievement is' (Maclellen, 1997, p. 34). In order to recite the counting string, as we have seen, children have to process and remember a string of arbitrary words in sequence. The researchers Fuson, Richards and Briars (1982) have shown that a first difficulty is that two- to three-year-olds often process the counting string as one very long unbroken word, '*onetwothreefourfive*'.

Since many dyslexic and dyspraxic children have difficulties processing sequences of words, and some also have auditory processing difficulties, it may take them longer than other children to understand that the 'string' contains a number of distinctive small words. Learning the early 'meaningless' counting sequence also represents a very large sequential memory burden for young dyslexic and dyspraxic children. From parents' descriptions of their children's early number abilities, it would appear that many dyslexic and dyspraxic children acquire the early counting sequence, and certainly the sequences from 10 to 20, and then to 100, noticeably later than other children. A number of studies have shown that proficiency at reciting the sequence of counting words correlates with greater ability in all aspects of number-work in the first years of schooling (Aubrey, 1997). This is possibly because the whole process of working through the stages of counting inevitably takes time: recitational delays can delay the development of counting overall. For example, dyslexic children and dyspraxic children often begin the process of enumerating larger quantities of objects somewhat later than other children. Ongoing recitational difficulties will also impact on counting efficiency and counting automatization.

Enumeration difficulties

While many dyslexic and dyspraxic children understand the *one-to-one counting principle*, they often find it hard, in practice, to synchronize the sequence of number names with the objects they are trying to count. Many commentators point out that it is easier for children to manage a 'count' involving small quantities of physical objects which may be moved or which are already presented in an ordered way. In real life, in 'how to count' picture books, and in maths text books, the objects to be counted are often not presented in such easily managed ways. Dyspraxic children invariably count 'scatters' of objects in a disorganized way: they may miss out objects, count objects more than once and become confused about which objects they have counted. Children who become confused often start over again from the beginning and become even more confused about which objects have already been counted, and which may still need to be dealt with. Secondly, as Karen Fuson (1992) and Brian Butterworth (1999) show, most very young children spontaneously represent numerosities on their fingers. In fact, however, fingers can be difficult for many dyspraxic children and for some dyslexic children to manage . This seems to be because fingers are 'fixed', because an index finger from one hand is often used to touch counted fingers in early counting, because fingers may be 'presented' for counting in many different ways, and because children with visuo-spatial weaknesses find it hard to 'read' and remember any finger configurations, including their own. This means that young children with specific learning difficulties can become confused in the process of presenting or counting their own fingers.

General sequencing difficulties also make the *enumeration* aspects of counting particularly difficult for many dyslexic and dyspraxic children. Counting objects is, in fact, cognitively quite demanding for children with sequencing weaknesses. Managing a count is a process which takes place in time and which, as we have seen, involves mapping a memorized and conventional sequence of words on to a to-be-created physical sequence of objects. A number of children with specific learning difficulties commonly 'miscount' by failing to manage the 'mapping' process itself. Typically, for example, children allow the counting sequence to 'run ahead' of the objects being counted; sometimes, however, children will allow the objects to be counted to 'run ahead' of the related sequence. Some children make the mistake of mapping the syllables within number words on to the objects being counted: thus the two syllable word 'seven' may be mapped on to two objects rather than one. Most children will allow their ability to subitize small quantities to correct miscounting of up to four objects within an overall larger quantity to be counted: some severely dyspraxic children will allow early miscounting to proceed completely unchecked, however.

Enumeration difficulties impact on general counting proficiency and number development in at least three important ways. First, children with specific learning difficulties may master the 'count–cardinal transition' (Fuson and Hall, 1983) and a more developed understanding of cardinality later than other children. Persistent miscounting means that a proportion of six to seven-year-old dyspraxic and dyslexic children fail to grasp the cardinal 'stability' of numerosities in a consistent way. Secondly, even when all of the relevant cardinal understandings may ultimately have been acquired, difficulties synchronizing counting means it is very much harder for many children with specific learning difficulties to count efficiently or achieve concrete counting automaticity. Because of these problems, counting confidence may be eroded. In a subtle way, for example, it is possible that a degree of counting dissonance may arise between children's formal understanding that counting should yield consistent results and the practical experience that counting, in fact, does not yield reliably consistent results for them. Children may have an unsettling sense that what they have counted as '7' may not be 7 after all. (Indeed, some children with specific learning difficulties will volunteer that they seem particularly unable to manage to count very well, although they don't understand why this should be the case.) Thirdly, even when 'mapping' mistakes are not made, the difficulty of managing and completing a complex and effortful sequencing process means, to borrow Eddie Gray's (1997) formulation, that counting *input* is probably not linked with counting *output*. In the context of basic counting, itself, difficulties automatizing the counting process means that counting will require so much working memory space that children will often fail to link a given object array, or quantity to-be counted, with the actual counted outcome. In other words, children with poor counting skills rarely manage to 'take in' counted numerosities: instead they will generally stop counting with relief, give or record the 'how many?' answer, 'switch off' once this is done, and fail to pause to pay attention to the overall quantity which has been counted.

In summary, the consequences of *enumeration* difficulties are likely to be very significant, indeed. One critical implication – and an implication which will be seen to impact considerably on children's ability to reason about numbers – is that, unlike most ordinary children, many dyslexic and dyspraxic children have difficulty acquiring *number-sense*. Even when dyslexic and dyspraxic children have achieved a formal understanding of the stability of numbers (and may be said to have acquired a *basic abstract number concept*) the laboriousness of the counting process often works to prejudice their ability to develop of a *feel* for numerosities and abstract numbers. As we have seen, this 'feel' for numbers helps children pay attention to the patterns within and the connections between numbers.

The counting development paradigm and dyslexic and dyspraxic children: basic number concept and number-sense

Generally speaking, it would seem that many dyslexic and dyspraxic learners enter the respective counting stages later than other children and seem to take longer to master each stage. While such developmental delays in counting difficulties are clearly significant, complex difficulties to do with *enumeration* also appear to have a profound long-term impact on the maths abilities of many young dyslexic and dyspraxic learners: as we have just seen, difficulties managing the organizational and sequencing demands involved in counting quantities would seem to be related to the fact that children with learning difficulties often have a markedly poor basic *number-sense*.

With regards to children's basic concept of number, it is important to reiterate that at quite a late stage (at seven years old, and sometimes even later) some children with specific learning difficulties have not fully grasped the cardinal aspect of numerosities. However, this is generally not the norm: by six-and-a-half or seven years of age the majority of children with specific learning difficulties may be said to have attained an adequate grasp of the counting process. By the age of six-and-a-half years or so, the majority of dyslexic and dyspraxic learners understand that counting establishes the stable numerosity of a group of objects and demonstrate a basic relational understanding of numbers. They are able to grasp the notion of purely abstract numbers such as *five* and *seven* and may thus be said to have a *basic abstract number concept*. Because they are able to work with abstract numbers, they are ready to understand – and indeed often use – relatively simple reasoning strategies such as *counting on* in addition. On the other hand, it is a marked characteristic of many dyslexic and dyspraxic maths learners that they have a very poor basic *number-sense*. In the maths and specific learning difficulties literature, Mahesh Sharma (1990a, 1990b, 1990c), Chinn and Ashcroft (1998) and Eva Grauberg (1998) all comment on this feature of a significant number of children with specific learning difficulties. Teachers and parents confirm these observations. Parents and infant school teachers also often indicate that primary school children with poor basic *number-sense* usually show evidence of such tendencies from a very young age.

As we have seen, *number-sense* is difficult to define in any precise way although a very broad description of the concept has been offered above. From a teaching point of view it is important to note that poor basic *number-sense* is associated with a number of significant numeracy-related characteristics. First of all, children with poor basic *number-sense* have a very poor, 'fuzzy' sense of quantities and numbers between 5 and 10, and above. Secondly, children with poor basic *number-sense* usually find estimating quantities very difficult – they cannot judge the size of quite small quantities and will often try to insist on counting the quantities; indeed, requests to estimate even relatively small quantities may make some children anxious. Thirdly, children often show, or overtly articulate, a dislike of all very basic number-work. Finally, children often display a lack of practical *number-sense* at home and at school.

Teaching basic counting

Where children with specific learning difficulties are experiencing, or have experienced, significant counting difficulties, counting related issues are important to address. In more specific terms:

1. children who do not adequately understand the principle of cardinality will need to be helped to do so;
2. the ability to count objects accurately is an important component element of building up an understanding of various aspects of number-work and is also obviously important in 'real life';
3. it is very important, indeed, that children with poor *number-sense* begin to develop a more confident *feel* for numbers.

There are three different types of counting activities, based on three different models of numbers, which are useful to engage in with children. These models are: the linear counting model, the staircase model and the number pattern model.

The linear counting model

Many commentators point out that basic number difficulties may arise from insufficient or inadequate concrete counting experiences. In fact, because all aspects of the counting process may present difficulties for dyslexic and dyspraxic children, they may require considerable amounts of concrete counting practice. Parents and teachers often unwittingly emphasize recitation and pure *enumeration* (execution skills) at the cost of an understanding of numerosity (the counting result) and of fostering *number-sense*. To build counting competence and *number-sense* children need to have lots of experience of counting objects in an ordered way. They also need to be encouraged to stand back from and 'take in' the overall quantities they have counted. In general terms, some research (for instance, Fuson and Hall, 1983; Fuson, 1992) shows that very young children process overall numerosity better when collective nouns or terms are used to refer to sets of objects to-be-counted: for example, 'How many pigs are there in this very large pig family?' According to Thompson (1997a,

p. 129), the use of collective terms may 'focus the child's attention upon the set as a whole rather than the individual objects within it'.

More specifically, there is a very large body of research to show that whenever quantities of objects need to be counted, children should be encouraged to move and count objects in an organized, relatively measured and rhythmic way. This helps ensure that the relevant number words and the counted objects are synchronized. To ensure that the counting process remains ordered, children can be encouraged to count objects into a simple row, 'line' or 'track'.

Secondly, children can be encouraged to 'take in' the quantity they have counted in a number of simple ways:

1. Children can be asked to estimate quantities first. As we will see in Chapter 5, many children enjoy the simple activity of estimating a 'disordered' scatter of *ones* and then counting the *ones* into an ordered line to check the closeness of their estimate. 'Estimating and checking' help predispose children to focus on the actual numerosity of the count.

2. In activities which require a specific number of objects children can be asked to simply take the quantity they which they 'guess' is the correct amount and then check and adjust the quantity by counting the objects methodically. Again, guessing or 'estimating', first, encourages children to pay attention to the actual 'count'.
3. After children have successfully *enumerated* a quantity of objects they can be encouraged to pause between completing the count and articulating 'how many 'n's there are' to give them time to take in the overall *how-many-ness* of the count. In working with younger children, or with children who have not consistently grasped cardinality, it is important to make a point of asking and emphasizing the 'How many 'n's are there?' question. As suggested above, many researchers note that adults will often ask children to count arrays of objects without necessarily directly asking the children how many objects there are.
4. Playing a competitive 'accumulation game', in which quantities of *ones* are placed on simple number tracks, is an excellent way of focusing children's attention on numerosities – and, indeed, such games also focus children's minds on comparative or relative numerosities. Some quite advanced calculation games (for example the 'First to 25' game,

described on p. 220) have the additional bonus of building up children's *number-sense*. However many five- to eight-year-old primary school children, or children with quite severe maths learning difficulties, both enjoy and benefit from ʾhe simplest form of track accumulation game (see generic games descrᵢptions, p. 000). In this very basic accumulation game, each player has his or her own 'track' to play on. Each player takes turns to throw a dice to generate the quantity of small *ones* he or she 'wins' in each turn. The *ones* are then placed on the player's own track. The tracks are drawn on to one 'playing board' so that quantities can be readily compared. The game works very well with two players, but can usually accommodate up to four players. Very young children will happily use a die numbered 1 to 3, and play on a simple 'Ten Track'. Most five- to seven-year-old children prefer to play using a 0–5 or 1–6 die on a tens-structured 'Twenty Track'. Accumulation tracks are usually not numbered. This encourages children to 'take in' and process quantities in terms of their relative position. It is important to carefully demarcate the *tens* structures or to leave a small 'gap' between *tens*. In short tracks it can also be helpful to give an additional structuring cue by highlighting the '*two fives*' structure within each *ten*.

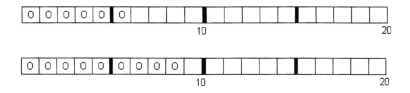

After a turn is completed, each player is required to articulate how many counters he or she now has. The winner is the player who covers his or her track first: some children prefer to play that an exact throw is needed to win; others are happy with a more economical 'first past the post' principle. It should be clearly noted that this game is not intended to be an addition game (though children should not be discouraged from adding, if they do so). As suggested above, the game is designed as a vehicle for paying attention to specific numerosities: in the game illustrated above, for example, 6 is contrasted with 9.

The staircase model

As we have seen, children begin to develop a more consistent concept of number as they develop an understanding of specific numerosities in relation to other numerosities. As an intrinsic part of this process, it is important that children grasp the basic relationship between successive numbers in the counting sequence. The fundamental principle, here, is that each successive number in the counting sequence is *one more* than the number before. Constructing a 'staircase' representing the basic counting sequence allows children to recreate and experience this relationship. Such staircases can be built in different ways: interlocking cubes, building block cubes, or Cuisenaire rods, can be used in concrete 'staircase' activities. In slightly more abstract activities, children can draw, and colour, a 'staircase' on squared paper.

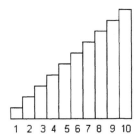

Working with concrete materials allows children to rediscover the basic staircase relationships in the most natural and flexible way: in figuring out how to build the sequence from a spread of 'unordered' materials – and in correcting the inevitable mistakes which are made along the way – children also learn that making the staircase correctly is a process which *orders* numbers. Repeated staircase- building activities helps foster an intuitive understanding of the concept of *transitivity*: that, for example, if 9 is larger than 8, and 8 is larger than 7, then 9 is larger than 7. After building uninterrupted sequences, children can be asked to put 'incomplete' sequences in order. Questioning children about what they are doing will help them to translate actions, which may be largely intuitive, into deductions which they can then use. For example after ordering a few quantities from smallest to largest, children can be asked some questions relating to *transitivity*. For example: 5, 2, 3 and 8 would be ordered 2, 3, 5 and 8:

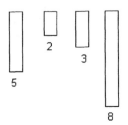 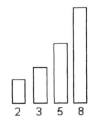

Following this, children can be asked whether 8 is bigger than 5, whether 5 is bigger than 2, and whether this, in turn means that 8 is bigger than 2. This kind of concrete activity paves the way for much more difficult task of ordering an abstract set of numbers (for instance, 'Put these numbers in order from largest to smallest: 5 3 2 8').

Cuisinaire rods are particularly well suited to 'staircase' building precisely because the rods are designed to represent numerosities through their relative size and colour. Indeed, because children usually understand from the outset that rods embody an intrinsic or inbuilt order, they will often spontaneously 'invent' a staircase if they are given a set of rods to explore. Rod 'staircase' building can be used to serve two important functions. At the same time that children explore the 'plus-one steps' in ordering a spread of rods, they can also be helped to become familiar with, and learn, the rod–number equivalences – for example, they will learn that the 'bright' colours, 'orange' and 'yellow', represent *ten* and *five*, respectively, and so on.

Most children enjoy the simple activity of building Cuisinaire rod staircases, and can be encouraged to build a staircase from 1 to 10, and then back down again to 1. (As Eva Grauberg points out, rod work depends on children laying rods flat on a table or 'mat', rather than – as some children intuitively do – standing them up vertically.) Younger children, or children with severe maths difficulties, may also benefit from playing a simple rod staircase game. In the *rod staircase game* each player sets out to build a staircase as rapidly as possible. Rods are secured by rolling the respective dice number on a 1–10 die: a rolled die 5, for example, will secure the rod *five*. Two to four players may play the staircase game, and each player takes it in turn to generate a number which represents a rod value to place in the staircase format. The rods do not have to be secured in sequence: players simply 'guess' the position for each rod they earn. A player 'misses' a 'turn' if s/he has already secured a particular rod. When time is limited, it is possible that 4 consecutive rod stairs 'in-a-row' will win the staircase game.

The number pattern model

Examples of simple counting activities and of 'staircases' which are designed to represent number ordering are very familiar in contemporary teaching approaches. On the other hand, as we saw in the introduction, the use of readily recognized *number patterns*, in early counting-related number-work, is rather less familiar. While children with learning and maths difficulties can benefit greatly from practising ordinary counting skills, a number of maths educators have found that working with clearly defined *number patterns*, which represent the counting numbers to 10, also helps children acquire a *feel* for quantities and numbers.

It is often pointed out that the majority of children – and this usually includes children with specific learning difficulties – seem to feel 'at home' with very small quantities up to the subitizing limit of 4. Mahesh Sharma (1981a) argues that this is especially true of children who play dominoes or who play games using conventional 'dot' dice. As we have seen, very young children are able to subitize very small quantity configurations and children encounter small and instantly recognizable quantities far more often in 'everyday life' than they do large quantities (or indeed large numbers). It can be argued that children feel more confident and comfortable with small numerosities since they are able to recognize them in a very immediate way and thus they feel 'at home' with the related number symbols such as 'three' or '3' because they have an image of them based on quantity recognition.

Although the *number track* model is a very useful, simple and ordered model for representing and visualizing the numerosities above 5 – and is one to which we will return in the next chapter – it has the important drawback that images of slightly larger numerosities, or larger numbers, are potentially unclear or imprecise:

$$\bullet \; \bullet \; \bullet \; \bullet \qquad\qquad = 4$$

$$\bullet \; \bullet \; \bullet \; \bullet \; \bullet \; \bullet \; \bullet \; \bullet \; \bullet \quad = \boxed{?}$$

In fact, as we have seen briefly in the introduction, children's perception of quantities above 10 can be rendered less imprecise – and can also be situated in terms of *Base Ten* number structures – by employing simple 'tens-structuring' devices, or 'tens-structured' models.

Nonetheless it remains true that linear images of the crucial basic counting numbers between the upper subitizing limit of about 5, and the first decade number, 10, can remain rather too 'unclear' or imprecise to be sufficiently helpful as *number-sense* fostering images on their own. In mainstream maths education writing, Karen Fuson (1992) suggests that it would be beneficial for all young maths learners to become familiar with images for numbers larger than 5 which are based on instantly recognizable patterns and which build on the natural subitizing strengths of the

human brain. Examples of possible *number patterns* for '8' which are based
on instantly recognizable component patterns include:

```
o o     o o     o o
             o           o
o o     o o     o o

o o      o       o
         o        o
o o      o         o
         o
```

   In the field of maths and learning difficulties, Sharma (1981a; 1990b),
Chinn and Ashcroft (1998) and Henderson and Miles (2001) have found
that children with specific learning difficulties do, indeed, benefit from
being exposed to patterned visual images for the larger numbers to 10 –
patterned images which can then be stored in children's visual memory.
Sharma points out that children who are familiar with *number patterns*
intuitively match other arrangements of the basic numerosities to 10 to
the *number pattern* models which are familiar to them. He points out, too,
that *number patterns* provide children with images which can be 'matched'
to the abstract number words and abstract number symbols to 10.
Working with number patterns helps children with specific learning
difficulties feel almost as 'at home' with the numbers between 5 and 10 as
they do with the numbers below 5.
   In fact, for children with specific learning difficulties and poor *number-
sense*, there are a considerable number of additional and quite subtle
advantages attached to working with number patterns. First, while structured linear models and images of numbers can be useful, basic linear
images can also perpetuate an unhelpful 'one number after another' view
of numbers, as we have already suggested. We will see that this can have
serious implications for the way in which calculation is conceived. *Number
patterns* offer a helpfully 'different' or alternative model of numerosities.
On one hand, each number pattern is a very distinctive whole with a very
distinctive identity and a very distinctive *feel*. On the other hand, each
pattern is also made up of unique combinations of immediately recognizable and familiar components. Thus, in the most natural or 'osmosis' like
way, children who become familiar with *number patterns* also begin to view
numbers as internally patterned constructs – as 'wholes' which can be
built up and broken down (decomposed) and built up (recomposed) again.
In other words, children develop images for numbers which are components-based rather than *ones-based*. This emergent understanding that
numbers can be viewed in part-whole ways, represents the beginnings of

an important development in children's early number concept and helps pave the way for what one could call 'reasoning readiness', as we will see in the next section of this chapter. A related advantage of working with *number patterns* is that the human brain would appear to be able to process quantities between 5 and 10 quite rapidly as long as they are made up of smaller and immediately recognized component quantities. This capacity of the brain means that *number patterns* can be processed more rapidly as patterns than they could through counting each individual unit.

For dyslexic and dyspraxic learners with basic number difficulties, using *number patterns* as number referents continues to have important advantages in subsequent concrete cognitive groundwork – for instance working with *repeated patterned groups* helps dyslexic and dyspraxic children develop a *feel* for the basic concepts of multiplication and division.

It is clear from the available literature on *number patterns* that the *number pattern* idea can be put into practice in rather different ways. In working with secondary school children, for example, Chinn and Ashcroft (1998) found that it worked best to ask pupils to design or select their own preferred, and therefore individualized, versions of the counting numbers to 9. Other educationalists prefer to design and work with 'in-house' standardized patterns, which can be used by all of the children they teach. A clear advantage of standardized patterns is that they can be used to help children visualize key internal components of the counting numbers, as well as a range of basic addition and subtraction facts, as we will see.

Standardized number patterns can be designed with a number of slightly different basic premises or maths educational criteria in mind. For instance, Sharma sometimes has children superimpose the symbols for numbers on to the standardized quantity patterns they work with. For example:

Patterns may also be selected to reinforce a *5-plus* patterning for the numbers between 5 and 9 or 10. *Five-plus* patterns are one set of patterns illustrated in Chinn and Ashcroft's *Mathematics for Dyslexics*; and Steve Chinn's subsequent (1999) 'What to do when you can't add and subtract' illustrates *5-plus* patterns as a way of explaining and supporting helpful calculation strategies, too.

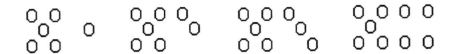

Another option for designing standardized number patterns is to build on the very familiar canonical dice or 'dominoes' patterns. Genuine canonical patterns extend only as far as 6, of course, but they have the advantage of being pleasingly symmetrical and the patterns for 4 and 6 are structured as patterned *doubles*:

4 = 2 plus 2 or   O O   6 = 3 plus 3 or   O O
                  O O   O O
                                                     O O

Chinn and Ashcroft (1998), Sharma (1990b) and others illustrate similar *doubles* based patterns for 8:

8 = 4 plus 4 or   O O
                  O O
                  O O
                  O O

While all the evidence seems to confirm that dyslexic and dyspraxic children benefit from the experience of working with standardized patterns it is not a particularly easy task to select which particular patterns to employ. For instance, *5-plus* patterns have very distinctive advantages: very significantly the *5-plus* patterns reiterate in a different form the two-hand and five-finger structure which humans naturally possess (and intuitively refer to in counting) and which probably informed the *base-ten* structure of our number system in the first place. However, although *5-plus* patterns merit serious consideration, many younger primary school children with maths difficulties do not easily process some of the *5-plus* patterns 'in one go' nor can they readily differentiate between them 'at a glance'. Instead they often need to *count on* beyond the 'base' canonical 5 pattern in order to determine which pattern is illustrated. For this reason, young primary school with specific learning difficulties generally prefer symmetrical dice-related number patterns: in essence, primary school children seem to find dice-based number patterns easier to process and considerably easier to remember than the *5-plus* patterns.

The *number patterns* to 10 which seem to work particularly well with all primary school children (and with children from as young as four years of age, upwards) are consequently *doubles* and *near-doubles* based patterns; these patterns are also, in the main, built of two easily recognizable canonical components:

Some specific 'number pattern' teaching suggestions

Although the visual images of dot *number patterns* are very distinctive and can be used to great advantage in wall displays, friezes, posters and on playing cards and home-made dice, it is also important that children actually have the experience of constructing the larger number patterns, themselves, and consequently have a practical understanding of the way in which each pattern is structured or built up. It is usually best to begin practical pattern building work by building even numbers. Depending on the age and ability of the child, the numbers 4 or 6 (which are often familiar from dice games, anyway) are good numbers to begin working with. For example, to construct the pattern of '6' each child should be given *6 ones* such as glass nuggets. The children can then be asked to 'split' or share the nuggets into absolutely equal or even groups. Once the children have created two groups of 3 they should be asked if they can organize the 2 *threes* into the dice pattern of '6'.

Although the majority of children manage this task very easily, it is worth ensuring that a conventional dice model is available, in case this is needed. The patterns for '8' and '10' can be established in a very similar way. Once children have 'split' the two quantities into their respective 'even' components they can be encouraged to invent or copy the illustrated dice-related standardized patterns for themselves.

Building the odd-number patterns derives from and links to the *doubles* components idea: since the standardized patterns for '7' and '9' illustrated above are *near-doubles* patterns, it is through a *near-double* partitioning process that they are introduced to children. For example, to establish the pattern of '9' children are given 9 counters and asked if they can manage to split them into two absolutely equal groups. When it has been established that this is not possible, children are asked to 'split' the 9 as 'fairly' as they possibly can – in other words, they are asked to partition the '9' into two 'nearly equal' groups, or into two groups which are as equal as possible. Following this, the majority of children will invent, or are able to copy, the standardized pattern which is based on the canonical components.

On the other hand, designing the *near-double* pattern for '7' is not quite as straightforward as the *number pattern* of 9 turns out to be. Instead of building the illustrated pattern, children often invent slightly different versions:

Any of these patterns could, of course, be adopted for use with children. The pattern of '7' chosen for illustration is simply the one which the majority of primary school children seem to recognize most rapidly and is also the one which most younger children seem to remember best.

From the beginning, children can be encouraged to pay attention to the components which make up the patterns: for example, teachers should emphasize that 10 'equals' 5 plus 5; 8 is 'built from' 4 plus 4; 9 is 'made up of' 5 and 4; 7 can be 'made from' 4 plus 3. The emphasis on components can also be fostered by recording the component relationships in non-canonical ways. This helps promote flexible thinking about numerical relationships: instead of sticking with the more usual '4 + 4 = 8', children can be introduced to number sentences such as '8 = 4 + 4', and presented challenging problems such as 9 = □ + 4. Although the triad model of representing numbers really comes into its own slightly later on, as we will see, it can be useful to introduce children to this form right from the outset .

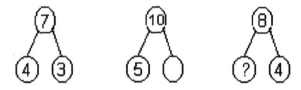

Some 'number pattern' card games to play

Snap! Snap! is played by two players only. The number patterns should be drawn on to individual cards. To play Snap! effectively, 4 sets of each number pattern are needed. The basic Snap! rules should be followed but it is important to lay cards side-by-side.

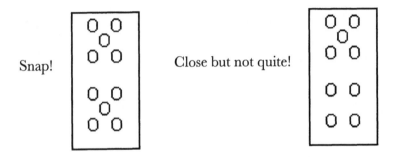

Number Pattern Card 'War' This is a game for 2–4 players. Four full sets of *number pattern* cards are needed. The rules for 'card wars' can be found on p. 431. Players are dealt one *number pattern* card in each consecutive round. The overall winner is the player with the most cards at the end of the game.

Number Pattern 4-in-a-row Again, this is a game for 2–4 players. The basic rules for **card lotto** can be found on p. 429. In this game each player has a set of *number pattern* cards, 1–10, laid out in sequence. Each player takes it in turns to throw a number 1–10 die (0 = 10), and the matching card is turned over. The winner is the player who first turns over 4 cards in a row.

Number Pattern Pairs, or Pelmanism The rules for pelmanism can be found on p. 432. *Number pattern* pelmanism is played with one set of number pattern cards and a matching set of digit cards.

CHAPTER 4

Counting in basic calculation

The importance of counting in calculation

The use of counting to work out simple addition and subtraction calculations is a very important first phase in children's developing understanding of numbers. It would appear that the use of counting to calculate is also a universal phenomenon: children in all cultures go through a fairly prolonged period of counting in order to calculate (Butterworth, 1999; Dehaene, 1997). Because counting is understood to be the foundation of calculation, this particular aspect of counting and of calculation has received a great deal of attention in recent research and in mainstream maths learning literature. It is widely accepted that just as children's general counting skills go through important developmental phases, so, too, do their counting skills in learning to work out simple arithmetical calculations. In general terms, two important kinds of development take place in early calculation. First of all, counting tends to become increasingly abstractly executed. In brief outline, studies show that most children first use small objects to count out addition and subtraction problems. Next, most children generally use their fingers to work out addition and subtraction answers. Finally children count their addition and subtraction solutions 'mentally' or 'in their heads'. Secondly, children's counting procedures usually become increasingly sophisticated. In essence, studies show that most children naturally 'discover' how to execute counting procedures in ever-efficient and cognitively more complex ways. In the process of becoming more efficient, children may temporarily 'fold back' to using concrete materials (objects or fingers) to support their cognitive progress. Overall, though, the developmentally significant cognitive advances in counting allow children to move through and beyond counting to more cognitively advanced and much more efficient ways of calculating.

We have already seen that 'ordinary' counting experiences do not seem to allow significant numbers of children with learning difficulties to develop *number-sense*. We have also noted that a defining characteristic of dyslexic and dyspraxic children's approach to calculation is that they remain dependent on counting. Once again, it is important to understand in some detail the ways in which 'ordinary' children's basic calculation skills develop. This helps make sense of the calculation difficulties which classically characterize a very large number of dyslexic and dyspraxic learners – difficulties which set them apart, in maths learning terms, from most of their peers.

The stages of calculation: addition and subtraction

There is general agreement in the literature on children's early calculation development that children's progress in learning how to add and how to subtract proceeds in broadly parallel ways and through broadly equivalent stages – although it is also generally recognized that development in subtraction turns out to be somewhat more complex than the equivalent progress in addition.

Addition

There is widespread consensus in research literature that children go through three important and clearly defined stages of development in learning how to add quantities or numbers together. In the process of trying to solve simple word problems (Carpenter and Moser, 1982) or simple calculation problems (Hiebert et al., 1997), children often spontaneously 'invent' or devise these stages for themselves. Alternatively, as Gray (1997) points out, the stages may be specifically taught or children may be 'guided' by adults to develop them for themselves.

Counting all

In this earliest and most basic addition stage, children count out both of the quantities to be added, combine the two quantities, and then count the total of the combined quantities from the beginning. For instance to work out 3 + 5 children represent both numbers concretely, ooo and ooooo, and then count them together, oooooooo – 'one, two, three, four, five, six, seven, eight.' The *counting all* stage of addition is usually associated with the pre-cardinal *enumeration* stage of counting.

The counting on stage

The *counting on* stage can be broken down into two phases. The first phase is often called *counting on from the first number*. At this stage, children are able to hold the first number in working memory and then count on the second number: 3 + 5 = 'three ... four, five, six, seven, eight'. *Counting on from the first number* is conceptually more advanced than *counting all* because it depends on an understanding of the basic *cardinality principle*. It also requires the management of a complex double-counting procedure: whilst counting on from the first number, children have to devise some way of keeping track of the second number so that they know when to stop counting. The second phase is *counting on from the larger number*. Counting on from the larger number is significantly more advanced than counting on from the first number. In this addition phase children select the larger of the two given addends and then *count on* from this larger number. This approach is sometimes called the *min* procedure because it requires 'minimum counting'. To solve 3 + 5, children select the larger addend, 5, as the starting point for the calculation, and count, 'five ... six, seven, eight'. It is often argued that the *min* procedure rests on an implicit understanding of the commutativity of addition – in other words, many researchers believe that children intuitively grasp that the order in which any addition calculation is undertaken will not affect its *outcome*. The *min* procedure is certainly more efficient, involves less working memory, and is less conducive to procedural counting errors than 'first phase' *counting on*.

Knowledge of facts

Ultimately, most children begin to know easier facts *by heart*: the earliest known facts are often pattern-based facts such as the *doubles* facts or facts which involve small amounts of counting, such as n + 1 and n + 2. At the same time, many children begin to harness their growing relational understanding of numbers and start to use their small repertoire of known facts to work out further 'unknown' facts. Thus, for instance, children will begin to reason that if 2 + 2 is 4, then 2 + 3 will be 5; or if 5 + 2 is 7, then 5 + 3 will be 8. Reasoning in this way involves using a known fact together with very small amounts of counting (Thompson, 1997c).

Fact-derived reasoning is quite efficient and does not involve very large amounts of working memory. Active, creative cognitive processes are also involved and children tend to pay more attention to the *input* (or question) and *output* (or answer). For these reasons, children usually begin to internalize more and more facts. Although the overall tendency is for children

to know increasing numbers of facts *by heart* it is increasingly acknowledged that some children may continue to derive some of the 'hardest'
facts from known 'easier' facts: for instance 8 + 9 may continue to be
derived from 8 + 8 or 8 + 10.

Subtraction

The counting out stage

At this very basic stage, children use objects or fingers to 'count out' the
whole 'start out' number or minuend. From the 'start out' number
children then 'count out' the number to be taken away, which is also called
the subtrahend. The second number, or subtrahend, is removed. The
number (or quantity) which remains is counted and is understood to give
the answer to the subtraction problem. For instance to work out 7 – 4,
seven is 'counted out', a group of 4 is 'counted out' from within the 7 and
then removed. The remaining 3 are counted and '3' is given as the answer.

The counting back stage

At the *counting back* subtraction stage, children are usually less dependent
on access to physical objects, and they learn to hold the 'start out' number
(the minuend) in working memory and *count back* the subtrahend. Children
may employ *counting back* in slightly different ways. More commonly
children employ a method of *counting back* which mirrors *counting on* procedures and involves counting back to each prior number in turn: to work
out 7 – 4, for example, they will count back from seven, 'six, five, four,
three', so 3 will remain.

7–4 4 have been *counted back* and 3 remain

This method is often reinforced by adults through the use of simple
'jump' representations on an ordinary number-line.

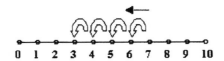

Less frequently, children use an abstract version of the *counting out* model and 'say out loud' each individual number subtracted. In this instance, to work out 7 – 4 children count, 'seven, six, five, four', so 3 will remain.

O O O Ø Ø Ø Ø
1   2   3   4   5   6   7

7–4 4 have been *counted back*, so 3 remain

Like *counting on, counting back* involves a double counting procedure in which children simultaneously count backwards while keeping track of the second number, or subtrahend. Counting backwards is harder than counting forwards and most children find *counting back* very much harder to manage than *counting on*.

Counting up to

Since most children first understand subtraction as *taking away* and picture *taking away* as subtracting back, the majority of children intuitively use one of the *counting back* methods as the equivalent procedure to *counting on* in addition. However some children – usually children with a strong relational grasp of numbers – also devise the alternative, and in many subtraction calculation instances, more manageable, *counting up to* subtraction procedure for themselves. In the *counting up to* subtraction procedure children start from the second number (the number to be taken away, or subtrahend) and *count up to* the first number (the minuend) while keeping track of the number counted up. The number *counted up* is the *difference* between the two numbers and the solution to the subtraction question. For example, in *counting up* to work out the answer to 7 – 5, children count up from 5 'six, seven', keeping track of the fact that two numbers have been counted up, so 7 – 5 = 2.

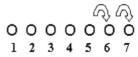

Counting up as 'jump' representations on a number-line:

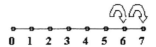

When relatively large subtrahends are subtracted, *counting up to* is much more efficient than counting back and minimizes the number of counting errors that children make. *Counting up to* is far less frequently taught or modelled by adults than *counting back* and some children find the logic which underpins *counting up to* very difficult to understand when it is abstractly taught.

Knowledge of facts

In time, children begin to know certain subtraction facts *by heart*. At first, children tend to internalize the 'easy' *counting back* facts, such as n − 1, and n − 2. Many children also begin to use well internalized addition facts to work out the related subtraction fact: for example, to solve 8 − 4 children may reason '2 fours are 8, so 8 − 4 must be 4'. Children who use the *counting up to* subtraction procedure will know *by heart* that subtracting adjacent numbers (for example 8 − 7, or 7 − 6) equals 1. In time, children become increasingly flexible in their use of 'easy' subtraction facts or known addition facts to work out further subtraction facts. For example, to solve 10 − 6 children may reason, '2 *fives* are 10, so the answer can't be 5, it must be 4'.

Dyslexic and dyspraxic children and the stages of calculation

Once again, unfortunately, there are no detailed developmental studies charting the progress of dyslexic or dyspraxic children's early calculation skills. Once again then, too, the attempt to outline the earliest calculation progress of dyslexic and dyspraxic children has to depend on reports from parents and teachers, from classroom observations, and from teaching assessments of younger dyslexic and dyspraxic children.

In general terms there would seem to be some important connections and parallels between the basic counting development of dyslexic and dyspraxic children and the profile of their early counting and calculation development. First of all, as in their basic counting development, the calculation development of dyslexic and dyspraxic children would seem to be typically delayed. It is often noted that the basic calculation progress of dyslexic and dyspraxic children is considerably slower than that of most 'ordinary' children. Parents, nursery school teachers and reception teachers report that many children with specific learning difficulties do not easily progress from the *counting all* stage of calculation to the *counting on* and *min* stages of addition or certainly to the *counting back* stage of subtraction. Parents and teachers report, further, that children with specific learning difficulties often need explicit teaching and considerable amounts of overlearning practice before they are able to master *counting on* and *counting back* procedures. Children with specific learning difficulties seem to rely longer on concrete materials or on their fingers in order to complete basic addition and subtraction calculations.

Secondly, although early calculation development is slow, in the same way that significant counting milestones are finally attained, it should be acknowledged that some of the important calculation milestones are also finally reached by the majority of dyslexic and dyspraxic children. Thus, although a small number of severely dyslexic or dyspraxic children cannot *count on* in addition by the time they are 7 to 7$\frac{1}{2}$ years old, this is certainly not the norm. Diagnostic assessments show that by the time they are about 7 years old, most dyslexic and dyspraxic children have understood the cardinal significance of numbers and know how to *add on*. Indeed, most children with specific learning difficulties fairly consistently *add on* from the larger number in simple addition situations from about 7 years old onwards. They can thus be said to have acquired a very basic abstract *number concept*. On the other hand, progress in subtraction is rather harder to achieve. Assessments show that subtraction development presents obstacles for quite a large number of children with specific learning difficulties. Since counting backwards is a particularly difficult skill for many dyslexic and dyspraxic children to acquire, the development of counting back procedures is often significantly delayed. Children as old as about 7$\frac{1}{2}$ years of age, or older, will sometimes rely on *counting out* subtraction methods where subtrahends greater than 2 are involved. Children who generally use fingers rather than objects for *counting out* and who achieve persistently incorrect answers this way will often declare '0' to be the outcome of any 'difficult' subtraction problem . Ultimately, however, and nearly always by about eight years old, or so, the vast majority of children with learning difficulties finally master *counting back* in subtraction work, too.

Nevertheless, it is also very important to acknowledge that the overall calculation profile of dyslexic and dyspraxic children is strikingly different in many significant regards from the calculation development of 'ordinary' children. In other words, there is rather more involved in the calculation difficulties of many dyslexic and dyspraxic children than could be attributed as a general developmental delay. By contrasting the calculation development of dyslexic and dyspraxic children with the expected or 'ordinary' pattern of development, three further characteristics of learners with specific learning and maths difficulties are foregrounded:

1. As the majority of primary school children begin to enter the third calculation phase, subtle differences in the way many dyslexic and dyspraxic children relate to numbers begin to be apparent. Ordinary children with good *number-sense* and a familiar feel for numerosities begin to see patterns within and between numbers. They understand, for instance, that 8 comprises 8 *ones*, and certainly grasp the *eightness* of 8, but they also begin to notice and internalize the fact that 8 comprises the special pattern of 'two 4s' or is 'made' of '7 and 1'. In more general terms, what may be said to begin occurring is that children with 'good' *number-sense* begin to develop a more flexible and sophisticated number-concept. In other words, ordinary children become increasingly sensitive to part–whole relationships, as well as to any connections or logical relationships between numbers. In contrast, sequencing difficulties, working memory difficulties and difficulties automatizing counting and 'taking in' numerosities mean that many dyslexic and dyspraxic children fail to begin viewing numbers as constructs which comprise internal patterns and do not start to see numbers as complexly related entities, either. Instead, it is highly characteristic that they continue to see numbers in quite basic or primitive counting-based and ones-based ways. While most dyslexic and dyspraxic children grasp the cardinal *eightness* of 8, the sequential and working memory demands of counting mean that they fail to develop beyond perceiving 8 as '8 *ones*' or as all the *ones* it would take to reach the number 8. As we have seen, Karen Fuson describes a ones-based number concept as a primitive *unitary* number-concept.

2. Whereas most children progress beyond using purely mechanical counting procedures, many dyslexic and dyspraxic children do not. Many children with specific learning difficulties do not spontaneously and readily begin using 'easy' and known facts to work out harder addition facts nor do they come to know steadily increasing numbers of addition and subtraction facts 'by heart'. In other words, many children with specific learning difficulties do not seem to move in any conclusive way into the third and most advanced calculation stage. Instead, to borrow Eddie Gray's (1997) terminology, many dyslexic and dyspraxic learners seem to become 'stuck' or 'arrested' at the second calculation stage or the stage of *counting on* and *counting back*.

3. The third very significant characteristic of dyslexic and dyspraxic

maths learners is that although *counting on* and *counting back* procedures constitute their preferred method of calculation, and are therefore extremely well practised, many children with specific learning difficulties make repeated counting errors when they try to work 'harder' basic addition facts (such as 8 + 7) or quite basic subtraction calculations (such as 9 – 6). In counting-to-calculate many dyslexic and dyspraxic learners regularly achieve answers which are incorrect by a margin of one or two, particularly in subtraction problems.

The importance of understanding the 'counting trap'

It is clear that the pivotal point at which most 'ordinary' children enter the third calculation stage is essentially the point at which they begin to use more reasoning, or thinking, and less counting. As we have seen, children begin to use already known facts and much shorter sequences of counting to work out 'unknown' facts. Once children begin to reason in this way, it seems to quite rapidly follow that more facts begin to be known *by heart*. The ability to reason in the development of most children usually leads to increasingly competent facts knowledge. As we have seen, however, dyslexic and dyspraxic children do not make this important cognitive leap in calculating.

This particular cognitive weakness would seem to represent a very significant key to understanding the ongoing calculation difficulties of many dyslexic and dyspraxic children. To gain some sense of how addition and subtraction should be presented to children with specific learning difficulties, it is important to try and understand why it is that the calculation development of children with learning and maths difficulties seems to stop short before the final developmental stage in addition and subtraction calculation is reached. In other words, a fundamental teaching question to try and make sense of is why it is that mathematically able ordinary children usually progress through and beyond counting-based procedures whereas many dyslexic and dyspraxic learners do not.

In fact, as Eddie Gray suggests, the likely reasons for these enormously important developmental differences are very complex and seem to involve a vicious cycle of cause and effect which are quite difficult to disentangle.

The repercussions of difficulties managing counting on and counting back procedures

As we have seen, older primary school children with specific learning difficulties nearly always *count on* or *count back* to work out addition and subtraction facts but counting-based procedures represent a much harder and much more demanding form of calculation than many adults realize. The key difficulty with relying on *counting on* and *counting back* to work out addition and subtraction facts – and to reach the ultimate goal of knowing addition and subtraction facts *by heart* – is the sheer difficulty of managing the procedures.

Counting on and *counting back* are, by definition, sequential or linear counting processes which take place in time and which tend to use substantial amounts of working memory. As we saw earlier on in this chapter many dyslexic and dyspraxic children have difficulty managing the most basic sequential and working memory demands of ordinary counting. In general terms, the counting processes involved in *counting on* and *counting back* are far more difficult than ordinary counting because double counting processes are involved and because it is difficult to count and simultaneously keep track of where to stop counting. In fact, classroom-based research shows that most ordinary primary school children, including mathematically able children, find lengthy *counting on* and *counting back* sequences difficult to manage. Of course, sequencing problems compound key aspects of 'keeping track' difficulties: most children with learning difficulties are able to manage small addends (plus one, plus two and, usually, plus three) and small subtrahends (minus one, minus two and sometimes minus three) but larger addends or subtrahends are hard for many children to visualize and dyslexic and dyspraxic children are often not clear about where they should start *counting on* or *back* from. This particular problem is often especially acutely felt in subtraction. As Gray remarks, the demands of extended sequences of counting back are especially 'horrendous'. In subtraction, too, children are often particularly unclear about where they should start and stop counting. Indeed, many dyslexic and dyspraxic children seem unable to visualize the subtraction counting back process, at all: in working out a subtraction such as 7 – 5, for example, children are often unable to decide whether to start counting from 7 or from 6 and frequently fail to make sense of whether the final answer would be the number which is stopped on in the counting back process (for example 3, in 'six, five, four, three'), or the number before this (and in this given instance, 2). In other words, many dyslexic and dyspraxic children are confused between the two different models of subtracting back, which are described on p. 109.

The problems which many children with specific learning difficulties experience in managing longer *counting on* and *counting back* sequences have a number of extremely important further consequences – consequences which are so important, in fact, that they also need to be described in detail. Firstly, *counting on* and *counting back* difficulties help explain the significant fact that dyslexic and dyspraxic children make basic calculation mistakes, particularly in subtraction. At the most obvious level, achieving consistently incorrect answers is inevitably demoralizing. It means, too, that children are disinclined to trust their calculation *outcomes* and wrong answers can make children anxious about, and mistrustful of, all calculation, especially of subtraction. A second quite complex consequence of the difficulties entailed in *counting on* and *counting back* is closely intertwined with the related problems of poor *number-sense* and a weak *number-concept*. In essence, difficulties in the execution of *counting on* and *counting back* procedures further compound and confirm the tendency for children with specific learning difficulties to go on seeing calculations as instructions to count.

We have already noted that it is the recognition of quite simple patterns in number-work – such as *doubles* patterns or *plus-one* patterns – which form the basis for children's earliest reasoning about numbers. Children who see, take note of and internalize patterns, and notice connections with patterns (such as *near-doubles* connections, for instance), begin to develop a relationship-based conception of numbers which underpins the ability to think about calculations in increasingly sophisticated ways. As we have seen, children with specific learning difficulties have a *unitary number-concept* and often fail to see patterns within or connections between numbers. In the context of calculation development, this is very significant. It means that dyslexic and dyspraxic children usually continue to see both of the component numbers in addition and subtraction number-fact calculations as individually separate or isolated entities. In other words, the component numbers in most calculations are viewed in monolithic or ones-based ways. It needs to be emphasized that children who are struggling with the mechanical demands of *counting on* and *counting back* find it very hard to 'take in' the nature of the two (or more) numbers making up a calculation, and certainly find it very hard to perceive any significant or memorable patterns within the numbers. Thus, the demands of managing complex double counting procedures underscore difficulties seeing connections between closely related facts and also make it hard for children to make connections between given calculation problems and any 'easier' known, facts.

All of this links closely to a third consequence of difficulties managing *counting on* and *counting back* procedures. The particularly heavy working memory demands of difficult and lengthy double counting procedures mean that children with specific learning difficulties often fail to link *question* and *outcome*, or *input* and *output* in a form which is remembered as a new fact. In essence, as Gray (1997) argues, the large amount of working memory, which is required to execute longer stretches of *counting on* and *counting back*, contributes towards making it very difficult for children with specific learning difficulties to put addition or subtraction facts into long-term memory, and thus to know them *by heart*. Overall, then, it can be seen that a *unitary number-concept*, combined with the particularly demanding nature of *counting on* and *counting back*, mean that demands to provide answers to given number fact calculations will be interpreted by dyslexic and dyspraxic children as instructions to count. In other words, all 'harder' addition or subtraction *questions* are understood to call for a counting response. Thus, for example, a very simple calculation, such as 4 plus 5, is invariably seen to require the action of counting the two numbers, 4 and 5, together.

To illustrate the way in which dyslexic and dyspraxic children are 'doomed' to count it is, perhaps, helpful to explore in some detail the specific '4 plus 5' calculation briefly touched on a moment ago. On one hand, a child with a strong intuitive feel for numbers – who has a growing understanding that there are patterned relationships within and between numbers and who has internalized *doubling* and *halving* relationships – is likely to 'discover' or grasp that the calculation '4 plus 5' can be processed as the *near-double* calculations, '4-plus-4-plus-1'. In other words, the ability to understand numbers in terms of their components and to step back to notice logical connections means that children increasingly understand that they could choose to simply count to work out '4 plus 5', if they wanted to, or they could rearrange the numbers – for instance, break down the 5 into 4-plus-1 – to make calculation easier. Children who start developing in this more flexible way, increasingly process numbers as objects which can be manipulated in different ways and consequently understand requests to solve 'unknown' number facts as opportunities to think, or to reason. In essence, an increasingly sophisticated basic *number concept* (which builds on an intuitive and growing *number-sense*) is accompanied by an increasingly sophisticated understanding of calculation.

In contrast, as we have seen, the child with poor *number-sense* and a weak *number-concept* will not usually 'see' the *double* in '4 plus 5' even if the double '4-plus-four' fact is well known. Instead, the '4' and the '5' are usually processed as two initially *monolithic* entities which are then counted together. In this particular instance since '4 plus 5' does not involve a particularly lengthy sequence (especially if it is processed as '5 plus 4') many dyslexic and dyspraxic learners are likely to count correctly and are therefore also likely to achieve the 'right' answer. On the other hand, the *counted on* sequence is lengthy enough and onerous enough in sequencing terms to involve quite large working memory demands: the final *outcome*, '9', is thus unlikely to be consciously linked to the initial problem and is therefore also unlikely to be remembered. Indeed, as we suggested above, requests to add '4 plus 5' on subsequent occasions will be interpreted as further, repeated, commands to perform the mechanical counting together process all over again.

Many dyslexic and dyspraxic children believe that basic addition and subtraction calculation is synonymous with a counting response. The illustration of the two very different counting-based and reasoning-based approaches to the simple 4 plus 5 addition example helps crystallize what Gray (1997) calls the 'proceptual divide' in calculation. The term 'proceptual divide' is intended to encapsulate a clear distinction between those children who view calculation solely as the *process* of counting – and who therefore remain 'stuck' at the *counting on* and *counting back* stage of calculation – from those more mathematically able children whose developing *number concept* enables them to view numbers as complex *concepts* and thus allows them to 'take off' in maths.

The teaching implications of the calculation 'divide'

Understanding what Gray calls the 'dual face' of counting means understanding that it is important to distinguish between those children for whom counting is an appropriate way to work out number facts – and part of the normal and necessary process of development – and those children for whom an over-reliance on counting is impeding progress and leading to a calculation 'dead-end'. In very broad terms, as we have seen, counting is the calculation norm until children are between 6 and 7 years old. Although the majority of 'ordinary' children subsequently use less and less counting, most teachers and parents become resigned to the fact that a great many dyslexic and dyspraxic children rely on counting long beyond the age of 7 years old. This general acceptance of counting-based strategies is also informed by the belief that repeated practice at counting will lead in the end to automatized number fact knowledge. In other words, it is widely believed that overlearning practice at *counting out* facts will ultimately result in *by heart* knowledge of the facts. As Eddie Gray argues, this widely held assumption that counting will lead to knowledge of the number facts means that much seemingly 'commonsense' and pragmatic teaching intervention actually reinforces counting-based methods of calculation. A number of common teaching-support practices are based on mechanical counting models. For example, when teachers offer support to children who cannot keep track of *counting on* and *counting back* processes, teachers often suggest that they use counters or unifix cubes to 'help' them. In fact, children generally use counters and cubes in the most primitive *counting all* ways. Some teachers prefer to teach less able children to use *counting on* and *counting back* responses. They may thus encourage children to use their fingers to *count on* or train children to use a simple 'ordinary' *number-line*, such as a ruler.

However, there is a lot of evidence to show that long-term use of concrete counting supports often has unforeseen results. First, mechanical use of concrete supports often leads to calculation mistakes. Dyspraxic children, in particular, are often baffled by finger methods of calculation. As we have seen, many young dyspraxic children cannot 'read' or remember fingers and finger patterns easily and certainly become further confused if different and conflicting finger methods are demonstrated by different people offering them support. As we have seen, *number-lines*, too, can lead to faulty calculation. This is because dyslexic and dyspraxic children remain characteristically unsure about where to start *counting on* and *counting back* 'from'. Secondly, even when counting tools are used accurately, they do not normally lead to automatization of the number facts. The short-term pragmatic result of using a counting tool may be that the child works out the answer, so that progress appears to have been made, but, in fact, the child ultimately remains dependent on the tool. In large part this is because counting-based procedures employ tools in non-thinking and mechanical ways. It is also true that *input–output* 'linkage' is also often undermined by distracting 'clutter' and the time it takes children to organize and execute a concrete 'count'.

A summary of the limitations of counting in calculation

In brief, the teaching and learning disadvantages of perpetuating counting-based ways of working out addition and subtraction facts are that:

1. children with specific learning difficulties often have a primitive, ones-based, or *unitary concept* of numbers;
2. counting-based procedures reinforce *unitary* conceptions of numbers;
3. children with specific learning difficulties and maths difficulties do not naturally progress beyond counting-based methods of adding and subtracting numbers;

4. many children with specific learning difficulties cannot rely on counted outcomes;
5. repeated practice at counting addition and subtraction facts does not result in automatization – *by heart* knowledge – of the number facts.

Teaching basic addition and subtraction facts

Of course, it is clearly not the case that all dyslexic and dyspraxic children, who experience difficulties learning maths, have no knowledge of 'harder' basic addition and subtraction facts. Like proficiency at counting, acquiring some knowledge of the very basic number facts is a very early maths skill and children start working towards internalizing the facts from their earliest days at school. Although many children with learning difficulties depend heavily on counting, as we have seen, it is also important to acknowledge that a number of children with maths difficulties – and especially somewhat older primary school children – will have managed to internalize some, or even most, of the very basic addition and subtraction facts to 10.

The reasons for this are quite straightforward. In brief, comparatively short stretches of counting are needed to work out the most basic number facts. Addition and subtraction calculations below 10 are fairly easy to visualize and the 'double counting' and 'keeping track' aspects of smaller calculations are consequently relatively manageable. Because of this, many children with number difficulties are able to count those facts quite accurately and since comparatively small amounts of working memory are needed, the counted *outcomes* are not impossible to put into long-term memory.

Nevertheless, while all of this is true, diagnostic assessments and classroom observations show, as we have seen, that many primary school dyslexic and dyspraxic children do, in fact, have difficulties with very basic calculation to 10. These usually require to be addressed for genuine maths progress to be made possible. Generally speaking, broad differences can be identified between the basic number fact abilities of younger dyslexic and dyspraxic children and those of somewhat older dyslexic and dyspraxic children. Assessments and observations show that a great many younger primary school dyslexic and dyspraxic children have difficulty working out the majority of the addition and subtraction facts in acceptably efficient ways. Assessments also reveal that younger primary school children have a very narrow and inflexible grasp of number relationships. Thus, while they may be able to work out 'easier' addition and subtraction problems which are posed in more conventional linear ways (e.g. 3 + 4 = ☐ or 6 − 2 =☐) they are often unable to answer more challenging missing number or component number questions, such as 3 + ☐ = 7, or 6 − ☐ = 4. Likewise, younger children are very often unable to solve logically challenging word problems. The profile of older primary school children with learning and maths difficulties is often slightly different. It is common for older children to know a good proportion of the basic addition facts by *heart* but many still have difficulty with harder subtraction facts, such as 8 − 5, for example. Many older children can figure out non-linear calculations and word problems but may still use counting to do so.

In summary, then, teaching decisions about whether the most basic foundation stage of calculation will need to be covered at all and, if so, how much time would need to be allocated to work at this level, will depend on the abilities and needs of the individual child or group of children who require number-work help. A very broad guideline is the very simple one that all children who rely on counting to work out the basic facts to 10 would benefit from learning to reason about them. However it is also helpful to give a slightly more detailed overview. Younger or less able children with specific learning difficulties usually need to pause for some time at this basic calculation stage. They generally need time to grasp the new flexible ways of thinking about numbers and to absorb a more sophisticated approach to thinking, reasoning, and talking about numbers. Older or more able children with some maths difficulties may be helped to speed through certain selected areas, such as basic subtraction and *missing number* competence, at the same time as working on subsequent and more advanced areas of maths. Part of the skill of helping older children calculate more efficiently involves devising ways of having children apply basic number knowledge to larger, more 'grown-up' calculations, as rapidly as possible. For instance, knowing how to calculate 9 − 7 efficiently, may be applied to calculations such as 99 − 7 or even, when appropriate, to calculations such as 6539 − 7!

Adding and subtracting very small quantities such as one, two and three

Although requiring children to engage in long sequences of *counting back* should, in principle, be avoided as much as possible, some children need direct teaching intervention in order to be able to move on from the *counting all* and *counting out* stages of calculation. There are a number of reasons for ensuring that children are able to *count on* and *count back*. First, as we have seen, an understanding of *counting on* and *counting back* forms part of important cognitive developments in calculation. Secondly, *counting on* and *counting back* form a sensible basis for the addition and subtraction of small quantities. Thirdly, *counting on* and *counting back* procedures can be understood to provide useful 'fall-back' strategies when alternative 'thinking strategies' have been temporarily forgotten. Finally, as we will see in the next chapter, understanding *counting on* is thought to facilitate an understanding of the *Base Ten* composition of larger numbers.

Teaching suggestions for *counting on* and *counting back*

Certain counting activities are well known to help prepare children for *counting on* and *counting back* procedures. For example, instead of asking children to count from 0 or 1, or to count backwards from 10 or 20, children can be asked to count forwards or backwards from a range of different starting points. 'Broken chain' counting, in which a child is asked to take over a 'count' at any point in the counting chain, is also very useful.

In ordinary counting activities or in *number track* work children may be given a specific number and asked to say which number is the *next number* or which number is the *number before*. The link between the *next number* and 'plus 1' and the *number before* and 'minus1' is relatively easy for children to make. To prepare the way for 'plus 2' and 'minus 2' children may also be given a number and asked to articulate 'not the next number, but the number after', or 'not the number before, but the number before that'. For example: 'I'm pointing to the number 7. Can you tell me the number which is not the number before 7, but is the number before that?'

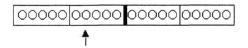

'Hidden quantity' activities (for instance, Martin Hughes's (1986) very famous **Tins Game**) are very popular with children and offer successful ways of promoting *counting on* procedures. In basic **Tins** work, a first specific and reasonably large quantity of *ones* is counted into a container with a lid. The first quantity needs to be out of view and is either to be held in working memory or, alternatively, the container may be labelled. Children are given a small second quantity which remains in view. They are then asked to add the two quantities together by *counting on* from the larger quantity in the container. Children who have a poor understanding of the cardinal principle may need a *counting on* response to be modelled first.

7 glass nuggets are put into the 'tin', then 3 nuggets are added on to the '7':

In 'classic Tins' activities, the teacher starts out by placing the larger of two quantities in a container. However, some dyslexic and dyspraxic children do not seem to have developed an intuitive grasp of the commutativity of addition. In this context this means that they may be able to work out 7 + 2 by *counting on* successfully but they perceive 2 + 7 as a 'hard' calculation because they believe that they have to *add on* 7 to the 2. The *components of numbers* activities which are described shortly are partly designed to help children gain a better sense of the commutativity of addition and enable them to start *adding on* from either addend in an addition calculation. Nevertheless, a modified 'hidden quantities' game is also enjoyed by children who like the **Tins Game**. In the modified activity, children are given two quantities: one very small quantity, such as 2, and one relatively large quantity, such as 8. Children are asked to select the most sensible quantity to place in the 'tin' and then the activity proceeds as before.

The beginnings of fact-derived strategy use. Introducing children to the power of logico-mathematical thinking

The key argument which lies at the heart of much of the discussion about counting procedures in this chapter is that if children with learning difficulties and maths difficulties are going to move beyond counting as a central calculation strategy, they need to be given explicit and carefully structured teaching so that they are able to reason to figure out number facts. They have to be released from the burden of having to mechanically count facts. As we have seen, counting strategies are not a useful basis for learning the majority of facts *by heart*, especially where children have sequencing and working memory weaknesses. Furthermore, since most dyslexic children and many dyspraxic children have difficulties remembering language-based fact associations, a strong and efficient reasoning ability is all the more central to their ability to make progress in basic number-work.

Thus, instead of perpetuating counting-based approaches to calculation, it is important to prepare dyslexic and dyspraxic children for the more forward-looking and exciting maths world of thinking about numbers and number relationships. Children with specific learning difficulties, who are 'stuck' with counting, need to be helped to understand that numbers are flexible and manipulable entities; they need to see patterned relationships within and between numbers; and they need to be helped to feel that thinking is more reliable, often quicker, and can be infinitely more fun, than counting. They need to learn, and to trust, that thinking becomes 'easy once you know how'.

Confident use of efficient thinking strategies, supported by over-learning practice at using the strategies, helps the majority of children with specific learning difficulties learn the foundation facts *by heart* – or at least work them out very quickly. Once children really begin to understand that they can use known facts to work out unknown facts they can begin to participate in the positive cycle of reasoning, knowing increasing numbers of facts *by heart* and reasoning in more and more confident and sophisticated ways.

A key teaching question, of course, is to decide where to start the new cycle of reasoning-based calculation work from – in other words, it is important to decide which aspects of addition or subtraction are the most appropriate ones to start the reasoning and understanding-based learning process with. In fact, there are no really hard-and-fast rules concerning which aspect of early calculation are 'best' to teach first. It is possible to begin, for example, by teaching certain strategies or ways of thinking which are the most helpful ones in basic addition work. For instance, many children particularly enjoy learning the *near-doubling* addition method which was mentioned earlier.

However, as we have seen in some detail, it is the fact that many dyslexic and dyspraxic children have a primitive *unitary* concept of numbers which lies at the heart of their calculation difficulties. For this reason, many teachers have found that it is most beneficial, in the longer term, to target work which fosters children's *concept of number*, right from the beginning. The process of learning to think in number-work can begin by building children's understanding that numbers are not just built of *ones*, but, rather, that they comprise patterned relationships, as well. In other words, for children with specific learning difficulties it is often most helpful to introduce reasoning-based calculation through work designed to highlight the internal patterns or 'components' of numbers – to start out by exploring all of the ways in which the numbers to 10 can be 'partitioned', 'chunked', 'broken down' or 'decomposed' into two parts.

In fact there are quite a number of educationally compelling reasons for starting with, and particularly emphasizing, component number knowledge – especially whenever vulnerable children with poor intuitive *number-sense* need to be introduced to thinking about numbers.

1. As we suggested a moment ago, component number-work is a key way to help children understand that numbers are complex entities which can be broken down (or decomposed) and built up (or recomposed), in a variety of different ways. Through component number-work, children are better able to understand that numbers can be broken down or 'split' into parts to make addition and subtraction easier.

2. Component work helps children absorb, in intuitive ways, some very important foundation mathematical principles. For example, as Nunes and Bryant (1996) argue, structured partitioning work helps children grasp the *commutativity* of addition. (As we saw a moment ago, *commutativity* is the important principle that the order in which numbers feature in an addition problem, or a multiplication problem, will not affect its outcome – in other words, that 5 + 2 is equivalent to 2 + 5, and the answer to both 'sums' is 7). Thus, for instance, the process of partitioning an individual number, such as 7, into all its constituent pairs, makes the equivalence of differently ordered pairs of numbers relatively easy to see – indeed, in many instances, working with concrete materials to partition numbers enables children to 'discover' the *commutative principle* in addition for themselves. Secondly, the process of 'chunking' specific numbers into all of their parts can help children grasp the key principle that if one component of a target number is made larger, for example by 1, then the other component is necessarily smaller, by 1, as a result. For example, if 8 is comprised of '4 plus 4', then 5 will require 3 to 'build' 8. In this very simple way, children may be introduced to the idea that component numbers can be adjusted by small amounts to work out equivalent component pairs and that this can be done in entirely logical ways. In the longer term, a general proficiency at adjusting calculations in simple and logical ways is an important aspect of many fact-derived strategies and is a key number skill to acquire.

3. Component work helps children grasp other important logical relationships in intuitive ways, as well. Very significantly, learning to reason about the paired components of numbers helps children understand *missing number* or *missing addend* types of problems. Children who genuinely understand that 9 is 'built' from '5 plus 4' will also understand that 5 will require

4 to 'build' 9. In other words, children will understand the connections between conventional 'linear' addition problems, such as 4 + 5 = ☐, and less conventional problems such as 4 + ☐ = 9, or ☐ + 5 = 9. Secondly, working on the internal paired relationships within numbers, helps children understand the relationship between addition and subtraction. In particular, concrete partitioning work helps children see that if a number comprises two parts – for instance if 8 comprises 4 plus 4 – then removing one part will leave the other part as the remaining portion, or answer. Thus, if 8 = 4 plus 4, then 8 minus 4 equals 4; or to express this in a more conventional form, if 4 plus 4 = 8, then 8 minus 4 = 4. Understanding the link between partitioning and subtraction allows children to develop a flexible model of subtraction. As we will see, the most basic foundations for the *adding up to* (or *complementary addition*) model of subtraction are put into place through partitioning work and children are also able to understand the concept of *difference* more easily.

Acquiring and developing an understanding of the logical principles and ideas which are outlined above has two enormous pragmatic advantages. First of all, having an intuitive grasp of the *commutativity* of addition represents a very large step forward in reasoning potential: it means that children understand that addition calculations can be organized to make them as 'easy' and efficient as possible. Secondly, a pragmatic understanding of the link between components knowledge and subtraction means that children can use their components knowledge to work out subtraction problems. They do not need to learn, or practise, a separate set of skills. Finally, knowing the paired components of the numbers to 10 *by heart* gives children the foundation skills and the knowledge which they need to be able to use more complex fact-derived strategies: for instance, to use the common *bridging-through-ten* strategy to figure out 8 + 7, or 48 + 7, children need to know that 8 + 2 = 10 and that 7 can be partitioned into 2 + 5.

A discussion of partitioning

Although partitioning work does not occupy a very central position in some contemporary understanding-based classroom approaches to teaching maths, its value is generally acknowledged. Partitioning work certainly features in the Numeracy Strategy Framework and most foundation maths textbooks and commercial schemes of work contain some partitioning exercises. In particular, children's knowledge of the patterned components of 10 is widely considered to be important, and the 'story of 10' tends to be quite comprehensively covered in the majority of primary school classrooms.

While most children will have some partitioning experience in the early primary years, it is important, nonetheless, to strike a somewhat cautionary note. Partitioning exercises can, and often do, descend into rather meaningless mec̄anical exercises, if they are not carefully monitored. The key argument behind emphasizing partitioning work is that many children do not easily see patterns within numbers. In many partitioning activities, which are certainly intended to foster part–whole understanding and knowledge, children may not necessarily make the important connections and logical 'discoveries' which educationalists want them to make. As some writers point out, children often derive story-of-numbers answers in a range of purely mechanical ways, in which very little real thinking is involved. For example, many children with specific learning difficulties simply count to find missing components. Alternatively, children may perceive 'plus 1' and 'minus 1' patterns in written component number exercises and use them in the most pragmatic ways to derive the *missing component* answers.

For example: The *story* of 6

6
1 + 5
2 + ☐
3 + ☐
☐ + 2
5 + ☐
☐ + 0

In this common layout, children may notice that the first numbers in each component pair ascend in order while the second numbers descend in order.

With particular regard to working with children with specific learning difficulties, the major drawback of unstructured partitioning work is that if patterns and connections are not genuinely grasped, children cannot, and will not, begin the process of automatizing the component number-facts – especially for the larger and less easily visualized numbers, such as 7, 8 and 9. Of course, if children have to *count* to work out missing components, this takes a relatively long time and requires so much additional and 'draining' working memory that children are unlikely to use components-based routes in subsequent fact-derived reasoning strategies. They will obviously depend, instead, on the well understood, familiar, linear and *unitary* counting methods.

For these reasons, partitioning activities work best with the majority of dyslexic and dyspraxic children if the following teaching conditions are met. First of all, clear models for partitioning need to be used and early work needs to be based on using concrete materials. Secondly, important logical principles (for example, commutativity) should be carefully and explicitly taught. Thirdly, children's initial memory load needs to be reduced by teaching the minimum number of *big value* internal component facts. Reasoning to derive component pairs should also taught in a careful step-by-step way. Finally, the component facts need to be thoroughly overlearned. so that they are genuinely internalized.

Suggested teaching models for partitioning work

Although alternative teaching tools can be valuable, two effective models for component number-work include:

1. The doubles-based *number patterns* described earlier which children might already be familiar with.
2. Linear 'step' models of the components of numbers which primary school children enjoy calling '*number sandwiches*'.

In general, it works particularly well to use both of these models to help build children's knowledge of the components of numbers. As we will see, each model has its own particular strengths, both in helping children visualize the component pairs making up individual numbers, and in supporting children's ability to reason to work out 'harder' *missing component* and subtraction facts. On the other hand, it is also sometimes best to select and use just one of the models – for example, in trying to speed through components-based work with an older child with specific learning difficulties.

Suggestions for number pattern and number sandwich partitioning work

The number patterns: key 'inside' facts

In all basic calculation work, as Thompson (1997d) frequently notes, children have to have a foundation of well-known facts in order to be able to reason to work out 'unknown' facts. For this reason, it is often particularly fruitful to begin exploring the patterned components of numbers by working, in a structured way, with the standardized *number patterns* described in the earlier part of this section. Familiarity with the *number patterns* gives children ready access to a set of *key double* and near-double component facts for the numbers to 10.

For example, the *number pattern* for 10 reinforces the 'easy' component fact that 10 can be partitioned into 5 plus 5:

The *number pattern* for *9* – which is very closely related to *10* – establishes the '*key*' component fact that 9 can be partitioned into 5 plus 4, or 4 plus 5.

The first structured teaching step in component work ensures that children know the *key* component facts 'by heart'. The games described on pages 104–105 are one way to familiarize children with the *key number pattern* facts. Children can also be asked to 'build' the *number patterns* using small concrete materials or to draw the patterns from memory. It can be explained that the *key number pattern* pairs will prove very useful in reasoning about numbers. As children become familiar with the *number patterns*, children can be asked to visualize each one individually and to name the *key* constituent parts. In early oral work very concrete phrasing such as 'Can you put the *number pattern* of 'x' in your head, and tell me what it is built from', can be very helpful, indeed. In time, it is important to ask slightly more abstract *questions*, such as 'What is the *key* fact of 7?'

A further and very significant feature of working with the *number patterns* is that knowledge of the *key components* translates very readily into knowledge of a fairly large number of basic *missing number* and subtraction facts. For instance, the components of the *number pattern* for 7 are the two smaller and canonical patterns, 4 and 3. If 3 is removed or taken from 7, 4 will obviously remain:

Likewise, if the number 9 needs to be 'built', and one part, or 4, is in place, then the other part required to complete the pattern of 9, is the component 5. Questions which suggest actions should be asked first. For example, 'You want to build 9. You have built 4. What do you still have to put down to build 9?' As soon as children become more familiar with using the number patterns to solve *key* component problems, questions can be phrased in more familiar ways. For example, children can be asked questions such as '5 plus what equals 9?' or 'What plus 4 equals 9?'

Key component fact work can be recorded in a range of different ways. To emphasize the part–whole idea it is particularly useful to record components of numbers in the non-canonical form, 9 = 5 + 4. Written overlearning exercises should be designed to foster maximum flexibility: 4 +☐ = 9, 5 + ☐ = 9, 9 – 5 = ☐, 9 – ☐ = 5. The increasingly popular triad form of recording component facts, which was touched on earlier, is a particularly successful, newer, method of recording internal number relationships. As we will see in subsequent chapters, the triad representation of component facts offers an extremely useful shorthand model for recording *key* 'chunking' steps in many of the big value fact-derived strategies.

9, recorded in triad form, is represented as

Written exercises can be presented in the triad format:

More component facts of the numbers to ten

Once children have acquired a confident and flexible knowledge of the *key* component facts, these well-known facts are established as the starting point for reasoning to figure out the other component pairs of the basic counting numbers to 10. Since the *doubles* facts, such as '8 equals 4 plus 4', are relatively easy to visualize, it works particularly well to start by partitioning the *even numbers* to 10. For instance, younger or less able children could begin by partitioning 6 (or even 4) into all of its component parts. Older children, who already know the facts of 6, may start out by partitioning the larger and 'harder' even numbers, 8 or 10, instead.

In early practical pattern-based partitioning work concretely built *number patterns* or drawn images of *number patterns* can be used. Using the *key* component fact of an even number as a starting point, children can be helped to see how the other paired relationships relate to, and can be built from, the *key* fact:

Here, for instance, what children are able to see is that 'since 3 plus 3 equals 6, 4 plus 2 equals 6, and 2 plus 4 also equals 6'. In written number form, there relationships can be expressed as: $6 = 3 + 3$, so $6 = 4 + 2$ and $6 = 2 + 4$.

However, while the *key facts* certainly offer a valuable starting point for much part-whole reasoning, it is also important to bear in mind that reasoning processes should be kept as efficient as possible. The *key facts* are especially helpful in understanding and visualizing the generally trickier component fact pairs around the 'middle' of a specific number, for instance '3 plus what equals 8?' or '6 plus what equals 10?' Visualizing the facts at the 'outer edges' of numbers should also be emphasized, too. For instance, it is particularly effective for children to be able to visualize and reason that 'if 1 plus 7 is 8, then 2 plus 6 also equals 8'

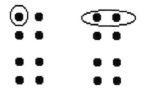

Likewise, *number patterns* can help children understand that 'If 9 plus 1 equals 10, then 8 plus 2 will be 10, too.'

In conjunction with ongoing *number pattern* based work, it is in working to build children's knowledge of all the paired relationships that it is particularly helpful to introduce children to the second model, the 'sandwich' or 'component steps' model, for understanding part–whole relationships. We have noted a number of times that teaching suggestions for structured *number pattern* work are not very common. On the other hand, a variety of versions of 'components-steps' can be found in contemporary teaching guides and textbooks. If Cuisinaire rods are not available for component steps work, the step patterns can be drawn on to squared paper and then shaded with coloured pencils. However, Cuisenaire rods are a particularly effective tool for working to construct the component number pairs.

It will be remembered that one common drawback of much components-of-numbers work is that the component pairs are often derived in unthinking, mechanical ways. In the special 'sandwich' model referred to earlier, the core idea modifying rather more conventional step-building work is that children are encouraged to start building from the *centre* of the model – in other words, they are encouraged to start building from the *key* component fact which is already overlearned from *number pattern* activities. Thus instead of building each step in sequence, the first step in rod 'sandwich' work is to establish the number fact 'outer casing' (the bread of the 'sandwich', so to speak), and the *key* fact 'middle'. The middle or core filling provides the starting point for structured reasoning-based pattern building. Some of the steps towards building the '*sandwich*' of *eight* include the following:

The key 'four-plus-four' is placed in the middle.

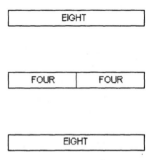

Children build out from the four-plus-four layer. 'Four needs four to make eight, so five needs three to make eight. Five needs three to make eight, so six needs two to make eight.'

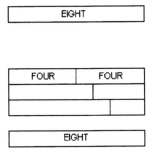

To complete the '*sandwich*', children are also shown that 'Seven needs only one to make eight, so six needs two to make eight.'

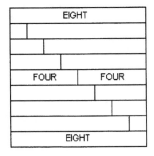

Within the overall framework of the *key* fact starting point, rod 'sandwich-building' activities are largely self-teaching and self-correcting exercises. In instances in which children make a mistake and select an incorrect component, the rod will not fit the step framework and the children will have to try again. Although children should be encouraged to build sandwiches as independently as possible, some children may need a little help, at first, with establishing the full range of component pairs. Once again, it helps to use very concrete and action-based language in the beginning: for example, 'You want to build 10. You've put down 4. What do you need to build 10? 5 needs 5 to build 10, so 6 will need ... 4!' However, as soon as children become successful at using effective reasoning paths, the ordinary abstract language of maths should be introduced. For instance, it is certainly important to pose conventional 'shorthand' questions, such as '6 plus what is 10?', or 'What is 8 minus 7?' (It is helpful to note, too, that if a child is unable, at any stage, to answer oral questions, the first step would usually be to offer a reasoning 'cue' or 'prompt'. Nevertheless, it may also be necessary to return to a concrete model to reaffirm and reinforce a clear and appropriate reasoning route.)

Quite soon, of course, children will need to become familiar with the *odd number* component facts. Knowledge of the *odd number* component relationships is structured in the same way as the *even number* component relationships. Using the same *key-fact* principle children learn to use the near-double *key* fact from a specified *odd-number* pattern to figure out many further unknown facts. In brief then, for example, since 7 equals 4 plus 3, 7 minus 5 will leave 2:

Likewise, since 9 is 'built' from 4 plus 5, 3 plus 6 also equals 9. Children also learn to reason from the 'outer edges' or 'extremes' of the *odd number* models. Thus, if 1 plus 8 equals 9, 2 plus 7 will be 9. Similarly, 7 minus 1 is 6, so 7 minus 2 is 5:

		Seven
X		Six
	X	Five

It should be noted that as children internalize the 'sandwich-based' way of visualizing relationships, shorter step sequences can be built and foregrounded just in the way in which 7 − 2 is illustrated above. In other words, it is not always necessary to construct the whole '*sandwich*' to reinforce a specific reasoning point.

Two important notes on subtraction

Subtraction and partitioning

Although most children with specific learning difficulties are encouraged to use a *counting back* model of subtraction, the model which *number pattern* and '*sandwich*' work makes possible, is, in fact (as we suggested before) a very economical components-based model of subtraction. In the kind of structured components work described above, children learn (and can be reminded) that they have all the knowledge which is required to be able to figure out any basic subtraction problem efficiently, so long as they are able to generate the relevant component pairs of the number. To figure out a problem such as 9 − 7, using a components knowledge approach, children visualize the first number (or minuend), 9, and 'chunk' or 'split' it into the component parts, 7 (the number to be subtracted, or subtrahend) and its – initially unknown – component pair, 2. Since 7 is subtracted, the paired component, 2, remains. The triad form of recording component parts is a very handy way of transcribing and reinforcing the thinking process involved:

$$9\text{–}7 = \underset{\textstyle\widehat{7}\quad\bigcirc}{\overset{\textstyle 9}{\diagup\diagdown}} \;\rightarrow\; \underset{\textstyle\widehat{7}\quad\widehat{2}}{\overset{\textstyle 9}{\diagup\diagdown}} \;\rightarrow\; \underset{\textstyle\widehat{\cancel{7}}\quad\widehat{2}}{\overset{\textstyle 9}{\diagup\diagdown}} \quad 9 - 7 = 2$$

Using a *components* model of subtraction has the very big advantage that children do not have to rely, at all, on difficult, slow, counting back procedures.

The language of subtraction

An important aspect of the reasoning-based approach described in this book is that children's understanding needs to be secured, at the outset, by careful, transparent and 'concrete' language usage. It is also emphasized that part of the learning process involves a conscious teaching commitment to building up children's knowledge of appropriate and increasingly complex maths vocabulary. In general terms, all of this applies to subtraction, too: for instance, concrete language certainly needs to give way to abstract terms like 'minus' and 'subtract'. However, in most primary school classrooms, the most frequently used colloquial terms for subtraction are the very common terms 'take away' or 'taking away' – for example, 'What is ten take away four?' or 'Take four away from ten'. Since the commonly taught model for subtraction or 'taking away' is a *counting back* model of subtraction, children generally identify the phrase 'take away' with a process of subtracting backwards. As Fuson (1992) points out, this 'take away' understanding of subtraction limits children's conceptual understanding of subtraction and often holds children back from understanding *counting up to* models and *difference-based* concepts of subtraction. Since 'taking away' is fairly universally identified with the *counting back* concept and model of subtraction in children's minds, teachers should try to use the associated terms as sparingly as possible. To help children become familiar with less conceptually 'loaded' subtraction vocabulary, it is best that the components-based model for subtraction is accompanied by the terms 'minus' and 'subtract' just as soon as possible – although, to be sure (as we saw in Chapter 2), children might need reassurance for some while that 'minus' or 'subtract' do, indeed, mean 'taking away.' Similarly, children's use of the term 'take away' should be accepted but also rephrased, whenever possible: 'Yes, the answer to 9 take away 2 – which also means 9 subtract 2 – is 7.

Addition facts to ten

Why teach addition facts?

It has already been acknowledged that, of all the number facts to be learned, the basic addition facts are the set of facts which are most likely to be known *by heart* by dyslexic and dyspraxic children. However, when children are asked how they figure out their addition answers, it turns out that a surprising number of children with specific learning difficulties *count on* to work out these facts, too. While many children may count quite accurately at this level, the basic addition facts, like the component facts, are such important building blocks within subsequent reasoning strategies that it is very helpful, indeed, if they are known as automatically as possible. As we have seen, *by heart* knowledge of addition and subtraction number facts is much more likely to be achieved through reasoning to figure out the facts than through repeated practice at lengthier sequences of counting. Thus, at the same time that children are consolidating their ability to reason logically about the patterned relationships within numbers, it is also often important to work on, and to consolidate, their knowledge of basic addition strategies, too.

Fortunately, there are a number of important links between structured partitioning work and the basic addition 'thinking' strategies. Many of these links contribute towards helping children to make rapid progress in mastering the addition facts to 10. Nevertheless, these links between partitioning and addition are not, in fact, entirely straightforward. On one hand, it is clearly true and important that addition facts represent relationships which children have already encountered in structured partitioning work. Thus, for example, the addition fact '2 plus 4 equals 6' involves exactly the same set of relationships as '6 equals 4 plus 2':

Six	
Four	Two

On the other hand, it is also important to understand and acknowledge that there is a very big difference between the way in which the 'problem' or 'unknown' aspect of an addition question is structured and the way in which the 'unknown' aspect of the problem features in a subtraction or *missing number* question form. In subtraction and *missing number-work*, as we have seen, the 'unknown', or answer to the problem', is actually a part of a whole which is represented by the principal or focal quantity in the number sentence. In other words, to solve problems such as $7 - 4 = \square$ or $4 + \square = 7$, children start generating the correct solutions by visualizing and/or partitioning the given number, 7. In an addition question, by contrast, the ultimate outcome or solution involves a combination of the two quantities within the problem, and it is the result of this combination which is the unknown. In the example $3 + 4 = \square$ children have to reason towards the unknown and completely new solution, 7. In simple terms, then, a child who has worked on partitioning numbers may recognize that the answer to $3 + 4 = \square$ is, in fact, 7, and this may occur because the child has remembered the verbal association, or because the component numbers '3' and '4' have successfully triggered an image of the appropriate *number pattern* or 'sandwich'. (Children will often volunteer that they know an addition outcome 'because of the pattern' or 'from the sandwich'.). However, some children have difficulty making associations between component-number knowledge and addition questions and many dyslexic and dyspraxic children fail to make such associations in a sufficiently consistent way. What this means, then, is that structured addition work has to offer children who continue to have poor basic addition facts knowledge reliable ways of reasoning which will help them to figure out addition questions.

Near-doubling

One set of addition facts which children with specific learning difficulties often know (or manage to internalize from the symmetrical patterning of the even number patterns) are the 'easy' *doubles* addition patterns to 10: for example, $2 + 2 = 4$, $3 + 3 = 6$, and so on. These *doubles* addition facts can be used as the basis for the fact-derived reasoning strategy which is widely known as *near-doubling*. In an earlier section of this chapter we have seen that ordinary children with good basic *number-sense* will often intuitively invent *near-doubling* ways of thinking for themselves. In contrast, children with learning difficulties who generally *count on* to figure out simple additions usually need explicit teaching to make sense of the *near-doubling* idea. In essence, using *near-doubling* strategies involves remembering a known *doubles* fact and then adjusting the *doubles outcome* by adding or subtracting very small quantities – usually 1, but sometimes 2, and, occasionally, even 3. Thus in the *near-doubling* approach, as we saw above, the specific addition problem 'what is 4 plus 5?' can be processed as the calculation '4 plus 4 plus 1'. Likewise, the problem 'what is 5 plus 7?' is sometimes processed as the easy-to-figure-out '5 plus 5 plus 2'. To prepare vulnerable dyslexic and dyspraxic children for some of the procedural aspects of the *near-doubling* strategy, it is helpful to introduce work based on the addition principle of *associativity*. This fosters children's ability to add three or more quantities together. In brief, the principle of associativity means that the outcome of complex addition calculations is not affected by the order in which the constituent parts are added. In adding three (or more) quantities or numbers together, children can be encouraged, for instance, to look for *doubles* patterns first, and then, in a final step, add the third quantity. Cuisinaire rods are a particularly efficient tool for exploring these ideas.

Most children with specific learning difficulties find the *near-doubling* pattern of doubling-plus-one relatively easy to grasp where small numbers are involved. Again, Cuisinaire rods are 'classic' tools for teaching children the *near-doubling* concept.

Three	Four	
Three	Three	one

$3 + 4 = \square$

$3 + 3 + 1 = \square$

The written triad form of representing component parts of numbers can be used to highlight the *doubles* pattern, which is contained within the *near-double* calculation:

$$3 + 4 = \square \qquad 3 + \overset{4}{\underset{(3)\ (1)}{\diagup\ \diagdown}} = 3 + 3 + 1 = 7$$

Small *ones* arranged in carefully structured linear patterns can also help children grasp the *near-doubling* idea.

oooo ooooo $4 + 5 = \square$

oooo oooo o $4 + 4 + 1 = 9$

Once children have grasped the *near-doubling* concept, 'harder' *near-doubling* situations, in which *near-doubling* choices have to be made, can be introduced. In many *near-doubling* situations the first addend is larger than the second addend, for example, 5 + 4 = ☐. In these situations conventional linear left-to-right processing will mean that it is necessary to employ a *doubles-minus-one* idea:

Five	Four	
Five	Four	one

To work out 5 + 4, using doubling-minus-one reasoning, one can say, '5 plus 5 equals 10, but 5 plus 4 is one less than 10, and is thus 9'. On the other hand, however, children can, of course, apply the *commutative* rule in addition and they can opt to process the calculation from the second and smaller addend. This means that they proceed from right to left: 4 + 4 = ☐ so 4 + 5 = ☐. In this instance, children will again be using the slightly easier *doubling-plus-one* strategy:

Five	Four	Four
one Four	Four	Four

Harder additions below 10: addition 'leftovers'

Once children are able to add 1 or 2 to numbers and have mastered the *key doubles* facts and the *key near-doubling* strategies, the only addition facts which may remain slightly difficult to figure out are 3 + 5, 5 + 3, 4 + 6, 6 + 4, and, especially, 3 + 6 and 6 + 3. However by the time that children have become familiar with the idea of reasoning to work out addition facts they can often indicate their own preferred methods for figuring out these slightly 'harder' facts. Many children happily use *near-doubling* to embrace 3 + 5, seeing it as 3 + 3 + 2, or seeing 5 + 3 as 5 + 5 – 2. Some children prefer to see 5 + 3 as (5 + 2) + 1. The facts 4 + 6 and 6 + 4 are usually processed as a 'doubles-plus-two' pattern, but in time, these facts should also be recognized as two of the *key facts* of *ten*. The additions, 6 + 3 and 3 + 6 are slightly less easy to figure out. 6 + 3 can be *counted on* or processed as (6 + 2) + 1. Once children recognize the facts of *ten*, 6 + 3 and 3 + 6 may also be seen as 1 less than a *key* fact of 10. Children who are already familiar with the most familiar 'three by three' pattern for 9 enjoy visualizing this classic pattern in responding to 3 + 6 and 6 + 3 addition facts:

● ● ○
● ● ○   6 + 3 = 9
● ● ○

The special case of the facts of ten

Our number system is a *Base Ten* system, as we will see in some detail in the next chapter. In other words, the number system is structured in *tens* and multiples of *ten*. This means that the ability to quickly access the component facts of 10 is an especially important foundation skill to have. Secondly, many of the most accessible fact-derived strategies in subsequent calculation work exploit the *Base Ten* structures to 'decompose' calculations and in this way make the calculation processes easier to manage. For example, the facts of 10 are central to children's ability to use *key* strategies, such as the big value *bridging-through-ten* addition and subtraction strategies. In using 10 to work out 8 + 7, for instance, 8 requires 2 to 'reach' 10, 5 remains from 7, 10 + 5 is 15, so 8 + 7 = 15. Thirdly, the basic foundation components of 10 can also be used to help children understand and access the larger-value *tens* facts of 100 and the even larger component *hundreds* of 1000: thus, for example, if 4 plus 6 equals 10, then 40 + 60 equals 100 and 400 + 600 equals one thousand. Likewise, since 10 minus 6 equals 4, 100 minus 60 equals 40, and so on.

The component facts of 10 are thus particularly important for children to study, and automatize:

1. *Number-pattern* and 'sandwich-building' work should emphasize the 'facts of 10', in particular.
2. Many 'facts of 10' overlearning opportunities should be provided.
3. Children's knowledge of the facts of 10 should be frequently reviewed, both in the shorter and in the longer term.

Building children's 'by heart' knowledge of the number facts to ten

In the early stages of mastering new ways of thinking it is important that children are given plenty of time to figure out each unknown calculation. In the beginning it is to be expected that many dyslexic and dyspraxic children will calculate quite slowly and sometimes more slowly than they would have done had they been counting. Nonetheless, of course, it is also important that children begin to learn to calculate more efficiently. Calculating very slowly predisposes children with specific learning difficulties to lose track of what they are doing when they have to manage more complex calculation demands. As we indicated when we discussed *counting on* the ability to figure out facts efficiently – and use less working memory space – also facilitates *by heart* knowledge of facts. We saw in Chapter 2 that it is common for children with specific learning difficulties to require a lot of overlearning practice at using reasoning routes in order to become familiar with them – and certainly to automatize them. It should be noted that children with severe or compound processing difficulties, or with severe working memory difficulties, may always reason quite slowly.

1. Frequent and short 3–5 minute oral 'quizzes' are very helpful ways of practising thinking strategies because children can also provide information about how they are thinking. Where children are working in a group situation, oral reviews can be organized so that children take turns to explain the way they reasoned to work out the given calculations. In one-to-one sessions adults may need to model alternative ways of calculating to encourage children to become more flexible or to help children consider alternatives to *counting on*: 'This is the way I did it ...' or 'Some children work it out like this ...'
2. In time it is important to provide children with 'mixed bag' oral or written calculation exercises so that they practise remembering and selecting appropriate strategies. At first, many children with learning difficulties find it difficult when different types of problems are 'mixed together'.
3. Completing written exercises also affords very useful overlearning practice. In closely monitored written exercises, and particularly in one-to-one teaching situations, children can be asked to explain their thinking by being asked simple *questions*, such as 'How did you do it?' In early independent written practice (for example, in exercises set for

homework) it is helpful, at first, to provide children with reasoning 'cues'. For instance:

$$6$$
$$\boxed{3} + \boxed{3}$$
$$\boxed{2} + \square$$

$8 - 4 =$ $\qquad$ $9 - 5 =$
$8 - 5 =$ $\qquad$ $9 - 6 =$

$7 = \boxed{4} + \square$ $\qquad$ $7 = \square + 4$
$7 = \boxed{5} + \square$ $\qquad$ $7 = \square + 5$

4. In general, as we have already noted in Chapter 1, some of the most successful calculation practice is afforded by playing carefully selected calculation games with children. Since games meet considerably less resistance than other forms of overlearning practice and are usually positively enjoyed, they provide painless ways of helping children automatize reasoning processes. From the outset it will need to be clear to children that games are intended to practise the 'thinking' methods they have learned. However, simple and quick overlearning games afford children invaluable practice at figuring out facts in the most palatable – and often genuinely fun – ways. Games can also be reintroduced at subsequent intervals to provide opportunities for children to review their knowledge of the basic number facts.

Components of numbers games

Simple missing number card lotto

The general **card lotto** rules are described on p. 429. For **missing number card lotto** a target number, for instance 9, should be selected. If the target number is 9 each player has a set of digit cards numbered 0–8. Players take turns to throw a 1–8 dice. Players need to give the 'missing' component of the target number. For example, if a player rolls a dice 3, he or she needs to give the missing component '6'. The player can then turn over his or her '6' card. This is a very good game to play for overlearning the components-of-10: in this instance players require digit cards numbered 1–9, and a 1–9 dice should be used.

'Clear the deck' components game (one player)

In a game to practise the components of 9, four sets of digit cards, numbered 1–8, are required. The cards should be carefully shuffled. From the shuffled pack of cards the top 12 cards should be placed in 3 rows of four.

2	1	2	3
5	7	6	5
4	3	6	4

The pupil removes any pairs 'making 9' which he or she finds. Each card which is removed is replaced by the teacher (or another child) from the remaining face-down pile of cards so that the 4 x 3 'grid' of cards is replenished for as long as possible. The player has completed the activity when all the cards have been paired The components-of-10 can be practised this way: in a components-of-10 game, four sets of digit cards, numbered 1–9 are required.

'Pairs of a number' components game (2–4 players; Pairs of 8 game)

To play this game, five sets of digit cards, numbered 1–7, are required. The cards should be carefully shuffled. Each player is dealt 7 cards from the shuffled pack. The remaining cards are placed face down in a 'home' pile. The top card from the 'home' pile is turned over and placed next to the home pile. Each player takes it in turn to 'make 8' using the turned over card and a card from his/her hand, e.g. if the turned-over card is 2, then the player may 'play' 6 to make a pair equalling 8. The player removes each pair he or she has made to a separate 'store' of pairs cards. Another card is turned over from the 'home' pile. Whenever a player can make a pair of 8 he, or she, may have another turn; alternatively, play passes to the next player. The winner is the player with the most cards at the end of play.

Ten Snap (two players only)

To play Ten Snap, four packs of digit cards, numbered 1–9 are required. The cards should be well shuffled and the cards equally shared between the two players. The game is played in a similar way to ordinary Snap! but instead of requiring that the two cards match, the two cards should have a sum of 10, instead. To actually win the cards which add up to 10, players are required to shout Ten!, or Snap!

Addition games

The simplest dice war ever (2–4 players)

General instructions for dice wars can be found on p. 431. Two 0–5 or 1–6 dice should be used and the two dice 'rolls' added together.

Addition card war (2–4 players)

General instructions for **card wars** can be found on p. 431. Four to five sets of digit cards numbered 1–6, respectively, should be used. In each round (battle) each player should be dealt two cards. The two numbers on the cards should be added together.

Shut the Box

This is an excellent addition and component-number game. Commercial versions of **Shut the Box** can be bought from good toy shops: larger versions (often made from wood) are available, and smaller travel versions are available, too. However, **Shut the Box** can be played simply and effectively using digit cards, and two dice. Ordinarily, two 1–6 dice are used. For reinforcement of the facts to 10, two 0–5 dice may be used in exactly the same way, although 1–6 dice should be used as soon as possible. Usually one player at a time has a go at trying to 'shut the box'. To play the card version of **Shut the Box**, one set of digit cards numbered 1–9 are laid out in sequence, face upwards. In the card version, 'shutting the box' involves turning over all the cards in the sequence. The player rolls the two dice and finds the sum of the two rolls: for example, dice rolls of 2 and 4, respectively, have a sum of 6. The player turns over the 6 digit card, or turns over digit cards equalling 6 for instance, the '2' and '4' cards. The player rolls the two dice again, finds the sum, turns over a card, or cards, and so on. Whenever no single card is available to match the dice score, alternative combinations of cards equalling the sum should be turned over. The player continues until he or she has 'shut the box' or is unable to turn over a card, or card combination. In other words, the player is 'out' when he, or she, cannot match any card, or combination of cards, to the dice sum. Where two or more players are playing competitively, the player who 'shuts the box', or who is closest to 'shutting the box' (has turned over the most number of cards) is the winner.

Track games

Different kinds of **track games** are described on p. 433. For simple addition track games two 1–6 dice should be used. For basic **subtraction track games**, a 0–9 and 1–6 dice can be used, Alternatively, teachers can make specially designed sets of addition and subtraction cards, instead.

Word problems

An overview and discussion of word problems, and their role in maths teaching, in general, may be found in the introduction on pp. 000-00. Helping children to solve meaningful addition and subtraction word problems plays an important role in consolidating and enlarging children's understanding of addition and subtraction and in helping them to begin developing problem-solving skills, in general. As soon as children begin to acquire more flexible calculation skills it is important that they should be given appropriate, and appropriately varied, addition, subtraction and *missing number* word problems to solve. Thus, as early as possible, abstract number problems and genuinely engaging word problems can and should be interwoven in number-work sessions: the numbers chosen for use in word problems can be selected with children's fact and strategy knowledge-base in mind.

As we have seen, many discussions and analyses of typical 'school' addition and subtraction word problems, and of children's overall word-problem-solving abilities, make the point that children are mostly given a rather limited range of problem types to solve. The further point is often made that if children's conceptual understanding of addition and subtraction is to be extended, and if children are to be helped to become more flexible and sophisticated problem-solvers, then teachers (and parents) need to be made aware of the broader range of problem types that children could encounter.

In fact, a very useful and influential descriptive framework for classifying addition and subtraction situations has been available since the late

1970s. The framework, which has been broadly accepted by subsequent researchers, was initially proposed by Riley and Greeno et al. (1983). In essence, the basic classification schema, established by Greeno and his associates, suggests that addition and subtraction word problems can be categorized as belonging to one of three broad problem types: *change*, *combine* and *compare* problems. The researchers Verschaffel and Corte, who have analysed and built on Greeno and Riley's work, offer a very clear description of the three basic categories of addition and subtraction word problems:

> Change problems refer to active or dynamic situations in which some event changes the value of an initial quantity. Combine problems relate to static situations involving two quantities that are considered separately or in combination. Compare problems involve two amounts that are compared and the difference between them (Verschaffel and Corte, 1997, p. 70).

Riley et al. also offer a rather detailed schema of the large number of problem types which fit into the three basic addition and subtraction word-problems categories. The three main categories of addition and subtraction word problems are subdivided according to the identity of the unknown quantity (which term is the 'unknown'), and, in *change* and *compare* problems, according to the direction of the change (whether the answer will involve more or less). Other researchers, such as Karen Fuson (1992), have suggested some important amendments to the Riley et al. schema. Most significantly, Karen Fuson introduced the *equalize* subtraction type – as we will see shortly, *equalize* problems are a problem type which is part of the *compare* category but which is distinct, in important ways, from ordinary *difference* problems.

From a teaching point of view, the detailed classification schemas on offer can feel very daunting because there are so many sub-classifications to come to terms with.. However, it is also true that most teachers feel quite overwhelmed at the prospect of trying to devise a broad enough range of suitably challenging word problems for children to solve and many teachers welcome specific help and direction in this regard. To make sense of a synthesis of Riley et al.'s and Fuson's proposals, it is most useful – at least from a teaching point of view – to refer to specific examples of more familiar and common word-problem subtypes within each broad category, first, before going on to examine the range of rather less common word-problem variants. The 'chocolates' problems described here are very similar to Riley et al.'s famous 'marbles' problems but formal and informal solution forms are also given. It should be noted that informal solution forms often relate more closely to concrete models of the problems than do formal number sentences.

Common addition and subtraction subtypes

1. **Change word problems: outcome or result unknown**

(a) *Addition*: Sam had 5 chocolates. His sister gave him 3 more chocolates. How many chocolates does Sam have now? Formal solution: $5 + 3 = \square$. Triad representation:

(b) *Subtraction*: Sam had 8 chocolates. He gave 3 chocolates to his sister. How many chocolates does Sam have now? Formal solution $8 - 3 = \square$. Triad representation:

(c) *Missing addend* (change subset unknown): Sam had 3 chocolates. His sister gave him some more chocolates. Now Sam has 8 chocolates. How many chocolates did Sam's sister give him? Formal solution: $8 - 5 = \square$. Informal solution $3 + \square = 8$. Triad representation:

(d) Missing subtrahend (change subset unknown): Sam had 8 chocolates. He gave some chocolates to his sister. Now Sam has 3 chocolates. How many chocolates did he give to his sister? Formal solution: $8 - 3 = \square$. Informal solution: $8 - \square = 3$. Triad representation:

2. Combine word problems (These are also often referred to as part–whole problems)

(a) *Addition* (combination set unknown): Sam has 5 brown chocolates and 3 white chocolates. How many chocolates does Sam have altogether? Formal solution: 5 + 3 = ☐ . Triad representation:

(b) *Subtraction* (part unknown): Sam and his sister have 8 chocolates altogether. Sam has 3 chocolates. How many chocolates does Sam's sister have? Formal solution: 8 –3 = ☐. Triad representation:

3. **Compare word problems**
(a) *Difference* (difference set unknown): Sam has 8 chocolates. His sister has 5 chocolates. How many more chocolates does Sam have compared with his sister? Formal solution: 8 – 5 = ☐. Informal solution: 5 +☐= 8.
(b) *Equalizing* (strictly speaking, a mixture of compare and combine problems; equalizing set unknown): Sam has 8 chocolates. His sister has 5 chocolates. How many chocolates will Sam's sister need to be given to have the same number of chocolates as Sam? Formal solution: 8 – 5 = ☐. Informal solution: 5 +☐= 8.

Less common, addition and subtraction word-problem types

The logical forms of the 'less common' problem types are generally more difficult to make sense of. Quite often, the initial or original quantity or 'start set' is the 'unknown'. Less common problem types which involve *decreases* rather than *increases* can be particularly difficult for children to solve.

More change problems

(a) *Missing initial quantities* (start set unknown): Sam had some chocolates. He gave 5 chocolates to his sister. Now Sam has 3 chocolates. How many chocolates did Sam have in the beginning? Formal solution: $5 + 3 = \square$. Informal solution: $\square - 5 = 3$. Triad representation:

$$\overset{\bigcirc}{\underset{\textcircled{5}\ \textcircled{3}}{\diagup\diagdown}}$$

(b) *Missing initial quantity* (start set unknown): Sam had some chocolates. His sister gave him 5 more chocolates. Now Sam has 8 chocolates. How many chocolates did Sam have in the beginning? Formal solution: $8 - 5 = \square$. Informal solution: $\square + 5 = 8$. Triad representation:

$$\overset{8}{\underset{\bigcirc\ \textcircled{5}}{\diagup\diagdown}}$$

More compare word problems

(a) *Difference* (compared set unknown): Sam has 3 chocolates. His sister has 5 chocolates more than Sam. How many chocolates does Sam's sister have? Formal solution: $3 + 5 = \square$. Informal solution: $\square = 3 + 5$.

(b) *Difference* (compared set unknown): Sam has 8 chocolates. His sister has 5 chocolates less than Sam. How many chocolates does Sam's sister have? Formal solution: $8 - 5 = \square$.

(c) *Difference* (initial reference set unknown): Sam has 8 chocolates. He has 5 more chocolates than his sister. How many chocolates does his sister have? Formal solution: $8 - 5 = \square$. Informal solution: $\square + 5 = 8$.

(d) *Difference* (initial reference set unknown): Sam has 3 chocolates. He has 5 chocolates less than his sister. How many chocolates does his sister have? Formal solution: $3 + 5 = \square$. Informal solution: $\square - 5 = 3$.

Some teaching recommendations: addition and subtraction word problems

Children who are limited to a conventional linear *counting on* and *counting back* conception of the addition and subtraction operations ($5 + 3 = \square$; $8 - 3 = \square$) generally have great difficulty understanding and solving non-linear word-problem forms. This includes *missing addend*, *difference* and *equalize* problem forms. Since many introductory maths textbooks and workbooks model addition as *change* problems, which are slightly easier to understand than *combine* problems, a number of younger children with learning problems have difficulty with *combine* addition and subtraction problems, too.

By contrast, children who have – or who are systematically building – a good knowledge of the component pairs of numbers and who are able to figure out basic *missing number* questions will be better prepared to make sense of all these 'difficult', but common, word-problem forms. As dyslexic and dyspraxic children begin to reason in the ways described earlier, they can be given appropriate word problems based on the subtypes described in the first list. The less common word-problem types are certainly more difficult but many children who are confidently reasoning to solve addition and subtraction word problems enjoy the challenge of solving these 'puzzle-like' word problems, too.

The early stages of working on addition and subtraction word problems

An overall description of how to introduce word problems in meaningful, 'bottom-up' ways is given in Chapter 2. Some addition and subtraction word-problem reminders include the following:

1. At first, the specific addition and subtraction problem forms which are selected for children to solve should be given in spoken form, and in very clear, transparent language. Words which are part of the common vocabulary of word problems but which children often fail to understand (such as 'each' or 'altogether') should be carefully explained, using concrete materials. The situations which are represented in the word problems should be as lively, meaningful and as accessible to the children as possible. Children respond particularly well to exaggeration and humour in word problems.

2. Concrete materials should always be available. The very earliest word problems should be built around specific materials such as miniature teddies, coins, 'pretend' (or real) sweets, and so on. In some instances (for example, where children are not yet able to visualize *equalize* and *difference* problems – see below) children may use concrete materials to model the word-problem situation so as to help them figure out a solution. In the main, however, as suggested in Chapter 2, children should be asked to picture the given problem, figure out an answer, if they can, and then use the materials to model the problem and check the answer they have given. Concrete modelling of the problem will allow children to confirm, or

self-monitor and self-correct, the answer they figured out. Quite soon, slightly more 'abstract' materials such as counters or cubes can be used to represent objects and to model the word-problem situations. Once children's understanding of individual word-problem types is consolidated, concrete modelling will no longer be necessary.

3. The list of word-problem types can be used as a checklist for word-problem forms to be covered. Whenever possible, children should have some experience of solving examples of all the common word-problem forms. If children are asked to solve three or more word problems in any one 'go', it is best to mix the types of word problems selected.

4. In time, children can be encouraged to represent individual problems in written form, and to record their solutions to the word problems in written form. At first, many children enjoy using informal written forms, which include triad representations. As children become increasingly sophisticated and able thinkers, they can be encouraged to represent the 'harder' addition and subtraction word-problem types in the formal linear, operational ways.

5. As children become competent problem-solvers, addition and subtraction word problems need to be made increasingly formal or school-like. For instance, word problems will need to be presented in written form. However, in early written word-problem work, care should still be taken to ensure that the word-problem situation is described in the clearest and simplest possible way. Conventional word-problem formulations, and typical word-problem language, such as in the 'chocolates' problems described above, should certainly be encountered by children, but these stylized formulations should be introduced in a structured and gradual way.

The special significance of difference and equalizing problems

In her analyses of children's conceptions of subtraction, Karen Fuson often points out that children who have a conventional 'take away' conception of subtraction can find compare (difference and equalize) word problems difficult to understand. Like other researchers in the field, she also points out that many children fail to discover that a counting up to or complementary-addition subtraction procedure is easier to manage, in a great many subtraction instances, than counting backwards subtraction procedures. In fact, research by Karen Fuson herself, as well as by others, has long since shown that meaningful compare problems will usually be solved quite readily by children who have access to concrete materials and that concretely modelled compare problems are usually worked out by using *counting up to* procedures. Furthermore, some children who discover that *compare* problems can be solved by *counting up to* go on to generalize the *counting up to* procedure to appropriate abstract subtraction problems, (such as 9 – 6 etc.).

Research also seems to show that children find *equalize* versions of *compare* problems somewhat easier to solve than conventional *difference* problems. In other words, it is easier to solve a problem such as, 'By half-time, Jim had scored 8 football goals and his friend had scored only 5 football goals; how many goals does Jim's friend have to score so that he can equal Jim's score?' than, 'By half-time, Jim had scored 8 goals and his friend had scored 5 goals; how many more goals did Jim score compared with his friend?' This is because classic *difference* problems involve static comparisons, which children can find difficult to comprehend, whereas *equalize* problems suggest the action, and procedure, of counting up from the smaller quantity to the larger quantity to make the situation 'fair'. Of course, children who have been helped to develop a part-whole conception of subtraction intuitively understand the links between addition and subtraction, as we have seen. Nevertheless, *compare* problems involve making sense of relationships between two quantities, rather than reasoning about logical part-whole patterns within one quantity, and the *compare* problem forms are therefore important for all children to encounter. Furthermore, solving *equalize* and *difference* problems serves to emphasize the *counting up to* or *complementary addition* subtraction procedure (and conception of subtraction) and thus helps pave the way for subsequent, more advanced, *complementary addition* strategies, as we will see at a number of subsequent points in this book.

In early *equalize* and *difference* work it is important that children work concretely, and can see the direct one-to-one relationship between the different quantities in the problem. The quantities involved are thus best laid out in two rows, and in one-to-one correspondence.

Equalizing made very simple

In working with younger or less able children with specific learning difficulties it works best to develop the *equalizing* concept from an initial 'fair' or temporarily *equal* situation. For example, 'We're going to start with the same number of jelly beans. I have 5 jelly beans and you have 5 jelly beans. But now I'm going to give myself some more jelly beans. I've got 8 jelly beans, and you've still only got 5.

'How many more jelly beans do I need to give you so that you can have 8 too?' (Note: This can be recorded in a *missing addend* written form as 5 + □ = 8).

More equalizing problems

A concrete equalizing problem: Your sister has 10p. You've only got 6p. How many more pennies do you need to be given so that you can have the same amount of money as her?

0000000000
000000

An abstract equalizing problem: You are playing a computer game with your friend. Your friend has destroyed 9 aliens. You've only destroyed 6. How many more aliens do you need to destroy to equal his score?

Difference problems

Concrete difference work: Early concrete *difference* work can be linked to the simple activity of estimating two quantities. For instance, 'We've both got a pile of jelly beans. How many jelly beans do you think you've got? How many do you think I've got? Who do you think has more? Let's check to see, by counting. You count first into a neat row, then I'll count mine using your row to help me.'

| Child: | 000000000 |
| Adult: | 0000000 . |

An abstract difference problem: I've played the new computer game 5 times and you've played it 8 times. How many more times have you played the game than me?

A final note on word problems and the *complementary addition* procedure: meaningful *missing addend* problems, where the 'change set' is unknown (in other words, *change* (c), above), can also help foster *adding up to* conceptions of subtraction. Problems in which an appealing target goal needs to be reached are particularly successful. For example: 'You are playing a computer game. Your goal is to wipe out 10 monsters. So far, you have wiped out 8 monsters. How many more monsters do you need to wipe out?'

PART III

The Number System

CHAPTER 5

Defining the difficulties

Introduction

Most people tend to take the ways larger numbers are structured – how numbers which are larger than 10 are spoken and how they are written – for granted. In time, most of us become so familiar with the conventions of the number system that we begin to see them as entirely natural and inevitable: it is hard to conceive of any other way of saying the number 'three hundred and sixty-five', or of recording it, except as '365'. Of course our way of structuring numbers is actually not natural or inevitable at all. As we have seen, what does seem to occur spontaneously in most cultures, and in the development of most young children, is a very basic form of counting in a simple one-to-one correspondence. In Western European cultures, however, our particular ways of expressing and representing large numbers are, in fact, complex and largely arbitrary cultural inventions which have to be taught to each new generation of children.

In some approaches to maths learning, children are not introduced to numbers beyond 10 in the first year of formal maths work. In more recent understanding-based approaches to learning maths, young children are introduced to aspects of large numbers from the very earliest stages. There are important reasons for deciding on an early formal or classroom introduction to large numbers. First of all, most young children are surrounded by large numbers. They frequently encounter them in spoken and in written form. Many young children are fascinated by the large numbers they encounter and may even be in awe of them. They will consequently use spoken larger number forms colloquially and quite spontaneously from very early – pre-school or nursery-school – days. It is important that children begin to understand the large numbers which are part of their everyday experience. Secondly, it is widely acknowledged that an understanding of the ways larger numbers are structured is an integral part of understanding how to calculate with large numbers. In approaches which emphasize learning with understanding, a sound grasp of the spoken and written number structures is one of the most important ideas about numbers which children need to be given access to. The notion that understanding the conventions of the number structures underpins an understanding of calculation applies, in particular, to informal *mental* methods of calculation, Children do not have the basic ability to calculate *mentally* if they do not understand how large numbers are built up or may be broken down, or fail to understand how large numbers relate to each other. Of course, an understanding of the number system and, in particular, of the written number system, is really a prerequisite for making sense of traditional forms of column-based calculations, too. As we have seen, children can learn formal methods of calculation in entirely procedural ways but they are able to calculate more confidently and are likely to make fewer calculation errors if they have an understanding of how number structures 'work'.

However, while an understanding of the number structures is one of the essential keys to making sense of numbers and of calculations beyond 10, the structures are difficult for the majority of children to master. While primary school children are fascinated by large numbers, they are also puzzled and bewildered by many aspects of them. It usually takes time for children to understand how large numbers are structured and where it is that they fit in to the overall 'number picture'. Furthermore, it is well established that dyslexic and dyspraxic children have particular difficulties with many of the conventions which govern the larger number structures. At the deepest level, the fact that many dyslexic and dyspraxic children have difficulties processing sequences – and therefore have difficulties understanding patterns or structures within sequences – means that it is not surprising that many children with specific learning difficulties seem to retain a very poor understanding of large numbers and of the structures they fit into.

In understanding-based approaches to learning maths it is often reported that children with specific learning difficulties struggle to make sense of counting work and that thy find all work which involves finding patterns in sequences very difficult, indeed. In more traditional approaches to maths learning it is often noted that children with learning difficulties have difficulty understanding '*place value*' and that they therefore have problems working with the written number conventions and with formal calculation in columns.

Since many problems are encountered by children in the lengthy process of learning about large numbers, and since children with learning difficulties struggle longer and harder than most 'ordinary' children to make sense of them, it is important to start out by exploring, in some detail, some of the intrinsic difficulties of the number system. This will highlight the aspects of the system which need careful teaching. It will also illuminate the kinds of mistakes which are commonly made by children and which often require particular attention.

The spoken number system

A very significant feature of the number systems which are found in all industrialized cultures, including our own, is that they are actually made up of two related but distinctive systems – the spoken number system and the written number system. Our spoken number system – like our written number system – is, at its very core, based on two fundamental structuring principles. The first important principle is that we use a range of counting units of different sizes, or of different intrinsic values, and that these special units of value are organized according to what is called a *base* structure. In a base structure, a specified number of smaller units make up a larger value. While alternative bases have been used by different cultures the fact that we have 10 fingers means that our counting system (like those of most present-day cultures world-wide) is organized according to a *base* of 10: thus when we have 10 units of one value we regroup them into one unit of the next value. The special units of value which we employ to count are: *ones, tens, hundreds, thousands* and so on. The structure functions so that 10 *ones* are regrouped into one *ten*, 10 *tens* into one *hundred*, 10 *hundreds* into one *thousand* etc. The second fundamental principle of our spoken number system is that the individual larger numbers within the structuring base *ten* framework are consequently made up – or 'built' – from component units of different value. This is the principle of *additive composition* in which value units are joined together to create larger composite numbers. The specific spoken number 'three hundred and sixty-five' is made up of three *hundreds*, six *tens* and five *ones*.

The deeper underlying structure of our spoken number system is thus highly structured and consistent. There is a very clear, deep 'syntax' according to which large numbers are structured (created or composed) and articulated. This is true of most number systems. Since the majority of spoken number systems throughout the world are *Base Ten* systems this deep syntax is a very widely generalized one – in other words, a largely uniform 'deep structure' underpins the vast majority of number systems. While all of this is true, however, the factor which complicates spoken number systems is that the actual languages in which numbers are expressed are always organic developments which are specific to individual cultures. Thus many specific 'surface' aspects of individual spoken number systems are expressed in different cultures in rather different kinds of ways. As Nunes and Bryant (1996, p. 45) explain: 'among Base Ten representation systems there are considerable variations in the way that that the structure is represented in different languages'. This means that while the deepest logic of the spoken number system is universal across most cultures and most languages, the surface ways this logic is expressed varies from culture to culture and language to language. The significance of this is twofold. First, and most obviously, different languages tend to have somewhat different ways of expressing the under-lying structure: for instance, whereas the two-digit number, 24, is expressed in German as four-and-twenty – or *vier und zwanzig* – we say twenty-four. But also, and ultimately much more importantly, different language systems can vary in terms of two important criteria:

1. in terms of how internally *consistent* they are;
2. in terms of how *transparently* they represent the deeper logical structures.

The English spoken number system is largely consistent and largely trans-parent in the later parts of the system but – and this represents a large learning problem for young children – it is particularly inconsistent and opaque in the earliest encountered parts of the structure. By contrast, there are other spoken number systems which are both consistent and transparent from the very outset.

To make the significance of these important variations clear it is helpful to compare what Dehaene (1997) describes as 'the headache' of the early stages of the English spoken number system with the transparent early stages of more elegantly consistent systems, such as those of the Chinese or Japanese systems – or, closer to home, of the Welsh language spoken number system. In purely structural terms, as we have seen, all *base-ten* spoken numbers beyond the first nine counting numbers and below 100 are organized into rounded decades or *tens* and, for non-rounded numbers, into a basic tens-and-ones pattern. In transparent languages the rounded decades or *tens* are represented as: ten (or one-ten), two-ten, three-ten, four-ten and so on. The basic tens-and-ones pattern is apparent from the second decade onwards. The numbers eleven, twelve and thirteen are articulated as: ten-one, ten-two and ten-three (or one-ten-one, one-ten-two, and so on). Similarly the numbers twenty-one and twenty-two are articulated as two-ten-one and two-ten-two, and thirty-one and thirty-two as three-ten one and three-ten-two.

In the English counting system, on the other hand, the *tens* or rounded decade words are much less obviously transparent. There is, in fact, a significant 'cue' pointing to the informing *tens* structure in that *tens* are compressed to 'ty' in the decade words beyond ten itself. But while this may be clear when we reflect on the structure as adults, this is not an obvious connection for children to make in the early stages of learning to count to 100. This relative lack of transparency is further complicated by the variations on 'two', 'three' and 'five' which are buried within the idiosyncratic decade words, *twenty, thirty* and *fifty*. As Thompson (1997a, p. 124) clearly explains:

> Because they do not have the regular form *two-ty, three-ty* and *five-ty* as do *sixty* and *seventy* these particular number words do not make it easy for children to see the way in which the words two, three etc., are re-used in the naming of the decades. The words conceal the relationship between the decade names and the first nine counting numbers, a connection which is more clearly observed in larger numbers such as sixty, seventy, eighty and ninety.

This is not the only difficulty. In addition to the lack of transparency of the *tens* words, children also have to contend with a great number of irregularities in the very early second decade – the decade which immediately follows the first nine counting numbers and a decade which is consequently encountered very soon in the business of learning to count. Here, in this very brief counting stretch alone, the usual tens-and-ones structure of the English spoken number system is overturned and the *ones* are articulated first. In this decade we say thirteen, fourteen, and so on – rather than something like ten-three ten-four, and so on. It is only from third decade onwards that the usual 'tens-first' structure is established: from here we say twenty-one, twenty-two, thirty one, thirty-two, ninety-one. Secondly, the digit-teen reversals are further complicated by the 'thir' and 'fif' corruptions of *three* and *five* in the words *thirteen* and *fifteen* respectively. Thirdly, and finally, there are the two entirely eccentric number words, 'eleven', and 'twelve', 'which give no indication whatsoever of the fact that they, mean ten-and-one and ten-and-two respectively' (Thompson, 1997a, p. 124).

Before we go on to look at the implications of the lapses in transparency and consistency, which are embedded in the English spoken number system, we need to touch, briefly, on yet another common and very important language-based source of difficulty. It further complicates already confusing counting issues that the two spoken cues for *ten* – 'teen' in the second decade and 'ty' in the decade-words – can be hard to distinguish between. As Eva Grauberg (1998, p. 166) points out, 'the salient difference between "ty" and "teen" is one of stress. If a child's perception of stress is poor, discrimination is almost impossible.' This particular confusion is one further result of the already difficult digit reversals in the 'teens', and is certainly compounded by the idiosyncratic pronunciations of three and five which *thirteen* and *thirty*, and *fifteen* and *fifty* share. It is very common then, for children to 'hear' and interpret 'teens' as 'ty's', for example, believing *thirteen* to be *thirty*, or counting 'eleven, twelve, thirty, forty etc.'. Likewise, although slightly less commonly, 'tys' may be interpreted as 'teens' – thus the spoken number *fourteen* may be believed to be the much larger number, *forty*.

Some implications of the difficulties contained within the English counting system

In the rather vast literature concerning children's understanding of the counting system some doubts have been raised about the degree to which language, by itself, could shape such understanding (Towse and Saxe, 1998). With these doubts in mind, it is important that one should not overstate the consequences of operating within different number languages and make too glib a link between the presence of a transparent number language and a resulting ease of understanding of the structures. As a way of maintaining a balance, it is important to bear in mind that the *Base Ten* structure and *additive composition* principles are, in themselves, complex inventions which are intrinsically difficult to understand – in other words, it needs to be borne in mind that, regardless of the language within which children happen to be working, most children would, in fact, benefit from careful and explicit teaching of the structures.

Nevertheless, while this is true, the practicalities of teaching extended sequences of counting and the counting structures to English speaking primary school children, makes it abundantly clear that the language anomalies in the English number system greatly contribute to the difficulties that children experience in learning how to count. In practical learning terms, Nunes and Bryant (1996) argue that the historical purpose and main advantage of a *Base Ten* number system is that the structure makes it possible for the learner to generate number names instead of having to memorize them all by rote. 'We only have to remember a few number words the rest we can generate for ourselves' (Nunes and Bryant, 1996, p. 45). In the English counting system, however, the greatest inconsistencies occur (as we have seen) in the part of the structure that children encounter – and need to master – very early on. The first important consequence of this is that very young English-speaking children have to memorize a significant proportion of the early 'counting string'. As we saw in the last chapter, they have to memorize the first nine counting words, as well as those between 11 and 19. (On its own, mastering the pivotal, but very difficult 11–19 slows down counting progress enormously.) They also have to rote-learn the decade words and the precise order of the decade names at the 'decade boundaries' or 'crossover points'. For example, children have to memorize that we count 'nineteen, *twenty*', 'twenty-nine, *thirty*' and so on.

There are two very important further consequences of all of those difficulties. Cross-cultural studies have shown that English speaking children manage to master the counting sequence to 20, and then the subsequent counting sequence to 100, much later than, for example, Japanese or Chinese-speaking children. Children with memory difficulties and with difficulties processing and remembering sequences learn to count even later still. While reciting the counting string is not synonymous with 'true counting', as we saw in Chapter 3, a delay in learning to recite the counting sequence does have serious consequences. Lack of 'counting string' knowledge means that children are unable to count larger quantities. This clearly impacts on their development of *number sense* for larger numbers and this, in turn, seems to constrain aspects of further number development. We have already noted that studies show that children with good recitational counting skills tend to do well in all number tasks in the early maths years. On a purely pragmatic level, the need to learn so much of the early counting sequence *by heart* can consume a great deal of valuable teaching time.

Secondly, while a transparent number language does not guarantee an understanding of the number structures, it certainly facilitates children's ability to see the patterned logic underpinning it. Conversely, the irregularities and idiosyncrasies of the English counting sequence – which pushes much of the business of early number sequence generation into the domain of rote memory – contributes to a sense of the arbitrariness of the sequence and also of its 'sameness'. Children who fail to grasp the presence of structures are likely to see number sequences in ones-based or *unitary* ways. The counting sequence to 100, for example, is frequently interpreted in the most basic 'one number following after another' kind of way. This means that children have an intrinsically 'fuzzy' or indistinct sense of larger numbers and tend to miss all of the structured cues for interpreting them. There are classic experiments (Kamii, 1985) which show, for example, that many children will build two-digit numbers from *ones* even where materials representing *tens* are available. From a teaching point of view it is genuinely difficult to convince many young English-speaking children to accept that the numbers 11–19 are composite numbers. Failure to grasps the *Base Ten* structure – and the related compositional nature of all numbers beyond ten – also profoundly affects children's ability to calculate. For example, as we will see in Chapter 7, if children cannot visualize eighteen as ten-plus-eight, an 'easy' calculation such as eighteen minus four is usually 'counted back' even when 8–4 is known *by heart*.

The written number system: place value

In historical terms, written number systems arise out of spoken number systems. In our number system this means that the conventions for written numbers have the same 'deep structure' as spoken number systems – in other words, they are also informed by the most basic *Base Ten* and *additive composition* principles. However, written numbers also encode another rather different and more difficult principle. In contrast to a system in which the different units of value which make up numbers are essentially (though not always transparently) *named* or *tagged*, the value of any one digit in the written number system is purely determined by its *place* – or, in other words, by the relative position of the digit within the overall number. As Stanislas Dehaene (1997, p. 98) writes, 'Thus the three digits that make up the number 222, though identical, refer to different orders of magnitude, two hundreds, two tens and two units.' Unlike other number systems – for example the widely-known Roman numeral system, in which 222 is represented as CCXXII – a *place value* system does not use special symbols to act as markers for words.

Although the label 'place value' is loosely (and inaccurately) used to refer to all aspects of multidigit number-structure work it should really only be used to apply to the *written number system* in which *place* or position alone determines and denotes value. The significance of understanding this distinction is the recognition that children have to learn about two systems and build two conceptual structures, not one. The very basic fact that there are two systems within one overall structure – introduces difficulties from the start. It means that there are two systems, each with their own complexities, which children have to master. It also means that they have to learn to relate the two systems to each other: in other words they have to learn to 'translate' or *transcode* between them. Brian Butterworth (1999, p. 133) makes this point particularly clearly. In learning about large numbers, he writes:

> The child has to confront the conflict between two conflicting representational principles: name value in words and place value in numerals. This makes learning difficult especially, as we have seen, where the name-value system is irregular, as it is in English and other European languages.

The place value principle

The *place value* principle was essentially an Indian invention which has brought to Europe in the twelfth century by Arabs – hence the name 'Hindu-Arabic' numeral system. As Butterworth (1999) and others point out, it was an invention which had had taken many centuries to devise and perfect. Of course, in cultural-historical terms, the *place value* construct was a very significant development – not only was *place value* notation an extremely economical way of writing numbers, but its compactness also facilitated difficult multidigit calculations, such as those required by business transactions. Thus Stanislas Dehaene (1997, p. 98) writes: 'Place value coding is a must if one wants to perform calculations using simple algorithms. Just try to compute XIV × VII using Roman numerals. Their invention revolutionized the art of numerical computation.' And it is precisely because place value coding is the best available notation that it is the one which has been adopted in most countries worldwide.

Nevertheless, despite its many arithmetical advantages, it is also widely recognized that the *place value* principle is so abstract, compact and hence difficult to understand that most young children experience at least some problems in the process of coming to terms with it. First of all, it is important to acknowledge that many young children, and quite a number of children with specific learning difficulties, have difficulty understanding the basic idea that 'place equals value' at all. From a child's point of view it can be hard to grasp and accept the idea that a familiar digit such as '2' has to be given a different value in a number like '23' simply because the '2' has been placed 'in front' of the '3'. Children with a *unitary* number concept are often not conceptually ready for the idea that a '2' placed before another digit has to be understood as 2 *tens*, or twenty. Some children who have not made the 'place equals value' cognitive leap, tend to interpret the digits making up written multidigit numbers as mini-sequences of individual ones quantities – for instance, the number 23 may be interpreted as 'two three' or even as 'two plus three.' Further difficulties processing and interpreting direction also compound the complexity of interpreting the place value idea.

In addition to all of the difficulties which children can experience in making sense of the *place value* idea, it can also prove difficult for children to apply their developing *place value* understanding in a consistent way. In the long-term process of learning to work with larger numbers children often revert or 'fold back' to assigning *ones* values to the component digits making up larger numbers. For example, a child may be able to read an individual number, such as '36', perfectly competently, but may then treat '30' as '3' in a 'harder' two digit addition situation such as 36 + 36. It is not uncommon for a child to argue that the answer to 36 + 36 is 18, because 3 + 3 is 6, and 6 + 6 is 12, and 12 + 6 = 18! It is also not uncommon for a child to be mindful of the place value conventions most of the time but then 'lapse' into *ones*-based interpretations when he or she is tired or distracted.

The complex function of '0' in the place value system

As children begin to make sense of *place-value* coding they have to confront certain aspects of the structure of the written number system which are harder to understand than other aspects and which consequently take longer for most children to learn. The role that 'zero' plays in the *place value* system is a very significant one. It is often pointed out that a *place value* system cannot be fully efficient without using zero as a 'placeholder' or, in other words, without using zero to indicate the absence of units of value in any specific value position (or positions). Without a zero placeholder many numbers would be ambiguous: for example, the digit 2 could represent 2 units, 20, 200, 2000 and so on, ad infinitum. Likewise a gap between two digits, for instance 2 2, could mean that the two 'twos' represent 202, 2002, and so on, or the space could even be a mistake and the numbers could actually represent 22. This placeholder function of zero often causes children particular difficulties. Zero is, of course, used in another way, as a number in our system of numerals, and in this context represents an empty set or 'nothing'. In this easier *number context* zero means 'zero quantity' and most children understand this quite early and, generally, quite easily. In its *place value* context, however, it is hard for children to grasp that each zero in a written number suddenly functions to make the digit immediately preceding it ten times larger: thus the '3' in 305 is 3 hundred, and the '2' in 2085, two thousand. Written numbers which contain 'empty' value positions are consequently much harder for children to make sense of than their spoken *named* equivalents.

Although 'zero' functions in exactly the same place-holding way in written rounded numbers, such as 20, 200 and 2000, many children learn to understand rounded numbers in a rather different light. Since rounded numbers are much more frequently encountered in everyday contexts than non-rounded numbers, children tend to focus on, and memorize the 'meaning' of, the number of zeros represented in the numbers: thus children learn that '0', in rounded number contexts means 'ten', '00' means 'hundred', '000' means 'thousand' and so on. While this informal 'learning process' means that children are often competent at reading and writing rounded numbers from quite early on, attributing a label to round zero chunks is actually very similar to a process of *naming* in determining spoken number values. Children believe that '00', 'means' hundred, just as 'C', in the Roman system 'means' hundred. This misunderstanding can lead to written transcoding errors, as we will see.

Transcoding difficulties

The problems of 'reading' written multidigit numbers

The ability to read written numbers or to know, for example, that '35' means 'thirty-five' and '101' means or 'says' 'one hundred and one', involves transcoding one set of number conventions, the *place value* conventions, into the *named value* conventions of the spoken number system. In essence, there are two main areas of difficulty in transcoding written numbers to spoken numbers. First of all, it is an important feature of the written number system that it is an entirely consistent system whereas, as we have seen, the spoken system is not. In practical terms this means that children have to come to terms with the fact that the early encountered and difficult spoken number reversals in the second decade are not (and cannot be) represented in their written number equivalents. While '13', '14' and so on, are written according to the *place value* rules, giving them their spoken number meanings involves having to transcode them in reverse order, with the *thir* and *four* (or in other words, the *ones* values) articulated first. By the third decade children have to adjust to the further idea that the rules for transcoding second-decade numbers do not represent the norm. From the third decade onwards, children have to apply the

'usual' conventions for transcoding written numbers which involve articulating the largest value first. While the process of transcoding written
numbers into spoken numbers is generally systematic beyond the 'teens'
decade many children remain unsettled by the very difficult 'teens'
transcoding demands. Once again, of course, left-right confusions will
exacerbate uncertainties about the written-to-spoken transcoding order.
Dyslexic and dyspraxic children quite commonly reverse the correct
written to spoken transcoding sequence, reading '38' as 'eighty-three', for
example, or, in the very common 'teen' mistakes, reading '16', as 'sixty-
one', rather than as 'sixteen'.

Secondly, even when both the *place value* idea and the written to spoken
transcoding order have, in principle, been understood, they can be difficult
to interpret and articulate. As Derek Haylock (1991), Cockburn (1999) and
others point out, numbers are generally spoken from largest to smallest
value, in the order in which they are written as numbers, and in the same
direction as use for reading words; in contrast, we actually designate and
determine value from right to left, in relation to the smallest *units* position.
While this is not usually a problem when smaller written numbers need to
be transcoded, larger numbers can be much harder to 'read'. Thus we
determine that the first value in 36257 is 'thirty thousand' by working 'up
left' from the '7' in the far left *units* position but we have to say 'thirty-six
thousand' first. Sequencing difficulties, poor understanding of the overall
Base Ten structures, left-right orientation difficulties and working memory
difficulties contribute towards making this aspect of 'reading' numbers a
particular difficulty for many dyslexic and dyspraxic children.

**Transcoding difficulties: the problems of transcoding spoken
numbers into written numbers**

Children usually learn to 'read' numbers first, before they begin the
process of learning how to write them. Although reading very large
numbers can remain difficult, children are generally more proficient at
reading numbers than they are at writing them: In other words, it is generally somewhat harder to transcode spoken number forms into the written
number conventions than the other way round.

Yet again, it is the inconsistencies of the spoken number system in the
second decade which are the source of many written number difficulties.
Although *thir* and *four* in *thirteen* and *fourteen*, respectively, are heard first,
it is the 'ten' of the 'teen' syllable which has to be recorded first. This
difficulty leads to very common written digit reversals: while children may

reverse all of the 'teens' numbers, writing '31' instead of '13' is especially common, and it is perhaps significant that '13' is the first 'teens' number. Interestingly, too, the idiosyncratic '12' is very frequently written as '21' by dyslexic and dyspraxic children. Such digit reversals in writing numbers often persist long after children are able to 'read' the written number forms without any apparent difficulty. It is worth noting that many slightly older dyslexic and dyspraxic children overcome the difficulty of written 'teens' reversals by continuing to write the digit for the first syllable first – the norm, of course, for most spoken-to written transcodings – and then squeezing in, or interposing, the '1' afterwards.

Secondly, while children are often able to apply the basic 'place equals value' rule and are able to read three-digit numbers, such as '365', or even four-digit numbers, such as '1365,' correctly, writing the equivalent numbers often proves much more difficult. In the more open-ended process of transcoding spoken numbers to written numbers, children often forget the *place value* coding rules and apply 'rules' which are much closer to the spoken number *naming* conventions, instead. For instance, when children transcode larger numbers such as 'three hundred and sixty-five' or 'one thousand three hundred and sixty-five' into written numbers, they often translate or represent the values *hundred* and *thousand* in a *naming* or more directly symbolic way. We have seen that children tend to understand the zeros in rounded numbers as labels or tags. The misleading belief that '00' means *hundred* and '000' means *thousand*, and so on, very often surfaces when children transcode spoken numbers to written numbers. Thus 'three hundred and sixty-five' may be written as 30065: here '3' is followed by the '00' symbol or tag for hundred, and then, using the principle of *additive composition*, '65' is tacked on, at the end. Likewise, the spoken number, 'one thousand three hundred and sixty-five' may be recorded as 1000365. It should be noted, however, that although children frequently wish to 'mark' the big values they are working with by using special signs or signals, the actual *tags* which they use quite regularly end up being symbolic *naming* compromises. Thus, while some children's representations of spoken numbers may well include the whole cluster of zeros usually used to represent rounded values, other children realize that using entire chunks of zeros 'looks wrong' and make the pragmatic decision to reduce the number of zeros they are using: thus three hundred and sixty-five is often recorded as 3065, and one thousand three hundred and sixty-five as 10365, or 103065.

There is a further difficulty, which can arise in relation to the ways that rounded numbers are written, which may also affect the *tagging* decisions which some children make. While most children memorize the visual 'look' of rounded numbers, such as 20, 200 or 2000, quite easily, children with visual memory difficulties often do not; they may, therefore, find rounded numbers particularly difficult to record. For example, children with visual memory difficulties frequently have extended difficulties learning how to record the 'ty' (or 0) of rounded decade values, such as twenty, thirty and so on. While some children are simply confused and have to ask for help, others, as Nunes and Bryant point out, seem to resolve recording difficulties by using a one-to-one correspondence between a number-word and a digit. Children who apply a one-to-one correspondence principle transcode the number 'twenty-two', which is made up of two words, correctly, as the two-digit '22', whereas 'twenty', which is one word, may be transcoded as '2', and 'two hundred', which is two words, may be transcoded as '20' (Nunes and Bryant, 1996, p. 71). The use of a one-to-one correspondence between number words and digits may also help explain why many children use a single zero to 'tag' both of the very different value words 'hundred' and 'thousand,' as we saw in the examples given above.

CHAPTER 6

An understanding-based approach to teaching the number structures

Because written calculations and standard procedures in columns have dominated maths teaching until recently, many practical teaching guides focus principally on children's written number difficulties. In more recent understanding-based approaches – in which the importance of oral and mental activities is emphasized – it is acknowledged that children make the best progress in primary school number-work if the spoken number system and the written number system are both given careful consideration.

One way to ensure that both aspects of the number-system are given adequate attention, is to identify two sets of number-structure activities and cluster them, roughly speaking, under the rubric of two basic headings. In the practical work which follows, the first set of activities are best defined as *counting* or *counting-related* activities; the second set of activities can be described as *number-building* activities – activities which are designed, in large part, to help children understand the *place-value* aspects of written numbers.

Counting activities

In counting-based activities, as I have suggested, the main focus is helping children learn about the *spoken number system*. Because dyslexic and dyspraxic children usually understand numbers as *unitary* constructs, a key emphasis in all counting work is to foreground the Base Ten counting structures. Counting activities help provide an overview of the 'overall' number structures: in other words they help provide an overview of the framework within which individual counting numbers and 'mini-sequences' are situated. Counting activities are designed to emphasize the relationships between individual numbers and the number structures;

children are encouraged to understand individual numbers in terms of where they are located in the counting structures. This helps children understand the real size of different numbers.

To make sense of the complex *Base Ten* structure of the counting system, children are also helped to understand the way in which different counting sequences fit together. Since many children with learning difficulties have difficulty understanding how sequential structures 'work' and many children have difficulties memorizing aspects of the spoken counting sequence, special attention is paid to the *Base Ten* counting 'crossover' points.

Early counting beyond 10; understanding the counting system to 100

All structured counting activities beyond 10, and to 100, involve a dynamic interplay between counting in *ones* and counting in decades, or *tens*. To begin making sense of the *Base Ten* aspects of the number system (and of the way in which numbers can be partitioned into their *Base Ten* components) children need to build up a picture of the two-way exchange in which *ones* build up into the *tens* or decades and the decades can be broken into *ones*. As part of this process, children have to be able to count in *tens*.

Tens alone: counting the decades

Helpful materials for practising counting *tens* include materials such as: a 100 bead string, a bead abacus, rods placed in *100 square* or *100 track* number formations, and 10p coins. As counting proceeds, it is important for children to handle the *tens* in some way: for example, children need to touch each successive decade on the 100 bead string or move across each line of beads on an abacus. If *tens* rods are used, they should be counted as they are laid down in the chosen formation.

It should be noted that some writers suggest that it is better to introduce children to a systematic counting sequence such as *one-ty, two-ty, three-ty* and so on, all the way to *ten-ty*, rather than have children count using the conventional and rather opaque decade words in the early stages of learning to count. There are advantages in using such 'systems words' at the beginning of structured counting work (Grauberg (1998) uses the term 'system words'). 'Systems words' highlight the structural meanings of the decade words and enable children to see the repetition of the basic 0–10 counting sequence in the decade words, in a way that the 'proper' words do not. In practice, however, as Anne Cockburn (2000) has noted, such teaching suggestions are not always successful. Most children will, of course, know that system words are entirely artificial teaching constructs. On one hand, it is possible to make artificial constructs work in a 'whole classroom' context because an entire alternative counting culture can be created. In the very different context of individual or small group sessions, on the other hand, dyslexic and dyspraxic children can feel that they are being taught a different, 'baby' form of maths because they have maths difficulties. In addition to this, children with specific learning difficulties are often made anxious by any suggestion that they will have an extra learning load – they will know, of course, that they ultimately have to learn, and use, the conventional 'grown-up' counting words. Yet again, some children in special teaching and learning contexts enjoy engaging in 'dual' counting practices. For instance, counting activities can be organized so that children can practise counting in the 'proper' economical way, most of the time, but they may also enjoy using the 'systems words' in a fairly light-hearted or humorous way.

Estimating 'gestalts' of ten

In the same way that children can be helped to develop a *feel* for small numbers by developing their subitizing skills for small quantities to 10, it is also helpful to encourage children to develop a *feel* for the relative size of *tens* numbers within the frame of *one hundred*: in other words, it helps for children to sense how close 90 really is to 100 and, by contrast, how close the number 30 is, relatively speaking, to zero or 10. For this purpose, a simple structured concrete number track, a 100-bead string, or rods placed on a 100 square 'frame' can be used. Instead of counting ten-by-ten, children are encouraged to estimate or guess the number of *tens* selected. To start with, children should be asked to judge quantities which are relatively easy to take in at a glance: for example, quantities such as 10, 20, 80 and 90. As the 'guessing' is made harder, the important number fact that 50 is half of 100 should be explored and emphasized. It should be acknowledged to children that estimating quantities such as 40 and 60 is quite hard but that mentally-splitting the 100 'frame' in *half* helps a great deal in this regard.

Counting tens and ones: simple estimation and counting activities

One of the simplest and best ways of introducing the idea of counting patterns and structures to children is to engage them in very straightforward estimation and counting activities. Although some children equate maths with having to produce a 'correct' answer, and can find estimation work quite unnerving, at first, most children thoroughly enjoy it and cannot believe that something so 'easy' could be considered a serious activity. Estimation activities can be used as helpful 'ice-breakers' at the beginning of sessions, as time-fillers, or as final 'fun' activities. They can even be brought into 'everyday life' situations: 'I wonder how many chocolates there are in this packet? ...' As well as building up children's understanding of how counting 'works', estimation of quantities larger than 10 help build up children's *feel* for larger numbers. In this regard it is important that children encounter a range of rather different kinds of *ones* to estimate and count – for example, glass nuggets, small counters or buttons can be used on certain occasions, and much larger *ones* – such as pebbles, or playing cards – on others. To give the activities sufficient focus, it is also important to select reasonably contrasting quantities to work with: for instance, one of the quantities to be estimated and counted could be a relatively small 'teens' quantity, while another may be as large as 'in the thirties' or 'forties'. (It is important, however, that the actual counting does not become too long and tedious; it can help to take 'counting turns', when particularly large quantities require counting.)

As Sharma (1993b) argues, the estimation aspect of estimation and counting activities can be structured in one of two basic ways. The first method is to 'throw out' a number of *ones*, ask children to estimate the quantity and then ask them to check their estimate by counting. The second method is to ask children to take a specified number of *ones* without counting – for example, 30, once again – and encourage them to check their estimate by counting. In the counting part of the activity children will, of course, have to count the *ones* in a simple one-by-one fashion. However, from the outset, the powerful structuring aspect of the counting system should be emphasized by teaching children to count the *ones* into clearly differentiated tens-based formations. Children are usually introduced to structured counting through counting *ones* into a tens-structured *number-line* (or strictly speaking, *number-track*) formation. They can be introduced to the idea of counting into a *100 square* formation slightly later.

1. Tens-structured number-line counting

(a) 14 =

(b) 26 =

2. Tens-structured *hundred square* counting

 = 27

In practical terms, in the process of counting, the *ones* should be moved one-by-one into the structured rows of ten. After a clear break or gap beyond each ten, counting should continue as usual, 'eleven, twelve, thirteen', or 'twenty-one, twenty-two, twenty-three' and so on. When the *ones* have been counted in this way, the overall amount is then checked and confirmed by counting (or 'taking in') the number of whole *tens*, together with any partial row of *ones*.

Simple 'estimating and counting' activities can be extended to include 'number- tracking' activities, in which children are asked to 'track down' a few individual numbers within the simple number track which they have built. Before beginning number-tracking activities, it is important that children understand that they will be able to locate numbers most quickly by referring to decades and decade boundaries rather than by counting from the beginning, slowly in *ones*. To facilitate this 'tracking' process it is important that children are first asked to 'track down' the decade boundaries themselves, followed by easily located numbers, such as 32 (2 more than 30) or 19 (1 less than 20). Once children have become used to working and 'thinking' within the decade structures they should be helped to understand that 'the fives' – 15, 25, 35, and so on – are exactly half-way through each decade stretch, and they should be encouraged to estimate or judge, rather than count, the half-way 'points'. Children can then be asked to find the 'hardest' numbers, such as 24 or 36, as quickly as possible or by employing as little counting as possible. Number-targeting activities are good activities for exploring possible aural confusions such as the very common confusions between *thirteen* and *thirty*. The location of the 'teens' numbers in the second decade can be contrasted with the very clearly foregrounded decade boundary, 'tys'.

●●●●●●●●●● ●●●●●●●●●● ●●●●●●●●●●
             13   30

Since children actively construct the *number-line* and *100-square* formations, estimation and counting activities help give children a real insight into the ways in which these important models for thinking about numbers are built and how they work. Children who understand the 'tens-structuring' principle and who can locate numbers relatively easily on their own simple 'models' can easily transfer to work on structured bead strings, or on to a *hundred frame*.

Foregrounding that decades structure

Since the English spoken decade words are not transparent, many children do not grasp the relationship between a given quantity of *tens*, say 40, and the equivalent number of *ones*, in this case 4. As we will see, understanding this relationship is an extremely important element of the early stages of two-digit calculation. The neatness of the *100 square* formation makes it a particularly useful model for illustrating this relationship. While some children are able to extract the relationships from the written numbers on a completed *100 square*, it is usually more beneficial for children to actively construct the relationships. In one simple but effective activity, children work with rod *tens* and *ones*. Children lay down *ones* on one sheet and the equivalent number of *tens* on the second sheet and continue laying down the *ones* and the *tens* until 10 and 100, respectively, have been made. The relationships and the number language that we use needs to be carefully discussed as children proceed, but the *systems words* (*one-ty*, *two-ty* etc.) may also be used in order to help reinforce children's appreciation of the structure. It helps to record the quantities in digits as the matching patterns are built: one very simple way to do this is to record the values on to the sheets as they are laid down:

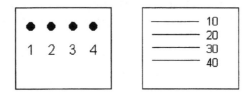

Targeting the teens

The 'teens' decade can be emphasized by building an extended Cuisinarie rod 'staircase', from 1 through to 20. (The basic staircase is illustrated on p. 000). The number 11 will need to be built from an orange *ten* and a *one*, 12 will need a rod *ten* and a *two*, and so on. To reinforce this *Base Ten* understanding of this second decade, a lotto game, based on the extended staircase idea, can also be played. Players require a spinner base displaying the numbers 11–20. Players take turns to spin a number, for example 14. The player takes the relevant rods (here a *ten* and a *four*) and places them in the approximately correct place in the staircase formation: Players have to 'miss a go' if they have already secured and built a particular step. The winner is the player who manages to build four adjacent steps first – or, in other words, he or she is the player who has managed to build '4-steps in-a-row'.

Counting to and beyond Base Ten 'crossover' points

As we have seen, many dyslexic and dyspraxic children find the idea that the counting system is made up of a complex and hierarchical system of structures-within-structures very difficult to grasp. While many primary school children with specific learning difficulties have managed to internalize the counting fact that 100 follows 99 in the ones-based counting sequence to 100, other 'crossover points' within counting sequences can be much harder to learn. Many dyslexic and dyspraxic children have difficulty remembering that 100 follows 90 in the *tens* counting sequence and it is not uncommon for aural confusions between the spoken '19' and '90' to lead to the count, '80, 90, 20 ... 30' etc. Later on, counting sequences such as 800, 900, ☐ are very difficult for many dyslexic and dyspraxic children to remember and *ones*-based sequences 'in the hundreds', such as 197 198 199 ?, can prove extremely difficult, too. Furthermore, even when *Base Ten* 'collection points' (or counting 'crossover') words are finally articulated, many children with learning difficulties become confused about how to continue counting beyond the 'collection point'. In fact, dyslexic and dyspraxic children very typically switch to an illegitimate higher value count when a higher value collection point is reached: thus the mistaken counting sequences, '98, 99, 100, 200, 300' or '90, 100, 200, 300,' are very common, indeed.

The first kind of activity which helps children grasp the complexities of the *Base Ten* structures, is practising counting up to, and beyond, the important value 'crossover points'. For counting in *tens*, Base Ten 'longs', or *tens* and (photocopied) *100 square* 'bases' are probably the simplest materials to use. As before, children count as they lay the rods down on to the framing *squares*. Once they have reached *one hundred* and need to count on to the next framing *square* children will have another *ten* in their hands to lay down. It is surprisingly difficult for a number of children to say 'one hundred and ten' and to continue along the 'track' of the *tens* count. For many children this seemingly simple activity will need much concrete overlearning practice. (It is very worthwhile to continue counting beyond 200, and even further, still, especially if children are enjoying the activity.)

Sequencing difficulties and working memory difficulties mean that activities which involve counting backwards are experienced by most dyslexic and dyspraxic children as much harder than counting forwards.

The ability to count backwards is a very significant pre-skill for flexible mental calculation and especially for mental subtraction from rounded numbers. Once children are able to count forwards through *Base Ten* collection points, counting backwards, or reversing the counting exercises described above, will need to be overlearned. Since counting backwards represents a very significant sequencing burden, it is worth targeting 'crossovers' carefully and limiting the length of the 'backwards' counting sequences required.

As soon as children are proficient at counting forwards and backwards through targeted 'crossover' points, the idea of switching between different value counts can, and should, be introduced. In simple terms, structured 'cross-counting' exercises help children understand that larger denominations can always be broken into smaller denominations, and vice versa. The most effective way to introduce the idea of 'cross-counting' is to allow children to experience the differences between 'quick counting' and 'slow counting' (Grauberg, 1998). For example, counting in *tens* can be seen as quick counting compared with 'slow' counting in *ones*. Likewise, counting in *hundreds* is 'quick' counting compared with counting in *tens*, and counting in *hundreds* is extremely quick in comparison with counting in *ones*. To practise concrete counting in *tens* and *ones* it is possible to use an abacus or a structured hundred-bead string but using Base Ten 'longs' and 'ones,' together with a number of *100 square* 'bases', allows the activity to encompass the all-important 'crossover' transitions, too. In essence 'cross-counting' activities are extremely simple. Children are asked to start counting in a certain specified denomination such as *tens* and to stop at a certain given signal – for example, the word *stop!* – and then to continue the 'count' in an alternative denomination, such as *ones*. Thus children may count 'ten, twenty, thirty, forty ... forty-one, forty-two, forty-three, forty-four, forty-five, forty-six, forty-seven, forty-eight, forty-nine, fifty ... sixty, seventy, eighty, ninety, one hundred, one hundred-and-ten ... one hundred and eleven, one hundred and twelve ...' and so on.

It may be helpful to note that many dyslexic and dyspraxic children find the task of counting larger denominations away from the *Base Ten* boundaries – for example, counting '22, 32, 42, 52, 53, 54 etc.' – very hard, indeed. It is thus important to secure children's understanding of the core *Base Ten* counting structures well before such very difficult counting patterns are attempted.

Early cross-counting activities can include presenting children with a very simple mixed array of coins to sort, and count. At the most basic level, a child could be given two or three 10p coins and about 15–20

1p coins to 'count together'. In time, the 'scatters' of coins, which children are asked to count, can be made increasingly complex: a more difficult count could include a 50p coin, two 20p coins, a 10p coin and 30 1p coins.

Concrete counting at higher levels, in larger denominations

Most of the counting that children engage in is oral or recitational counting. This is especially true of larger quantities. Children seldom count more than 20 'things' and rarely count concretely beyond 100 in any informal or real-life context. It is important that children develop the genuine *feel* for larger quantities that concrete counting can offer. Most children have no real sense of the actual size of large numbers. Indeed, because they have not experienced the complex way in which smaller quantities build up to make larger rounded quantities – and in which more of the smaller quantities are needed to build up more of those rounded quantities before an even larger rounded quantity and different denomination is reached – large numbers are often foreshortened in children's minds. This means that children have no real grasp of the distance between, say, 100 and 1 000, or 1 000 and 1 000 000. While counting and cross-counting to 100 is an invaluable experience, 100 is nevertheless a relatively small number. To grasp the scale of larger numbers, it is counting and cross-counting to and beyond 1000 that is often the really illuminating experience for children. Building up the 10 *hundreds* needed to make a *thousand* at least partially out of *tens* and slowing down even further, on occasion, to count in *ones*, makes children view 1000 with some awe and certainly with new respect. It should be noted that it is also surprisingly difficult for children to count in *hundreds* through one *thousand*. In a simple counting activity, children can be asked to count, Base Ten *hundreds*, stacking them on top of each other to build the equivalent of a *thousand* cube. After counting 'one thousand', and from 'one thousand, one hundred', children start building a second *thousand* cube. Again, children often struggle to articulate the 'one thousand, one hundred', even when they have the *hundred flat* in their hands.

    In concrete work beyond 1000 (as we will see, again, when we discuss teaching suggestions for understanding the written number system) there is the obvious problem of which materials to use. As far as Base Ten material is concerned, it is hugely beneficial if children have at least two or three *thousand* cubes to work with. While wooden cubes are expensive, they can be supplemented by paper cubes, constructed from proportional paper 'nets'. Most children are genuinely interested to see what a tower of

10 *thousand cubes* looks like. However, it is also generally true that once children have counted and cross-counted beyond 2000 or so, scale analogies begin to make sense. As Chinn and Ashcroft (1998, p. 47) point out, 'Base Ten blocks follow a repeating pattern in the thousands'. Children can see and feel the analogy between a *one* and a *one-thousand* cube; if 10 *thousand cubes* are not available, children can use a metre rule to try and envisage the dimensions of a *ten-thousand* 'long'; and creative use of masking-tape to mark out the area which a 'to-scale' *one-hundred thousand* cuboid would take, together with the use of a metre rule to suggest the length of one side of the cuboid, helps give children some purchase on the analogy between an ordinary *100 flat* and the size of *one-hundred thousand*! Base Ten material is proportional and it is therefore the best available teaching material to use to help children gain a *feel* for the relative scale of large numbers. However, counting 'fake' large value money denominations also offers additional valuable counting experience. It is worth noting that many counting activities have to be given some prior thought: 1p and 10p coins can be used for counting into the *hundreds* (100 = £1) but in the earlier stages of counting larger numbers, it confuses children to have to accept a £10 note as the equivalent of 1000. For counting large denominations of money, £1 needs to be considered the basic unit. or *one*, and 'fake' photocopied 'banknotes' can be used for subsequent larger denominations. Paper denominations all the way up to *millions* can be designed and 'printed' or photocopied on differently coloured paper. At first only *rounded* value notes should be used: £100, £1000, £10 000, and so on (and not amounts such as £20, £50 or £5 000). The idea of National Lottery 'wins' gives much impetus, and often excitement, to the activity of counting money: many children also enjoy playing 'bank' and granting requests for large amounts of money paid out in specified denominations.

   Specific and simple counting suggestions for counting larger denominations include the following:

1. Ask children to count Base Ten *hundreds*, or 'flats', stacking them into a *thousand* cube formation. Children enjoy making exchanges between *hundreds* and a single *thousand* cube. Count beyond 2000, and preferably to 3000, or so. Alternatively, count Base Ten *hundreds* into a long *thousand number-track* formation.
2. Ask children to count backwards from a specific number, such as 2 300 built from Base Ten *thousand* cubes and hundred 'flats'. Children will

discover that it is necessary to decompose' (break down) one of the *thousand* cubes. Children who find counting backwards very difficult should not be asked to count back beyond 1 600, or so.

3. Have at least 100 £10 notes, count them into £100s, bundle them, exchange them, but also 'bank' them once £1000 has been reached; the single £1000 note can be compared with the 10 bundles of £10, and then 10 x £100 bundles.

Counting from different starting points

It is important that counting activities do not always begin from 0. It is a precondition for using counting as a starting point for basic calculation that children can 'pick up' and continue a count from any given starting point. In early two digit addition work, for example, children can figure out 60 + 30 by counting from 60 in *tens*, (60), 70, 80 and 90. Although other concrete materials may, of course, be used, activities which are designed around counting money are very good ways to practise this skill. Most children enjoy counting money, and for children who are not yet familiar with the different value of coins, counting money provides a good opportunity for reinforcing an essential life skill.

In money-based counting activities; children are given a selection of coins (an early example may be a 50p coin, and three 10p coins) and asked to determine their overall value. Certain pre-skills may need to be put in place, first. Children may need to practise sorting coins, and then learn to order them, highest value first. They may also need to learn to count the coins from highest to lowest value. Finally, younger or less able children may need to count 20p coins initially as 2 tens, touching the 20p twice. For example, 50p + 20p + 20p may be processed as (50), 60, 70 ... 80, 90.

Oral sequence counting activities

Most children with specific learning difficulties fail to 'intuit' structures from oral counting activities alone, and need plentiful experience of concrete counting in order to grasp how the spoken system really 'works'. Nevertheless, a significant part of children's flexibility in working with numbers derives from a very thoroughly internalized knowledge of the spoken number system. Quick oral counting activities help consolidate, reinforce, and extend children's growing understanding of how to count 'properly'. Many helpful oral counting activities can simply be based on the concrete counting activities already described. Since oral counting is a fast-moving and generally relatively brief activity, it is particularly suited to the very first opening moments of the *mental maths* section of any maths session. Specific oral counting suggestions include the following:

1. It is especially valuable to ask children to count from a starting point which is relatively close to a *Base Ten* 'collection point'. In this way different value 'crossover' points can be targeted. For example, 'Please count in 100s, starting from 700.'
2. Oral 'cross-counting' can be extensively practised. For example, 'Please count in 100s from 800. Stop! Count in 10s. Stop, count in 100s again.'
3. Counting backwards should also be practised. 'Backwards sequences' should be kept relatively short. As children become proficient at counting backwards at each level of difficulty, it is important to target *Base Ten* 'collection points'. For example, 'Count backwards in 10s from 230.'

Building two-digit and multidigit numbers

As we have seen, counting work foregrounds the *spoken number system*. Counting work helps children to situate numbers in relative or 'relational' ways and consequently helps children develop a *feel* for the relative size of numbers and the relative distances between them. In developing an understanding of large numbers, it is also important for children to have a sound understanding of the internal structure of individual larger numbers. Understanding the component structures of individual large numbers is an important precondition for understanding the *written number system* and for understanding many aspects of two-digit and multidigit calculation. Much of the 'building work' described in this section is designed to help children understand the complexities of the written number system and the *place value* aspects of calculation.

Two preconditions for understanding written numbers

In the context of exploring the difficulties inherent in the spoken number system we have touched on research observations that young English speaking primary school children often perceive individual two-digit numbers in ones-based or *unitary* ways. This means that young children are likely to choose *ones* to construct an individual number, such as 16, rather than select materials which represent units of larger value, such as a *ten* together with the relevant number of *units* or *ones*. As we have seen, many dyslexic and dyspraxic children retain a *unitary* concept of numbers well into the primary school years.

Further research studies have been concerned to explore the way in which children are able to move beyond a *unitary* number concept. In other words, some researchers have set out to understand the nature of the pre-understandings which inform the more mature understanding that numbers can be constructed from units of different value – for instance that the number 16 can be seen as one *ten* and six *ones*. Studies by Nunes and Bryant (1996) and Cakir and Saxon (1999) show that before children are in a position to understand the very abstract *place value* principle they need to have grasped two rather more basic concepts: they need to understand the principle of *adding on*, as well as the principle of exchange.

Adding on

In order to understand the written number conventions, children have to understand the principle of *adding on* – in other words children have to understand the idea that component quantities can be combined without having to count both quantities all the way from the beginning, or all the from 'one'.

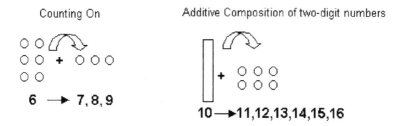

From a practical teaching point of view, this means that *counting on* needs to have been internalized before written number conventions are tackled; it also means that work aimed at helping children understand the written number system should almost certainly be delayed if the principle of *adding on* is not understood. (*Adding on* is comprehensively covered in Chapter 4.)

The principle of exchange

For children to have a clear understanding that 16 equals one *ten* and six *ones*, they need to grasp, first, that 10 *ones* is also one *ten* or that ten *ones* can be exchanged for one *ten*.

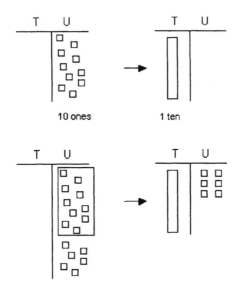

In some regards, *exchange* can be said to feature in counting activities: the principle of exchange is certainly *implicit* in many of the counting activities suggested in the previous section of the chapter. However, while concrete counting activities are sometimes carried out as processes which involve making some exchanges along the way, counting really draws on the idea of a *base* as a 'grouping into sets' or as a 'collection point' for the *units* which higher values are made up of:

Many children, and certainly many children with specific learning difficulties, benefit from participation in activities and games with a rather more explicit focus on exchange itself – on the idea that a specific number of items can be physically exchanged for a single item or token which then represents that initial number or quantity. Very basic exchange activities include the following ones:

1. Younger children enjoy simple activities in which they are asked to make piles of ones 'shrink' by exchanging them for larger values. Piles of Base Ten *ones* can be counted into *tens*, and exchanged for *tens* 'longs'. Piles of 1p coins can be counted and exchanged for 10p coins. *Tens*, or 10p coins, can, of course, also be exchanged for *hundred* 'flats' or £1 coins, respectively.

2. Most younger primary school children enjoy playing **the simplest exchange game ever**. To play this game, attractive materials in two sizes, such as two sizes of marbles, or two sizes of colourful counters, are needed. Alternatively, 1p coins and 5p coins can also be used. A slightly more advanced exchange game (see p. 196) introduces the idea of *Base Ten* exchanges. However, 10 is quite a large quantity to work with. Many children benefit from exchanging a smaller quantity than 10 for a larger 'value unit' and, in fact, 5 is an especially good quantity to work with. In the **simplest exchange game**, a 1–4 spinner, or die, should be used. In each round, each player generates a number and takes the number of small *ones* indicated. As soon as a player has accumulated 5 small *ones*, he or she can exchange the *ones* for a larger token (marble or counter). After a certain number of rounds, the player with the greatest number of larger tokens is declared the winner.

The unique aspect of the written number system: the place value principle

The most difficult aspect of understanding the written number system (or, in other words, of transcoding between the earlier learned spoken number system and the written number systems) is the principle that *place* alone determines value. However, while *place value* is hard to understand when it is abstractly taught, there is a great deal of well-respected research (for instance, by Fuson and Kwon, 1991; Fuson, Smith and LoCicero, 1997) to show that children can make good sense of the complexities of the *place value* system so long as they are taught using 'concrete representations'.

Within approaches advocating a 'concrete approach' to learning about written numbers, there has been some debate as to which 'concrete representations' are best to use. Recommended materials include: straws or cocktail sticks, money, Base Ten material and a *place value* abacus.

Straws or cocktail sticks: bundling activities

Many classroom teachers like to introduce written number conventions through the active, 'homespun' and relatively inexpensive activity of bundling *ones* into *tens*. For instance, 25 straws would be bundled as two *tens* and one *five*.

While many children thrive on 'bundling' activities, there is some evidence to show that children with learning difficulties can find 'bundled ones' hard to perceive as *units* of a larger value: strictly speaking, the bundles of *ten* remain ten straws because they are not exchanged for a special unit of *ten*. Bundles of 100s (ten *tens*) are also unwieldy to construct and to work with.

Money

The principle of exchange is a significant and intrinsic or inbuilt feature of different value coins. Thus 10 one pence coins can be exchanged for one 10p coin.

Money is certainly a useful tool for two-digit written number-work. It is also possible to use coins to represent three-digit numbers: in place value work 10 ten pence coins equal £1 or 100 pence.

To represent 'thousands' using the 1p coin 'equals' 1 unit analogue, £10 is needed: as we have suggested, however; most primary school children find this very confusing and it is consequently not recommended.

Instead, as we recommended earlier, one pound coins can be used to represent one *unit*, or *one*, and fake banknotes can be used to represent higher values once the four-digit number stage has been reached.

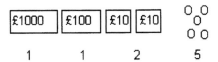

Base Ten material

Base Ten materials were specifically designed by Zoltan Dienes to illuminate the structure of the written number system. As a representation of written numbers, Base Ten materials have a number of important advantages. First of all, like money, the principle of exchange is an inbuilt feature of the materials. Secondly, Base Ten materials are designed to embody exchange in a directly proportional way: children can physically explore the fact that 'ten *ones* make a *ten*' and that 'ten *tens* make a *hundred*'. The fact that these equivalences can be explored, is reassuring to many primary school children with learning difficulties; they often find more arbitrary and abstract equivalences (for instance 'trading' chips, such as poker chips) rather more difficult to accept. Thirdly, the large value, *thousands*, are represented as clear units of value. And, finally, the building blocks of Base Ten material – the 'ones', 'longs', 'flats' and 'cubes' have a readily visualized identity which make the representations particularly useful: for example, it is possible to ask children to 'picture' 1 900 constructed from Base Ten material. With regards to the structure of the written number system, the only potential drawback of Base Ten materials is they do not specify the *place* element of the different values embodied in the materials. Thus while 'three hundred and sixty-five' is clearly represented by 3 'flats', 6 'longs' and 5 'ones', there is nothing intrinsic to the materials which indicates the relative place positions of the materials. (This disadvantage applies to the money and the 'bundles' analogues too, of course.)

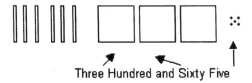

Three Hundred and Sixty Five

The place value abacus

The principal advantage of the place value abacus is that it clearly foregrounds the *place* element of the written number system.

In all *place value* work, as we will see shortly, it is important to ensure that children understand from early on that very large values are structured in 'classes' of 'three' (see below). For this reason it is important to use an abacus with six spokes – and not widely available four spoked ones.

Nevertheless there are also disadvantages which are intrinsic to the *place value* abacus and which make it unsuitable as a principal teaching tool for children with specific learning difficulties. First, although it is possible to make exchanges from 'lower' to 'higher' value positions, the attribution of values is entirely arbitrary (for instance, red 'equals' one hundred) and the 'bead units' are not, of course, proportional at all. And, secondly, while the bead abacus can help children visualize the 'grid' or 'column' structure of the written number system it cannot help children develop an analogous 'feel' for the size of large written numbers.

To sum up:

Base Ten material has a very strong visual and physical identity and is a particularly successful material to use in working with children with specific learning difficulties. Because of this, nearly all of the activities which are outlined below employ Base Ten materials. Nevertheless it is also important to bear in mind that children generally benefit from having some experience of alternative concrete embodiments. In many 'place value' activities and games, coins and paper money can be used. Some work with a place value abacus should also supplement Base Ten *number building* activities.

Base Ten materials, and place value: the place value 'mat'

While Base Ten material does not, in itself, indicate the *place* aspect of written values (and can, consequently not be used as a 'self-teaching' tool for understanding written numbers), this element can be introduced by the simple action of building numbers on headed 'mats' or 'boards'. The headings represent the columns of values to be worked with:

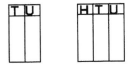

In 'spoken to written' transcoding activities the written representation of numbers are much clearer when the selected materials are placed in their correct positions on a mat. Thus 'three hundred and sixty-five' is represented, in the appropriate columns as:

H	T	U
▢▢▢	I I I I I I	••••
3	6	5

Working on headed mats also helps make the placeholding function of zero clear. For example, when the two-digit decade number, 30, or the three-digit number, 101, are built on mats, both have empty columns. Children readily accept that the empty columns have to be represented in the equivalent written form by using a placeholding '0 marker'.

T	U
III	
3	0

H	T	U
▢		•
1	0	1

Place value mats also introduce children to the conventional place value 'grid' or structure of place values. For instance, as soon as younger children have become familiar with the number system to 100, they can be introduced to activities on a place value mat which encompasses the *hundreds* position. Many children need practice at using '0' as a written-number *place value* holder, and at building and 'reading' numbers which incorporate the 'teens' (e.g. 213) and 'tys' (e.g. 230). Once these difficulties have been negotiated, however, primary school children can usually be introduced to much larger values quite quickly. Indeed, since 'millions'

feature prominently in 'money-talk' in our culture, children are generally
very keen to 'reach a million' as speedily as possible. However, before work
with 'thousands' values is rushed into, it is very important to note that
children will need to be introduced, first, to the hugely important idea that
the different units of value – all the way from the most frequently encountered smallest values – are actually organized into *broader classes* or *families*
of value. Indeed many adults are not fully aware that each *class* (or *family*)
of values is organized into a pattern of three component values. Thus,
from a structural point of view the basic and familiar HTU pattern is
repeated, but in higher and higher classes of value. Overall this structure
of *threes* includes the class of *ones*, the class of *thousands*, and only then the
class of *millions*.

For instance, 'Two hundred million, five hundred thousand, eight
hundred and fifty':

Millions	Thousands	Ones
2 0 0	5 0 0	8 5 0

A discussion of the conventional 'grid' of place values

Introducing the idea that there is a whole *class of thousands* in the very early
stages of working with units-of-thousands is not standard teaching
practice. It is more usual to introduce what is loosely called the 'thousands'
position once children need to encounter numbers which are larger than
three-digit numbers. At this stage, the grid of values is usually represented
as ThHTU. Children typically work with 'thousands' for many months
before the *tens of thousands* and *hundreds of thousands* value-positions are introduced. In the main, comparatively little time is devoted to the larger
thousands values. The major disadvantage of this is that when children with
specific learning difficulties acquire the habit of thinking about a single
'thousands' position they often have difficulty accommodating the idea
that there are additional and larger *thousands* values within the overall
structure of values. When dyslexic and dyspraxic children are asked to
describe the structure of *place values* they will often describe a very
foreshortened model in which 'the thousands' (and later 'the millions') are
represented by a single position or column. In other words, the structure
is usually thought to be one which contains *units, tens, hundreds, thousands,
millions* (and then *billions*); in column terms they represent this highly
contracted structure as MThHTU. Similar problems occur when children
are asked to read very large written numbers. For instance, if the class

structuring is not indicated in any way – through the use of a 'comma', or the present-day standard 'space' – a number such as 24537 is often transcoded as 'two million, four thousand, five hundred and thirty-seven'. On the other hand, a written number such as 127 353, which uses a 'space' to separate the two classes', often confuses children and many end up making rather wild guesses at what the number may mean.

The place value 'grid': teaching suggestions

In practical terms, children should be encouraged to label *place value* columns, for themselves, just as soon as they become more familiar with the way in which written values are organized. In time, as we will see, 'mats' can give way to columns drawn on squared paper. Labelling columns, or generating the conventional grid of place values for themselves, enables children to internalize the 'classes-of-three' structure of written values and consequently helps them read and write large numbers more efficiently. There is, in fact, no one completely standard way of representing the complex structures-within-structures contained in the number system. The most successful grid form is one which clearly foregrounds the repeated pattern of *threes* values. For example:

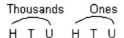

```
    Thousands    Ones
    ⌒⌒⌒      ⌒⌒⌒
    H  T  U   H  T  U
```

and later,

```
    Millions  Thousands   Ones
    ⌒⌒⌒   ⌒⌒⌒    ⌒⌒⌒
    H  T  U  H  T  U   H  T  U
```

Using 'boxes' to contain the *threes* is potentially neater but can be more time-consuming to construct. For example:

```
    Millions   Thousands    Ones
    |H  T  U| H  T  U| H  T  U|
```

Some children tend to record the grid structure in a way which highlights the values, rather than the repeated HTU structure: MMM, Th Th Th, HTU.

To forestall difficulties which children may experience in decoding very large numbers, it is recommended that *place value* mats or headed grids for games should always represent an *entire class* of values – even when all of the columns are not going to be used in a particular activity, or even when children are not ready to work, as yet, with the larger values in the class. Thus when the units-of-thousands position is introduced, place value 'mats' should still be structured and labelled. If so wished, the values 'up to' the units of thousands position can be highlighted in some way. Teaching in this way leaves the mental 'space' in children's minds for more 'kinds' of thousands to be learned about.

Working with 'thousands"

Thousands   Ones

H T U   H T U

Traditional number building and transcoding exercises

In the simplest concrete number-building activities, children may be asked to use materials to build specified individual spoken or written numbers on a *place value* mat or they may be asked to name and record individual concrete representations of numbers which have been built from materials for them. Thus, for instance, one might say to a child, 'Using these blocks, can you show me the number two hundred and five?' The child would then place (or may be helped to place) the relevant blocks in the correct positions; he or she could then record the number in writing, using the place-holding '0' to represent the 'empty' *tens* position.

"Two hundred and five'

H	T	U
□		•.•
□		•.•

H	T	U
2	0	5

Similarly, a child might be asked to represent the written number, 113, using Base Ten materials and to articulate the number in the spoken number form – 'one hundred and thirteen'.

H	T	U
□		••

= 113

On the other hand, in concrete work which starts the other way round, a child may be asked to identify a number which has been built from concrete materials. For example, a concrete array may be presented to a child, and the child might be asked, 'Can you tell me the name of the number I have built?' He, or she, would then give the spoken number form, 'one hundred and thirty' and record the number in written form.

H	T	U
□	III	

H	T	U
1	3	0

(As a slight variation, recording 'written' numbers can be made a little more exciting by having the child key the relevant number on to a calculator screen.)

These relatively widely used 'show me', 'tell me' and 'record for me' number-building activities are very useful because the numbers used can be very carefully selected. This means that simple number-building exercises are an excellent way of assessing children's understanding of the written number system, including the more difficult aspects of *place value*. Secondly, number-building exercises can be used to reinforce those aspects of the written number system which children have most difficulty with, such as the place-holding function of '0' and the 'teens' and 'tys' elements of composite numbers (all of which were deliberately highlighted in the examples give above).

There are two potential disadvantages, however, of limiting work on *place value* to ordinary number-building activities. In brief, the written number system is particularly complex, as we have seen, and many children with specific learning difficulties need a great deal of overlearning practice before they can be helped to master it. Sooner or later, children can find number-building exercises somewhat repetitive and even a little dull. Secondly, many dyslexic and dyspraxic children have grave difficulties with the mental calculation aspects of the written number system, as well as with the more fundamental aspect of making sense of it.

Place value and mental calculation

Many children with specific learning difficulties take time to understand that the written number system facilities the addition and subtraction of rounded values. A calculation such as 123 + 100 feels 'difficult' if children have not grasped that the 'hundreds' can be combined in the *hundreds* position. Likewise, the written number implications of mental calculations such as 999 + 1 or 890 + 10 can be very hard to grasp. In essence, while conventional number-building exercises are valuable learning exercises, they cannot help children with these important conceptual connections because they present each number to be built in an isolated and static way. Unless children are asked to build a particular *sequence* of numbers, conventional number building exercises do not foster a sense of the relationships between individual written numbers, nor do they touch on the ways in which written numbers can dramatically change – as in the sequence, 999, 1 000, 1 001, for instance. Some writers (for instance, Hiebert et al., 1997) argue that the more dynamic aspects of the written number system should be understood through calculation work itself. They claim that when children learn about two-digit addition they will also come to learn, for instance, what it means in 'place value' terms to add 20 to 36. Indeed, a number of prominent understanding-based approaches to maths learning adopt and promote a calculation-based perspective towards understanding the written number-system, itself. For instance, it is argued that in the process of actively 'figuring out' the answer to the calculation problem, 36 + 23 children will ultimately come to realize that '3' *tens* and '2' *tens* in the *tens* position can be combined as 5 *tens*, or 50.

For children with specific learning difficulties, the first and more general drawback of linking written-number-understanding to calculation, is that this can hold back children's understanding of the written number system; children's understanding of written number structures can start to lag quite significantly behind their knowledge of the spoken number system. Secondly, linking *place value* understanding to the process of solving calculation problems can represent an overwhelming learning load for children with specific learning difficulties. The very common 'dyslexic' and 'dyspraxic' combination of long-term memory and working memory difficulties means that if *place value* understanding and calculation understanding are combined, children often lose track of the relatively large number of different conceptual connections which they have to make. In Ashcraft et al.'s (1998) terms, the very many different demands which are made on children in these situations can end up 'draining' their working memory capacity. In fact, in sharp contrast to the *place-value-through-calculation* teaching approach, teaching experience shows that children with specific learning difficulties make much better progress in understanding written numbers *and* in managing the steps of multidigit calculation if the written number system is made an important and explicit separate teaching focus. It would also seem that the best progress is made in both of these areas if the *place value* conventions are presented in as dynamic a way as possible.

Concrete place value games

Fortunately, introducing dynamism into written number activities also makes them 'fun' for children to participate in. In the teaching suggestions, outlined below, the desired element of change and fluidity is introduced through playing *place value* games – usually on *place value* 'grids'. In other words, games in which numbers are made to grow and shrink are the activities which most successfully give children the same kind of experience of the written number system which the obviously dynamic counting activities provide for the spoken number system. In fact, it is through games – concrete games, first, and then pencil-and-paper games – that the bulk of learning about the written number system can take place.

A brief explanatory note on number-building games

Most of the games which are described in this section can be played by between 2 and 4 players. Some games can be played by more players and many of the games can be adjusted for whole-class teaching purposes. The 'running progress' of *number building* games should nearly always be recorded. Games using concrete materials should be played on place value 'mats'. Each individual player should have his/her own mat. Each player should also have his/her own *place value* 'grid' to record his/her own individual progress; place value grids should be drawn on squared paper. In a large number of the games which are described, different units of value are 'earned' and accumulated by players. The most efficient and flexible way of generating different values is to use a spinner which is placed on specially created spinner bases; however blank dice can also have the required values written on them, or specially created sets of cards may be used, instead. Most of the concrete number-building games can be played at a basic *tens-and-units* level; many may be adapted to include *hundreds*, or even *units-of-thousands* values. Pencil and paper games may be 'stretched' to include very large numbers indeed. (Readers specifically interested in helping children understand very large numbers should refer to the section on p. 179).

A classic exchange game, and many useful variations

The exchange games described, here, should be played once children have demonstrated an understanding of the basic concept of *exchange*. The games introduce the base of *ten*, and the 'grid' of *place values*. In a concrete **First to 30 game**, Base Ten material is accumulated and exchanged. Each player has a basic TU *place value* 'mat'. A 1–6 or 0–9 dice may be used. Players take turns to roll the dice: dice rolls indicate the number of *ones* cubes which the player should take to place on his or her 'mat'. As soon as 10 or more cubes are accumulated in the *units* position, 10 *units* should be exchanged for a *ten rod* and moved across to the *tens* position. Each player also records his or her running total in headed T/U columns:

	T	U
A record of two rounds		
		6 (+7)
	1	3

In the the **First to 30 game**, the winner is the player who first reaches (or overshoots) 30. Some variations include, (a) the **First to 100 game**: this game is played in the same way, but players have to accumulate 10 *tens* to exchange for the target, 100. Using a 4–9 dice helps speed up the game; (b) the **First to 300 game**: in this game *tens* only are accumulated. As soon as 10 or more *tens* are accumulated in the *tens* position they should be exchanged for a 100 'flat' and moved across to the *hundreds* position on the mat:

H	T	U
□	l	X

H	T	U	
	6	0	(+ 50)
1	1	0	

Some examples of accumulation games

Place value accumulation games are very valuable games because they compress a great deal of maths learning in a efficient and fun way. They encourage children to pay attention to the way multidigit numbers are constructed. They help children target the correct value position in mental calculations. They give practice at adding and subtracting units of different value to any number, and they also help children pay attention to the value differences of the numbers in play.

Open-ended accumulation games

The adding values game

In this game, a place value 'mat' is given to each player and a spinner is used to gain a *value unit* for each player in each round of the game which is played. For example, in a **tens and units accumulation game**, either a *ten* or a *unit* may be earned and accumulated: each time a value is 'spun' the player places the relevant Base Ten piece in the correct column, and records his or her running total. It is usually best to begin by having each player place a 'start out quantity', such as '5', on his/her 'mat'.

The game may be completed after a certain number of rounds have been played, or after a certain amount of time has elapsed. The player with the larger/largest number wins. After 8 rounds, a player's 'mat' and record of earned values may look something like this:

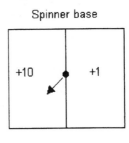

Spinner base

In **adding values** games, which are designed to incorporate *hundreds* values or *thousands* values, the spinner base will need designate the relevant values to be earned. A **subtracting values** game can be played. This is based on the **adding values** game, but is played in reverse. Players start with 99 (or with 999 etc.) in Base Ten Materials, placed on their mats. The values which players 'spin' in each round are removed from the mats, and the decreasing 'running totals' are recorded. The winner is the first player to 'reach' 0, or to have the smallest value number, when the requisite number of rounds have been completed.

Target number games

Specified 'targets': for example 'Four Throws'

'Four Throws' is described by Ian Sugarman (1997, p, 150). In 'Four Throws' *tens* and *ones* are accumulated. The goal of the game is to be the player to have a final total which is the nearest to the target number, 100. Each player, in turn, throws a 1–6 dice and has to choose whether to take the number indicated on the dice as *tens*, or as *ones*. The game is played in four rounds. An important rule of **Four Throws** is that each player *has* to have all four 'goes': thus, for example, a player may already have

accumulated 90 after just two 'throws', and may subsequently roll a dice
'1'. If one *ten* is taken, a fourth 'throw' will still have to be played, and the
target of 100, will, of course, be overshot. *Four throws* can be modified to
attempt to reach a target of 1000. In this game, each player has 4 dice rolls,
as usual, but Base Ten *hundreds* or *tens* are selected and accumulated.

Open ended target games

In **open ended target** games, the target number for each player is
unique to that player and is generated by throwing a specified number of
dice: two dice for a *tens and units* game, three dice for a *hundreds, tens and units*
game, and so on. Each player is asked to organize his or her dice 'throw',
largest digit first, to determine his or her own personal target number –
this represents the quantity which the player needs to accumulate in Base
Ten materials. For instance in a *hundreds, tens and units* version of the game,
the dices scores '3', '7' and '1' would be ordered as 731. Players use a
spinner to 'earn' Base Ten materials, which are placed on to the 'mats'. A
range of different spinner bases can be used. A very simple set of spinner
choices for a *hundreds, tens and units* game would be single units of *ones*, *tens*
or *hundreds* (+1, +10 +100). More complex versions of open-ended target
games involve the players in making choices between different values, or
different numbers of values: for example, (take) + 10 or +100; (take) +1 or
+100; or (take) +10 or + 20.

Further games foregrounding exchange

As children become increasingly proficient at understanding the basic
principles of the *place value* system, it is important to begin building more
advanced pre-skills for mental multi-digit calculation. The ability to
exchange values 'up' and 'down' is one very important prerequisite for
flexible calculation. Many calculations require that children are able to
translate between the standard written number form of numbers and their
equivalent, but non-standard, forms: in other words children need to
understand that 160 is also 16 *tens*, and, conversely, that 16 *tens* 'equal' 160.

A very simple dice exchange game: 'exchanging up'

In this game, players take it in turns to throw a 1–20 dice to earn numbers
of a specified concrete *Base Ten* value – for instance, *tens*. The quantity
taken is then expressed in standard written form. Thus, if a player throws
a dice 12, he or she will take 12 *tens*, exchange this for one *hundred* and two

tens, and record it appropriately. On the other hand, if a player 'throws' a dice '4', he or she will take four *tens* and record the 40.

$$12 \text{ } tens = \begin{array}{c|c|c} H & T & U \\ \hline 1 & 2 & 0 \end{array} \qquad 4 \text{ } tens = \begin{array}{c|c|c} H & T & U \\ \hline & 4 & 0 \end{array}$$

This particular game is not an accumulation game. After each round, players put the material away and a new round is begun; each round is won by the player with the larger/largest number in each round. The overall winner is the player who has won the greatest number of rounds.

A dice and spinner game: 'exchanging up'

In each round of this game, players take turns to roll a 1–20 dice to earn quantities of Base Ten materials as before, but the value of the materials earned in each round are determined by spinning a 'number value' spinner. For instance, the spinner base may represent *ones* or *tens*. Thus, if a player throws 13, and spins *tens*, he or she takes 13 *tens*, exchanges ten *tens* for a *hundred*, and records 130. On the other hand, another player may throw 6 and spin *ones*: he or she will earn 6 *ones*, which will be recorded as 6.

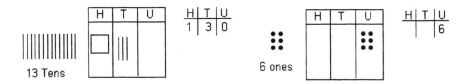

As in the previous game, material is put away after each round and a new round is begun; again, too, the player who has won the most rounds overall is the winner of the game. Quite quickly, children are able to play a faster-moving pencil-and-paper version of this game.

Games which combine accumulation and exchange

In basic accumulation games, as we have seen, values are usually acquired one at a time. Accumulating more than one of each value in a 'go' speeds up the likelihood that exchanges will need to be made. It is particularly worthwhile playing larger value versions of the classic exchange game described on p. 196. Thus players could roll a *tens* dice (0–90) to reach 500, or 'spin' hundreds (100–600, for instance) to reach 3000.

Open-ended accumulation and exchange games

These games are played in the same way as the accumulation games described on p. 196. Instead of acquiring 1, 10 or 100, however, players can, for instance, spin to acquire 4, 40 or 400 (or any other number of the relevant values). Players can also begin with a start number, such as the start number, 150, illustrated below.

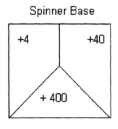

Th			Ones		
H	T	U	H	T	U
			1	5	0
			5	5	0
			5	9	0
			6	3	0
		1	0	3	0

In basic accumulation games, players generally start with '0' or a small quantity, such as 50. Another way to build in *place value* exchanges is to begin play with large 'start-out' numbers. To introduce greater competition, each player could generate his/her own individual start-out number by rolling a dice such as a 4–9 dice. Dice rolls can be ordered, largest value first. For instance, if '5', '7' and '6' are rolled, the player would begin play with the start-out quantity/number, 765. Individual values would be 'spun' for and accumulated as usual. As usual, too, the winner is the player who accumulates the largest overall value by the end of play.

Working with larger values

The games described, so far, have largely illustrated work with two-digit or three-digit numbers. As suggested earlier on, however, all of the two-digit games can be adapted to working with three digits, and vice versa, and most of the games can be adapted to work with very much larger values, too. It is often assumed that it is not necessary to use concrete materials in work with larger values. It is commonly argued that children will understand mental calculation problems, together with the relevant place value exchanges, by analogy with concrete work as lower levels. It is certainly true that establishing an understanding of the most basic *place value* principles and conventions is a priority and that, generally speaking, this foundation will pave the way for understanding how the written number system works. But it is also true, as we have seen, that children with specific learning difficulties have a particularly hazy grasp of the structure of the higher spoken and written number values. Furthermore, large number mental calculations, such as 999 + 1 or 990 + 100, are very challenging and need to be well rehearsed and frequently reviewed. It is certainly very helpful if dyslexic and dyspraxic children are able to work and to 'play' with larger-value quantity representations.

Games which extend to working with *units of thousands* should preferably employ wooden, plastic or paper *thousands* cubes. As we have seen, Base Ten material is visually memorable and playing games which include *units of thousands* representations helps children extend their *feel* for large numbers. Of course it is not possible to use Base Ten materials to represent larger-value *thousands*. Unfortunately, pieces of paper cannot match the experience of working with Base Ten materials but for very large value number-work children with specific learning difficulties benefit from concrete work with fake paper money – and value–colour associations can be additionally helpful for some children. However, while concrete experience is invaluable, it is important to note, too, that as soon as children have developed a *feel* for very large values and are competent at making large value exchanges, *place value* games at this level should preferably be played using pencil and paper only. Large amounts of different materials inevitably involves distracting 'clutter' and concrete games involving large values are certainly very much slower and are more cumbersome to play than abstract ones.

Fostering children's ability to round numbers

It is widely recognized that the ability to *round* numbers represents one indication that children understand the number structures; and the ability to *round* numbers is, of course, also an important element in the ability to approximate and check calculations. In many maths textbooks, however, *rounding* is treated as though it were a separate skill and activity and it is often taught in a very abstract and predominantly rule-based way. Furthermore classroom textbooks frequently introduce difficult *rounding* problems very rapidly indeed. As a result of this, many dyslexic and dyspraxic children have no real conception of what *rounding* work is for, and dislike, or even fear, formal or textbook-driven *rounding* exercises.

To help children acquire a natural *habit* of rounding numbers the idea, language and rules of *rounding* are best integrated into ordinary number-system activities and games. The fluidity of many of the games described above, together with the fact that they are played competitively, lend themselves to talking about the relative closeness or distance of numbers from the relevant Base Ten structures. By way of illustration, for instance, the *rounding habit* or *idea* can be built into a game such as the **First to 30 game**, described on p. 196. In a game played between two players, the teacher can make a point of drawing attention to the fact that a running total of 18, achieved by one player, is close to 20, whereas a score of 13, achieved by another player is closer to 10, and very far away from the ultimate goal of 30. Important *rounding* conventions can be introduced in such informal ways too. Children who experience in a concrete way that the '5's (such as 5, 15, 25 and so on) are exactly half-way between the *tens* also accept the maths convention that we round *up* to the next ten rather than *down* to the *ten* before. The 'halfway' *rounding* rule is readily extended to the '50s', '500s', and so on.

Other activities which particularly lend themselves to *rounding* discussions and explorations are emptier *number-line* and *number-track* activities. In early *number-track* work it often happens that when children are asked to locate 39 on a structured concrete model, for the first time, they locate 30 and then go back to 29, by mistake. With concrete *tens* to hand children readily accept that 39 will be much bigger than 30 and they can be helped to realize that it is actually 'next door' to 40. Children who have the opportunity to have many experiences of this kind – and who are also guided by appropriately questioning and informing language – begin to feel that the answers to *rounding* questions are self-evident.

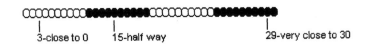

|
3-close to 0   15-half way   29-very close to 30

In time, it is important to ensure that children are able to respond to formal verbal or written requests to *round* numbers, too. For example, children should be asked conventional *rounding* questions such as 'Can you round the number 375 to the nearest *hundred*?' If children continue to need concrete support in rounding exercises of this kind, it is particularly helpful to provide appropriate and relevant *rounding frames*; for instance, *tens* should be placed on an empty *100 square* frame, and *hundreds* should be placed on empty *hundred square* frames.

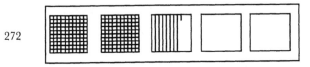

272

Rounded to the nearest *hundred* = 300, rounded to the nearest *ten* = 270

Working with digit cards and overlay cards

Digit cards

Many contemporary maths teaching approaches recommend that children use digit cards to 'build' individual numbers. For instance, the digit cards $\boxed{7}$ and $\boxed{1}$ can be used to 'build' $\boxed{7}\,\boxed{1}$ or $\boxed{1}\,\boxed{7}$. Digit cards are easily moved around and they can also be clustered in subtle ways to suggest place value *classes*: $\boxed{2}$ $\boxed{5}$ $\boxed{0}$ $\boxed{8}$. They are consequently very flexible tools for reinforcing place *value* work. Work with cards represents an excellent intermediate stage between concrete work, on the one hand, and 'fixed' pencil-and-paper work, on the other hand.

All of the accumulation games described above can be played by placing digit cards, instead of concrete materials, on the place value mats. It should be noted that any change in an existing value will require that at least one card from the mat will need to be 'swapped' for another one: for example, if 200 is to be added to 135 the $\boxed{1}$ card will need to be exchanged for a $\boxed{3}$, and the outcome will be 335:

Digit cards are especially useful in activities and games involving very large values, and they are also invaluable tools for use in classroom situations. Two very popular, quick and effective games using digit cards include: **Place value card war** games and **Place value boxes**.

Place value card war games are played by dealing a selected number of digit cards to each player in turn. The number of cards in play should reflect the size of written numbers currently under review. A three digit number game is described here. 4 sets of 0–9 digit cards are shuffled and 3 cards are dealt to each of 2–4 players. Before play can begin, the rule-for-play needs to be decided on: in any game either the biggest number wins or the smallest number wins. Each player then lays down and arranges his/her cards appropriately. For instance, in a game in which the *biggest number wins* Player A may lay down $\boxed{7}$ $\boxed{3}$ $\boxed{0}$, Player B may lay down $\boxed{9}$ $\boxed{1}$ $\boxed{0}$ and Player C may have $\boxed{4}$ $\boxed{1}$ $\boxed{1}$. In this round Player B 'wins' and takes all 9 cards to store in a separate pile. Play continues until all the cards have been used. The overall winner is the player with the greatest overall number of cards in his or her individual pile – he or she has won the most *battles* and is thus the overall winner of the *war*.

In **Place value boxes**, each player has his or her own individual base on which empty boxes represent place value positions. For example, in a game in which numbers in the *hundreds of thousands* are to be consolidated, each player would have six boxes. In a game in which 4-digit number-work is to be consolidated, 4 boxes on a two-class boxes base should be highlighted.

For 2–4 players, 4 sets of 0–9 digit cards are shuffled. The rule-for-play – whether the *largest number* wins or the *smallest number* wins – needs to be determined. Following this, one card at a time is dealt to each player in turn and he or she needs to determine straight away which the best position for that particular digit might be. In a *largest number wins* game, a $\boxed{9}$ received in the first round would clearly be placed in the largest available value position and a $\boxed{0}$ or $\boxed{1}$ in the lowest-value *units* position but the positioning of a $\boxed{5}$ or $\boxed{6}$, for example, would involve a degree of gambling on probabilities:

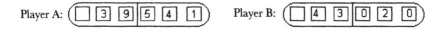

Boxes variations

Instead of playing **Place value boxes** in an open-ended way, the game can also be played with a specific target number as a number-building goal. For example, the goal could be a target number of 50 000. Play would proceed in the same way but the player whose cards show the number closest to 50 000 is the winner of that round. For instance,

Player A: $\left(\boxed{}\ \boxed{3}\ \boxed{9}\ \boxed{5}\ \boxed{4}\ \boxed{1}\right)$ Player B: $\left(\boxed{}\ \boxed{4}\ \boxed{3}\ \boxed{0}\ \boxed{2}\ \boxed{0}\right)$

Player B is the winner. 'Boxes' may also be played in written or pencil-and-paper versions of the games. In the pencil-and-paper versions a dice is rolled to generate the digits making up the multidigit numbers. The games may be played in the open-ended or target number versions. Each dice roll is recorded by writing the digit in a selected empty box: for example, in a Target of 500 'Boxes' game, an initial 8 would be recorded in the *tens* position:

Target = 500 dice roll = 8 | | 8 | |

Rounding skills and *number-building* skills are combined in a **place value lotto** game. For example, in a **Round-to-the-nearest-100-lotto game** each player has a board or base representing the *hundreds*, 0–1000. Depending on the number of players, four to six sets of 0–9 digit cards are shuffled and 3 cards are dealt to each player in each round. Players arrange their cards to build a 3-digit number. The *rounded* version of the constructed 3-digit number is then covered by a counter, or simply crossed off. For instance, the digit cards ⌐7⌐, ⌐6⌐ and ⌐3⌐ could be ordered as the 3-digit number 763, *rounded* to 800 and then 800 'crossed off' on the lotto base. Alternatively, if 800 and 400 have already been eliminated, the number ⌐7⌐ ⌐3⌐ ⌐6⌐, which is rounded to 700, would allow 700 to be 'crossed off':

763, rounded = | 0 | 100 | 200 | 300 | 400 | 500 | 600 | 700 | 8̶0̶0̶ | 900 | 1000 |

763, rounded = | 0 | 100 | 200 | 300 | 4̶0̶0̶ | 500 | 600 | 7̶0̶0̶ | 8̶0̶0̶ | 900 | 1000 |
736, rounded =
367, rounded =

As always, it is usually best to play a game in which 4-in-row (a sequence of 4 covered numbers) wins.

Overlay cards: expanded form card activities

Implicit in all of the digit card games described thus far is the idea that individual digits can be used to build a range of larger numbers. For example, by exploiting the place value principle, the individual digits, ⌐7⌐ ⌐4⌐ and ⌐1⌐ can be organized to build six three-digit numbers; 741, 714, 471, 417, 174 and 147. *Expanded form cards* (overlay cards or Arrow Cards) can also be used to build numbers. However, like concrete materials, *expanded form cards* make the actual values of the *places* or component values entirely explicit: in other words, overlay cards express seven as ⌐7⌐, seventy as ⌐70⌐, seven hundred as ⌐700⌐, and so on. When *expanded form cards* are used, the number 741 has to be 'built' by overlaying ⌐40⌐ and ⌐1⌐ on top of 700. In other words, the essential distinguishing feature of overlay cards is that the expanded form of each digit is represented and smaller values are built on top of larger ones.

Overlay cards: | 7 | 4 | 1 |

Overlay cards can be used to reinforce the simple concrete *number-building* activities described on pages to. 'Show me' activities work particularly well: for example, 'Using these cards, show me the number one thousand four hundred and seven.' Once again, the specific numbers that children are asked to build can reflect the areas of greatest difficulty. For instance, children could be asked to build a difficult series of numbers, such as 'four thousand and seven', 'four thousand and seventy', 'four thousand, seven hundred' and 'four thousand and seventeen'. Overlay cards can also be used to foster children's *rounding sense*. For instance, open-ended activities such as 'build any four-digit number between the numbers 2000 and 3000, but make the number you build closer to 3000 than 2000', are very useful activities to engage children in.

Written number activities

Calculator activities

Some calculator activities are becoming 'classic' *place value* number games. They are fun and appealing ways for children to consolidate their understanding of the ways number are constructed. Most calculators have a *constant facility*. In the context of *place value* work, this means that they can be programmed to *repeatedly add* or *repeatedly subtract* a particular value. For example, a calculator can be set to add *ten* repeatedly by pressing the keys 10 + + = =, in this order. In the next step, a start-out number, say '0', or '5' (or, in more advanced work, a much larger number) is entered. Following this, each time the 'equals' button is pressed, the number on the screen will have had 10 added to it: 370, 380, 390, 400, 410 ... Children may need encouragement to think, rather than simply press the *equals sign* in an unthinking and mechanical way. The phrase 'guess, *then* press' encourages children to reason, first, rather than punch the *equals sign* indiscriminately. To subtract 100 repeatedly, the keys 100 − − = = should be pressed. A start-out number, such as 5300, is entered and children then generate a stretch of the −100 sequence, checking each 'guess' on the calculator screen by pressing the *equals sign* button.

A very successful activity which involves 'knocking down' or cancelling values by subtracting them is often called **Calculator skittles** (Ashlock et al. (1983) call the same game 'Wipe out'). In **Calculator skittles** each child enters a given, specific multidigit number, such as 'two thousand, four hundred and thirty-five' in digits, 2435. The child (or group of children) is then asked to *knock down* a specific digit 'in one go' without cancelling the whole given number. For instance, to cancel the digit '4' in 2435, 400 will need to be subtracted. A round of skittles is completed when each digit of the number has been *knocked down* – although they should not be knocked down in order of value – and '0' registers on the calculator screen.

Accumulation games transfer well to the calculator. Since most children enjoy working on calculator, it is especially valuable to use a calculator for practising difficult written-number mental calculations which cross the *place value* 'crossover' points. With this in mind, children should start a game with quite large digits in each value position – a 'fun' number such as 7777 is a good example of such a start-out number. Children spin for additional values in the usual way; then, for instance, if 100 is 'spun' children will enter +100 but they will be required to predict the outcome, 7877, before the *equals sign* can be pressed.

Quick oral transcoding activities

Although concrete games and card games help give children the necessary conceptual underpinnings for reading written numbers, directional confusions and spatial orientation difficulties mean that a number of dyslexic and dyspraxic children can continue to have persistent difficulties with reading very large multidigit numbers. Practice at locating the groups-of-three which make up place value *classes* helps iron out these difficulties. In early multidigit number written-to-spoken-number transcoding activities, children can be encouraged to draw a 'loop' or 'box' around each class or group of three from right to left: 23 576 . The numbers within each group-of-three can be read in the ordinary way (in other words, in the ordinary way for reading, from left to right). For each *class* from the *class of thousands* upwards the overall *class* name will need to be given: Thus 23 in 23 576 is 23 thousand, and 576 is 576. The number 23576 is read as 'twenty-three thousand, five hundred and seventy-six'. In 200720005, or 200 720 005 , the 200 represents 200 million, the 720 is 720 thousand, and 005 is a mere '5'. 200720005 is thus two hundred million, seven hundred and twenty thousand and five. In time, most dyslexic and dyspraxic children become proficient at mentally 'boxing', 'circling' or clustering digits into *place value classes* and become expert at reading very large multidigit numbers.

Because mental two-digit and multidigit addition and multiplication calculation methods rely on children's ability to break numbers down into their component values it is very valuable if children are given practice at naming values and also at 'renaming' them in a variety of different ways. In a relatively open activity, for example, children could be asked to describe the '4'in 4019 in as many ways as possible. As well as describing it in the canonical expanded form as 4 *thousands*, the '4' also represents 40 *hundreds*, 400 *tens* and, of course, 4000 *ones*. Oral decomposition exercises of this kind are particularly useful 'filler' activities when a few spare minutes present themselves.

Written work

Recording counting-based activities

Although the emphasis in counting-based work is largely on exploring the spoken number system, certain written activities help consolidate children's understanding of the ways in which the number system, in general, is structured. For example, concrete *number-track* work can be followed up by consolidation work on emptier tens-structured drawn *number-lines*.

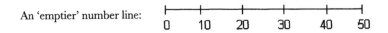

Most children do not have difficulty accepting emptier number-lines as a representation of a tens-structured concrete track, or tens-structured bead string. For example: draw a small cross on the *number-line* to show where these numbers would be: (a) 44 (b) 15 (c) 8 (d) 22

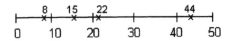

Children's understanding of where multidigit numbers are located within the number-structure can also be consolidated on the *emptier number-line* format. For example, activities based on counting in *hundreds* sequences can be followed by work on a hundreds-structured emptier number-line:

1. Write the missing numbers on the lines.
2. Show where these numbers would be. Draw a small cross above the line and label the number above the line:
   (a) 970 (b) 1005 (c)1290 (d) 704 (e) 1500

Difficult counting sequences – especially sequences through *Base Ten* collection points – can be consolidated in written work. For instance, children can be asked to complete counting sequences:

1.	10	11	12	☐	☐	☐
2.	70	80	90	☐	☐	☐
3.	203	202	201	☐	☐	☐
4.	1700	1800	1900	☐	☐	☐
5.	99970	99980	99990	☐	☐	☐

Some suggestions for pencil-and-paper 'place value' work

The quick oral transcoding exercises described above can also be translated into classic written *place value* activities.
  For example:

1. Write the following number in *words*: 1 203.
2. Write the following number using digits: three thousand and two.
3. Give the value of the underlined digit: 3 207.
4. Circle the digit which is found in the *units of thousand* position: 1 230.

Once children understand the *inequalities* signs, > and <, and are given a method for drawing them correctly, most dyslexic and dyspraxic children enjoy *inequalities* work. Children can be invited to view the inequalities signs as *hungry crocodiles*. They can also be invited to remember that the hungry crocodiles *always* open their mouths to the larger number: for example, 13< 31; 130 > 103; 2000 > 1990. In early *inequalities* work, many primary school children relish drawing 'crocodile' teeth and eyes on to the *inequalities* signs.

A hungery crocodile:

PART IV

More Addition and Subtraction: Working with Larger Numbers

CHAPTER 7

To twenty

Many of the addition and subtraction facts beyond 10 are difficult to internalize through *counting-on* and *counting back* procedures. In Chapter 4 we saw in some detail that a number of dyslexic and dyspraxic children:

1. know few addition and subtraction facts by heart;
2. do not often naturally invent reasoning-based calculation short-cuts;
3. often rely heavily on *counting-on* and *counting-back* to work out addition and subtraction facts.

We have seen that for dyslexic and dyspraxic children, in particular, counting procedures are a particularly unreliable basis for knowledge of the addition and subtraction facts. In counting to work out facts such as 8 + 6, or 15 − 8, quite long sequences of 'double counting' are involved. It is hard for dyslexic and dyspraxic children to manage long sequences of counting, while keeping track of the second addend (the '6' added on, above), or the subtrahend (the '8' subtracted in 15 − 8). Working out facts by *counting on* or *counting back* places a large burden on children's sequencing skills and working memory and the counting procedures are likely to be quite laboriously executed. Many dyslexic and dyspraxic children consequently make counting errors, especially when they execute *counting back* procedures. As we saw in Chapter 3, whenever children have to employ large amounts of working memory to achieve an addition or subtraction answer, it is very unlikely that they will remember the fact association. This is largely because the connection between *question* and *counted outcome* is lost.

For these reasons, a significant number of children with specific learning difficulties benefit from a teaching approach which aims to help them to reason to figure out the harder addition and subtraction facts. In the first part of the chapter we will explore the way in which confident practice at using 'logico-mathematical' thinking – using well known facts, simple logical principles and clearly understood reasoning routes – enables dyslexic and dyspraxic children to become competent at working out the addition and subtraction facts beyond 10. Through careful teaching, and with sufficient overlearning practice, most dyslexic and dyspraxic primary school children are able to quickly figure out all of the 'harder' addition and subtraction facts. Indeed, a number of dyslexic and dyspraxic children are ultimately able to automatize those facts beyond 10 which – through sufficient practice at reasoning – come to feel particularly accessible or 'easy' to them.

Newer ideas about teaching the addition and subtraction facts beyond ten

In traditional approaches to teaching maths, as we have seen, it is generally assumed that 'drilled' practice at *counting on* and *counting back* will ultimately result in *by heart* knowledge of the 'harder' addition and subtraction facts. In more recent years, maths educationalists have emphasized the importance of developing children's mental maths skills and it has become more common for teachers and textbooks to introduce children to one or two 'quicker' reasoning-based calculation strategies. These reasoning-based strategies are often called 'fact-derived strategies.' Before the introduction of far-reaching maths teaching initiatives, such as the National Numeracy Strategy, the most commonly taught fact-derived strategy, which can be used for figuring out some of the facts beyond 10, was the *rounding and adjusting* calculation strategy of treating 'n plus 9' as 'n plus 10 minus one'. Thus, for example, 6 + 9 may be quickly worked out as (6 plus 10) minus 1 = 16 minus 1 = 15. In the last few years, however, general attitudes towards calculation have changed enormously. Researchers who are interested in exploring how children's understanding in maths can be facilitated, have explored the quite broad range of 'informal' or *mental* strategies which 'ordinary' children with good *number-sense* will devise for themselves – at least under open and sympathetic teaching and learning conditions. Indeed, as Ian Thompson points out, there is a newly positive attitude to, and far greater acceptance of, fact-derived strategy usage. As we saw in Chapter 4, it is now widely accepted that the use of known facts to derive further facts precedes *by heart* knowledge of the basic number facts. It is also increasingly acknowledged that many adults employ *mental* strategies for working our 'harder' number facts. In fact, as Ian Thompson (1999a), among other commentators, notes, distinctions between facts which are fully automatized, and facts which have been very quickly worked out, are often hard to make.

Examples of fact-derived strategies which children (and adults) devise to help them figure out 'harder' addition and subtraction facts include:

1. the *near-doubling* addition strategy, already described in Chapter 3;
2. a 5-plus addition strategy, in which the fact that $5 + 5$ equals 10 is used to figure out slightly larger calculations such as $7 + 8$; in this instance $7 + 8$ is treated as $(5 + 2) + (5 + 3) = 10 + 5 = 15$;
3. *bridging-through-ten* strategies, in which 10 is used as a structurally significant and clear point for reasoning to figure out *through-10* addition and subtraction calculations; for example, to figure out $8 + 7$, 8 is made up to 10 by adding 2 from the 7 to the 8, then the 'easy sum', $10 + 5$, is calculated;
4. the *rounding and adjusting* strategy mentioned above, which some children extend to 'n-plus-8' problems, too.

Once it is accepted that familiarity with fact-derived strategies represent a valuable step in learning how to calculate efficiently, decisions have to be made as to how they may be presented to children. Fact derived strategies can, of course, be directly taught to children. However, following the example of many research project classrooms, children may also be encouraged to actively 'invent' quick ways of calculating; these 'invented' ways can then be shared with other children . In this way, a culture of thinking, inventiveness and idea-sharing is fostered. In maths settings which openly value thinking, teachers can encourage individual children to use strategies which make particular sense to them. Teachers can also model and encourage flexible approaches to calculation and thinking. In practice, as we noted in Part I, many classroom teachers choose to teach a selection of addition and subtraction fact-derived strategies directly to children. In principle, however, it is the latter, more open attitude to working out harder addition and subtraction facts which has, by and large, been put forward by contemporary understanding-based maths teaching guidelines, such as those contained within the National Numeracy Framework. All of the strategies outlined above are described in the Numeracy Strategy so that teachers can encourage and support their use.

Dyslexic and dyspraxic children and addition and subtraction calculation

For a number of children with specific learning difficulties a classroom emphasis on the use of fact-derived strategies, together with some individualized support from the teacher, is generally much more productive and successful than the traditional counting-based emphases. In strategy-oriented classrooms a number of dyslexic and dyspraxic children make real progress in learning to figure out the addition and subtraction number facts beyond 10. In other words, a classroom ethos in which value is placed on flexible calculation skills can help some dyslexic and dyspraxic children move beyond their typical over-reliance on counting to discover – sometimes for the first time – the advantages and power of thinking in mathematics.

This is not the full picture, however. Diagnostic assessments of dyslexic and dyspraxic children who have encountered fact-derived strategies at school, discussions with teachers and observations within classrooms all indicate that a significant proportion of children with specific learning difficulties do not seem to be helped by a an open ended thinking-orientated classroom culture – or by exposure to a number of specific calculation approaches. Despite encouragement to think flexibly, and sometimes in spite of teaching intervention to directly teach the addition and subtraction strategies which 'ordinary' children seem to absorb quite readily, many dyslexic and dyspraxic children continue to *count on* or *back* to work out harder addition and subtraction facts. A number of children become even more seriously disabled: instead of choosing to use counting procedures to figure out facts, they become confused about how to proceed at all. In assessments which have taken place since the Numeracy Strategy was introduced, some children have been able to indicate that they have become – to use the words of one nine-year-old dyslexic girl – 'totally strategied out'.

It is important to examine some of the deeper reasons which may explain why primary school dyslexic and dyspraxic children often fail to make progress in classrooms in which flexible thinking and fact-derived strategy use is supported. While teaching and learning aspects (such as the quality of teaching and the amount of additional support available) will obviously have an impact on children's learning progress, some of the core *cognitive* reasons for children's difficulties with fact-derived strategies include the following:

1. Fact derived strategies depend on a good knowledge of basic facts. Some primary school dyslexic and dyspraxic children cannot remember the *doubles* facts between 6 + 6 and 9 + 9 *by heart* and

therefore have difficulties with *near-doubling* strategies. Many dyslexic and dyspraxic children do not have efficient knowledge of the facts of 10 and most young dyslexic and dyspraxic children cannot quickly access the component facts of the basic counting numbers to 10. This makes *bridging-through-ten* strategies difficult to comprehend and use.

2. Fact-derived strategy usage requires good working memory skills. Many children with learning difficulties have poor working memories and can feel 'lost' or confused in the process of trying to follow a strategy, or in trying to execute a strategy. For example, a number of children with specific learning difficulties become frustrated by the working memory demands of *5-plus* strategies or of *rounding and adjusting* strategies.

3. Children with specific learning difficulties often have poor *number-sense* and a *unitary* conception of numbers. As we saw in Part II, it is hard for many dyslexic and dyspraxic children to perceive the possible patterns within numbers, or the relationships between numbers, which would give them a starting point for reasoning. Whereas an 'ordinary' child with a flexible number concept may see $7 + 9$ as $(7 + 7) + 2$ or as $(7 + 10) - 1$, many dyslexic and dyspraxic children feel blank or 'stuck' when they meet each new calculation demand. They consequently do not know where, or how, to begin reasoning.

4. A combination of all of these difficulties, together with typically weak long-term memory abilities for recalling sequential steps, means that many children with specific learning difficulties do not easily remember fact-derived strategy procedures. Difficulties remembering procedures have two significant further repercussions. First of all, children with specific learning difficulties often need considerable amounts of overlearning practice before they are able to grasp fact-derived strategies sufficiently well, or use them with confidence. Secondly, children who have an incomplete grasp of the fact-derived strategies, which are used in individual classrooms, can feel overburdened by the range of calculation choices on offer and by the culture of 'inventive' decision-making. In essence, they can feel excluded from what is intended to be an open, challenging and exciting classroom environment.

The 'key' strategy approach to fact-derived strategy teaching

As I have already suggested, some children with specific learning difficulties – very often *grasshopper* children with good visual-spatial skills – are able to select, absorb and successfully use at least one or two of the fact-derived strategies which make best sense to them. For all of the reasons given above, however, many primary school children with specific learning difficulties benefit from a more tightly structured and carefully sequenced approach to learning how to figure out the number facts beyond 10. For many dyslexic and dyspraxic children, an important first step in making progress in 'hard' fact learning involves building confident and proficient use of *one* strategy. Of course, for this approach to be successful in the longer term, the strategy which is selected for teaching has to be a strategy which can be applied to the widest possible number of calculations. It also has to be a strategy which is relatively accessible. In other words, it needs to be a *key* or *big value* calculation strategy.

The family of fact-derived strategies which can be used for all single digit addition calculations which cross the 10 boundary (e.g. 6 + 9, 7 + 5 etc.) and all 'teens' subtractions with single digit subtrahends which also 'cross through' 10 (for example, 13–5, 15–8, etc) are the *bridging-through-ten* strategies. Compared to other available strategies (such as *near-doubling*) a significant advantage of *bridging-through-ten* strategies is that children who understand the concept of *bridging* to ten, and who are able to apply *bridging* procedures efficiently, become as proficient at working out the 'harder' subtraction facts as they do at figuring out the 'harder' addition facts. The *bridging-through-ten* strategies are thus *big value* strategies, indeed. It should be clearly understood from the outset, however, that efficient (autotamized) strategy execution is just as important as a broad conceptual understanding of the strategies. In one sense, acquiring the ability to use *bridging-through-ten* strategies merely lays a foundation for further development. As children become more confident at using *bridging* strategies (as the strategies are increasingly automatized) three important developments usually take place. First of all, some 'harder' facts begin to be known *by heart*. Secondly, the facts which are not known *by heart* are increasingly quickly worked out. Thirdly, because children feel secure in the knowledge that they have internalized a way of reasoning 'which works' they very often become more inventive and flexible thinkers. Like 'ordinary' children, many dyslexic and dyspraxic children are increasingly able to 'see' alternative part–whole combinations in given calculations and are ultimately able to devise or to understand some alternative reasoning routes.

There is another very significant reason for selecting *bridging-through-ten* strategies as the *key* fact-derived strategies for figuring out the 'harder' addition and subtraction facts. Children with specific learning difficulties often have particular difficulty learning and managing *new* sequences of steps in calculation. *Bridging through ten* strategies have important long-term value, as well as the shorter-term benefits which have just been outlined. As we will see later on, *bridging-through-the-nearest-ten* or decade number is a very useful strategy for figuring out answers to addition calculations in which a single-digit number is added to a large number – for instance, 48 + 6 and 187 + 8. *Bridging-through-ten* subtraction strategies also lay the foundation for the *key sequencing* mental subtraction calculation strategies – strategies which form the basis of much *mental* two-digit subtraction work.

Introducing the bridging-through-ten strategy – addition

The *bridging-through-ten* strategy seems to be the commonest fact-derived strategy which is devised and used by numerate adults. To figure out 8 + 5 by applying the *bridging-through-ten* way of thinking, 8 is made up to 10 by 'splitting' (breaking down or decomposing) 5 into 2 plus 3, and the 3 is then added to 10 to make 13; thus 8 + 5 = 10 + 3 = 13.

In Chapter 4, it was noted that competent use of fact-derived strategies depends on children having a good foundation of known facts to reason from. As always, children with specific learning difficulties should not be required to learn too many facts *by heart.* In fact, to protect their vulnerable long-term memory for verbal fact associations, children with calculation difficulties should be obliged to know as few *key* facts as possible. The *key* facts, which underpin successful *bridging through ten* ways of reasoning are: (1) the component facts of 10 and (2) the component facts of all the counting numbers to 10. As we have seen, ways of helping children know, or work out, these facts are covered in Part II. Children also need to have an understanding of the *Base Ten* structure of the numbers between 10 and 20. This knowledge is covered in Chapter 6.

Although other 'tools' may, of course, be used, Cuisinaire rods are generally a good and particularly efficient choice of concrete tool for introducing children to the *bridging-through-ten* way of thinking and calculating. The *bridging* concept is most easily demonstrated by placing selected rods on an *emptier* tens-structured rod *track* to 20.

From the beginning, children need to understand that all *bridging* calculation work rests on the core idea that the structurally significant and helpful number, 10, is to be used as a part-way goal in reasoning. In other words, children have to build a 'bridge' to 10, first, before they continue reasoning. In terms of what happens with the rods, the vital point for children to grasp is that rods representing individual addends are not allowed to cross the 10 boundary. Instead, the second addend (or number to be added) has to be split into two parts. The first part takes the adding process up to 10; the second part of the addend is placed in the second decade portion of the *track* and is added to the 10.

In broad terms, it is often most successful to introduce the *bridging-through-ten* strategy by targeting the range of 9 + n calculations. The very pragmatic reason for this is that when numbers are added to 9, the splitting processes (or decompositions) are particularly easy to execute. In adding 9 + 7, for instance, 9 requires 1 to make 10 and if 1 is taken from the 7 (to make the 'bridge' to ten) the subtraction of 1 leaves 6.

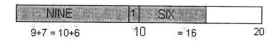

$$9+7 = 10+6 \qquad 10 \qquad = 16 \qquad 20$$

It can be very helpful to support and record concrete *bridging* work using the triad method of representing the component. Sometimes children wish to circle the first part of the calculation 'to 10' for additional conceptual emphasis.

$$9 + 7 = 10 + 6 = 16$$

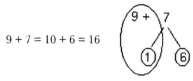

As soon as children are confident about *bridging* to 10 from 9, further concrete *bridging* work should be practised. The numbers '8' and '5' are excellent follow-on choices of initial quantities to start the figuring out *bridging* process from. Once children are beginning to understand and apply the *bridging* procedures successfully, a very simple but engaging game – essentially a tens-structured modification of the most basic **track accumulation game** – can be introduced. Since this game is usually very popular with children, it offers a valuable way of providing essential overlearning practice at using the *bridging-through-ten* addition strategy. The **bridging-through-ten track game** can be played by 2–3 players. Depending on the number of players, 2 or 3 rod-compatible tracks to 25 (or to 20) should be drawn directly beneath each other. The 10 and 20 boundaries should be carefully marked. Each player takes turns to roll a 0–9 dice and takes the equivalent Cuisinaire rod value to place on his or her track. For example, if a player rolls a dice '8' he or she takes an *eight* rod. The aim of the game is to cover the rod track. However the most important rule of the game is that rods may not directly crossover a *ten* boundary. For example, should a player roll '5', following an initial '8' roll, the *five* has to be 'split' into a *two* and a *three*. The *two* takes the player to the

10 boundary and the *three* is then placed on the 10–20 portion of the track. The *eight* and *two* can be exchanged for a *ten*. The player who first covers (or overshoots) his or her track is the winner. Some further points are worth noting. First, while this is not essential, it helps many pupils to 'exchange' rods along the way. For example, if a player secures *four* and then *three*, the resulting 7 can be exchanged for a *seven* rod. Secondly, it is helpful for teachers to encourage children to 'think ahead': for instance, children can be asked questions, such as 'What do you need to reach 10 (or 20)?' In this way children are already 'primed' for the first part of the next calculation. Thirdly, children should be strongly discouraged from mechanically working out rod exchanges by placing rods against the *gap* to be filled. Children need to be encouraged to reason, instead.

As we saw in Part I, a small number of dyslexic and dyspraxic children have difficulty making sense of Cuisinaire rod use in number-work. For such children it is best to devise an easy-to-visualize *ones*-based, but structured, experience of employing the *bridging-through-ten* strategy. Two simple suggestions include the following ones. First, some children enjoy adding a number of 1p coins to a first addend of 1p coins. The first quantity of *ones* should be placed on a tens-structured *track* before the adding process begins.

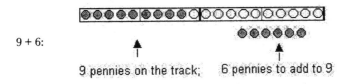

9 + 6:

9 pennies on the track;   6 pennies to add to 9

Secondly, some children respond to more situation-like *tens-structured* situations, such as 'adding passengers' to *tens-structured* train carriages.

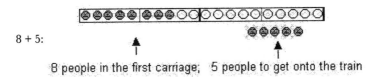

8 + 5:

8 people in the first carriage;   5 people to get onto the train

Again, such concrete *bridging work* can be supported and recorded using the triad method of representing components.

Bridging-through-ten subtraction strategies

In essence, the principle in all fact-derived *bridging* work is the same: reasoning first proceeds to 10 (or in larger number-work to the appropriate decade number) and then calculation continues beyond 10. In subtraction, however, there are two ways to reason or to subtract to 10. As we have already seen, there are two common basic models of subtraction. The first is a *subtracting back* model, which is based initially on *counting back* procedures, and often called a 'take away' model of subtraction. The second model is an *adding up to* model, based initially on *counting up to* subtraction procedures. The formal term for *adding up to* is *complementary addition*; it is often called 'shopkeeper's arithmetic' or 'shopkeeper's subtraction.' Likewise, there are two ways of *bridging through ten* in subtraction:

1. *Bridging-back-to-ten* and subtracting further back.
2. *Bridging-up-to-ten* and continuing to subtract *up to* the minuend or original number.

To work out 13 − 4, for instance, it is sensible to subtract 3 back to 10 and then subtract a further 1 from 10. To work out 13 − 9, on the other hand, it is much easier to *bridge up* from 9 to 10 and then continue reasoning from 10 to 13. Although it is important for children to learn both subtraction procedures, it does not matter which reasoning 'route' is initially presented to them. For instance, the *bridging-up-through-ten* model may well be taught, first, to tie in with *compare* work or to link in with concepts like giving change in shopping. On the other hand, children often identify with procedures which involve working 'backwards' in subtraction, more easily, and it may thus be decided to teach *bridging back*, first, before introducing the concept of *bridging upwards*. Whichever subtraction route is taught first, however, it is useful to reinforce the idea from the outset that *subtracting back* is most helpful when the number to be subtracted (the subtrahend) is quite small − for example, in the 13 − 4 example given above. By contrast, the *adding up to* subtraction model is likely to be much easier and safer to use when the number to be subtracted is quite large and the two numbers in the subtraction problem are relatively close together, as in 13 − 9.

Bridging-up-through-ten

Since many children strongly associate subtraction with *subtracting backwards*, the *bridging up* subtraction model can initially feel somewhat counter-intuitive. It can, at first, therefore be a little difficult for dyslexic and dyspraxic children to assimilate. Reinforcing all of the aspects of basic subtraction which suggest an adding up to procedure can help prepare children for the *bridging-up-through-ten* way of thinking. Certainly the *components* model of basic subtraction, which is outlined in Chapter 3, introduces children to the idea of thinking from a *part* which is to be subtracted, to an overall initial *whole*, in order to find that *part* of the *whole* which will remain. In essence, it is this same part–whole idea which underlies the *adding up to* model in subtraction. As we saw in Chapter 4, solving *equalizing, difference* and *missing addend* problems, and using money in concrete activities to give change 'the shopkeeper's way' all encourage children to devise and use *counting up to* or *adding up to* solutions to the problems. Some children seem able to generalize relatively smoothly from these less common models of subtraction to using *adding up to* as a preferred 'global' subtraction route in 'ordinary' subtraction situations. This is not always the case, however. A number of children with specific learning difficulties (who are able to generate *counting up to* solutions in all of the 'alternative' subtraction situations) do not easily transfer the procedures to abstract subtraction questions such as, 'What is 13 minus 8?' or 'Complete $13 - 8 = ?$'. These children seem to require more support than can be gained from simply exploring alternative concepts of subtraction. They seem to need to translate 'ordinary' subtraction questions into *adding up to* procedures as well as to complete work based on 'alternative' subtraction models.

It is often best to introduce the foundations for 'ordinary' subtraction 'upwards' by working with relatively small quantities. Cuisinaire rods can be used to support *adding up to* subtraction procedures. For example, $10 - 9$ can be modelled as:

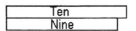

A number of children prefer to lay the *nine* rod on top of the *ten* and respond well to the metaphor of 'cutting off' or 'sawing off' the *nine* (the subtrahend) to understand that the *nine* is to be 'removed' or 'taken away'. Thus, for example, one can say something like 'In $10 - 9$, we start off with 10, but everything up to 9 is cut away. What we will be left with after this is the answer – the bit that hasn't been "cut off".' To begin with, though, the simplest, most direct, and often most effective model of taking away by 'working' upwards is a model in which *ones* are physically removed from the *start* (from the '*one*') of a *ones-based* structured number track:

Metaphors which help make sense of this particular 'taking away' model of subtraction are ones such as 'greedy monsters', 'hungry dragons' or 'mean people'(children's siblings work well as protagonists in these situations!) – who steal and steadily devour, in one-by-one succession, delicious *ones* items, like chocolates. In the beginning, the 'stealing' process can be executed in a slow one-by -one way. Soon, however, the number to be subtracted ('stolen', and taken away) can simply be swept away to leave the remaining answer. This idea can also be recorded on emptier number-line templates.

10 – 9 = 'Show where 9 is; remove the "chocolates" all the way up to 9.'

Both of these *number-line* models can be used to support the early stages of more advanced *bridging-up-through-ten* subtraction work. However, before 'bare' or 'ordinary' *through ten* subtraction questions are introduced, it is a good idea to return to conceptual work and introduce children to the *bridging up* procedure by extending concrete *equalizing, difference* and 'find the gap' work into the 'teens' decade beyond the 10 boundary. This is because these alternative subtraction situations quite naturally suggest *adding up to* solutions and help to give children valuable *through-ten* 'execution practice'. Children who have used *bridging-up-through-ten* for addition, and who have worked with *tens* and *ones* in some of the structured way described in the last chapter, readily grasp the idea that 10 can be used to structure thinking in these contexts. The steps in the *bridging-up-to* process can be recorded on *emptier number-line* templates: many children find that emptier number-lines help give valuable support in these sequential thinking processes. For instance:

1. You have 9 of your most favourite sweets. Your sister has 13 of your favourite sweets. How many more sweets do you need to be given to have the same number of sweets as your sister?

Emptier number-line recording:

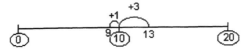

Informal number sentence: 9 + $\boxed{4}$ = 13

2. I have 8 golden coins. You have 14 golden coins. How many more golden coins do you have than me?

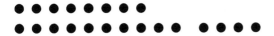

Emptier number-line recording:

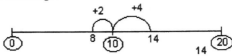

Informal number sentence: 8 + |6| = 14

3. You have 7. Your target is 12. How many more do you need to be able to reach your target?

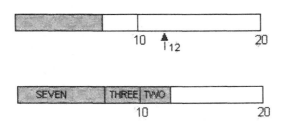

Emptier number-line recording:

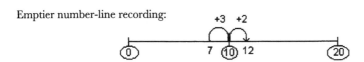

Informal number sentence: 7 + |5| = 12

To model 'ordinary subtraction' *bridging-up-through-ten* solutions, children can continue to use the structured ones-based *tracks*, or the Cuisinaire rod *tracks*, discussed a moment ago. We have noted that children are more likely to think of an *adding up to* solution rather than a *subtraction back* one, if the selected numbers in the subtraction question are quite close together – or, in other words, when the subtrahend is large in relation to the minuend. The examples selected for introductory *bridging-up-through-ten* subtraction work should thus contain numbers which are close together. In time, numbers should, of course, be selected to be further apart. Once again, recording the procedural steps on *emptier number-lines* gives valuable support to the thinking processes involved.

1.

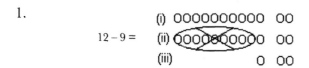

$12 - 9 =$

(i) OOOOOOOOOO OO
(ii) OOOOOOOOOO OO
(iii)   O OO

Emptier number-line recording: 9 → 12 = 3:

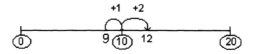

Formal subtraction sentence: $12 - 9 =$

$$12 - 9 =$$

Triad representation support :

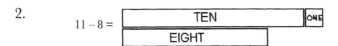

2.

$11 - 8 =$

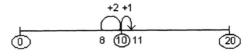

| TEN | ONE |
| EIGHT | |

The eight rod may be laid on top of the 10

Emptier number-line recording: 8 → 11 = 3:

Formal subtraction sentence: $11 - 8 =$

$$11 - 8 =$$

Triad representation support :

3.

14 sweets in a tube. 8 sweets disappear. How many sweets are left?

Emptier number-line recording: $8 \rightarrow 14 = 6$:

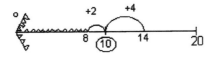

Formal subtraction sentence: $14 - 8 =$

Triad representation support :

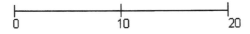

In early written subtraction practice, which is designed to help reinforce *bridging through-ten* solutions, it is often helpful to provide children with *emptier number-line* support. The triad representation can also be used to remind children of 'tens-structuring' of the 'teens' numbers. Finally, written work can set out suggest useful conceptual links:

1. Where are 9 and 14 on the number-line? What is $14 - 9$?

```
├────────────────┼────────────────┤
0                10               20
```

2.

$14 - 9 =$ $\begin{array}{c} 14 - 9 = \\ /\backslash \\ 10 \quad 4 \end{array}$

3. $9 + \square = 14$ $14 - 9 = \square$

Bridging back through ten: concrete examples and early written work

Although children do not need to be provided with large amounts of conceptual groundwork in order to understand the *bridging-back-through-ten* procedure, it facilitates the learning process if the subtracting back route is taught in a carefully structured way. In fact, it is the very first teaching step which usually helps children establish confident mastery of the *bridging back* strategy. In the *bridging-back-through-ten* procedure, the first step which children need to execute, is to *bridge back* to 10: in 13 − 5, for example, 3 is subtracted to 10, and then 2 is subtracted from 10.

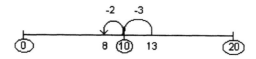

To manage the *bridging back* steps with ease, children need to be confident about the step back to the 10 boundary itself. In other words, children need to be absolutely sure that subtracting the unit component of a 'teens' number (for instance, 13 − 3, 14 − 4 etc.) leaves the number 10 itself. This understanding − essentially a number structure understanding − should therefore be consolidated, first.

Ten	Three

13 − 3 =   OOOOOOOOOO ⊘⊘⊘

Once children can confidently reason back to 10, it is generally advisable to select subtraction examples which extend back gradually *into* the 10 component. For example, if 13 − 3 = 10, then 13 − 4 will be one less than 10, or 9. Likewise, if 15 − 5 = 10, then 15 − 6 will be 9.

OOOOOOOOO⊘ ⊘⊘⊘⊘⊘

When this small 'one step back' step is clearly understood (and automatized), examples which extend further back into 10 can be given to children to solve. For example, children could be asked to work out:

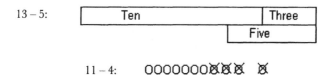

11 − 4:   OOOOOOO⊘⊘⊘ ⊘

Consolidation written work can be designed to suggest the crucial step back to 10. For example:

13 – 3 =	15 – 5 =	14 – 4 =	12 – 2 =
13 – 5 =	15 – 7 =	14 – 6 =	12 – 5 =

Further 'teens' addition and subtraction

We have seen that a common feature of dyslexic and dyspraxic learners is that they do not generalize maths knowledge easily. Many children with specific learning difficulties will count to work out addition questions, such as 14 + 4, even when the *units* addition fact is well known. Children need to be helped to understand that they can partition ten-structured numbers and use known basic facts to solve the *units* addition. The *'bridging'* game described on p. 220 provides a structured context for helping children master the strategy of 'holding' the 10 in working memory while working out the *ones* or *units* addition fact.

For example: 14 + 3 =

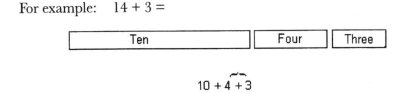

$$10 + 4 + 3$$

Teachers can also 'muse' reasoning solutions 'out loud' or model the *tens* and *ones* structures with Base Ten materials.

Figuring out component *units* facts by reasoning, rather than by counting, has three long-term advantages. First, reasoning in this context begins establishing an important sub-skill for the effective management of multiple number or 'string' additions, such as 9 + 3 + 2 + 4 (and, later on, 57 + 64 + 35 + 53 etc.). Secondly, working with component numbers in the 'teens' decade between 10 and 20 helps pave the way for 'non-bridging' teens *subtraction* work. Thirdly, practice at 'partitioning before calculating' establishes some very significant ground-rules for subsequent two-digit addition work, as we will see shortly.

'Teens' subtractions which do not require a *bridging-through-ten* step include subtraction examples such as 18 – 16, and 18 – 5. Dyslexic and dyspraxic children manage to figure out subtraction examples of this kind relatively easily as long as reasoning-based principles are consolidated and reinforced. Children may need to be reminded that it is easier, and therefore usually better, to use the *adding up to* model when the numbers in a subtraction problem are close together (e.g. 18 – 16). On the other hand, it is easier and quicker to *subtract back* when the number to be subtracted (the subtrahend) is quite small. In reasoning to figure out *subtraction back* subtraction examples, the 'teens' number is partitioned, and a known subtraction fact is used for the *units* subtraction components. In *subtraction-up-to* examples both 'teens' numbers are partitioned and the *difference* or *missing addend* is found between the two units numbers.

1. (a) 18 – 13 =

Ten	Eight
Ten	Three

Informal solution: $13 + \square = 18$ → $13 + \boxed{5} = 18$

(b) 19 – 16 =

Ten	Nine
Ten	Six

Informal solution: $16 + \square = 19$ → $(10) + 6 + \square = 19 = 16 + \boxed{3} = 19$

(c) 15 balloons were blown up for a party. 12 balloons popped. How many balloons were left?

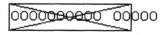

Informal solution: $12 + \square = 15$ → $\cancel{12} + \boxed{3} = 15$ →

3 balloons were left.

2. (a) 18 – 5 =

Ten	Eight
	Five

Consolidation written work can be designed to suggest the crucial step back to 10. For example:

13 – 3 =	15 – 5 =	14 – 4 =	12 – 2 =
13 – 5 =	15 – 7 =	14 – 6 =	12 – 5 =

Further 'teens' addition and subtraction

We have seen that a common feature of dyslexic and dyspraxic learners is that they do not generalize maths knowledge easily. Many children with specific learning difficulties will count to work out addition questions, such as 14 + 4, even when the *units* addition fact is well known. Children need to be helped to understand that they can partition ten-structured numbers and use known basic facts to solve the *units* addition. The '*bridging*' game described on p. 220 provides a structured context for helping children master the strategy of 'holding' the 10 in working memory while working out the *ones* or *units* addition fact.

For example: 14 + 3 =

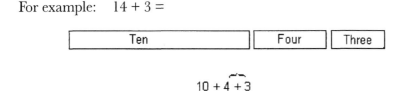

Teachers can also 'muse' reasoning solutions 'out loud' or model the *tens* and *ones* structures with Base Ten materials.

Figuring out component *units* facts by reasoning, rather than by counting, has three long-term advantages. First, reasoning in this context begins establishing an important sub-skill for the effective management of multiple number or 'string' additions, such as 9 + 3 + 2 + 4 (and, later on, 57 + 64 + 35 + 53 etc.). Secondly, working with component numbers in the 'teens' decade between 10 and 20 helps pave the way for 'non-bridging' teens *subtraction* work. Thirdly, practice at 'partitioning before calculating' establishes some very significant ground-rules for subsequent two-digit addition work, as we will see shortly.

'Teens' subtractions which do not require a *bridging-through-ten* step include subtraction examples such as 18 – 16, and 18 – 5. Dyslexic and dyspraxic children manage to figure out subtraction examples of this kind relatively easily as long as reasoning-based principles are consolidated and reinforced. Children may need to be reminded that it is easier, and therefore approach to addition that they will stretch the strategy to make it apply to as many addition calculations as possible. For example, as well as choosing to *near-double* in the classic and close *near-doubles* situations, such as 6 + 7 or 6 + 5, children will often employ *near-doubling* reasoning to figure out doubles-plus-2 addition facts, such as 6 + 8, or even doubles-plus-3 facts, such as 8 + 5.

Children who successfully and regularly *near-double* to figure out harder addition facts may initially acquire the strategy in different ways. Some children will already have internalized the *near-doubling* calculation approach. Many children encounter the *near-doubling* strategy in the class-room – a number of dyslexic and dyspraxic children absorb the strategy from classroom-based teaching and begin to employ the strategy indepen-dently and efficiently. A few children will have 'invented' the strategy on their own. Yet others may extend *near-doubling* from very basic *near-doubling* addition work. Some children devise the *near-doubling* approach as they become more proficient at *doubling* or at *bridging-through-ten*. As we have seen, children often become more inventive as they become confident at using familiar and automatized ways of reasoning.

On the other hand, a number of dyslexic and dyspraxic children (for example, in many private schools) are not taught to *near-double* in the class-room, and may not have come across the *near-doubling* idea. The teachers or adults wishing to support such children may feel it is important to directly introduce them to the *near-doubling* calculation approach. Since *near-doubling* seems to be the through-ten strategy which is most frequently invented by children (Thompson and Smith, 1999), and since children who employ *near-doubling* will often say that it is their most favourite strategy of all, teaching the *near-doubling* strategy can prove to be a partic-ularly successful and valuable aspect of addition fact work. Certainly children who are able to master the addition *bridging* strategy and the *near-doubling* strategies have the flexible option of selecting either of the two strategies in many 'harder' addition calculation situations.

Nevertheless, it is also important to strike a note of caution at this point. In practice, there are some dyslexic and dyspraxic children who struggle to learn the *near-doubling* strategy for 'harder' additions. In this regard, it is important to bear in mind that *near-doubling* is not a 'universal' *through-ten* strategy. While a number of dyslexic and dyspraxic children are able to absorb more than one fact-derived addition strategy for through ten thinking, others may need to take considerable amounts of valuable learning time to acquire what is ultimately an additional reasoning route. Furthermore, as we have already noted, above, some dyslexic and dyspraxic children can become confused and demoralized if they have more than one way of thinking to consider.

As a general guideline, the decision to teach the *near-doubling* addition strategy is likely to be successful when children know, or are able to *automatize*, the *doubles* facts between 5 + 5 and 9 + 9; when children understand *near-doubling* in simpler calculations such as 4 + 5; and when children are able to perceive *doubles* patterns within calculations. On the other hand, it is usually best to defer *near-doubling* teaching when children do not easily detect patterns within numbers and when they show signs of becoming confused if they have to learn more than one way of breaking down numbers. It is also best to defer teaching *near-doubling* when children have extremely poor memories for verbal associations and have to use reasoning strategies to work out the *doubles* facts. The working memory demands of double-strategy usage are far too burdensome for most children and may, in fact, serve to undermine the often fragile reasoning confidence of children who have very poor memory resources.

A useful set of facts: the doubles facts to 10 + 10

Whether the *near-doubling* strategy is ultimately learned or not, knowing (or being able to work out quickly) the *doubles* facts to 10 + 10 certainly helps to contribute towards the development of greater flexibility in the early stages of number-work. Efficient knowledge of this circumscribed and relatively easily visualized set of facts helps give children a sense of achievement and of growing competence. Discovering that the 'harder' *doubles* facts are actually 'quite easy' to learn is often an important moment in children's sense that number-work is something which they will be able to conquer, after all. In the longer term, efficient *doubling* also helps children with a number of multiplication reasoning processes, as we will see in the following chapter.

Children who do not already know the 'harder' *doubles* facts beyond 5 + 5 *by heart* can, of course, use the *bridging-through-ten* addition strategy to figure them out. For instance, 7 + 7 can be worked out as 7 + 3 → 10 + 4 = 14. However, there is an alternative and quicker reasoning route which usually speeds up the acquisition of *by heart* knowledge of the *doubles* facts. This alternative calculation route rests on the very simple principle that it is possible to reason from 'easier' and already known *doubles* facts to figure out those 'harder' *doubles* facts which are not yet known. In other words, children can be helped to establish reasoning paths which build on the *doubles* facts patterns, themselves.

Taking time to construct a *doubles pyramid* provides children with a very useful model for understanding and visualizing the ways in which *doubles* facts 'build up' and relate to each other. Cuisinaire rods can be used to build up a *pyramid* of doubles facts. (Alternatively, the *pyramid* can be made from *ones* constructed, or coloured, using squared paper.)

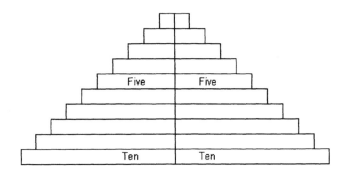

In a very clear way, the *pyramid* model establishes the *plus-2* pattern which is involved in each successive *doubles* step. For instance, each component '6' in the 6 + 6 step is clearly one more than each '5' in the 5 + 5 step above. Since each '6' is one more than each '5', the 6 + 6 step will consequently have an outcome which is 2 more than the 5 + 5 outcome. In practical terms, the *pyramid* model offers children a pleasingly direct, *doubles-based* way of working out successive *doubles* facts. For example, to figure out 6 + 6, one simply needs to add 2 to 5 + 5. Likewise, 7 + 7 can be worked out as (10) + 2 + 2. However, since the use of too many successive steps can place an unnecessarily heavy burden on working memory, equivalent *minus-2* relationships can be demonstrated and used in *pyramid-based* reasoning as well. Thus, the 'large' 9 + 9 *doubles* fact is best figured out from the large but equally 'easy' 10 + 10 fact. Since 10 + 10 = 20, 9 + 9 will be 2 less tan 20, which is 18.

Once the *plus-2 / minus-2 patterns* are established, known *doubles* facts can be used to work out all of the 'not-yet-known' or 'harder' doubles facts. In the beginning, 5 + 5 = 10 and 10 + 10 = 20 can be presented as the *key doubles* facts in the 'harder' layer of *pyramid* facts from 5 + 5. Thus, as we have already noted, 7 + 7 can be derived from 5 + 5: if 5 + 5 = 10, then 6 + 6 = 12 and 7 + 7 = 14. Likewise, 8 + 8 can be derived from 10 + 10: if 10 + 10 = 20, then 9 + 9 = 18, and 8 + 8 = 16. Although *by heart* knowledge of *key facts* represent an excellent starting point and safety net, children should, nevertheless, be encouraged to work from the 'closest' fact which they already know *by heart*. For example, if 6 + 6 is already internalized, the known '12' outcome can be used to work out the 7 + 7 *doubles* fact. As always, practice at generating *doubles* facts helps children work them out more and more efficiently. In time, overlearning practice should allow children to know all of the *doubles* facts *by heart*.

The simple lotto game, described on p. 429 in the Appendix, is a good *doubles* overlearning game. For **doubles card lotto**, sets of 1–10 digit cards represent the numbers to be *doubled*. Each player has his or her set of cards. A 1–10 die is rolled, the number rolled is *doubled*, and the relevant number card turned over. The first player to turn over four-cards in-a-row wins the game.

Halving and halving in subtraction

As children begin to have confident knowledge of the *doubles* facts to 10 + 10, they can be encouraged to understand and express the paired *doubles* relationships in *halving* terms, as well. It is generally helpful to introduce *halving* in a step-by-step way. For instance, many children can be encouraged to identify *half* of all the even numbers to 20 by thinking of their internal *doubles* components, first. Thus, many children find questions such as, 'Is 12 made up of a *double*? Which *double* is it made up of?' easier to visualize, initially, than direct *halving* questions, such as, 'What is *half* of 12?' Nevertheless, the concept and language of *halving* should certainly ultimately be covered, and can be linked to the pyramid model illustrated above.

A *halving* version of the lotto game briefly described above can also be played. In the **halving lotto game**, each player has a set of 1–10 digit cards which represent halves, and the even numbers from 2-20 have to be generated in some way. For example, they can be represented on a spinner base. Each number which is generated is *halved*, and the relevant card turned over. As always, 4 cards turned over in a row will win the lotto game.

It is often assumed that children will automatically extend their knowledge of well-known addition facts to working out subtraction facts. Because children with learning difficulties often have a *unitary* number-concept (and because they also often fail to generalize knowledge) they tend to perceive addition and subtraction as different and separate processes. While children may know *by heart* that 7 + 7 = 14, they may not recognize the 'known' doubles fact in 14 − 7 = ? Although 14 − 7 can, of course, be worked out through the key *bridging back* or *bridging up* strategies, a recognition of known *doubles* components, or an understanding of *halving* relationships, will usually help children answer *doubles* subtractions more quickly. Subtraction *doubles* can be presented to children through building on the patterned *component* model which was touched on in the *halving* discussion above. Thus, for example, children can be asked to say whether specific individual numbers are 'made up of' a *double*, and, if so, which *double* fact is involved. Next, children can be helped to see that since 14 is, indeed, built from the *double* pattern 7 + 7, then if one of the component '7s' is removed, the other '7' naturally remains. In concrete terms:

Five	Five
Six	Six
~~Seven~~	Seven

Once again, using the triad representation form usually works well to support this *partitioning-based* subtraction model:

$$14 - 7 = ? \rightarrow$$

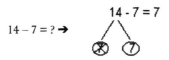

With the aid of the concrete *doubles pyramid*, the connection between subtraction *'doubles'* questions and *halving* can also be pointed out. It is helpful to consolidate the components basis for doubles subtraction in simple written exercises. Some examples of such exercises include the following:

Complete the doubles patterns

$12 = \square + \square$

$18 = \square + \square$

$16 = \square + \square$

Match

| 12 = | | 9 + 9 |
|------| |-------|
14 =		8 + 8
18 =		6 + 6
16 =		7 + 7

Complete

Complete

$$\square - 5 = 5$$

$$\square - 7 = 7$$

$$\square - 9 = 9$$

Children can also be guided to look for *doubles or halves* relationships in subtraction exercises which carefully target a 'mixed selection' of subtraction problems, – all of which contain readily identifiable patterned relationships.

Complete these problems. Look for useful patterns

$$14 - 4 =$$
$$13 - 10 =$$
$$15 - 10 =$$
$$16 - 8 =$$
$$13 - 3 =$$
$$14 - 7 =$$

Teaching 'near-doubling'

An explanation of the *near-doubling* strategy in addition, and a description of some ways to introduce the *near-doubling* strategy, may be found in Chapter 3. The important idea which children who are encountering the *near-doubling* concept, for the first time, need to grasp, is that 'using a *doubles* fact to help' can be a quick and efficient way to work out quite a large number of 'hard' addition facts. Very briefly, a calculation such as 7 + 8 can be 'made easy' with the help of a *doubles-plus-one* pattern, as long as the 7 + 7 component calculation is actually perceived 'in' the 7 + 8 question, and as long as it is also understood to facilitate the figuring out of the closely related 7 + 8 larger fact.

Seven	Eight	
Seven	Seven	One

OOOOOOO   OOOOOOO●   7 + 8 =
    7   +   7   +1

In other words children who are able to adopt a *doubling-plus-one* approach to working out the 'difficult' addition fact, 7 + 8, use the fact that if 7 + 7 = 14, then 7 + 8 must be one more than 14 and must therefore be 15. This *near-doubling* logic can be expressed in triad form:

As we have already seen in Chapter 4, the fact that addition is *commutative* means that it is possible to identify a *doubles* pattern which 'begins' from the 'second' number in the addition question: the 7 + 8 addition fact can be processed from the second addend, '8', and as a *doubles-minus-one* calculation. In this instance, children will reason that if 8 + 8 = 16, then 8 + 7 will be 15.

Seven	Eight
Eight	Eight

●OOOOOOO + OOOOOOOO

In early written *near-doubling* reasoning practice, at this level, it can still be helpful to foreground one of the possible *doubles* components calculations and in this way 'nudge' children to use a *doubles-related* reasoning route. For example:

6 + 6 =	7 + 7 =	5 + 5 =
6 + 8 =	7 + 6 =	5 + 7 =

However, as soon as children are better able to 'find' the helpful component *doubles* patterns within calculations, for themselves, it is also important to reinforce the understanding – which is made explicit in concrete work – that *near-doubling* reasoning routes can proceed from either of the two addends.

A brief note on *near-doubles* subtraction patterns: a small number of primary school children with specific learning difficulties – usually visually able *grasshoppers* – are able to extend their grasp of *near-doubling* patterns in addition to using *near-doubles* component patterns in subtraction. For instance, the minuend 15, in 15 – 7, may be recognized as the number which is 1 greater than double 7, or 14. Since $14 - 7 = 7$, $15 - 7$ must be 8. However, the majority of dyslexic and dyspraxic children have difficulty making sense of this rather abstract way of thinking. Since few dyslexic and dyspraxic children perceive the potentially useful *near-doubles* relationships which are 'hidden' within some subtraction questions it is generally not advisable to directly teach *near-doubling* subtraction routes.

A brief discussion of further addition strategies

In general terms, as we have seen, it is not a good idea to directly teach a wide range of fact-derived strategies to those dyslexic and dyspraxic children who have difficulty learning to reason in number-work. Nevertheless, we have also seen that practice at using well-understood reasoning routes allows some children to perceive alternative patterns within numbers and helps them to become more adventurous and inventive thinkers. Teachers and parents who recognize the creative ways in which children's thinking is developing, can give them valuable encouragement and support. While some children rely, by and large, on *bridging-through-ten* ten strategies, and others may depend on a combination of *bridging* and *near-doubling*, there are, as we noted earlier on, strategy variations which are fairly commonly 'discovered' or 'invented' by 'ordinary' children and by *grasshopper dyslexics*. In time, these strategies are quite often 'discovered' by *inchworm* dyslexic and dyspraxic children, too.

1. Children's understanding of the process of 'making 10,' in the *bridging-through-ten* addition strategy, quite often shifts towards the subtly different *rounding and adjusting* principle of adding a whole 10 to an addend, first, and then finally adjusting the ultimate outcome. In *bridging-through-ten* to work out 9 + 7, 1 is added to 9 first, and 10 and 6 are combined. In the *rounding and adjusting* approach to 9 + 7, as we saw earlier, 9 is rounded up to 10 so that 10 can be added to 7, and the outcome of 17 is then adjusted by 1 to attain the final answer of 16.

2. Children who 'love' the *doubles* patterns and who frequently use *near-doubling* procedures will sometimes notice that a *doubles* fact can be created from addends which are two digits apart. Thus, the addition 7 + 9 can be transformed into the double, 8 + 8, by subtracting 1 from 9 and adding it to 7. In fact, the underlying logic involved in creating *doubles* facts has much in common with the key *bridging-through-ten* way of thinking. As Ian Sugarman points out, the core idea which underpins both strategies is that the numbers may be adjusted to make them easier to work with 'by subtracting a bit of one number and adding it to the other' (Sugarman, 1997, p. 145). The *creating-a-double* strategy can be concretely modelled for those children who show an interest in making sense of it – for instance because a friend may have referred to it in the process of sharing calculation ideas. A good way to demonstrate the idea, practically, is to build two vertical columns to represent the addends. The column can be constructed from *ones* stacked on top of each other (e.g. wooden blocks) or from interlocking *ones* (e.g. unifix cubes). The two columns can then be transformed into an equal height column *double* by removing one unit from the taller *plus-two* column and placing it on the shorter *minus-two* column. The columns are then 'evened out' and their sum can be calculated as a known *doubles* fact.

3. The universally well-known and very easy 5 + 5 *double* and *10-component* fact is a particularly accessible starting point for reasoning in addition. A number of dyslexic and dyspraxic children discover that the '5 + 5 *key*' can be used to figure out any addition facts which happen to contain one 5 component: for instance, 5 + 7, 8 + 5, 5 + 3, and so on. A very small number of dyslexic and dyspraxic children go on to use the '5 + 5' *key* to break down addition calculations such as 6 + 7 (in which both component numbers are larger than 5) into *5-plus* components. Thus, for example, 6 + 7 can be broken down into (5 + 1) + (5 + 2), or (5 + 5) + 1 + 2. The working memory demands of *5-plus* calculation can prove quite onerous for many children with specific learning difficulties and it is probable that it is not a very popular strategy for this reason.

Helping children use strategies consistently

While many children can use strategies when they are 'cued in' – for example, when one particular strategy is being practised and the calculation examples have been selected accordingly – it can be a different matter when reasoning decisions need to be made. When children have mastered a number of reasoning routes, and need to practise thinking independently, they will need to remember how to begin the process of reasoning. Many dyslexic and dyspraxic children require considerable amounts of practice at remembering and applying calculation strategies. It can therefore take some time before dyslexic children become confident and fluid at working out mixed selections of addition and/or subtraction facts.

On the other hand, when children are afforded sufficient and varied 'mixed' calculation practice they will usually become efficient and assured strategy users. They will often become inventive thinkers, as well. As we saw in Part II, quick oral calculation reviews provide valuable overlearning practice. Alternatively, children can, of course, be given carefully selected, mixed written calculation exercises to complete in a maths session, or for homework. Introducing fast-paced Calculation Games will also contribute enormously towards making needed calculation practice a great deal more inspiring and fun.

Addition games

It should be noted that a number of useful generic games are described in detail in the Appendix. In brief, finding the sum of two rolled 0–9 or 4–9 dice is a quick way of livening up addition calculation practice. Working out dice *sums* can be the basis for very slightly more elaborate games such as dice 'wars'. Alternatively, sets of individual digit cards can be used as the basis for addition card war games. Additions can be restricted to 'harder' calculations by modifying sets of cards to omit easier addends, such as 1, 2 and 3. It is very useful to play a basic addition track game which is really an abstract version of the **Bridging through ten track game**, described on page 220. In the **basic track pencil and paper calculation game**, each player has a very simply drawn track to record his/her progress. It is most effective to draw tracks underneath each other. The tracks could comprise consecutive squares or 'caterpillar' circles.

Players take it in turns to throw a 0–9 dice. Each player's first dice roll

is recorded on the track. Dice rolls are subsequently added to the most recent sum shown on the track and this runnung total is recorded in the next square on the track. The first player to reach 30 is the winner. Since 30 can be reached quite quickly, it is best to play a number of rounds of the game.

Subtraction games

Subtraction dice games are slightly more difficult to devise than addition
games. Games which will involve a very wide range of subtraction calculations can be played using a 1–20 dice, and a 0–9 dice. The smaller
number (which may, in fact, be on either dice) is subtracted from the larger
number. To restrict subtraction practice to subtraction from 'teens'
numbers, six numbers between 13 and 19 will need to be written on a
blank dice and an ordinary 0–9 die can be used to generate the 'second'
number. Subtraction games which use pre-prepared special subtraction
operation cards allow specific subtraction strategies to be practised.
Children generally enjoy track games in which players move a marker to
the next 'square' which shows the answer to their subtraction card (see
Appendix, p. 433). A subtraction version of the basic addition track game
can be played, too. In the basic track subtraction game each player
records the 'start' number, 25, in the first square:

| 25 | 21 | 16 | 12 | | | | | | |

| 25 | 18 | 17 | 9 | | | | | | |

Players take turns to roll an ordinary 1–6 dice or a 0–9 dice and the
dice roll is subtracted from the most recent number recorded on the track.
The first player to reach 0 is the winner. It should be noted that the
commercially available game *Beelines*, which is made by Waddingtons,
successfully mixes addition and subtraction calculation. Subtraction
practice is limited to subtraction to 10, however.

CHAPTER 8

Two-digit addition and subtraction

In the discussion in Chapter 7 about the ways in which children learn, and come to know, the harder addition and subtraction facts, some very important contemporary maths teaching themes were touched on. In contrast to the traditional emphases on *by heart* knowledge of facts, a new ethos of valuing methods of figuring out solutions to calculation problems can be seen to inform contemporary maths teaching. In the early stages of working to solve addition and subtraction facts to 20, children are encouraged to employ reasoning-based ways of calculating. In general terms, there is a far greater interest in encouraging children to think, and a far greater interest in exploring how children are, in fact, thinking. In this sense, the 'mental' processes involved in figuring out solutions in maths can be seen to be much more highly valued than they were in the past.

In broad terms, these same themes can be seen to inform contemporary approaches to the next stage of calculation, in which children have to learn how to solve two-digit addition and subtraction calculations. However, when children reach the point at which two-digit addition and subtraction calculation require to be introduced, the contemporary emphases on thinking in maths and on performing calculations with understanding turn out to have very profound, quite radical – and for many adults quite unsettling – teaching implications.

Traditionally, as we have seen, two-digit addition and subtraction calculations have been performed on paper, in columns, and have been completed in standard ways. These standard methods for addition and subtraction in columns have also been acquired by each new generation of children as rote-learned step-by-step routines or 'drills'. For reasons which will be outlined in greater detail below, it is difficult to learn the standard column methods for addition and subtraction in genuinely understanding-based ways. In the search for two-digit addition and subtraction methods which young children potentially devise or invent for themselves – and which are open to greater understanding by all children – contemporary maths researchers and theorists have turned away from the standard column forms. Instead, more open, 'informal' or *mental* methods of calculating, which build on earlier acquired mental strategies, have been found to be more genuinely accessible to children and have been very widely advocated. Many contemporary national maths teaching guidelines – such as those contained in the National Numeracy Strategy – stipulate that young primary school children should be encouraged to add and subtract two-digit numbers using *mental* calculation strategies or *informal* ways of calculating. Furthermore, most contemporary recommendations, including those contained in the Numeracy Framework, suggest that it is only in the later primary years, and only once children are competent at *mental* addition and subtraction calculation, that they should ultimately encounter the traditional standard addition and subtraction methods.

In principle, at least, teachers would seem to be able to choose between two very different teaching approaches to introducing children to two-digit addition and subtraction. Teachers can continue to teach addition and subtraction in the very familiar traditional ways. In this approach, children can continue to be taught one standard way to add and subtract two-digit numbers and can be encouraged to perfect these standard ways throughout the primary years. Alternatively, teachers can opt for an approach to early two-digit addition and subtraction work which fosters and develops the reasoning processes which are begun in the very earliest years of number-work. Children can be encouraged to develop and automatize *mental* calculation strategies which are reasonably efficient but which are also well understood. In time, if this latter approach is adopted, children will also, in the main, need to be taught the standard formal ways of adding and subtracting in columns – this is largely because *multi-digit* calculation is generally more efficiently and accurately executed within the column framework and using the standard addition and subtraction procedures.

In practice, however, at present, the way in which primary school children are taught to work out two-digit addition and subtraction calculations is determined by the nature of the school which they attend. In England, for instance, state schools follow the National Numeracy Strategy Framework, as we have seen, and all children who attend state schools are introduced to the more open and reasoning-based methods for two-digit addition and subtraction. However, children within the private education sector are taught two-digit addition and subtraction in a way which is determined by the school itself. While few schools remain unaffected by the National Numeracy Framework and most schools broadly accept arguments for fostering mental maths proficiency, the majority of private schools continue to place a very great emphasis on teaching children traditional standard addition and subtraction procedures. Specialist teachers, tutors and parents who support dyslexic and dyspraxic children in schools which adhere to the traditional ideas about two-digit addition and subtraction are consequently placed in a very difficult position. As we will see in the discussion which follows, there are particularly cogent reasons for arguing that dyslexic and dyspraxic children should not be expected to master column arithmetic too early and that, to the contrary, it is generally advisable for them to learn the reasoning and understanding-based mental addition and subtraction methods which are so widely supported by maths educationalists.

Traditional addition and subtraction algorithms

The essential attributes of the standard methods for adding and subtracting two-digit (and multi-digit) numbers are very familiar to most adults. Addition and subtraction 'sums', or algorithms, are traditionally completed in written form. Numbers are laid out in *place value* columns. Calculation begins from the *units* position and proceeds from right to left, column by column, until a final answer is reached. In the standard addition algorithm whenever the number of unit values within any value position exceeds 9, the 'ten' is exchanged and 'carried' into the next position. In subtraction, whenever there are insufficient unit values within any position, a unit of value is 'borrowed' from the next value position so that the calculation process can proceed.

$$
\begin{array}{r}
8\ 7 \\
+\ 5\ 8 \\
\hline
1\ 4\ 5 \\
1
\end{array}
\qquad
\begin{array}{r}
{}^{5}\cancel{6}\ {}^{1}0 \\
-\ 3\ 7 \\
\hline
2\ 3
\end{array}
\qquad
\begin{array}{r}
4\ 5\ 6\ 9 \\
+\ 2\ 8\ 7\ 8 \\
\hline
7\ 4\ 4\ 7 \\
1\ 1\ 1
\end{array}
\qquad
\begin{array}{r}
{}^{5}\ {}^{9}\ {}^{'}{}^{4}\ 1 \\
\cancel{6}\cancel{0}\cancel{5}1 \\
-\ 2\ 9\ 8\ 3 \\
\hline
3\ 0\ 6\ 8
\end{array}
$$

The standard algorithms for addition and subtraction in columns are universal methods in the sense that they can be used to apply to all numbers. Although they are not always the most efficient methods for double-digit calculations, the standard addition and subtraction algorithms are generally very efficient paper-and-pencil methods for adding and subtracting very large numbers. While the addition and subtraction algorithms feel entirely natural and logical to most adults, they are, in fact, very difficult conventions for young children to learn. As many educationalists argue, standard addition and subtraction algorithms are extremely abstract and condensed forms. In the words of Thompson (1997b, p. 99)

> The standard algorithm for addition treats each number to be added as a collection of discrete digits, where those set out underneath each other in the same column have to be combined as if they were actually units digits. This leads us to say, 'four and three makes seven and one more makes eight' partway through calculating 47 + 36, when we actually mean 'forty and thirty makes seventy and ten more makes eighty.' Use of the standard written algorithm obliges the user to disregard the meaning that the individual units possess by dint of their position in the number, and forces them to indulge in pure symbol manipulation.

For the purpose of calculation, then, the standard addition algorithm (and, indeed, the standard subtraction algorithm, too), reduces all digits within the numbers to the status of *ones*. This divorces the digits within the algorithms from the real value which they possess and forces children to concentrate on localized partial calculations. The further result of this is that young children generally do not have any conception of what the likely outcome of the calculation will be. Completing step-by-step partial calculations in columns, working from right to left, means that it is very hard for children to have an overview of, or *feel* for, the final addition or subtraction outcomes.

The particularly abstract and condensed nature of the standard addition and subtraction algorithms has many important consequences for the ability of young children to acquire them. First of all, the logic of column-based calculation is very hard for young children to understand in any deep and meaningful way. This means that the algorithms are taught using a procedural, one step after another, teaching approach. 'You start ... next you ... then you ... then you ..., etc.' Ian Thompson describes the usual 'patter' which children are taught to use when they complete an addition calculation such as 'Seven and six make thirteen ... put down the three and carry the one. Four and three is seven ... seven and one makes eight ...' (Thompson, 1997b, p. 98).

$$\begin{array}{r} 4\ 7 \\ +3\ 6 \\ \hline \end{array}$$

Children are required to internalize the procedures through following the prescribed steps and through using the prescribed language. In other words, it is by and large true that children have to learn the procedural steps by rote, or in a 'recipe-like' way. Because the procedures for completing addition and subtraction algorithms are acquired by rote, children generally require many years of repeated practice or 'drill' to acquire them. This, in turn, means that completing addition and subtraction in columns takes up a considerable proportion of children's maths learning time, particularly in the crucial early primary years. To give children a head start in acquiring the standard algorithms, column-based work is often begun very early indeed. Despite this, research shows that children who are restricted to learning the formal addition and subtraction procedures, are often delayed in their ability to add and subtract two-digit numbers, compared with children who are *not* introduced to the formal procedures very early on, and who use alternative *mental* calculation methods, instead.

Secondly, despite huge amounts of practice, a significant proportion of primary school children continue to make calculation errors when they complete standard addition and subtraction procedures. Traditionally, it was assumed by teachers and by parents that most of the mistakes that children made were the result of insufficient practice, or of inattention or carelessness. Now, however, there is a well-respected body of research to show that children who consistently make mistakes in formal addition and subtraction work, do so largely because they are misremembering and misapplying the hard-to-understand 'rules'. In other words, research shows that most children try to remember the step-by-step procedures correctly, but some would appear to be less able (or even seem unable) to do so. A number of researchers in the US have studied and reported the spectrum of 'rule-led' calculation errors made by children (so-called calculation 'bugs'), some of which will be used as illustrations below.

There is also another way in which children can indicate that they are having problems learning the very abstract standard addition and subtraction procedures. Instead of 'misremembering' the rules, a proportion of children are unable to complete the standard addition and/or subtraction algorithms unless the step-by-step procedures are rehearsed before they begin calculating. In other words, some children cannot initiate the procedural rules, by themselves. Although they may perform well in class when they are 'cued in' for addition and subtraction procedures, such children perform very poorly in situations in which they have to work independently. Increased amounts of routine practice, or 'drill', helps some children iron out 'bugs' or learn to remember the procedures, but many children who finally learn the procedures 'by heart' continue to have almost no understanding of the steps which they finally learn to execute. Research and simple classroom observations show that a number of primary school children make little progress in formal addition and subtraction calculation, despite very large amounts of routine 'overlearning' practice.

Furthermore, the standard forms for addition and subtraction have unique and complex sets of structural rules which have to be internalized – for example, learning the rules for 'borrowing' from zeros in subtraction – and formal calculation tends to be taught in separate or discrete teaching 'blocks'. Learning to calculate formally does not usually contribute very much at all to children's overall understanding of how the number system works.

And, finally, because each step in completing the step-by-step procedures requires the expenditure of considerable amounts of working memory, the procedures are intended to be written down and young children need pencil and paper to execute them correctly. This means that children who are restricted to learning the formal procedures do not acquire the skills to add and subtract double-digit numbers mentally. In other words, children who learn to add and subtract formally often lack 'real-life' numeracy skills, such as the ability to add 59p and 69p, or to subtract 87p from £1.00 'in their heads'.

Dyslexia and dyspraxia and the standard addition and subtraction algorithms

It is a widely observed feature of dyslexic and dyspraxic primary school maths learners that it can be especially hard for them to acquire the standard addition and subtraction procedures. Dyslexic and dyspraxic children are prone to calculation 'bugs'. They also forget procedures and some dyslexic and dyspraxic children regularly refuse to 'have a go' at completing addition and subtraction calculations unless they are first reminded of the rules. Teachers and parents report frustrating and upsetting interchanges with dyslexic and dyspraxic children who have failed, yet again, to make sense of the procedures, despite hours of overlearning practice and often despite apparent mastery of the procedures at an earlier stage. It is true that many dyslexic children ultimately succeed in internalizing the procedures for adding and subtracting in columns but this often takes time and vast amounts of 'drill' – and the 'drill' can, at times, affect the teacher-learner relationship. Hours and hours of drill can also cause unnecessary emotional distress and loss of self-esteem.

The cognitive aspects of dyslexia and dyspraxia, which affect formal addition and subtraction work, have already been touched on in the introduction. They are so important, however, that they will be explored here, again, and fleshed out in slightly greater detail.

General sequencing difficulties, difficulties with short-term retention of sequential instructions, and difficulties remembering sequential steps contribute to the problems which many dyslexic and dyspraxic children experience in trying to learn the steps – the 'rigmarole,' in Thompson's words – of the standard addition and subtraction procedures. Long-term memory, working memory and sequential memory weaknesses undermine the ability of dyslexic and dyspraxic children to remember the procedures accurately. Many examples which illustrate these difficulties could be cited but the procedural steps which learning-disabled children 'forget,' most often, typically have to do with redistribution rules – or, in other words, with 'carrying' and with 'borrowing'. For example, in two-digit addition work, it is very common for dyslexic or dyspraxic children to record 'carried' *tens* in the designated answer area instead of 'on the doorstep'. In another common type of error it is also typical for children with specific learning difficulties to forget 'what to do' with digits which have to be 'carried' into otherwise empty value positions. Dyslexic and dyspraxic children often record the 'carried' digit below the line without understanding the need to place it in the *answer* in the next value position to the left. Working memory difficulties contribute to the common failure of dyslexic and dyspraxic children to incorporate 'carried' digits in the standard addition procedures. Some *grasshopper* dyslexic children, who need to visualize numbers and problems in order to be able to calculate confidently, and who are constrained by sequencing difficulties, actively articulate their dislike of these aspects of the standard algorithms.

$$
\begin{array}{r}
5\ 6 \\
+3\ 6 \\
\hline
8\ 1\ 2
\end{array}
\qquad
\begin{array}{r}
8\ 7 \\
+3\ 5 \\
\hline
2\ 2 \\
1\ 1
\end{array}
\qquad
\begin{array}{r}
3\ 7 \\
+5\ 7 \\
\hline
8\ 4 \\
1
\end{array}
$$

Spatial problems, difficulties with left–right orientation and difficulties with visual memory frequently affect the ability of children to internalize addition and subtraction procedures. One significant problem which contributes to directional difficulties is that large numbers are read from left to right, but the addition and subtraction algorithms 'oblige us to work in the opposite direction' (Thompson, 1997b, p. 99). Younger children with specific learning difficulties typically forget to begin working from the units position and start calculating from the largest value position instead. Such children generally fail to accommodate redistributed 'tens' correctly.

Another result of particularly severe spatial and left-right orientation difficulties is that children may end up calculating in bizarre ways. In two not infrequent examples of bizarre interpretations of addition algorithms, children calculate in horizontal rows, rather than vertical columns – or muddle vertical-to-horizontal forms of setting out two-digit calculations. For example: 36 + 28 =

```
  3 6          ┌─┐
 +2 8          3 6          ↓3 2
 ─────         ──┬─          
  514         +2 8         +6 8
             ─────         ─────
             9 1 0         9 1 0
```

Redistribution (carrying) and decomposition (borrowing) 'bugs' are often partly caused by visual memory weaknesses and visual organizational difficulties, together with general difficulties remembering sequential rules. It is very common for dyslexic and dyspraxic children to redistribute the 'wrong' digit into the *tens* position. Instead of carrying the *tens* digit into the next column, children often record the *ten*, and 'carry' the *units* digit in its place Some children who inadvertently transpose column sums in this way are not usually prone to such place value reversals. In fact, 'carried digits' cause many visual memory difficulties – in a very common 'bug,' for example, a 'carried' *ten* is incorrectly interpreted as '*one hundred*'.

```
  3 6              ¹3 6
 +2 8              +2 8
 ─────             ─────
     1             1 5 4
 ───
  4
```

Subtraction facts, too, are frequently affected by visual memory and visual-spatial organizational problems. In both spoken or written subtraction contexts many dyslexic and dyspraxic children are not able to visualize which number 'comes first.' In basic subtraction work (outside of the framework of column subtraction) many children solve this problem pragmatically by mentally placing the bigger number first in the process of calculating. Thus they may say, '2 take away 8,' or write 2 – 8, but they count back the 2 from 8 to give the correct answer, '6.' Formal subtraction in columns compounds this problem. In an example such as 82 – 28 the units position does, in fact, contain the initial calculation '2 take away 8'. When they meet a calculation like this, children are trained to try and remember, and say, '2 take away 8 you can't do'. Dyslexic and dyspraxic children, however, often inadvertently 'flip' the digits first, and subtract the smaller number from the larger number in exactly the way that they have grown accustomed to working to figure out answers in basic subtraction work. Some dyslexic and dyspraxic children who consistently 'flip' subtraction column digits in this way are actually able to execute the correct 'borrowing' procedures when they are first primed to do so. When they 'flip' digits illegitimately they are usually unaware of the mistake they have made.

$$
\begin{array}{r} 8\;2 \\ -\,2\;8 \\ \hline \end{array}
\qquad
\begin{array}{r} 8\;2 \\ -\,2\;8 \\ \hline 6\;6 \end{array}
$$

A further feature of subtraction, which may contribute to the difficulty children have with interpreting subtraction columns, is that subtraction is not *commutative* whereas addition is *commutative*. As Karen Fuson perceptively argues, column addition is usually taught first, and it is often practised for a long time before column subtraction, and certainly 'borrowing', is introduced. In the standard algorithm framework, addition within columns can proceed from either the top digit or from the bottom digit. Children become accustomed to having this choice and incorrectly exercise the same perceived choice in completing *non-commutative* subtraction calculations in columns.

In conjunction with the other cognitive difficulties mentioned above, working memory difficulties particularly affect the ability of dyslexic and dyspraxic children to have an overview of what a reasonable answer to specific addition and subtraction calculations might be considered to be. It is often noted of dyslexic and dyspraxic maths learners that they will accept, without question, answers which are extremely unlikely. Furthermore, because they are usually so relieved when the required calculation processes are completed, many dyslexic and dyspraxic learners are often unwilling to consider the possibility that a specific answer is incorrect. Whereas non-learning disabled primary school children will usually mentally check an answer in response to adult prompts such as, 'Are you sure?' or, 'Do you think that answer could be right?' many dyslexic and dyspraxic children will insist that the given answer is correct. Similar fears about the possibility of having to execute difficult and laborious procedures, twice, mean that dyslexic and dyspraxic children are very unlikely to approximate before they calculate, no matter how many times teachers or parents encourage them to do so.

Non-standard (mental) two-digit addition and subtraction procedures

In reaction to the documented shortcomings of the standard addition and subtraction methods, most understanding-based approaches to teaching primary school maths promote the use of non-standard or *mental* addition and subtraction calculation methods, as we have noted above. There are many arguments in favour of encouraging children to use non-standard *mental* methods in two-digit addition and subtraction calculation work. The principal argument is that *mental* methods are quite a lot easier for children to understand than the standard calculation procedures. They are far less abstract and far less condensed than column arithmetic. As Ian Thompson writes,

> Mental methods, on the other hand, almost always retain the place value meaning of the digits and remain true to the language used when the number is spoken. The number 43, which is, of course, read as 'forty-three' is treated as a 40 (forty) and a 3 (three) ... (Thompson, 1997b, p. 100)

In other words, the ways in which numbers are broken down to make *mental* two-digit calculation possible are transparent and not implicit and difficult to make sense of. Furthermore, large values are never treated as 'honorary' *ones* within the calculation processes. In *mental* two-digit addition calculation methods, children begin adding from a whole number such as 43, or from the largest and not the smallest value position. Thus children usually add from left to right in the direction that numbers are written. This also means that 'the initial stages of calculation give you a useful first approximation to the answer (Thompson, 1997b). In *mental* subtraction methods children work with the real values making up the given two-digit numbers, too.

A second advantage of *mental* calculation models is that they build on understandings which are gained in basic addition, subtraction and number-system work so children are often able to devise *mental addition* and *subtraction* methods for themselves. Part of the theoretical drive towards promoting *mental* methods of calculation arose from classroom-based research to investigate which methods children most frequently 'invent' to solve a broad range of two-digit addition and subtraction word problems. Because *mental* maths models can be seen as part of the general continuum of learning about numbers, children are often flexible in their choice of the *mental* calculation methods which they choose to employ. Many children are able to select *mental* methods which are appropriate for the specific numbers within a calculation. Children are also able to select *mental* methods which make particular sense to them. Thus many children develop favourite ways of calculating. In general, too, the greater transparency of *mental* two-digit addition and subtraction methods means that they do not require to be 'drilled' as much as standard calculation methods have to be. To be able to calculate efficiently, children certainly need sufficient practice at using *mental* methods but research shows that the majority of children who are educated in cultures which teach *mental* calculation methods, consistently outperform traditionally taught children in their ability to add and subtract two-digit numbers.

Finally, the label '*mental*' in '*mental* maths methods' indicates that informal calculation methods are often devised to be performed 'in the head'. In other words, they are designed for genuine 'in the head' calculation purposes. At first, young children usually need pencil and paper to record the steps in the informal *mental* calculation process. With practice, however, most children are quickly able to execute informal additions and subtractions *mentally* without any need for pencil and paper. In other words, *mental* addition and subtraction methods help equip children to become 'functionally numerate'.

Mental calculation methods and dyslexic and dyspraxic children

The key argument for promoting *mental* two-digit addition and subtraction methods in teaching 'ordinary' primary school children, is also the key argument for teaching them to dyslexic and dyspraxic children. As we have seen, the complex memory-related difficulties associated with dyslexia and dyspraxia make it extremely difficult for children with learning difficulties to learn the opaque, sequential steps of the standard algorithms by rote. Dyslexic and dyspraxic children succeed far better if they understand the steps they are required to follow in order to complete calculation processes. As we have already suggested, *mental* calculation methods ideally suit *grasshopper* dyslexic children who generally work best in mathematics when they are able to visualize the problems they are required to solve. For those *grasshopper* children who dislike, and often fail to learn, the standard methods properly, encouragement to use *mental* methods can feel like a revelation which suddenly opens up calculation for them and makes it very much more accessible. In general, the majority of dyslexic and dyspraxic children with maths difficulties need especially carefully structured teaching in order to learn the *mental* methods, but they, too, are able to master the *mental* two-digit addition and subtraction methods much more quickly and far more happily than they do the standard column procedures.

There are further advantages which follow on from choosing to introduce dyslexic and dyspraxic children to the *mental* two-digit addition and subtraction strategies. We have already mentioned some of the structural details of *mental* methods which make them easier for 'ordinary' primary school children to learn than the standard procedures. Of course, these advantages apply to dyslexic and dyspraxic children, too. However, in addition to the general *child-friendly* advantages of mental calculation methods, it is also important to emphasize that there are a number of key features of *mental* methods of calculation which make them considerably better suited to the very particular learning needs of dyslexic and dyspraxic pupils than the generally unsatisfactory standard column procedures. In this regard, it is helpful to draw together, and outline, the specific *dyslexia and dyspraxia friendly* aspects of *mental* calculation methods. They include the following characteristic features:

1. It is common for mental methods to be introduced in a horizontal rather than in a vertical format. For dyslexic and dyspraxic children one advantage of this is that horizontal calculations form part of a natural continuum with early calculation work. Another advantage – and one which has already been touched on – is that partial calculations are recorded from left to right in the same direction in which numbers are read: e.g. (a) $36 + 28 = 50 + 14 = 64$; (b) $30 - 12 \rightarrow 30 - 10 = 20 \rightarrow 20 - 2 = 18$. For dyslexic and dyspraxic children, this means that *mental* maths addition and subtraction methods do not present the same confusing directional hurdles as do the standard formal algorithms.

2. A very big benefit of using informal methods to add and subtract two-digit numbers is that there is seldom any need to 'carry' or 'borrow'. Instead, as we have seen, children work with the whole numbers, themselves, or with the actual value of the digits within the numbers. For example: (a) $57 + 58 = 100 + 15 = 115$; (b) $100 - 76 \rightarrow 76 + 4 = 80 \rightarrow 80 + 20 = 100 - 76 = 24$. This, in turn, means that a whole range of calculation 'bugs' which are related to 'carrying' and 'borrowing', and which undermine the ability of children with specific learning difficulties to complete two-digit addition and subtraction calculations, effectively, disappear as learning concerns. Significantly, too, since *mental* subtraction methods are not column-based, there is less

likelihood that dyslexic and dyspraxic children will inadvertently 'flip' individual digits within two-digit subtraction calculations.

3. A third very important advantage of working with the more meaningful real values f digits is that dyslexic and dyspraxic children are able to develop a firmer grasp of what is likely to constitute sensible or realistic answers to given addition and subtraction calculations. Thus, for instance, dyslexic and dyspraxic children who learn to accompany the process of calculating an addition problem, such as 58 + 57 with the common *mental* verbalizing 'patter', 'fifty plus fifty is a hundred, eight plus seven is fifteen' are unlikely to give an answer of more than a thousand at the end of the calculation process. The ability to have a 'rough ballpark' sense of what the final outcome to addition and subtraction calculations is likely to be helps children with specific learning difficulties feel that they are in greater overall control of the calculation process. It also helps foster the general *number-sense* of dyslexic and dyspraxic children.

The different mental two-digit addition and subtraction methods

We have noted a number of times that one of the central teaching tenets in learning to use standard addition and subtraction algorithms is that they have to be completed in one prescribed, correct way. In contrast, as we have seen, *mental* methods for two-digit addition and subtraction can proceed in a variety of different ways. From a learning point of view, we have already touched on the idea that children can benefit from the variety of mental addition and subtraction methods which are available. Briefly, for example, children can select *mental* methods which suit their ways of thinking, their general conception of numbers, and the skills and the number models they have at their disposal. Also, children can potentially select *mental* methods to suit the particular addition or subtraction calculation which needs to be solved. For example, 200 − 99 is a laborious calculation if it is performed using the standard subtraction method, but there are a number of *mental* methods which can be used to calculate the answer quite quickly.

It should be acknowledged, however, that, from a 'non-specialist' teaching point of view the advantages of the *mental* maths calculation methods may not be so readily appreciated. To teachers, and to parents, it can feel that there are some significant disadvantages associated with the newer ideas about encouraging children to use reasoning-based methods of calculation. This is largely because the changes in maths teaching, which have brought the *mental* methods to the fore, are generally new and unfamiliar and the more open-ended approach to calculation can be somewhat daunting for many of the adults who wish to support or develop children's *mental* calculation abilities. Many teachers and parents report feeling uncertain or somewhat out of their depth in the area of two-digit *mental* calculation.

It is helpful to explore, in a slightly more detailed way, some of the reasons that adults feel daunted by informal calculation methods. First as we have just suggested, adults are often completely unfamiliar with *mental* ways of reasoning. They are generally used to, and feel comfortable with, the traditional column methods of calculating. Furthermore, many adults do not have an overview of the different calculation methods which children may use. Adults may not easily be able to identify, or easily follow, a method which a child is using. Most adults do not have an overview of the advantages or disadvantages of the range of different *mental* methods. This means that most adults do not know which methods may be particularly good methods to support or encourage. Understanding which methods are generally successful for children to use, and which are less so, is particularly important when adults are supporting children are weak in maths.

To help make sense of the possibilities within *mental* approaches to addition and subtraction calculation, it is very helpful to have some way of analysing and categorizing the approaches. Although children devise and use a complex variety of approaches to work out two-digit addition and subtraction calculations, it is possible to identify broad overall categories or types of approach. Generally speaking, most researchers roughly agree that there are three main types of informal calculation methods. All calculation approaches – including the standard algorithms – are really ways of breaking complex calculations down into manageable components: the different approaches essentially involve different ways of 'simplifying' the calculations. In general terms, the three calculation categories apply to both addition and subtraction calculations. As we will see, two of the three broad calculation types may be considered to be *universal* calculation types since they can be used in any given calculation situation.

Informal partitioning calculation methods

In *partitioning* approaches to two-digit addition and subtraction calculation, each number is broken down, prior to calculation, into its place value components. The decomposed values are then added or subtracted separately and the individual partial outcomes are combined to achieve the final answer or outcome. For example: (a) $36 + 36 = (30 + 6) + (30 + 6) = 60 + 12 = 72$; (b) $83 - 41 = (80 + 3) - (40 + 1) = 40 + 2 = 42$.

Informal sequencing calculation methods

In *sequencing* calculation methods, one number from the calculation is always retained as a whole. Indeed, Karen Fuson often calls sequencing methods *'begin with one number'* methods. Children calculate by 'jumping' in a cumulative (or running total way) the number of *tens* and *ones* specified in the 'other' number. 'Jumping' can proceed forwards, for example in addition and *complementary addition (adding up to)* calculations. Subtraction 'jumping' can also proceed backwards. For example: (a) $36 + 28 \rightarrow 36 + 20 = 56, 56 + 8 = 64$; (b) $93 - 15 \rightarrow 93 - 10 = 83 - 5 = 78$.

Informal compensation calculation methods – also known as overshoot methods

Compensation methods are suited to a relatively limited range of calculations. This means that they do not really constitute a 'universal' calculation category. From an analytical point of view, compensation methods can be considered to be extensions of *sequencing* methods of calculation. In *compensation* methods, children modify one or both numbers to make the calculation easier to execute. This means that children 'overshoot' or 'undershoot' in the main calculation step, and then have to adjust the final outcome accordingly. Children most frequently devise *compensation* methods to figure out particular kinds of subtraction calculations. For example, $93 - 49 \rightarrow 93 - 50 = 43 + 1 = 44$. *Compensation* methods work best when the numbers which are modified are close to *tens* in two-digit work, or when they are close to larger *Base Ten* collection points when larger calculations are involved. Children frequently make mistakes or become confused if they overextend compensation methods. $83 - 26 \rightarrow 83 - 30 = 53, 53 + 4 = 57$. For instance, in the example, $83 - 26$, children often become confused about whether the '4' requires to be added, or subtracted.

Partitioning, sequencing and compensation methods are usually identified as the three main calculation types. Most commentators acknowledge that children sometimes devise *mixed* methods of calculation. We will touch on two commonly used mixed *partitioning/sequencing* methods later on in the discussion.

Introducing mental maths methods

Since the basic premise of most contemporary approaches to maths teaching is that children should be actively involved in the process of learning about numbers, it is not surprising that there are many parallels between the discussions about how *mental* two-digit addition and subtraction calculations are best introduced and the ideas, discussed earlier, about how fact-derived strategies are best acquired. As we have seen, children can be encouraged to actively 'invent' or devise strategies for working out the harder addition and subtraction facts – either individually or collectively through idea sharing. In exactly the same way, children can be encouraged to 'discover' *mental* addition and subtraction methods. In other words, teachers can encourage children to 'invent' their own methods for adding and subtracting two-digit numbers without ever formally or directly teaching them any one particular method, or methods. Many researchers and theorists believe that the majority of children remember methods they have devised by themselves, or with others, better, and also make fewer 'bug-like' errors when they use these 'actively invented' methods. Like other understanding-based approaches to teaching maths, the Numeracy Strategy suggests that *mental* maths methods should be introduced to children in creative and open-ended ways. In practice, as we saw when we discussed fact-derived strategies, many teachers in state school classrooms do, in fact, opt for a direct teaching approach towards mental calculation procedures – this is very often because they are not very familiar with methods of encouraging children to 'discover' reasoning methods more independently.

Once again, however, the same general arguments expressed earlier about 'harder' addition and subtraction fact calculation also apply to two-digit calculation methods. Since so many of the cognitive features which are part of the dyslexic and dyspraxic profile make all calculation processes difficult to manage, it is not surprising that open-ended approaches to two-digit calculations (or approaches in which many different methods are directly taught) do not suit all dyslexic and dyspraxic children. It is certainly true, as we have noted many times, that *grasshopper* dyslexics who have acquired a good understanding of number-structures and a reasonable knowledge of the number facts often flourish in open-ended calculation environment. It is also true that a second group of dyslexic and dyspraxic children can benefit from encouragement to be inventive 'discoverers' of mental maths methods, particularly in addition – and, later on, in multiplication and division work. These are children who have been able to respond relatively quickly to understanding-based teaching and whose *number-sense*, foundation skills and confidence have very significantly improved. On the other hand, it is very important to acknowledge that a significant number of dyslexic and dyspraxic children need a great deal of support in order to make headway in acquiring more advanced addition and subtraction skills and that they may consequently not succeed unless the teaching situation is carefully structured. In essence, this is because many of the problems which dyslexic and dyspraxic children experience in trying to learn methods for two-digit addition and subtraction are very similar to the difficulties they experience in trying to learn a number of fact-derived strategies. At the risk of some repetition, it is helpful to outline some of the particular and most common difficulties which dyslexic and dyspraxic children can experience in learning *mental* methods for two-digit calculation.

First of all, poor or slow access to number facts, significant working memory difficulties and general sequencing difficulties all mean that children with specific learning difficulties can find it hard to follow the steps of the different *mental* methods which other children or teachers may share with them. Secondly, exposure to many different possible reasoning routes may result in making children with specific learning difficulties confused about how to proceed, in large part because the two-digit addition and subtraction calculation methods will be imperfectly understood. It should also be noted that while children may become somewhat 'lost' in open-ended teaching situations, classroom contexts in which teachers directly teach a large number of mental approaches (and expect children to remember and use all of them) can seriously undermine the confidence of dyslexic and dyspraxic children. Written exercises in which children are asked to complete given calculations in a specified number of alternative ways can be very inappropriate for many children with specific learning difficulties.

Thirdly, while some children with specific learning difficulties are able to devise or understand *mental* methods in supportive learning contexts – for instance, when concrete materials are available – the complex memory difficulties which are so frequently associated with dyslexia and dyspraxia can mean that children with specific learning difficulties subsequently fail to *recall* the methods. Because they are so prone to 'forgetting calculation methods', dyslexic and dyspraxic children often ask to be shown 'one way' to calculate, a way which they will always be able to use, and which they can subsequently practise and internalize. In many instances, an apparent tendency towards rigid and inflexible thinking actually illustrates the child's intuitive understanding that he or she requires a degree of cognitive security. It is also important to point out that that children with specific learning difficulties frequently understand and regularly use methods for *mental* addition and subtraction which work well for 'easier' calculations below 100 but which are harder to execute in working with larger, 'harder' calculations. Some children with specific learning difficulties, who have begun automatizing a specific reasoning route, can have a great deal of difficulty adjusting to having to learn alternative ways of reasoning. Finally, writers like Ian Thompson point out that mental calculation proficiency is related to confident understanding and a willingness on children's parts to 'have a go' at calculating. For all the reasons detailed above, many children with learning difficulties increasingly lose confidence in their ability to add and/or subtract two-digit numbers and often give up before 'having a go'.

The main teaching implications of these difficulties are ones which are already familiar. In essence, many children with learning difficulties learn to add and subtract larger numbers more confidently if they start, in an explicitly 'contained' way, by acquiring *key methods* for addition and subtraction – methods which children can apply with confidence to all two-digit addition and subtraction calculations and which are suitable for genuine *mental* calculation. Once again, it is suggested that many dyslexic and dyspraxic children benefit from an approach which specifically teaches carefully selected *big value* two-digit addition and subtraction strategies. In the same way that this applies to confident fact-derived strategy usage, children with specific learning difficulties, who are weak at maths but who begin to master and automatize *big value* methods which consistently 'work', continue to learn a great deal about the ways numbers function. Very often, too, mathematically 'disabled' children who master *big value mental* calculation methods, are given the tools and the confidence to become increasingly creative mathematical thinkers.

Two-digit mental calculation methods

We have touched on the fact that there are a number of choices of *mental* methods for completing two-digit addition and subtraction calculations which children can opt for, and at first sight it is not obvious which calculation methods might be considered the best ones to support, particularly in working with dyslexic and dyspraxic children. Nevertheless, although open-ended teaching is almost universally recommended – and this implies of course, that children could opt for any method which suits them – there has, in fact, been a very useful debate in the 'mainstream' maths teaching literature about which *mental* methods might suit the majority of children best. There are three main reasons for this. First, from a practical teaching point of view, it is recognized that a number of children, including children with learning difficulties, will need to be given some support and guidance in the process of finding the calculation methods which suit them best. Secondly, it is also acknowledged that the kinds of foundation skills that teachers engage in with children – for example, the kinds of activities which are selected by teachers to help children understand the number system – will inevitably affect the ways that children are likely to reason, and will therefore affect the addition and subtraction methods that they are likely to devise. In other words, teachers inevitably have a significant influence on the ways in which children choose to calculate. Thirdly, it is important that the textbooks, computer software and so on, which are designed to foster understanding and to offer support to ordinary teachers in classrooms, are able to illustrate methods which the majority of children are likely to understand.

What makes the task of selecting the most appropriate two-digit addition and subtraction methods somewhat tricky, however, is that while there is a fair degree of consensus over the kinds of methods which children frequently use, it is also widely acknowledged that each of the main calculation categories has a number of potentially serious *disadvantages*, as well as advantages, for the children who choose to use them. To understand the debates surrounding the value, or otherwise, of particular addition and subtraction *mental* methods, it is important to have some understanding of what the main advantages and disadvantages of the principal calculation methods are considered to be.

The partitioning calculation method

According to Thompson and Smith (1999), the *partitioning* method is the calculation method which is most frequently devised and used by English primary school children to solve two-digit addition calculation problems. As long as children have a relatively good understanding of *place value*, the *partitioning* method is an addition method which is quite readily learned by most young primary school children. Children with specific learning difficulties also learn to *partition* in addition quite easily. A big advantage of the addition *partitioning* method is that the first stage of the calculation – for example, the addition of 20 + 30 in 26 + 37 – is relatively easy to calculate and children are thus able to start the 'multi-step' reasoning process quite confidently. On the whole, children make relatively few errors when they use the *partitioning* method for addition. Because children often enjoy using the method, most children are also generally quite willing to practise it. With practice and increased 'automatization' children are often able to hold the first *tens* calculation in working memory and work out two-digit addition problems purely mentally. The *partitioning* method also translates well into non-standard *column* addition methods (or 'low-stress algorithms' as Thompson aptly names them) and has significant elements in common with the formal methods for addition. As we will see shortly, this means that children are generally able to make a relatively smooth transition from *mental* addition partitioning procedures to the standard written addition procedures.

On the other hand, while *partitioning* is a natural and successful choice for working out two-digit addition calculations, it is generally quite hard to use for the majority of two-digit subtraction problems and is consequently much less frequently employed by children as a *mental* two-digit subtraction method. *Chunking* values into their place value components works deceptively smoothly for 'easy' subtraction calculations without decomposition complications, such as $46 - 22$. (40 minus 20 is 20; 6 minus 2 is 4; the answer is 24). But employing a *partitioning* calculation approach leads to classic decomposition difficulties in a great many subtraction situations – for instance, in trying to work out quite modest subtraction calculations such as $46 - 28$, or $50 - 24$. To work out $46 - 28$, for example, the first $40 - 20$ step is easily calculated, and gives an answer of 20, but then children are left with the question of how to resolve the second-step calculation $(6 - 8)$ since insufficient *units* are available to allow this subtraction to be completed straightforwardly. Indeed, children will often verbalize this step as 'six take away eight – but you can't *do* six take away eight!'

If children continue to wrestle with the logic of a *partitioning* approach to 'difficult' subtractions, such as $46 - 28$, there are, in principle, at least two possible ways to proceed as Karen Fuson (1992) demonstrates. First, children may – and sometimes do – continue in a way which closely mirrors the addition partitioning approach. Thus, children may *subtract everything first*, starting from the largest value position and deal with the decomposition problem by regrouping or readjusting everything afterwards. To work out $46 - 28$ in this way, children would reason, '40 minus 20 is 20, 6 minus 8 is minus-2 (-2), 2 has to be subtracted from 20; $20 - 2 = 18$; the answer to $46 - 28$ is 18. However, managing the demands of this approach successfully is clearly no easy task. At the very least, children have to recognize problem situations which require decompositions (such as $6 - 8$ and $0 - 4$), and cope with the conceptual and working memory demands involved in carrying through the adjustment of the intermediate *tens* answer: $6 - 8 = -2 \rightarrow 20 - 2 = 18$. For these reasons, the *subtract-everything-first* partitioning method is rarely devised by dyslexic and dyspraxic children and is not a suitable method to promote with children with maths difficulties. In the second partitioning subtraction method, as Karen Fuson points out, any decomposition problems are dealt with first, ahead of any calculation. Instead of partitioning, subtracting and regrouping, children partition, regroup and then subtract. In other words, in this approach, regrouping *precedes* subtraction. To work out $46 - 28$ using this *regroup first* partitioning method, children 'check ahead,' note that $6 - 8$ represents a decomposition problem, regroup 46 as $30 + 16$, and then work out the component calculations $30 - 20$ and $16 - 8$. However, this *'mental'* subtraction method is not very appealing to the majority of primary school children – not only is it extremely abstract and difficult to understand, it is also very difficult to orchestrate. Karen Fuson acknowledges that the working-memory demands of this *regroup first* method, together with the difficulties which generally arise in trying to devise suitable methods for recording it, mean that it works best as a *written 'mental'* method, and is best set out in column form. This means, in turn, that the *regroup first* method does not easily lead to genuine *mental* subtraction competence – children's ability to subtract 'in their heads' – or to helping children build 'real-life' numeracy skills. (This method does, on the other hand, have a great deal in common with standard decomposition methods for subtraction).

While 'pure' partitioning subtraction approaches, such as the difficult *regroup first* approach (favoured by Karen Fuson), generally have to be quite intensively promoted or taught, a *mental* method for two-digit subtraction which starts by partitioning, but resolves difficult decomposition problems by switching to a *sequencing-like* approach, is much more commonly devised by children. Some children with good *number-sense* and strong visualizing skills begin the two-digit subtraction solution process by partitioning and subtracting the *tens* values first (just as they do when they employ the addition *mental partitioning* method) but then deal with any second-stage decomposition problems by introducing a *cumulative* or *sequencing* reasoning approach. For instance, to work out $46 - 28$ using this particular mental method, children reason, '40 minus 20 is 20, put back the "6" (from 46) on to 20, 26 minus 8 is 18.' It should be noted that *grasshopper* dyslexic children, who are able to visualize two-digit subtractions holistically, are sometimes very proficient at using this *partitioning-plus-sequencing* subtraction method. Nevertheless, the *parti-*

tioning-plus-sequencing subtraction approach has important drawbacks. For example, many children have difficulty following or making sense of its complex sequence of back and forth reasoning or feel overburdened by its particularly heavy working memory demands. The method does not extend well to three-digit subtraction calculations either. Although children who devise *partitioning-plus-sequencing* solutions to subtraction questions should be supported and warmly praised, it is not a suitable subtraction method to promote more widely.

The sequencing calculation method

Research shows that the *sequencing* calculation method is fairly frequently used by adults to solve two-digit addition calculations. In Holland, where the *empty number-line* tool is promoted from the earliest primary years onwards, young children are 'guided' to use the *sequencing* addition method as their primary addition calculation method. Thompson's research, which is undertaken in English schools (in which *Base Ten* materials and/or pictorial representations of numbers quite commonly used as cognitive supports) shows that English children devise the *sequencing* addition calculation method far less frequently than they do the *partitioning* calculation method.

The major disadvantage of the *sequencing* mental addition method is that many children have difficulty with the very first component calculation in all but the easiest *sequencing* addition calculations. Most children will calculate a 'begin-with-one-number' component calculation such as 36 + 20, quite easily, but a larger component calculation such as 36 + 50 is experienced as quite difficult by many children, and larger still 'through-one-hundred' calculations, such as 47 + 70, are often found to be very difficult, indeed. These 'onset' calculation difficulties have important implications. Children who experience an immediate calculation obstacle or become 'stuck' on the first calculation step in a *multi-step* calculation task, often become disheartened and 'lose track' within the overall procedure. For this reason, many children do not find the *sequencing* approach to two-digit addition an appealing way to proceed and some children voice an active dislike of the *sequencing (jump)* addition method. It should be remembered that a significant number of dyslexic and dyspraxic children find basic *jump* counting from *tens-and-units* numbers a relatively difficult skill to acquire, as we saw briefly in Part III, and children with specific learning difficulties can therefore find 'harder' addition *jump* calculations particularly difficult to manage.

On the other hand, while *sequencing* methods are seldom children's preferred methods for two-digit addition in the UK, the picture is much more complex and mixed with regards to two-digit subtraction. Precisely because the decomposition issues which 'harder' two-digit subtraction calculations raise are hard to resolve, it is important to acknowledge that most two-digit subtraction calculations are simply very much harder for children to execute than two-digit addition calculations. Contemporary researchers have shown that nearly all children find *mental* two-digit subtraction method harder to use than *mental* addition methods. They have also shown that most children make many more errors in solving *mental* subtraction problems than they do in solving *mental* addition problems. It is certainly the case that dyslexic and dyspraxic children much more frequently refuse to 'have a go' at devising methods for two-digit subtraction than they do for two-digit addition.

However, research also shows that children who do manage to devise two-digit subtraction methods generally end up devising and using the 'start-with-one-number' *sequencing* or *jump* subtraction method. This is probably because decomposition problems can be side-stepped in *jump* approaches to addition. (For the same reason, mathematically able children much more frequently devise *overshooting compensatory* methods to solve subtraction problems than they do to solve two-digit addition problems.) Even here, though, there are complications which need to be raised: *sequencing* in subtraction can, of course, proceed *backwards* or *upwards*. In fact, most research shows that children seldom devise sequencing up/compensatory addition methods of subtraction. They are much more likely to 'start-with-one-number' and sequence *backwards*, e.g. $82 - 57 = 32 - 7 = 25$. But although *sequencing backwards* fits very well with 'take away' conceptions of subtraction, and could therefore be considered to be the most 'natural' mental subtraction method to promote, adopting this approach is – unfortunately – not without significant teaching and learning drawbacks as Karen Fuson shows. We have already seen that 'harder' addition *jumps* are difficult for many children to work out. The cognitive demands of 'backwards' sequential reasoning, and even counting, are much more onerous than those of addition sequential reasoning. We have noted many times that children with specific learning difficulties typically struggle with all forms of backwards sequential thinking. Karen Fuson points out that sequencing backwards becomes especially difficult when the number which is subtracted from (the minuend), is greater than 100; for example, in subtractions such as $123 - 78$. For dyspraxic children, in particular, the first calculation *jump*, $123 - 70$, can feel impossibly difficult to work out. This means that dyslexic and dyspraxic children, who rely on *sequencing back mental* methods of subtraction, are often confined to being able to complete a very limited range of two-digit subtraction calculations with any degree of confidence.

The search for a suitable mental subtraction method for dyslexic and dyspraxic children

To sum up the discussion of *mental* addition and subtraction methods: generally speaking, children prefer to *partition* to solve two-digit additions but choose to *sequence backwards* to solve two-digit subtractions. *Partitioning* in addition is 'easy' for most children to grasp, it is usually executed with relatively few calculation errors and it is enjoyed by the majority of children, including dyslexic and dyspraxic children. On the other hand, the major difficulty from the point of view of working with children with calculation weaknesses is that none of the *mental* subtraction methods which have been discussed so far can be said to suit most children in the same way – and this includes the most frequently used *sequencing back* method.

An overview of the research literature on subtraction, of teachers' comments, and of pupils' responses to two-digit subtraction, leads to the following conclusions:

1. Many of the most vulnerable children in maths are daunted by two-digit subtraction and give up or ask for help much more frequently than they do in all other *mental* calculation situations.
2. All of the commonly devised *mental* subtraction methods are objectively difficult to execute and many children make frequent mistakes in *mental* two-digit subtraction work.
3. Many children express an intense dislike of two-digit subtraction work – equalled only, in very many instances, by their intense dislike of division.

Thus, although mathematically able children can usually find creative ways to negotiate the difficult aspects of those *mental* subtraction methods which most frequently spring to mind, less able children, and a great many dyslexic and dyspraxic children, cannot.

However, and this is a big 'however,' there is one important *mental* method for two-digit subtraction which has not yet been considered. In earlier theoretical discussions of subtraction we have seen that although most children base their rather limited conception of subtraction on very early *counting back* or conventional 'take-away' subtraction experiences, subtraction procedures which are based on a *counting up to* understanding of subtraction are often very much easier to execute. As we mentioned very briefly a moment ago, sequential thinking can, of course, proceed *upwards* rather than *backwards* in two-digit subtraction work.. To work out 62 – 27, for instance, children can proceed to reason *upwards* from 27 to figure out the 'difference' or 'gap' between 27 and 62, instead of working backwards from 62, and instead of by proceeding by subtracting 20, then 7, from 62.

'Sequencing up' in subtraction

Technically speaking, the fact that large differences (subtraction answers) can result from two-digit subtraction calculation problems, means that *sequencing up* can usually proceed in one of two slightly different ways. The somewhat harder version of *sequencing upwards* directly mirrors the most common *sequencing back* subtraction method. In this method, the *tens* are *jumped* or *sequenced up* before the *ones*. To work out 62 – 27, reasoning starts with 27, 27 plus 30 is 57, 57 plus 5 is 62; the difference between 27 and 62 is 30 + 5 or 35, so 62 – 27 is 35. Although *sequencing up* is certainly easier than *sequencing back*, this particular *sequencing up* method has two disadvantages. First, children have to figure out right at the start how many tens need to be *jumped* to 'land' in the *ten* just before the target number. For instance, to subtract from 62, the initial *tens* jump has to 'land' somewhere in the 50s. Secondly, subtractions from numbers larger than 100 raise 'through 100' calculation difficulties which are similar to those experienced in two-digit addition sequencing methods. For instance, to work out 132 – 78, the onset '78 plus 50 = 128' *step* is very difficult for many children with specific learning difficulties to figure out.

It is the second *sequencing up* method which really has the key calculation advantages. In this method *ones* are 'jumped' first from the 'whole' subtrahend (the number to be subtracted) to reach the very next *tens* number; then, in the second calculation step, children figure out how many remaining *tens* and *ones* are needed to *jump* all the way *up* to the minuend, or 'start-out' number. Thus, to work out 62 – 27, reasoning starts with 27; 27 *plus* 3 is 30, 30 *plus* 32 is 62, the *difference* between 27 and 62 is 32 + 3, so 62 – 27 is 35. It is generally this second, and much more common, method of *sequencing upwards* which educationalists usually mean when they refer to *complementary addition* procedures for two-digit mental subtraction.

The complementary addition method for two-digit subtraction calculation

It is widely noted that the complementary addition method is a method for two-digit subtraction which is frequently devised by adults. *Complementary addition* is found to be particularly reliable in situations where 'mental' subtractions are necessary. It is used by many adults in 'real-life' situations, such as giving or checking change. It was the primary calculation method used by shopkeepers to give change before the contemporary shop tills, which work out change, became common – hence the colloquial term 'shopkeeper's method'. Many dyslexic adults volunteer that they have always remained weak at formal subtraction but that they ended up devising the *complementary addition* method for subtraction at some point after they left school.

While the *complementary addition* method for two-digit subtraction is commonly devised and used by adults, it is widely argued that it is seldom devised by children. Researchers and teachers generally confirm that complementary addition is not a subtraction method which is spontaneously used by children in purely numerical or 'abstract' subtraction situations. In this sense, complementary addition has not been an entirely 'natural' method for children to employ to work out ordinary subtraction calculations, such as $100 - 37$ or $62 - 38$. There are probably two main reasons for this. The first has already been discussed and has to do with the fact that children usually identify subtraction with *counting back* or 'take-away' conceptions of subtraction. The second and very closely related reason is that children are particularly inclined to 'fold back' to earlier learned responses in calculation situations which they experience as particularly challenging.

Nevertheless, it is also important to set into some perspective this finding that children do not naturally employ complementary addition procedures to work out ordinary subtraction calculations. It is important to remember that while more traditional approaches to primary school maths emphasize the limiting 'taking-away' and *counting back* conceptions of subtraction, all of the newer contemporary under-standing-based approaches now consciously set out to give children a more properly rounded conception of subtraction. As we have seen, conceptually oriented teaching approaches, which explore subtraction situations in a deeper way, set out to foster *difference* and *missing addend*, as well as '*take away*' conceptions of subtraction. Furthermore, important procedural skills are often consciously put in place in newer approaches, too. For instance, the commonly devised and taught big value *bridging-*

up-through-ten subtraction strategy – a *complementary addition* strategy in its own right – has a large amount in common with more advanced two-digit *complementary addition* work.

It is certainly important to acknowledge that *adding up to* conceptions and skills often have to be reviewed and rehearsed to prepare most children for using the *complementary addition* method, once children reach the two-digit subtraction level. On the other hand, the use of *complementary addition* procedures for two-digit subtraction can be seen, ideally at least, as a culmination of a carefully designed approach to subtraction – an approach which sets out from the very beginning to help children acquire a flexible understanding of subtraction and an approach which also helps prepare children from the earliest foundation stages to consider choosing *complementary addition* procedures to figure out appropriate subtraction questions.

Many researchers and theorists acknowledge that *complementary addition* is a much easier and 'safer' mental subtraction procedure to use than any of the other procedures for two-digit mental subtraction. Since execution difficulties lie at the heart of dyslexic and dyspraxic children's failure to make progress in subtraction work, it is helpful to look in further detail at the advantages of using the complementary addition procedure in two-digit subtraction situations.

First of all, as we saw in the very brief synopsis given above, *complementary addition* involves reasoning forwards from the whole subtrahend, or second number, to the next *ten*, or significant *Base Ten* collection point, and then from there on to the 'start-out' minuend, or first number. For example, to work out 91 – 63, 63 is the starting point for reasoning, 7 is needed to reach 70, and 21 is needed to reach 91, so 91 – 63 = 28. As we have seen many times before, it is always easier for children with calculation weaknesses to reason forwards rather than backwards. The particular bonus and special advantage of complementary addition procedures is that the larger calculation *jump*, which occurs in the second calculation step, begins from a *rounded* two-digit or *tens* number (such as 70) and is therefore relatively easy to figure out. This helps explain why children generally make few calculation errors when they are encouraged to use *complementary addition* procedures.

Secondly, since the very first '*bridging*' step, which takes children to the *rounded ten*, is small, very familiar and therefore 'easy' to work out, and the second step is not too difficult to figure out, either, *complementary addition* can quite quickly be used by children with significant maths weaknesses as a 'truly mental' ('in the head') calculation method for solving oral and *mental* two-digit subtraction calculations. In other words, since the working memory demands of *complementary addition* are not especially onerous, it is a very suitable method for genuine 'in the head' subtraction reasoning. In contrast, as we have noted, whenever dyslexic and dyspraxic children choose to employ alternative subtraction methods, they usually require pencil and paper support.

Thirdly, the fact that the *complementary addition* procedures are designed to take children to a suitable *Base Ten* collection point as quickly as possible, means that *complementary addition* is a particularly effective procedure for subtraction from numbers larger than 100. To subtract from numbers larger than 100, children learn to make 100 itself, or indeed any relevant *hundred*, an important part-way reasoning point or reasoning goal. At first, for example, to work out 121 – 87, children may reason in three calculation steps: 'Start with 87, 3 is needed to reach 90, 10 is needed to reach 100, 21 is needed to reach 121.' With practice, most children learn to '*bridge*' in two quite large *jumps*: 'Start with 87, 13 is needed to reach 100, 21 is needed to reach 121; 13 plus 21 is 34, so 121 minus 87 is 34.' Either way, since *Base Ten* boundaries are used as part of the structuring process (and do not therefore have to be 'crossed through' in the ways required by the alternative *sequencing* methods) *complementary addition* is a particularly appropriate method to use to work out three-digit subtraction calculations. For example, three-digit subtractions such as 900 – 264 are particularly easy to manage. 'We start reasoning from 264; 36 is needed to reach 300, 600 is needed to reach 900, 36 plus 600 equals 636, so 900 – 264 = 636.'

It should be noted that success at using *complementary addition* to work out 'hard' subtraction calculations can help dyslexic and dyspraxic children acquire increasingly hopeful and positive responses to subtraction. Children with specific learning difficulties, who experience the benefits of subtracting this way, are more likely to participate in a positive 'learning loop' in which they are increasingly likely to think of using *complementary addition* in ordinary subtraction situations, in which they actually manage to execute the procedure accurately and in which they gain the confidence that they can 'do' subtractions. This means, in turn, that they are generally more willing to 'have a go' at subtracting and therefore have more practice at working out harder subtractions. The ultimate result of all of this is that the *complementary addition* method of two-digit subtraction is more likely to become genuinely automatized than other subtraction methods.

Big value methods for addition and subtraction

A detailed investigation of the conceptual and calculation demands of each of the main two-digit addition and subtraction *mental* calculation methods has led to the conclusion that *partitioning* in addition suits children with specific learning difficulties best whereas *sequencing up*, or *complementary addition*, is the safest and most suitable two-digit mental subtraction method to teach to dyslexic and dyspraxic children. But there is a further issue which needs to be raised. The fact that the *partitioning* and *sequencing* methods proceed in entirely different ways, and have entirely different starting points, has to be examined and considered. It should be apparent that there would be advantages in the contrasting idea that dyslexic and dyspraxic children should acquire one uniform approach to both addition and subtraction. As we have seen, however, the task of selecting a uniform two-digit addition and subtraction method to promote is made difficult because no one single method for two-digit addition and subtraction is equally successfully learned. It is thus inevitable that the selection of *key* addition and subtraction methods involves a degree of compromise.

In contrast to the approach adopted in this chapter, it is quite common for maths educationalists to opt for consistency across addition and subtraction methods and promote one calculation method which is felt to have the most advantages overall – as well as the fewest drawbacks, overall. In essence, this is the approach to two-digit addition and subtraction calculation which is adopted in the newer curricula within contemporary Dutch Realistic Education classrooms and in at least one of Karen Fuson's projects. As we have mentioned a number of times, Dutch maths educators' commitment to promoting *sequencing* methods for two operations is supported by intensive use of the *empty number-line* tool. On the other hand, Karen Fuson's project classroom adopted a different uniform approach – Fuson and her teachers report that they supported *partitioning* methods for two-digit addition and subtraction, and used simple, 'home-made' tens-structured materials to do so (Fuson, Smith and Lo Cicero, 1997). While the argument that it is simpler and less confusing for children to learn one overall calculation method to figure out two-digit addition and subtraction calculations is a powerful one, on balance it is a second compromise approach – an approach which promotes two distinctive *big value* addition and subtraction calculation methods – which has been found to be the most successful approach to adopt in working with dyslexic and dyspraxic children. The reasons for this include the following:

1. As suggested earlier, an insistence on promoting calculation methods which are difficult for dyslexic and dyspraxic children to execute can be counterproductive. Children who find learning particular procedures difficult quickly lose confidence and often lose the will to practise calculating further.
2. Decisions to insist on promoting a *sequencing* method in two-digit addition work or a *partitioning* approach in two-digit subtraction work run counter to arguments that children should be encouraged to calculate in ways which make best sense to them.
3. As long as dyslexic and dyspraxic children have access to both *Base Ten* and *number-line* models of numbers, and are helped to develop a flexible understanding of numbers, they can be guided to 'discover' the strengths of the *partitioning* addition model as well as the *complementary addition* subtraction model.
4. Research shows that 'ordinary' children are quite flexible in their use of mental two-digit calculation methods and often use different methods interchangeably. Dyslexic and dyspraxic children, who automatize a *partitioning* approach for addition and a *sequencing up* approach for subtraction, also become increasingly flexible and inventive thinkers in two-digit and in three-digit calculation work. Thus, for instance, dyslexic or dyspraxic children will often choose to *sequence* rather than partition to add a smaller two-digit number to a larger two-digit number. For example, to work out 78 + 15, children may reason from the whole number 78, add 10, to 'make' 88, and then 5, to reach the answer, 93. In another common example of flexible thinking, children devise a '*bridging-like*' addition to figure out certain addition calculations. For instance, to work out 193 + 79, children may reason, 'Start with 193, add 7 from 79 to make 200, 200 plus 72 is 272. So 193 + 79 = 272.'

The beginnings of mental methods for two-digit mental calculation: two-digit numbers and single-digit numbers

In fact, before the *big value* strategies for 'true' two-digit addition and subtraction calculations (such as 56 + 27 and 60 − 28) are introduced, it is often a good idea to spend time working on two-digit additions and subtractions with *single-digit numbers*: for example, it is often helpful to foreground addition calculations such as 23 + 6 and 28 + 6 and the roughly equivalent subtraction calculations, 28 − 6 and 22 − 6. There are a number of reasons for making calculations which combine two-digit numbers and single-digit numbers a special area of consideration for dyslexic and dyspraxic children. First, the *key methods* for working with two-digit numbers and single-digit numbers represent a very natural progression from the *key strategies* which are used in working out the addition and subtraction number facts. Secondly, reasoning about calculations which combine two-digit numbers and single-digit numbers continues the process of building children's understanding of the number structures to 100. Thirdly, and most critically, adding two-digit numbers and single-digits numbers is an important sub-skill of other relatively demanding calculation situations. These include complex multi-number or 'string' addition calculations, such as 8 + 6 + 7 + 8 . They also include the *step additions* which underpin the ability of many dyslexic and dyspraxic children to generate times *tables* sequences, as well as their ability to work out 'unknown' *tables* facts from known *tables* facts (for example, 36, 42, 48; 7 × 6 = 36 + 6). Because the oral sequential memory of dyslexic and dyspraxic children is often very weak, many dyslexic and dyspraxic rely heavily on addition to figure out the harder multiplication *tables* – as we will see in Part V. Similarly, efficient subtraction of single-digit numbers from double-digit numbers is an important sub-skill of the ability to execute step subtractions backwards, as well as the ability to work out certain *tables* facts (for example: 60, 54, 48; 9 × 6 = 60 − 6). Again, these sub-skills contribute towards effective *times tables* derivation for the same reasons which were touched on a moment ago.

Addition: additions with two-digit addends and single-digit addends

For most children with specific learning difficulties, the most accessible two-digit calculations with single-digit addends are ones which do not require the skills needed to cross a decade boundary. Thus, for example, the answer to a calculation such as 32 + 7 remains within the framework of the 'thirties' decade. Calculations which do not necessitate crossing a decade boundary build very naturally on key understandings which children gain in working on foundation 'teens' addition calculations, such as 12 + 7, discussed on p. 000.

To recap briefly, the principal teaching focus in 'non-bridging' addition calculation work usually involves weaning children from slow, ones-based counting procedures and helping them to partition the two-digit addends so they can reason efficiently to work out the decomposed *units* addition fact: 32 + 7 = ☐ ➔ (30) + 2 + 7 = 39. Children respond well to oral and written exercises which highlight common calculation patterns – for example 2 + 7 =☐, 12 + 7 = ☐, 52 + 7 = ☐, 32 + 7 = ☐.

Additions through tens boundaries

For many dyslexic and dyspraxic children, the reasoning demands of addition calculations which require crossing a decade boundary – for instance, in a calculation such as 28 + 7 – are much more challenging than 'non-bridging' addition strategies. In fact, adaptations of one of two familiar strategies may be used to facilitate crossing the decade boundary. Some children prefer to calculate by *partitioning* the two-digit number in the way described above. For instance, 28 + 7 can be figured out by partitioning 28 into 20 + 8, splitting off and calculating the sum of the units, 8 + 7, and finally combining the sum, 15, with the 'tens' number, 20, to reach the answer, 35. 28 + 7 = ☐ → (20 + 8) + 7 → 20 + (8 + 7) = 35. Alternatively, 28 + 7 can be worked out by employing a version of addition *sequencing* or *cumulative* reasoning which is very familiar from prior '*through ten*' calculation reasoning. Instead of starting by partitioning 28, the reasoning process can begin by taking the whole number, 28, as the starting point for calculation, and then building a '*bridge*' from 28 to the next *tens* number, 30: 28 requires 2 to reach 30, 7 has to be partitioned into 2 + 5 so that 28 can be made up to 30, and the remaining 5 from the 7 is added on to 30, to reach the final answer, 35. In other words, larger *through-ten* calculations can be solved by using an extension of the big value 'harder number facts' *bridging-through-ten* addition strategy.

Although *grasshopper* dyslexic children often use both methods interchangeably, children with specific learning difficulties and significant calculation weaknesses usually do best when they learn the cumulative *bridging* model for adding a single-digit number to a double-digit number This is probably because the *bridging* model requires less working memory than the *partitioning* model does in this particular calculation instance. There are three main reasons for the relatively light working memory load of the *bridging* model. First of all, the partial calculations in the extended *bridging* model are easier than those involved in the *partitioning* model and the partial calculations are therefore more rapidly executed. Secondly, the cumulative *bridging* model proceeds in one direction and does not involve any complex 'backtracking' steps. Thirdly, as we have seen, efficient *through-ten* two-digit calculation is often required in cumulative contexts such as generating multiplication tables sequences (35, 42, 49) or in adding *strings of numbers*. It is therefore a particular advantage that bridging itself is cumulative and requires no 'backtracking' reasoning..

Teaching advanced 'bridging' addition calculation

Quite a large number of dyslexic and dyspraxic children, who have learned and have automatized the *key bridging-through-ten* addition strategy, actively enjoy the very manageable challenge of extending '*bridging*' to more advanced or 'grown-up' calculations. In fact, as the 28 + 7 calculation example, given above, demonstrates, advanced *bridging* reasoning is very similar to the basic *bridging-through-ten* strategy. The only real difference is the fairly obvious one that more advanced calculations, such as 28 + 7, require that a 'bridge' is built to the *next decade* number – to 30, in the 28 + 7 example – rather than to 10 itself. To ensure that children are able to extend basic *bridging* work as smoothly as possible, it is useful to check that they have internalized the 'pre-skill' number-structure understanding which enables them to quickly determine the '*next ten*' after any given two-digit number. (It is useful to note that some children with specific learning difficulties confuse *bridging* with *rounding*. Children need to be clear that the *next ten* after a 'low twenty,' such as 23 or 24, is 30, and not 20.)

Although most children rapidly grasp the basic idea that *bridging* reasoning can be extended in this way, figuring out two-digit-and-single-digit additions is also a skill which often needs to be quite intensively overlearned. Children who have learned to reason in single digit (maths facts) situations often revert to counting in *ones* when they meet larger numbers. This is possibly because most children with specific maths and learning difficulties have spent many years relying on counting in *ones* to solve arithmetic calculations and also because the counting habit typically re-emerges as a familiar, well-worn reasoning 'route' in situations which children experience as somewhat challenging.

The *basic bridging* game, described on p. 220, can be adapted to help consolidate 'advanced' *bridging* thinking. The particular advantage of cumulative, dice-based, calculation games is that they afford children addition practice which is fairly similar to multi-number or 'string addition' calculation situations. The basic game has to be extended to accommodate the addition of single digits to larger two-digit numbers. To do this, parallel tracks to 50, or 60, can be used in place of the more circumscribed basic track. Alternatively, rods may be placed on an empty *100 square* base. The extended track game, or *100 square* game, is played in exactly the same way as the basic game. (In the *100 square* version the rods are not allowed to transgress the 10 by 10 frame.) Although a 0–9 die may be used as usual, selecting a 4–9 die in its place will help speed up the game. Using a 4–9 die will also slightly tip the calculation balance in favour of additions which require the use of *through-ten* reasoning.

A simple 'pencil-and-paper' number track addition game

The *abstract track game*, referred to on p. 241, can also be extended to cover more advanced addition calculation. In this open-ended game, players take it in turns to roll a die, as usual, but players simply record their own running total in the consecutive squares which make up the very simple tracks:

Player A: | 9 | 15 | 22 | 30 | 34 | 41 | 45 | | | | | | | | ∞∞ |

Player B: | 5 | 9 | 18 | 24 | 32 | 41 | 48 | | | | | | | | ∞∞ |

Player A rolled '9' first. This was followed by die rolls of 6, 7, 8, 4, 7 and 4. Player B rolled '5' first. This was followed by die rolls of 4, 9, 6, 8, 9 and 7.

A Card War game

In a 'bridging' card war game designed to practise adding two digit numbers and single-digit numbers, each player should be dealt three cards from a well-shuffled pack of ordinary cards. After receiving the cards, each player should arrange his/her cards in order, smallest digit first, e.g. 2   6   8 . The first two digits should be moved aside to represent a two-digit number, while the third, and largest, digit card represents a single-digit addend: 2 6 + 8 . The player with the larger/largest addition total within a specific round (or 'battle') wins that particular round, and takes all the cards in play. As always, the overall winner of the game (the 'war') is the player with the greatest number of cards.

To help children acquire an intuitive understanding of the principle of associativity, very simple 'easy addition' tracking activities were suggested on p. 138. For example, 5 + 3 + 5 = 5 + 5 + 3 = 10 + 3 = 13. Tracking for easier addition combinations, such as components of ten, or doubles-combinations, is a very important aspect of encouraging efficient multi-number or 'string' addition. To support working memory weaknesses, children can be encouraged to 'cross out' digits as they are added.

$$⑥+⑦+⑦+④+8$$

$$6 + 7 + 7 + 4 + 8 \qquad = 10 + 14 + 8 = 32$$

As always, providing children with meaningful calculation patterns can help them to remember useful, efficient ways to reason:

9 + 7 =	8 + 5 =	5 + 7 =
29 + 7 =	28 + 5 =	25 + 7 =

Subtraction: two-digit numbers and single-digit numbers

Fortunately there are many parallels between the strategies which are most successfully used in two-digit and single-digit additions and in two-digit and single-digit subtractions. Like the equivalent addition work, the 'teens' subtractions (for example, 18 − 6) provide the model for relatively straightforward subtraction calculations, such as 28 − 6. Rather than counting the '6' back in *ones* − 27, 26, 25, 24, 23, 22 − 28 can be split into 20 plus 8, and the 8 − 6 can be quickly calculated: 28 − 6 = □ → (20 + 8) − 6 → 20 + (8 − 6) = 20 + 2 = 22.

$$28 - 6 \;→\; 8 - 6 = 2 \;→\; 28 - 6 = 22$$

TEN	TEN	EIGHT
		SIX

While *partitioning* is a calculation option which some children may choose to use to work out *through-ten* two-digit and single-digit additions, very few children choose to *partition* to subtract single-digit numbers which cross the decade boundaries. To solve a subtraction problem, such as 22 − 6 for instance, *partitioning* 22 into 20 plus 2 results in the usual awkward redistribution problems. To subtract a single-digit number across a decade boundary, it is much more manageable and obvious to *bridge back* through the previous *ten*. To use the *bridging* approach to figure out 22 – 6, 2 is subtracted back to 20, then 4 is subtracted further back still, from 20.

$$22 - 6 = \boxed{} \rightarrow 22 - 2 = 20 \rightarrow 20 - 4 = 16$$

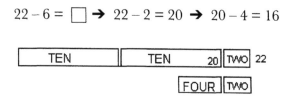

In the same way that the more advanced addition *bridging* strategy builds on basic *through ten* addition work, *bridging back* through decade boundaries builds on one of the *big value through-ten* subtraction strategies which was recommended in the earlier part of this chapter – namely, the *bridging-back-through-ten* subtraction strategy. The parallels between basic *bridging* and advanced *bridging-back* work can be made clear to children through concrete and abstract exercises which set out to highlight the patterned similarities:

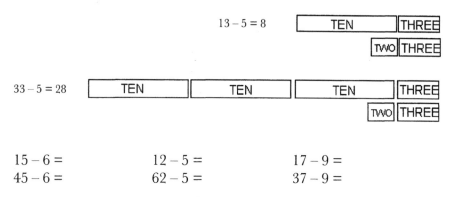

15 – 6 =	12 – 5 =	17 – 9 =
45 – 6 =	62 – 5 =	37 – 9 =

It is worth noting that many children with specific learning difficulties, who are able to subtract from *10* efficiently, nevertheless count back in *ones* when they are required to subtract single digit numbers from rounded decade numbers, for example, 30 – 6. Dyslexic and dyspraxic children very often do not make the connection that the *tens* making up '*tens-numbers*' can be 'split' in exactly the same kinds of ways as 10 in basic facts-of-10 work. Concrete and abstract work should be designed to make the parallels between 10 and the *tens* (or decade numbers) as transparent as possible.

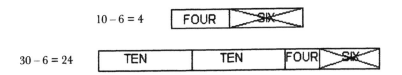

$$10 - 6 = 4 \qquad \boxed{\text{FOUR} \quad \boxed{\text{SIX}}}$$

$$30 - 6 = 24 \qquad \boxed{\text{TEN}} \quad \boxed{\text{TEN}} \quad \boxed{\text{FOUR}} \boxed{\text{SIX}}$$

In other words, the mental calculation understanding which concrete work should make clear to children is that it is the basic facts of 10 – the component facts of 10 – which help children to work out any subtraction of a single-digit number from a 'tens' number. The reasoning involved can also be explained in sentences, such as, 'The answer to $30 - 6$ has to be in the 20's because it is less than 30, and it is 24, because $10 - 6 = 4$.' Simple oral and written 'overlearning' work helps reinforce the essential 'tens knowledge' connection.

$10 - 8 =$ $10 - 4 =$ $10 - 7 =$

$50 - 8 =$ $20 - 4 =$ $30 - 7 =$

Since a 'subtracting back' approach is the key method for subtracting single-digit numbers from two-digit numbers, the **bridging** games which are recommended for 'advanced' *through-ten* addition work can be used in extended subtraction work, too. In a **concrete subtraction 'bridging' game**, players begin with an equivalent number of rod *tens* which are placed on matching rod *tracks* – for example, each player could start play with a rod *track* of 50. The object of the game is to clear away all of the rods from the track. Players take turns to roll a 0–9 die to determine the size of the portion of track which may be removed. For example, an initial dice roll, 6, means that a 'six portion' can be removed from the 50 track. The rod *ten* representing 40–50 (or the fifth decade) is removed and the remaining 4 substituted:

In the subtraction game, players cannot, in fact, physically subtract across a *tens* boundary. For instance, if a second dice roll indicates that 7 is to be subtracted from the 24, the player subtracts and removes the 4 from 24 first, then subtracts a further 3 from the $10 - 20$ stretch of track. In a **simple written number-track subtraction game** players also start with a given two-digit number (for instance, 50) from which single digit numbers are repeatedly subtracted. In the written game, the *start-out* number is recorded in the first square of a simple track. A dice determines the number to be subtracted, and each running total subtraction answer is recorded in the adjacent square along.

Player A Player A rolled 6 first, followed by die rolls of 7, 2 and 8.
Player B Player B rolled 2 first, followed by die rolls of 5, 6 and 9.

| 50 | 44 | 37 | 35 | 27 | | | | ⸰ ⸰ |

| 50 | 48 | 43 | 37 | 28 | | | | ⸰ ⸰ |

The **card war addition game** described above can also be adapted to practise subtracting single digits from double-digit numbers. In subtraction games, children usually prefer the smaller/smallest outcome to win each round.

CHAPTER 9

More on two-digit addition and subtraction

The partitioning or chunking model for two-digit addition

It will be remembered that the *partitioning* or *chunking* strategy is the *big value* 'true' two-digit *mental* addition strategy. As we have seen, the basic structuring principle of the *partitioning* model is that each of the two-digit numbers is split into its component values and the different values are calculated separately. In two-digit addition calculations the component outcomes are then finally combined: 28 + 35 → 20 + 30 = 50 → 8 + 5 = 13 → 50 + 13 = 63. Two-digit additions with sums below 100 are much easier to execute than larger addition calculations.

Working on additions to 100

As part of the earliest stage of working on two-digit additions, two important pre-skills may need to be introduced or reinforced. First of all, children have to be able to add larger values. In two-digit partitioning addition work children have to be able to add *tens* values: for example, 'What is thirty plus forty?' or 30 + 40 =   . This skill is not a feature of standard addition procedures. In traditional addition algorithms, as we have seen, all digits, whatever their real value, are treated as *ones* within the column framework.

From a teaching point of view, some of the games which are described in the previous chapter encourage proficiency at adding *tens* values. However, many children also benefit from additional pre-skill support. For example, in helping children with the concept and the mechanics of adding *tens* numbers, it is very valuable to show them that although a larger value than *ones* is obviously involved in *tens* calculations, a familiar,

281

basic fact still applies. To add 30 + 40, for example, 3 + 4 is the basic fact
but 3 *tens* are being added to 4 *tens* so 7 *tens* or 70 is the resulting answer.
This can be demonstrated by laying out the relevant values in contrasting
Base Ten material:

$$\Box\,\Box \atop {}^{\Box}\; +\; {\Box\,\Box \atop {}^{\Box}} \;=7 \qquad\qquad |||| \;+\; ||||| \;= 7\text{ tens} = 70$$

The simple sentence, 'It's the same *fact*, but a different *value*,' – which
can be used while children are working with concrete materials or with
abstract numbers – helps reinforce the core teaching point. The understanding that familiar facts, but different values, structure larger value
calculations can be underscored by demonstrating the calculation parallels between basic *ones* calculations and calculations involving particularly
large values.

$$\Box\,\Box\,\Box \;+\; \Box\,\Box\,\Box\,\Box \;= 7\text{ hundreds} =700$$

$$\square\!\!\!/\;\square\!\!\!/\;\square\!\!\!/ \;+\; \square\!\!\!/\;\square\!\!\!/\;\square\!\!\!/\;\square\!\!\!/ \;= 7\text{ thousands} = 7000$$

Although the central teaching focus at this point is two-digit addition,
young children, and children with poor number skills, generally enjoy the
feeling of power that this simple way of visualizing large value additions
gives them: 'So 3 million plus 4 million will be 7 million' is the excited
insight which often follows such very large value work.

Secondly, children may need to work on their ability to add 'teens'
numbers to decade numbers – for example 70 + 12 = 82. Working on
relatively simple two-digit calculations of this kind helps prepare children
for the second step of two-digit calculations. As we have seen, children
who are familiar with the structure of the partial calculations which make
up two-digit calculation methods, have fewer working memory demands
to cope with and therefore manage to learn the mental methods more
easily. Modelling calculations such as 70 + 12 with Base Ten materials or
Cuisinaire rods clarifies the reasoning steps which children need to take.

Working on 'tens-and-teens' additions has the further advantage that
it represents a manageable way of practising the partitioning model just

before children encounter more demanding two-digit calculations such as 34 + 35 or 37 + 48.

Structuring the partitioning addition strategy

It is important to ensure that the early two-digit addition calculation examples, which dyslexic and dyspraxic children with calculation weaknesses are given to solve, are carefully sequenced in terms of difficulty. This generally enables children to learn to add two-digit numbers with confidence. The key calculation steps are outlined in the specific teaching examples which follow. Some children will be able to progress through the steps, quite quickly; others will need time to consolidate each step. At each stage of difficulty, it is very helpful if the earliest calculation examples contain two-digit *doubles* addends, e.g. 24 + 24 and 36 + 36 etc. While the long-term memory difficulties associated with dyslexia and dyspraxia mean that it is unlikely that very many of the two-digit doubled outcomes will be remembered *by heart*, there are important working memory advantages associated with having children work with *doubles* two-digit addends. First, by the time children reach two-digit addition work, the doubles facts are usually well internalized and are therefore considered to be 'easy' facts to recall. Secondly, by employing the same number twice for each addend value, the 'load' on children's working memory is very considerably lessened. In effect, children have to remember just one repeated value rather than two different values. For example, 24 + 24 = ➜ 20 + 20 = 40 ➜ 4 + 4 = 8 ➜ 40 + 8 = 48. (Of course, it goes without saying that 'ordinary' non-doubles addends will always need to be given to children to solve later on, too.) All of the calculation steps which form part of a carefully structured approach to learning the *partitioning* addition strategy are concretely modelled below. It should, however, be noted that the majority of children are able to grasp the logic of the *partitioning* calculation steps with relative ease. This means that concrete materials are usually needed as support in the very first examples of each partitioning step, or stage, only.

Step one: Two-digit additions containing tens to 100, and ones to 9

Examples:
24 + 24 = ☐   32 + 56 = ☐

At this very basic stage of two-digit-plus-two-digit addition calculation, the emphasis is on helping children learn the fundamental steps of the *partitioning* addition strategy. In other words, children are encouraged to 'sort' two-digit addends into their component values and then add the values, separately, before finally combining them. Although most children quickly learn to work out calculations, such as 24 + 24 or 32 + 56, 'in their heads' it is often worth exploring children's preferred methods of recording the calculation stages, on paper, while the calculations remain 'easy'. Children who are not used to recording calculation steps will sometimes resist the request to record partial calculations later on, when calculation and working demands become more onerous and when children actually need the written support. One helpful tactic in this regard is to ensure that children have designated *written practice* sessions, as well as *oral mental* practice at working out similar kinds of addition calculations. It may help to inform children that one important aspect of mathematics is learning how to leave *records* of the ways we have thought and that 'real' mathematicians are trained to do this, too. Written methods of recording calculation can be presented as 'ways of showing how you thought'. Children can be helped to select or devise the method of recording the key calculation steps which suits them best. Examples of useful written methods of recording the partitioning addition strategy include the following most popular ones:

1. 24 + 24 = 40 + 8 = 48

2.
$$\overset{8}{\overbrace{24 + 24}} = 48$$
$$\underset{20}{\underbrace{}}$$

On the other hand, of course, it also needs to be made clear to children that developing genuine 'in the head' *mental* calculation skills in mathematics is very important. Written work should not be allowed to overshadow *mental* work.

Step two: Additions containing tens to 100, and ones to 18

Examples:
36 + 36 = ☐   27 + 33 = ☐   47 + 29 = ☐

The working memory demands of the second step 'tens and teens' calculations are slightly greater than the second step 'tens and ones' calculations, which are illustrated in the example above. Some children have to maximize working memory support in their attempts to figure out harder calculations, such as 36 + 36, and may opt to record each partial calculation step, particularly in the early stages of completing such work: for example, 36 + 36 = 60 + 12 = 72. On the other hand, a number of children with specific learning difficulties find it tedious and time-consuming to record each successive stage on every occasion that they are required to complete written work, but they may still need some support in recalling the initial *tens* calculation. One solution to the difficulty concerning how much children should write down is to introduce children to the increasingly common mental calculation convention of using a small arrow (→). The small arrow can be used to 'link' progressive calculation steps. It has already been used in this context in many of the calculation examples given in this text. It can, however, also be used to indicate that additional but 'internal' calculation processes have continued to take place. In 36 + 36, the partial calculation, 60, can be recorded and then an arrow can be used to indicate that the second 6 + 6 calculation, plus the further 60 + 12 calculation, have taken place 'in the child's head': 36 + 36 = 60 → 72. In this example, the 'arrow' represents the '6 + 6 = 12' and '60 + 12' part of the calculation.

Working on additions beyond 100

We have seen that the *partitioning* two-digit mental addition method requires that children are able to add *tens* numbers together. The ability to add together numbers of *tens* with outcomes beyond 100 (for example, 80 + 60) requires two additional skills. First, children need to be familiar with the principles involved in exchanging *tens values* from the *tens position* into the *hundreds position*. For example, 12 *tens* equals 10 *tens*, or 100, plus 2 *tens*, or 20, and therefore equals 120. Secondly, it is very helpful if children know, and are able to use their knowledge of, the *tens* components of 100. In other words, it is useful if children are able to 'bridge' numbers of *tens* through 100. For example, since 80 + 20 equals 100, adding any quantity of tens to 80 can be handled by making a 'bridge' first to 100. Thus, to solve the initial '*tens*' stage of a calculation such as, for instance, 86 + 75, children may choose either one of these two reasoning routes:

1. The *same fact, different value* route:

80 + 70 = 8 tens = 7 tens + 15 tens = 150

8 tens   7 tens   15 tens   100 + 50 = 150

2. The '*bridging*' route:

80 + 70 → 80 + 20 = 100 → 100 + 50 = 150

Of course, both reasoning routes may have been encountered before: '*place value*' exchanges feature in the *place value* work which was described in the last chapter. Secondly, it was suggested, earlier on in this chapter, that basic *through-ten bridging* work should be reinforced and extended by including reasoning *through 100*. However, many children with specific learning difficulties benefit from additional reinforcement practice at adding quantities of *tens*.

Step one: Additions containing tens calculations to 180 and ones calculations to 9

Examples:
64 + 64 = ☐   83 + 54 = ☐

64 + 64 =

Some examples of reasoning about and recording these two-digit addition calculation problems include the following:

(a) 64 + 64 = 12 *tens* + 8 = 128
(b) 64 + 64 = (100 + 20) + 8 = 128

(c)

(d) $64 + 64 = 120 + 8 = 128$
          $\overset{\wedge}{40\ \ 20}$

Step two: Additions containing tens calculations to 180, and ones calculations to 18

Examples:
$78 + 78 = \square$ $64 + 56 = \square$ $57 + 85 = \square$

$57 + 85 = $ ||||| ⋮ ||||| ⁚

Examples of ways of thinking through and recording 'harder' two-digit addition calculations include:
(a) $57 + 85 = 130 \rightarrow 142$
(b) $57 + 85 = (100 + 30) + 12 = 142$

(c) $\overset{12}{\overline{57 + 85}} = 142$
          $\underline{130}$

(d) $\overset{12}{\overline{57 + 85}} = 130 \rightarrow 142$
          $\overset{\wedge}{50\ 30}$

It is helpful to note that although many dyslexic and dyspraxic children prefer to follow each step of the *partitioning* model very carefully, some children intuitively devise the most commonly used *mixed method* of addition calculation in which *partitioning* is followed by *sequencing*. In the mixed calculation approach the $57 + 85$ example illustrated above is calculated by adding the *tens* first, $50 + 80 = 130$, then the *units* are added on cumulatively: $130 + 7 = 137$, $137 + 5 = 142$. As much as possible, dyslexic and dyspraxic children who use second-step *sequencing*, to combine a *partitioned tens* outcome with the *ones* values, should be encouraged to continue reasoning in the final *sequencing* stage rather than count on the *ones* values *in ones*. For example, $137 + 5 \rightarrow (140) \rightarrow 142$.

Working on additions of more than two two-digit numbers: 'string' additions

It is important to ensure that dyslexic and dyspraxic children are given sufficient examples of multi-number or 'string' two-digit additions to solve – for example, 37 + 47 + 42. Once again this is because the complex organizational demands and working memory demands of two-digit 'string' addition mean that many dyslexic and dyspraxic children, who are able to reason confidently to solve 'ordinary' two-number additions, nevertheless revert back to slow counting in *ones* when they are required to add more than two numbers together. Helping children feel confident about their ability to add many numbers together involves building on and combining three previously acquired skills. Firstly, as we saw above, calculation is often facilitated if children look for helpful calculation patterns. In the 38 + 47 + 42 example given above, selecting and figuring out the *doubles* 40 + 40 fact, first, could help speed up calculation. Children should also be encouraged to look for components of 10, 100 and so on. In this calculation problem, the two units digits, 8 + 2 equal 10. 38 + 47 + 42 → 80 + 30 → 110 + 17 = 127. Secondly, whenever children with specific learning difficulties remember to use patterns to facilitate the process of adding two-digit numbers – in other words, whenever they add values out of sequence – it is important that they remember which digits have already been 'added'. This is a particularly vital skill to possess in situations where children are required to add four or more two-digit numbers together. Children's working memory is protected in a simple way if they are encouraged to 'cross out' numbers as they add them. In the following example, the *tens* values have been added:

$$58 + 73 + 66 + 39 + 47 = 240$$

Thirdly, it may be helpful to offer a quick review of *through-ten* methods of calculating – it is especially important to ensure that children can add 'strings' of *tens* numbers confidently. The simple pencil-and-paper *bridging* track game can be adapted so that children have practice at adding lengthy sequences of tens numbers. In this game, a *tens* dice would, of course, be used:

Player A rolled 40, followed by 30, 50, 70 and 40.
Player B rolled 20, another 20, 70, 50 and another 50.

40	70	120	190	230				

20	40	110	160	210				

Emphasizing 'place value': vertical addition formats and the standard addition procedure

Most contemporary understanding-based maths approaches encourage children to record two-digit calculations horizontally, particularly in the early stages of two-digit addition and subtraction calculation work. The main advantages of horizontal two-digit addition layouts are that: children usually devise horizontal jotting and recording methods rather than vertical ones; horizontal layouts reinforce continuities with earlier reasoning-based work and horizontal layouts also seem to encourage children to remain cognitively active. In other words, as Karen Fuson (1992) points out, horizontal layouts encourage children to actively think about possible solutions. Children are less prone to reducing values to *ones* and then proceeding in purely routine ways.

In contrast, of course, as we saw in detail earlier, children in traditional maths classrooms are taught to add two-digit numbers in columns, using standard right-to-left procedures. While it is generally advisable that dyslexic and dyspraxic children are not taught standard procedures too early, it is also important to acknowledge that there are advantages to knowing how to use the standard formal procedures. We have already noted that the standard procedures are generally quite efficient, particularly as numbers become larger or as the calculation demands become increasingly complex (for example, when numbers of very different sizes require to be added: 47 + 1237 + 63 + 158). The standard procedures are also widely used and widely understood cultural conventions. Numerate adults and children have used standard addition methods – with slight variations, here and there – for many centuries. Dyslexic and dyspraxic children, like 'ordinary' children, often have an awareness of this, and wish to be taught 'grown-up' ways of calculating. For these reasons, many educationalists argue that children should learn standard addition methods, sooner or later, and certainly before the end of primary school. The Numeracy Strategy suggests that children should begin the process of understanding the way in which the standard procedures work in the latter part of Year Three (when children are 8–9 years old).

In brief outline, then, a very common argument about how primary school two-digit and multi-digit addition work should be structured overall is that:

1. Children should learn informal addition methods first. This is so that children acquire a good grasp of the calculation demands and difficulties entailed in adding larger numbers.

2. The introduction of standard addition methods should be delayed until children understand at least one mental addition method and until they are able to use it competently.
3. When children are conceptually ready for formal work, they should be introduced to the compact standard method for addition. Children should become proficient at using the standard method before the end of primary school.

While the broad thrust of these guidelines is very widely accepted, there have been subtle but important modifications in more recent understandings of how the shift from informal to formal procedures should be managed. Early advocates of informal addition methods assumed that an understanding of *mental* addition methods would allow children to learn the standard addition methods in a fairly trouble-free or seamless way. It is now understood that many children adapt to formal work best if they are introduced to the standard procedures in a more gradual way. It is increasingly widely argued that many children benefit from an intermediate period of working to solve two-digit additions by using *non-standard* column addition methods (Ian Thompson's 'low-stress' algorithms, see Thompson, 1999b).

In essence, there are three important characteristics of non-standard column-based addition algorithms:

1. The addition calculations are set out in formal-looking column-based ways.
2. Non-standard column algorithms proceed from left to right in the same basic way and direction as *mental* addition methods. Children add the largest value digits first (*partitioning*) or they add from the whole first number (*sequencing*).
3. Non-standard addition algorithms may be said to be 'low-stress' largely because no redistribution ('carrying') is involved.

It should be noted that some *grasshopper* dyslexics use a *sequencing* 'begin-with-one-number' approach to addition. The informal horizontal recording process can be translated into the more formal-looking vertical format:

1 (a) 38 + 38 = 68 + 8 = 76   (b)
$$
\begin{array}{r}
3\ 8 \\
+\ 3\ 6 \\
\hline
6\ 8 \quad (38+30) \\
+\quad 8 \\
\hline
7\ 6 \\
\end{array}
$$

The *big value partitioning* addition model also translates very directly into a column-based format:

2 (a) 38 + 38 = 60 + 16 = 72   (b)
$$\begin{array}{r} 3\ 8 \\ +\ 3\ 8 \\ \hline 6\ 0 \\ +\ 1\ 6 \\ \hline 7\ 6 \end{array}$$

3 (a) 576 + 396 = 800 + 160 + 12   (b)
$$\begin{array}{r} 5\ 7\ 6 \\ +\ 3\ 9\ 6 \\ \hline 8\ 0\ 0 \\ 1\ 6\ 0 \\ +\ \ \ 1\ 2 \\ \hline \end{array}$$

As mentioned earlier, one advantage of the *partitioning* 'low-stress' algorithm is that it is not very different from the standard addition algorithm. In essence, the difference between the standard procedure and the non-standard *partitioning* method of calculating rests on where one begins calculating – from the smallest value position or from the largest value position. The degree of similarity between non-standard and standard *partitioning* approaches means that it is not very difficult to introduce children to the standard addition method, once they are familiar with the non-standard partitioning algorithm. The standard procedure can be introduced as an alternative and quicker or more economical way of calculating. In the beginning, it often works well to allow children to make the choice about how they wish to proceed. For example, children may be asked, 'Do you want to begin calculating from the *tens*, or from the *ones*?'

Standard and non-standard addition column work, and dyslexic and dyspraxic children

Although standard calculation procedures have clear long-term advantages, there is some debate in contemporary maths-teaching literature about whether all children, including children who are very weak at maths, should have to learn the standard addition procedures. On one hand, the National Numeracy Strategy expresses the expectation that all children will learn the standard addition algorithm. On the other hand, however, there is some evidence that a small proportion of primary school children do not adjust well to learning the standard formal procedures. In The Netherlands, less mathematically able children are allowed to continue calculating in informal ways.

Although it is early days yet, the teaching evidence thus far is that the majority of children with specific learning difficulties adjust well to learning the standard addition algorithm, especially if the non-standard column *partitioning* method has been used. Indeed, our own teaching experience shows that many dyslexic and dyspraxic children become flexible enough to use standard and non-standard methods interchangeably, depending on the size of the calculation and depending on whether the calculations are presented as *oral* questions or as part of a *pencil-and-paper* exercise.

On the other hand, there is mounting evidence to show that there is a small proportion of children with specific learning difficulties who seem unable to master the standard addition procedures. Children with very severe left/right orientation difficulties, very severe sequencing difficulties and/or serious school-induced anxieties related to learning the standard algorithms, 'hate' the standard addition procedure and fail to make sense of it. It would therefore seem wise for teachers and parents to accept that dyslexic and dyspraxic children, who make endemic 'bug' errors in formal addition work, or who have a deep aversion to the standard addition procedure, should be allowed to calculate in the formal-looking, column-based, but non-standard ways.

It should also be noted that because it suits their particular way of visualizing addition problems, a number of dyslexic *grasshoppers* do best in formal multi-digit addition work if they are allowed to continue adding from the largest value position. Able *grasshoppers* often adapt well to what is often loosely called a *checking-ahead* model of column addition. In other words, children add each column in turn from right to left, checking ahead, first, to see if they have to adjust the particular column sum they are working on.

Checking ahead in addition:

$$
\begin{array}{r}
3\ 3\ 5\ 0\ 8 \\
+\ 4\ 9\ 7\ 5\ 6 \\
\hline
8\ 3 \\
\rightarrow \rightarrow
\end{array}
$$

The big value two-digit subtraction model: complementary addition

We have already briefly mentioned that learning to use the *complementary addition* model for two-digit subtraction is made easier if children have learned to reason *through ten* to solve subtractions such as $13 - 9$. A great deal of the work which is designed to prepare children for *bridging-up-through-ten* also builds the essential groundwork for successful two-digit subtraction. However, because much of children's early subtraction work – and hence their most basic concept of subtraction – tends to link subtraction with counting backwards, it is important to review many of the key concepts and skills which help children hold on to alternative *adding up to* conceptions of subtraction. In brief, to help children succeed at each new level of difficulty in subtraction work, children should be given sufficient opportunities to solve *compare* word problems (both *equalize* problems and *difference* problems), they should solve *missing addend* word problems, and they should give change, using the 'shopkeeper's' method.

As we have seen in some detail, the cognitive demands of subtraction are decidedly greater than those of addition, and children with specific learning difficulties usually require significant working memory support in two-digit subtraction work. To help make the process of learning two-digit subtraction as smooth as possible, it is important to establish ways of supporting and then recording the partial calculation steps involved in each type of problem mentioned above. Karen Fuson (1992) points out that most mental subtraction methods are harder to record in ways which make sense to children than mental addition methods. *Complementary addition* procedures and informal *compare* problem solutions present the particular problem that the partial calculations are, in fact, partial *additions* rather than subtractions.

Cognitive tools supporting 'compare' concepts of subtraction and complementary addition

For subtraction work, at the two-digit and three-digit level, it is possible to use one of two cognitive models, and two related diagrammatic representations, to help support the stages of thinking in the calculation processes, namely, Base Ten models and diagrammatic representations, and linear track or *number-line* representations.

The Base Ten model

At the two-digit calculation level, Base Ten materials are often used to support *partitioning* calculation models. In two-digit subtraction work, Base Ten materials (or indeed money) can also be used in carefully structured ways to support *compare* work and informal *complementary addition* procedures. For example,

'What is the difference between 18 and 35?' $(35 - 18)$:

In this example, '35' can be built from Base Ten materials and Cuisinaire rods can be used to cover the *18* portion of 35. The uncovered portion represents the *difference* or 'what is left' after 18 has been subtracted. Later on children can also use a diagrammatic representation of Base Ten *adding-up-to* procedures:

'What is the *difference* between 23 and 42?' (42 – 23):   ✗✗||| ✗|| ○○ = 19

                                                                    ↑
                                                                    7

Here, the number to be subtracted is crossed out. The difference, or what is left, remains intact and can be 'added up'. Money can also be used as a 'Base Ten' material. Some children enjoy drawing diagrams of giving change using the shopkeeper's model: 'Find the change from 40p if you spend 16p' (40p – 16p).

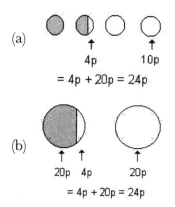

(a)
      ↑   ↑
      4p   10p
= 4p + 20p = 24p

(b)
  ↑   ↑   ↑
  20p 4p   20p
= 4p + 20p = 24p

In general, however, it should be noted that concrete and diagrammatic representations of Base Ten *adding-up-to* models are somewhat cumbersome to use, especially once children reach the level of three-digit subtraction. At the three-digit level the diagrammatic representations are also time-consuming to sketch. Nevertheless, the Base Ten subtraction model is a valuable model to employ with those children with specific learning difficulties who do not particularly enjoy, or understand, the linear *number-track* or *number-line* concept.

The linear number-track / number-line model

As we have seen in early subtraction work, *compare* problems, *target* problems and 'ordinary' subtraction problems lend themselves to linear *track* representations. It will be remembered that linear *tracks* include simple ones-based tens-structured tracks, Cuisinaire rod tracks and tens-structured bead strings. Simple, uncluttered *number-line* representations are excellent models for recording and supporting sequential or cumulative thinking. In earlier sections of this book, the 'emptier' structured number-line model features prominently as a supportive teaching tool. For example, the 'emptier' number-line is used to consolidate children's understanding of the relational nature of numbers and is a key tool for representing *through-ten* methods of reasoning. 'What is the *difference* between 23 and 42?' (42 – 23) can be figured out on an 'emptier' number-line:

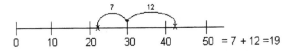

It has been noted many times that the *empty number-line* model features prominently in the Dutch Realistic Education maths approach and is used to support children in using sequential calculation procedures. In Numeracy Strategy materials the *empty number-line* model is also put forward as a potentially useful tool for supporting and representing sequential procedures. Although the *empty number-line* model was briefly illustrated, in the introduction, it is, in fact, the 'pared down' version or 'emptier' model of the *number-line* – rather than the completely empty *number-line* – which has been used and illustrated until now. In working with dyslexic and dyspraxic children, there are three main reasons which explain why *empty number-line* work is best delayed. First of all, children with specific learning difficulties often take time to develop an understanding of the relationships between individual numbers and the number structures. It is thus helpful for children to have a lot of experience at situating numbers in relation to the structures. The small demarcations representing *tens* (or *hundreds*, and so on) remind children of the importance of the structures. Secondly, most of the calculations which have been studied thus far have involved relatively small numbers. Drawing the *tens* demarcations is consequently not too much of a burden for children and represents valuable overlearning practice. Thirdly, and most importantly, our teaching experience has shown that children with specific learning difficulties do not understand the very abstract *empty number-line* idea if it is introduced too quickly.

However, by the time that children have reached two-digit addition and subtraction, they are generally ready for the *empty number-line* idea and there are good, pragmatic reasons for introducing it at this stage. The *empty number-line* is obviously very quick to draw. In contrast, drawing the *tens* demarcations for emptier *number-lines* takes time when larger two-digit numbers or three-digit numbers are involved. As calculations become more complex, children are much more likely to use a model which can be very quickly sketched than one which takes time to set up. Many children with specific learning difficulties are anxious about the difficulty of subtraction. It is often reassuring that a 'tool' which is as simple as a short line, which they can draw for themselves (and which does not even necessarily have to be very straight), can offer as much support as it does. Also, as contemporary Dutch educationalists point out, the *empty number-line* supports *active* thinking processes. Answers cannot be 'read off' in the way that concrete tools sometimes encourage. This means that using the *empty number-line* can form a central part of consolidating children's understanding of subtraction and of subtraction procedures. This in turn means that *empty number-line* use often helps children develop competent, purely *mental,* subtraction skills.

In all of the previous chapters, we have seen in some detail that dyslexic and dyspraxic children with maths learning difficulties often have a ones-based or *unitary* number-concept and that they have a deep-seated tendency to think of calculation as a process which involves counting in *ones*. This core and rather primitive understanding of numbers has two important implications in terms of *empty number-line* conventions. First of all, dyslexic and dyspraxic children frequently have difficulty with the idea that an empty horizontal line (————) is able to represent any chosen stretch of the number system and that one can place any individual number near to the 'start' or to the 'end' of the short bit of line.

(a) $36 + 10$ =

$$\overset{+10}{\overset{\frown}{\underset{\underset{36 \qquad\qquad 46}{}}{\bullet\qquad\qquad\downarrow}}}$$

(b) $36 - 10$ =

$$\overset{-10}{\overset{\frown}{\underset{\underset{26 \qquad\qquad 36}{}}{\downarrow\qquad\qquad\bullet}}}$$

Secondly, the natural inclination of many dyslexic and dyspraxic children is to draw individual ones dots or loops on to the empty line to try to exactly represent the quantities which are to be added to or subtracted from the focal number:

$$36 + 10 \quad = \quad \underset{\underset{36 \qquad\qquad\qquad 46}{}}{\text{ᴖᴖᴖᴖᴖᴖᴖᴖᴖᴖ}}$$

Alternatively, children may pedantically measure *imaginary* individual dots or loops to work out how big the required calculation 'loop' should be. For all of these reasons, it is generally a good idea to engage children in activities which prepare them to 'loosen up' and relax into the idea that quantities can be represented on a line in a very approximate way and from many different starting points. One simple, popular way of doing this, is to play yet another version of the **simple track addition game**, which has already appeared in a number of different guises and at various points in the book. In a basic version of the **empty number-line loop game** a target number is declared, for example, 50. Each player starts out with his or her own 'long' empty *number-line* which represents a 'line' from 0. The target is to reach 100 (or a smaller decade number). Before play begins, players construct a rough 'key' or 'guide' giving the approximate size of a 'ten loop' and a 'one loop'. Children need to understand that loops representing the quantities, in between, will be drawn in very rough proportion to these guides. Each player in turn rolls a 1–10 (0 = 10) or 1–12 die, draws an appropriate 'loop' and records the running total which results following each die roll. Most children will mentally *bridge* through the *tens*, as usual, to calculate *through ten* additions. Some children prefer to represent *through ten* loops on the line; others find this distracting.

Rough size of loops: 10 = 1 =

A loop game record:

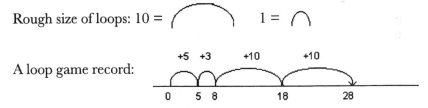

Two variations on the empty number-line loop game can be played. It is useful to play a target game from a starting point which is not zero. For instance, the starting point could be 35 and the target could be 90. The game is played in the same way as the basic game. Teaching strategies which may help children who feel insecure about the idea that '0' is not represented on the line include the following – children can be reminded that they are often asked to count from different starting points; they may locate the starting point and target for the current game on a tens-structures bead-string or they may draw a few dots to represent the numbers between 0 and the starting point.

In a second variation, just four 'loops' (each representing a dice-generated addition) are drawn on an empty number-line. In four loops children try to beat their opponents by attaining the highest overall total sum. In one version of four loops, children may begin from the same starting point; for example, they may start from 35. In a more exciting version the players each start from different starting points, generated by rolling two 1–6 die. Play proceeds using a 1–10 (0 = 10) or 1–12 die as usual. Players should play 3–5 rounds of the four loops game. In the example below, the player rolled a '4' and a '1' and started play from '41':

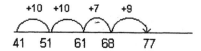

Similar but more prosaic pencil-and-paper activities can help prepare children for confident use of the empty *number-line*. For example, 'Add these numbers together. Show each number you are adding as a loop on the line drawn for you.'

$$7 + 7 + 5 + 8 + 4 =$$

Pencil and paper support in subtraction work

In two-digit subtraction work, the key issues to do with cognitive support and written recording of procedural steps turn out to be almost the opposite of those which arise in two-digit addition work. Whereas many dyslexic and dyspraxic children resist having to record partial calculations in addition, and wish to work purely mentally from very early on, children with specific learning difficulties often fear, and prefer to avoid, mental two-digit subtraction work. The danger in subtraction work is that children can end up relying too heavily, and for too long, on the security of working with tens-structured materials. The central challenge in teaching two-digit subtraction is to encourage children to reason increasingly abstractly. In early work, and whenever children reach a new level of difficulty, concrete materials should, of course, be available, but as soon as possible, children should be encouraged to use diagrams to solve subtraction problems and then pencil and paper 'jottings', or recordings, of key procedural steps.

In most progressive approaches to teaching primary school mathematics it is accepted that clearly legible diagrammatic representations of calculation steps are acceptable methods for children to show their methods of working out two-digit calculations, especially in the early stages. For example:

How much larger is 50 than 27?

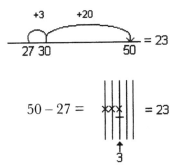

In completing early written work it also helps children maintain a 'feel' for the procedure they are following if they accompany their subtraction answer with the word 'left':

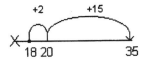

$$35 - 18 = = 17 \text{ left.}$$

Some children choose to cross out the 'subtrahend' on the empty number-line model:

In time, those children with specific learning difficulties who continue to need the support of diagrams to subtract successfully can be encouraged to draw them in a special 'rough workings' margin area, which they can create on the right-hand side of the page. Many children with learning difficulties are fairly quickly able to record the partial steps of complementary addition in numbers, with, or without, diagram support. For the reasons mentioned above, however, there is no one ideal method of recording informal compare methods of reasoning, or the complementary addition steps. Where 'plus' signs are used in recording the partial calculation stages in subtraction-related procedures, it is helpful to encourage children to make the sign as small as they possibly can – this helps children maintain the distinction in their minds between the *adding-up-to* steps in subtraction procedures and the 'ordinary' addition steps in addition procedures. For example, 'What is the difference between 15 and 40?' 15 ➔ 40 = + 5 + 20 = 25.

Finally, although it should be acknowledged that some dyslexic and dyspraxic children might not be able to figure out challenging subtractions without written pencil-and-paper support, all children should be encouraged to develop their mental subtraction skills as far as they can. Mental subtraction from *key tens*, such as 20, 50 and 100 should be made a priority for all children, including children who are especially weak at maths. Special activities for subtraction from 100 are outlined below.

A suggested sequence of teaching steps for two-digit subtraction

In previous discussions of subtraction we have seen that children are more likely to remember to use *complementary addition* procedures in subtraction work if the numbers in the subtraction questions are close together, for example, 50 – 47. In early work at each level of difficulty the numbers chosen for subtraction problems should be very close together and then, as children learn to reason 'upwards' more confidently, the numbers can be selected to be further and further apart. It should be noted that each stage of abstract subtraction work should be preceded by *compare* work and *target* (missing added) work at that particular level of difficulty.

Step One: Subtraction from rounded decade numbers; subtraction from one selected decade number*

(a) 50 – 47 = 3

(b) 50 – 42 = 8

(c) 50 – 39 = 11

(d) 50 – 34 = 16

(e) $50 - 27 = 23$

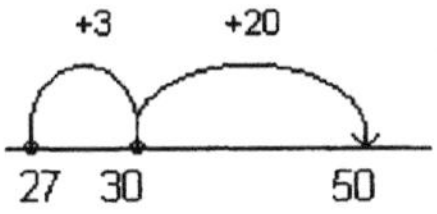

(f) $50 - 18 = 32$

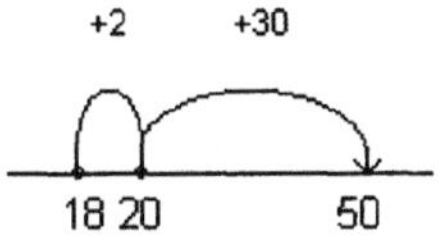

Step Two: Subtraction from rounded decade numbers; subtraction from a range of different decade numbers

(a) $70 - 65 =$

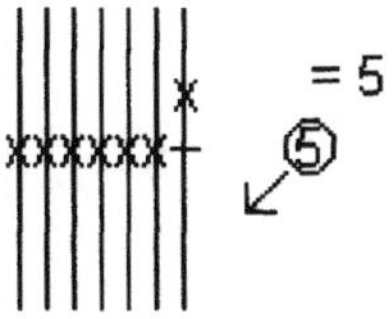

(b) $40 - 31 =$

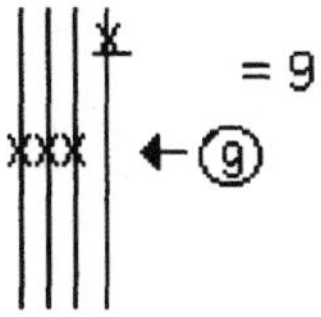

(c) $60 - 49 =$

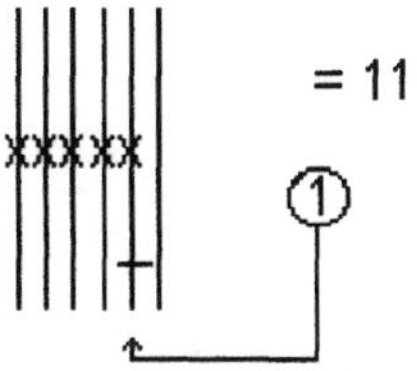

(d) $90 - 73 =$

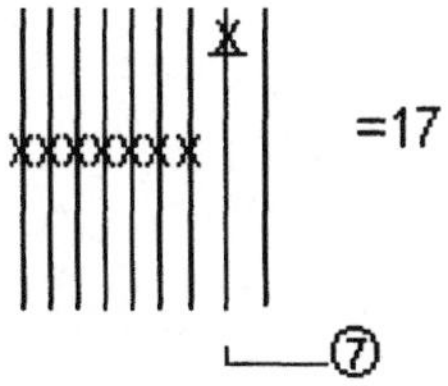

(e) $50 - 28 =$

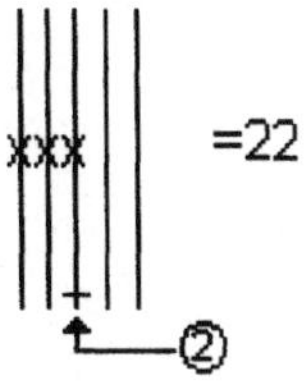

(f) $80 - 52 =$

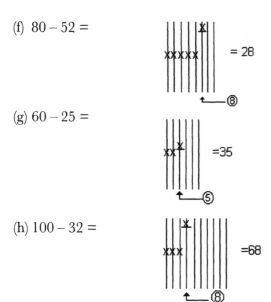

$= 28$

(g) $60 - 25 =$

$=35$

(h) $100 - 32 =$

$=68$

Step Three: Subtraction from tens-and-ones numbers; subtraction from one selected tens-and ones-number, 63

(a) $63 - 59 = 4$

+1   +3

59 60   63

(b) $63 - 54 = 9$

+6   +3

54   60   63

(c) $63 - 47 = 16$

+3   +13

47 50   63

(d) $63 - 41 = 22$

+9   +13

41   50   63

(e) $63 - 35 = 28$

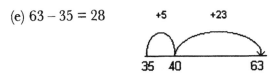

(f) $63 - 26 = 37$

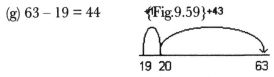

(g) $63 - 19 = 44$ {¶Fig.9.59}+43

Step Four: Subtraction from tens-and-ones numbers; subtraction from a range of different tens and ones numbers

(a) $21 - 19 = + 1 + 1 = 2$
(b) $34 - 25 = + 5 + 4 = 9$
(c) $67 - 48 = + 2 + 17 = 19$
(d) $46 - 23 = + 7 + 16 = 23$
(e) $51 - 16 = + 4 + 31 = 35$
(f) $72 - 27 = + 3 + 42 = 45$

'Adding up to' 100 and beyond

In many 'everyday' contexts, and certainly in many mathematical contexts, the ability to mentally subtract from 100 is a very useful skill to have. For instance, a facility at working out change from £1.00 gives children a great deal of confidence in shopping situations. The ability to work out the components of 100 efficiently has enormous benefits in advanced subtraction work. As Karen Fuson (1992) points out, children who are able to quickly reason to 100 have a very big advantage in learning to use *complementary addition* procedures to subtract two-digit numbers from numbers larger than 100, and they have an advantage in three-digit subtraction work, too. Reasoning to 100, or subtraction from 100, should therefore be practised as often, and in as many ways, as possible – in oral and in written work, in quick mental maths reviews within maths sessions, and in 'overlearning' homework exercises, too.

A great many activities can be devised for practising the two-digit components of 100. A particular favourite is called 100 Ping-Pong: The purpose of 100 Ping-Pong is to generate as quickly as possible the specific 'missing component' of 100 which matches any given two-digit number. For instance, if a questioner says, 'thirty-nine' the person targeted has to respond 'sixty-one' as quickly as he or she can. Ping-Pong should be played for a good few minutes, at least. Adults working with an individual child should give the child equal 'turns' at being the questioner. (Ping-Pong can, of course, be played to 20, 50 and so on.)

The particular advantage of the *complementary addition* procedure, in 'harder' subtraction situations, is that the *jumps or loops* beyond 100 (or beyond larger *hundreds*, and later, *thousands* etc.) to the start-out minuend, or target number, are very easy to work out. For example, $141 - 67 = + 23 + 41 = 64$. In three-digit subtraction problems, the first *jump*, or loop, will be to the next *hundred*. For example, $623 - 259 = + 41 + 323 = 364$. At this more advanced level of subtraction, the *empty number-line* model continues to provide very good working memory support. It can be also be used as a method for recording reasoning steps. The *empty number-line* can, of course, be drawn in a special margin area of the child's exercise book, if so required.

1. $1010 - 738 = 272$

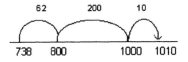

2. $2375 - 986 = 1389$

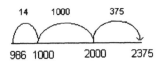

Alternative subtraction models

It has to be acknowledged that the basic conception that subtraction involves 'taking away' or reasoning backwards is such a powerful 'root' conception for some children with learning difficulties that their first instinct in most purely numerical situations (e.g. $100 - 67$) remains that of 'taking away' or sequencing backwards. This is often the case despite overlearning practice at using the *complementary addition* procedure in just such situations. Of course, children who devise sequencing back procedures and who are able to execute them without error present no teaching difficulties. As we have seen, many children who sequence backwards do make calculation mistakes, however. With such children it is generally wise to adopt a pragmatic approach. Alongside practice at using complementary addition procedures, the calculation 'bug' areas of easier *sequencing back* procedures can be targeted and worked on whenever children generate *sequencing back* solutions. Thus, for example, the steps in sequencing backwards from rounded numbers such as 50, 100, 600 and so on, are not particularly difficult to execute, or, at least, they can be relatively easily 'de-bugged'. To work out 50 – 27, for example, the first *jump* is the very manageable mental calculation *jump* 50 – 20. The next calculation *jump* is also not especially difficult since no challenging 'through-ten' thinking is involved. Nevertheless it is in figuring out this second component calculation that calculation 'bugs' tend to creep in. Instead of subtracting the *units* number (the 7, in this example) dyslexic and dyspraxic children frequently add the *unit* number, instead: 50 – 20 = 30, 30 + 7 = 37). The understanding that the *unit* number also needs to be subtracted or 'taken away' often needs to be repeatedly reinforced. Thus, if a child begins with 50 chocolates in a box, but 27 mysteriously disappear, 20 have disappeared certainly, but 7 *more* have disappeared, too:

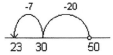

It is certainly true that *sequencing back* in 'regular' two-digit subtraction situations below 100 (for example, 54 – 27) is somewhat harder for dyslexic and dyspraxic children to manage, especially purely mentally, but practice at subtracting and subtracting again, and at negotiating the *through ten* calculation, will generally help to iron out calculation 'bugs': once more, it is the need to work out the second '34 – 7' step which generally causes working memory difficulties:

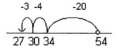

On the other hand, subtracting back from numbers larger than 100 generally proves difficult from the first onset calculation or jump, and many children's first instinct at this point is to give up. For children who do not easily adjust to the practice of adopting *compensatory addition* procedures as their 'global' subtraction procedure, it is this instinct which provides a relatively natural teaching 'cue'. In other words, just as overlearning reinforcement helps children learn that *adding up to* is a very easy calculation procedure in subtractions situations where 'the numbers are close together', so, too, they can be helped to see and accept that *adding up to* always works when 'the numbers in subtractions are difficult', or when 'the numbers in subtractions are very big'.

A few dyslexic and dyspraxic children (usually dyslexic *grasshoppers*) devise or absorb 'overshooting' subtraction strategies. This usually occurs once they have become more proficient at and more confident about two-digit subtraction. Children who generate a *compensation* solution but then 'forget' which way to compensate can be encouraged to try to resolve their dilemma by using *empty number-line* support. The internal or external verbalization which accompanies 'overshooting', and *empty number-line* support often runs something along the lines of, 'I'm taking 30 from 73, which leaves me with 43, but 29 is smaller than 30, so I've got to put back 1, 43 plus 1 is 44.'

73 − 29 =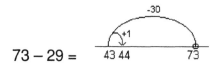

Vertical subtraction formats: non-standard column subtraction

In broad terms, the general arguments about the ultimate value of learning standard column methods, apply to multi-digit subtraction procedures in the same way that they apply to multi-digit addition procedures. From the outset, however, it has to be acknowledged, yet again, that subtraction is harder to learn than addition. The standard subtraction procedures are certainly much more difficult to understand and learn than the standard addition procedures. The transition to formal subtraction is also much more difficult to teach, and to manage, than the transition to formal addition. There are two main reasons for this. First of all, setting out numbers in columns suggests *place-value* based or *partitioning* methods of subtraction. This is not a problem in addition work – as we have seen, the *big value partitioning* strategy in addition and the standard addition algorithm are both *partitioning* procedures. On the other hand, as we noted earlier, subtraction methods which involve having to subtract values in separate *place value* columns inevitably introduce decomposition difficulties. Indeed, the subtraction methods which work as genuine *mental* methods do so

precisely because they sidestep the decomposition problem: they are therefore very different from the standard formal methods.

To help children acquire standard addition calculation procedures confidently, it was suggested that children learn non-standard 'stress-free' addition
methods first. It is very valuable to proceed in a similar way in subtraction
work. However, as we have seen, the transition from non-standard to
standard column addition procedures is able to occur relatively smoothly.
Unfortunately, a smooth transition is not as easy to achieve in subtraction
work. In fact, there are different possible ways to proceed in the transition
from mental subtraction methods towards more formal subtraction work.
The central dilemma involves deciding which non-standard algorithm to
introduce, first: in essence, it needs to be decided whether it is best to introduce an interim *non-standard* column stage which is continuous with *mental*
subtraction methods or whether it is best to prepare the way, from the beginning of column work, for the *standard* decomposition method.

Example 1: complementary addition in column form – a written mental
method.

$$
\begin{array}{r}
3\ 5\ 6 \\
-1\ 8\ 9 \\
\hline
1\ 1\ \text{(to 200)} \\
1\ 5\ 6\ \text{(to 356)} \\
\hline
1\ 6\ 7
\end{array}
$$

Example 2: Decomposition with meaning – a written, but non-standard
partitioning method of subtraction:

$$
\begin{array}{l}
3\ 5\ 6 \\
-1\ 8\ 9 \\
\hline
\end{array}
=
\begin{array}{l}
3\,0\,0\ +\ 5\,0\ +\ 6 \\
-1\,0\,0\ +\ 8\,0\ +\ 9 \\
\hline
\end{array}
=
\begin{array}{l}
2\,0\,0\ +\ 1\,4\,0\ +\ 1\,6 \\
-1\,0\,0\ +\ 8\,0\ +\ 9 \\
\hline
1\,0\,0\ +\ 6\,0\ +\ 7 \ = 1\,6\,7
\end{array}
$$

The decision about how to introduce 'stress-free' vertical subtraction work
in columns is a complex one but (for now at least) the decision is likely to
be influenced by two key factors – by the general mathematical ability of
the child, and by the nature of the maths approach adopted by the child's
school. At present, while there is such a big divide between traditional and
understanding-based maths-teaching approaches, the following
pragmatic suggestions may be helpful.

1. It is generally best to 'fast-track' children who are required to learn
   traditional subtraction methods at school on to the non-standard

decomposition methods. This means that they can progress on to standard *decomposition* methods as quickly as possible.

2. Younger children who learn maths in an understanding-based environment benefit from a slower progression towards *decomposition* subtraction methods. Such children do well if they learn the *complementary addition* or ' non-decomposition' stress-free column method first.

3. Some dyslexic and dyspraxic children do best if they avoid decomposition subtraction methods altogether. Dyslexic and dyspraxic children, who have severe working memory difficulties and severe sequencing difficulties, can find decomposition methods impossible to understand and it can therefore be entirely counterproductive to try and introduce them. A number of intrinsically able *grasshopper* dyslexics whose maths work is affected by severe sequencing difficulties thrive on 'low-stress' algorithms if they are allowed to use them. Both categories of children should be encouraged to continue to use the *complementary addition* method. It should be noted that there is anecdotal evidence that a number of dyslexic and dyspraxic children, who fail to grasp the standard decomposition method in their primary school years, are able to make sense of it later on – and often in their 'teen' years.

Work on standard subtraction *decomposition* can be accompanied by a classic and popular Base Ten decomposition game, Break the 100 square. In this game each player starts with a Base Ten 'flat' or 100-square which is placed on a HTU 'mat'. Players take turns to throw a 0–9 die to determine how many *ones* from the hundred square – or subsequent smaller values – they will be able to remove. Subtraction from 100 itself, and some subsequent subtractions, will necessitate 'decompositions'. The object is to achieve '0'. The winner is the player who gets rid of his or her 'hundred' first.

Two variations are also popular. Break 30 is a simpler game which is played in the same way. Players start with 3 *tens* ('longs') placed on a TU base. Break the 1000 cube involves challenging decompositions but again the rules of this game are essentially the same. To ensure that the game doesn't take too long, it is worth using a 4–9 die, or even, where possible a 1–20 die.

Multiplication and Division

CHAPTER 10

The theoretical debates

The 'times tables' debates

Because emotive and confusing *times tables* debates are regularly aired in the public domain, it is necessary to begin this chapter with a clear statement of the approach adopted here. It should be made clear that the approach to multiplication and division which is set out in Part V is consistent with the understanding-based approach which informs the whole book. In general teaching terms this means that the approach to multiplication and division is strongly conceptually orientated. It starts from the very familiar premise that children should understand the relationships involved in the operations of multiplication and division. It emphasizes that children should be taught to understand how multiplication and division 'work' and that they should develop a *feel* for multiplication and division relationships. Children should be also helped to recognize and solve multiplication and division word problems.

Understanding the relationships is not considered to be 'just' a conceptual matter, however: right from the outset the work on multiplication and division is fundamentally practically orientated. The approach recognizes that multiplication facts – like addition and subtraction facts – are very important building blocks. Ongoing experience in working to solve multiplication and division questions is structured towards encouraging children to come to know a range of specific facts *by heart*; in time, on the basis of an ever-deepening understanding of multiplication and division structures and principles, children learn how to derive increasingly difficult multiplication and division facts from the ones which they already know. They also learn to achieve this knowledge of the multiplication and division facts in increasingly efficient ways. Efficient fact derivation aids the process of automatizing many of the *tables* facts.

While it is clear that an understanding-based approach to multiplication and division has much in common with the reasoning and strategy-based approaches to addition and subtraction described in Parts II and IV, such an approach is very different from more conventional methods of teaching multiplication and division.

A central premise of understanding-based approaches to multiplication and division (and one which has already been hinted at) is that each child's understanding of multiplication and division relationships needs to be fully integrated with the entire process of building up a repertoire of known and 'derivable' facts. This is in marked contrast to conventional approaches in which the 'understanding' and 'knowledge of facts' strands of learning tend to become separated from each other quite quickly. In most approaches to multiplication, the promotion of children's conceptual understanding is considered to be a foundation stage through which children should move quite rapidly. This means that in conventional approaches to multiplication the more conceptually orientated foundation stage is soon superseded by abstract multiplication and division work for which children are expected to rote-learn the *tables* facts.

A second major implication of the emphasis on understanding – and of the related principle that each child's knowledge of the multiplication facts can, and should, be constructed in an understanding-based way – is that multiplication facts are not, and do not ever need to be, learned in a purely rote manner. This is in marked contrast to more conventional teaching approaches which rely on culturally embedded and traditional ways to help children learn and remember the *times tables* facts.

The persistence of traditional approaches to multiplication and division

At this stage it is important to note the seemingly curious fact that while there has been a marked and widespread shift in attitudes about how maths, in general, is best learned, in multiplication and division work it is very common for much more conventional views – particularly with regards to learning the *times tables* – to remain very powerful. Indeed, conventional views about *times tables* learning have been particularly resistant to change. In this regard it is also important to note that the *times tables* facts and concerns about whether or not children know the *times tables* tend to dominate debates about multiplication and division. On one hand, the whole rather complex area of multiplication and its allied concepts is often reduced to a mastery of the *times tables*. In this view, basic multiplication is 'in place' if children know their *times tables*: and because the ability to divide is believed to rest on *by heart* knowledge of the multiplication facts, the operation of division tends to be pushed into the background.

On the other hand, when discussions about multiplication draw particular attention to the importance of ensuring that children understand multiplication and division concepts and relationships, very common responses include, 'But what about the *times tables?*' or 'But how is understanding multiplication going to help children acquire a good enough knowledge of the *times tables?*' Even when teachers accept the principle that multiplicative (multiplication and division) concepts need to be understood, the argument that the *tables facts* will ultimately have to be learned *by heart* often ends up determining actual classroom teaching practices. Because of the widespread and enduring appeal of traditional ideas about *tables* facts learning, it seems important to explore some of the unique features about *tables* facts which contribute towards making traditional arguments so persuasive and so difficult for teachers to leave behind.

The broader cultural-historical suggestions and neuroscientific studies of Stanislas Dehaene help put some of the potentially divisive educational issues in a more objective (and consequently less emotionally charged) cultural and scientific context. With regards to dyslexic children, in particular, there is an additional and very significant bonus to pursuing these more broadly defined *times tables* debates. Dehaene's suggestive contribution to the *times tables* debates would seem to offer some insights into the particular and extreme difficulties which most dyslexic children– and some dyspraxic children – experience when they come to learn the *times tables*. In other words, the broader cultural-anthropological reasons which help explain why the *tables* are so widely rote learned, contribute towards one plausible explanation of the well documented fact that they are almost impossible for dyslexic children to learn that way.

The difficult task of rote learning the times tables sequences

One aspect of Dehaene's work which makes it relevant to the concerns of this book is that he is interested to understand why some aspects of conventional number-work seem to cause so many more problems for maths learners than other aspects. In his book, *The Number Sense*, Dehaene makes the important point that *by heart* knowledge of the *times tables* facts is considered to be a key element of basic number-work but *tables* knowledge is an aspect of maths which cause very widespread teaching and learning problems. Dehaene argues that an important feature of *tables facts* is that they are objectively difficult for the human brain to learn *by heart*: most people have difficulty trying to internalize the *tables* facts, in the first place, and they also have difficulty trying to remember them in the longer term.

In Dehaene's view, the explanation for these widely experienced difficulties lies partly in the nature of the facts themselves. The difficulties are also related to the structure of the human brain. First of all Dehaene argues that *tables* facts are very hard to learn because individual facts can easily be confused with other facts. Confusions occur through apparent but actually misleading associations with other facts. Dehaene calls these misleading associations 'false regularities, misleading rhymes and confusing puns' (Dehaene, 1997, p. 127). In the earlier maths learning years, as Dehaene points out, children often confuse multiplication and addition facts. Dehaene argues that it is more likely that an addition problem is answered with the corresponding multiplication fact so that a child may, for example, say that 2 + 3 equals 6. In fact, responses such as 3 × 3 = 6, 4 × 4 = 8 and 3 × 4 = 7, in which an addition answer is given to a multiplication problem, are also commonly given by younger primary school children. The important point, though, is that children often have 'a hard time keeping addition and multiplication facts in distinct compartments' (Dehaene, 1997, p. 129).

Dehaene also argues that *tables* facts are hard to learn because they are located within so many different *tables tracks* or number sequences. This means that trying to learn them is like trying to remember nightmarishly 'twisted lists'. For example, 7 × 6, understood as 7 *sixes* is not directly related to 7 × 5 or 7 *fives* but 7 × 6, understood as 6 *sevens*, is certainly related to 7 × 5 when it is understood as 5 *sevens*. As multiplication work becomes more complex, children often become muddled between *tables* sequences. In mixed *tables* review sessions it is quite common for a child to refuse to 'have a go' altogether: 'I don't know' or 'I've got confused' are very common responses from primary school children to questions which have been selected from a range of *tables* sequences. And primary school children quite frequently give a wrong answer from the 'wrong sequence' For example, a child may answer that 'eight *threes* are twenty-eight' or later on, and even more plausibly, that 'seven *eights* are fifty-four'.

Dehaene argues, further, that an important and very broad 'brain factor' which complicates and compromises *times tables* learning is that the tendency – or indeed the predisposition – towards making connections and seeking associations is a fundamental feature of the way the brain works. According to Dehaene, in general evolutionary terms, one of the distinctive advantages of the human brain has been its capacity to make associative links; but it is this very feature of the brain which can become a problem within the framework of very specific educational tasks such as *times tables* learning. In other words, the tendency of the brain to make associations reinforces the tendency of children (and adults) to register 'false puns' and 'inappropriate associations,' and this often results in the wrong answer being selected. To illustrate *tables* memory confusions, Dehaene quotes studies of the mistakes which students and adults tend to make. These studies show that when adults make mistakes – which they do 25 per cent of the time when 'harder' facts, such as 8×7 are presented to them – they do not tend to muddle operations or sequences in the way that younger children tend to do but, instead, they tend to give a wrong *tables* answer from the 'right' sequence. In other words they usually give an answer from the table (or column) from which the original question was selected (for example, a student may say that $8 \times 7 = 49$).

Learning the times tables facts: a common cultural solution

In his discussion of how the *tables* facts come to be learned, Dehaene explores traditional responses to the difficult task of helping children to learn these 'twisted lists' *by heart*. Dehaene argues that in most cultures in which there is an emphasis on very quick access to memorized *times tables* facts, the educators and teachers turn to the resource of children's *verbal memory* capacities. This helps explain the typical form that traditional *tables* learning takes. It is, in fact, relatively uncommon for *tables* facts to be learned as pure lists of facts. Instead whole *tables* sequences are usually acquired through chanting them in a carefully prescribed way. Thus many children chant, 'One times six is six, two times six is twelve, three times six is eighteen...' Others may be taught to chant, 'One six is six, two *sixes* are twelve, three *sixes* are eighteen,' and so on. The point which Dehaene emphasizes is that it is precisely because the *tables* facts are so hard to learn and to remember that they are so often turned into a form of chant or poem. In traditional *tables* learning, children learn the multiplication *tables* just as they learn a poem or song – for example, 'Twinkle twinkle little star' – by using their ability to remember patterns of sound. Thus the chant 'line', 'six *times* three is ...' should, in time, automatically evoke the response 'eighteen'. As Dehaene (1997, p. 130) points out, this whole solution to *tables* learning is 'not unreasonable' because, 'for the majority of individuals, verbal memory is vast and durable'. Indeed, Dehaene continues, 'who does not still have a head full of slogans and songs heard earlier?' For many children, then, learning the *times tables* in the traditional ways largely involves the educational gamble of relying very heavily on pure verbal memory.

The brain and knowledge of the times tables facts

In a recent scientific study of the brain, Dehaene (1999) has reported findings which seem to have important implications for discussions of how the *tables* facts are usually memorized. As we saw briefly in the introduction, Dehaene's study seems to confirm that the brain stores immediately known exact calculations – instantly known facts such as 6 × 3 = 18 – in verbal form. In other words, according to Dehaene's study, automatized and retrieved exact facts such as the fact that '6 *times* 3 equals 18' are stored in language or 'in a language-based format' and very possibly in the form of exact sequences of words. Dehaene's study also seems to show that memorized and immediately known maths facts are stored in a part of the brain which is known to make associations between words and which is situated in the left frontal lobe of the brain. Dehaene's study appears to demonstrate that the way immediately known maths facts are stored involves 'language-dependent coding ... as verbal associations' and in a language-association part of the brain (Dehaene et al., 1999, p. 284). At the moment, then, Dehaene's study appears to validate an assumption which traditional *tables* learning is intuitively based on, which is that an exact fact known *by heart*, and which can be recalled 'in one', is a fact known as a verbal association. Thus Dehaene is suggesting that to know instantly that '6 × 3 equals 18' is to associate the words ' six times three' very quickly with the word 'eighteen'. In making this 'in one' connection, a language part of the brain is accessed.

However, two important qualifications need to be made. First of all, acknowledging that immediately known exact facts are represented, stored and retrieved as verbal associations is not to say that traditional *tables-learning* approaches are the only ways or even the best ways to internalize the *tables* facts. Rather, what is illuminating to understand is that learning to recite the *times tables* is *one* way – and an obviously powerful way – of helping appropriate verbal associations to be formed. In order to try and speed up the process of encoding the verbal associations, and in order to minimize the risk of allowing 'false connections' to be made, *tables* recitation works to make the 'verbal links' as binding and as long-lasting as possible. Looking at it this way helps explain why traditional methods can be said to 'work' as teaching methods for many ordinary children.

The second qualification is that there are, in fact, some important drawbacks to the verbal association or chant-based approach. For example, since *tables* chants are not really very poem-like – they do not contain proper rhymes or other artificial memory hooks – they need to be very intensively practised. However, despite the many justified criticisms which can be made of traditional approaches to tables learning (and many additional criticisms will be outlined later), it has to be acknowledged that traditional tables recitation ultimately allows many ordinary children to 'just know' as a verbal association, for example, that 'eight times four is thirty-two' and that 'seven times eight is fifty-six'. By the time that children in traditional classrooms are about 8 years old, a substantial proportion of them will know most of their *tables* facts *by heart*. Sufficient repetitive *tables* drill will allow these children to generate the correct associations to most *times tables* questions and often in a matter of split seconds.

Dyslexia and learning the times tables

Unfortunately, as we have seen, Butterworth, Dehaene and others, have not directly studied the particular ways in which dyslexic or dyspraxic children represent numbers and number facts in their brains. However, it is extremely widely acknowledged and very well documented that dyslexic children usually know considerably fewer *tables* facts *by heart* than their age-matched and ability-matched peers. For example, many studies show that dyslexic children know fewer multiplication facts *by heart* and take longer to give answers to *tables* questions than their age and ability-matched peers. Teachers and parents also report that when dyslexic children learn or revise a 'new' *tables* sequence most of the previously known *tables* sequences disappear from memory.

In *Dyslexia and Mathematics* Tim Miles discusses some very significant findings to do with *times tables* learning which emerged from quite a large-scale and broad-ranging study of dyslexic children undertaken at Bangor University. Like other researchers, Miles found that dyslexic children have poorer *tables* knowledge than their non-dyslexic peers. Very significantly, too, he also found that many dyslexics 'respond in unusual ways when asked to say their *times tables*' (Miles and Miles, 1992, p. 12). Miles catalogues these unusual ways. In brief, Miles found that many dyslexics lost their place in conventional recitations, many preferred to step-count instead of giving the prescribed 'proper' recitational form; many allowed a chain of incorrect associations (such as 'six threes are twenty' to 'seven *threes* are twenty-three') and many switched into a different, wrong *tables* sequence without noticing that they had done so. Since these behaviours are relatively infrequent in non-dyslexic children, Miles found that he could score such traits as an indicator of dyslexia. Indeed, he refers to these traits as 'dyslexia-positive' behaviours (Miles and Miles, 1992, p. 12).

Miles's findings concerning 'unusual' *tables* behaviours are overwhelmingly corroborated by teachers and parents of children who are known to be dyslexic. It seems to be characteristic of dyslexic – and some dyspraxic – children that they cannot remember sufficiently accurately the stylized form which is intended to help them. Thus it is difficult for many dyslexic children to hold on to the associative structure (the *chant*, or *poem*) which holds the facts together. Dyslexics also typically fail to remember many of the vital step-by-step or line-by-line associations which join up to make the chant. Thus while the 'vast and durable' verbal memory of non-dyslexic children generally comes, in time, to associate a line-opening such as 'six *times* three' with 'equals eighteen' and, in time again, disallows a pairing of 'six *times* three' with 'equals twenty', this process breaks down with dyslexic children. In effect, what teachers and parents find is that no matter how many times the *tables* sequences are practised, the poor verbal memories of dyslexic children often fail to generate the appropriate association.

While out of the ordinary behaviour in *tables* sequence recitation may help adults identify and characterize dyslexic children, these observations also have enormously significant maths teaching implications. As we have seen, the central feature of traditional approaches to *times tables* teaching is that they use a chant-like form of verbal associations to help encode the *tables* facts in language and in a language association part of the brain. This is to say that traditional *tables* approaches rely on verbal memory resources to get the *tables* facts into the brain's long-term and verbally-based immediately known 'exact fact' storage system. But in relation to dyslexic or dyspraxic children, the question that necessarily arises is what is to happen to children if their exact fact verbal memory is fundamentally and consistently unreliable? Setting aside, for the moment, the broader maths-educational and understanding-related maths educational problems which often arise as a result of a *rote* approach to learning the number facts it has to be acknowledged that traditional *times tables* methods do not 'work' with dyslexic children in the most limited, instrumental ways.

The implications of the above considerations are clearly very profound. As Chinn and Ashcroft have argued for more than a decade, if dyslexic children are to be given reliable access to the *tables* 'building blocks' – access which many non-dyslexic children can and do obtain through traditional rote-learning methods – it is clear that they will have to approach learning them in an entirely different way. The simple and bald fact about *times tables* learning is that dyslexic children cannot and should not be required to learn the *tables* facts in any ˙ urely rote-learned way.

Rote learning the 'times tables' in contemporary classrooms

Until fairly recently nearly all children in the UK learned *tables* facts in very traditional and purely rote-learned ways. In more recent years there have been some important changes – although we have already touched on the fact that, generally speaking, the changes in multiplication *tables* learning are not as great or as sustained as they are in other areas. Since the advent of reform-approaches such as the Numeracy Strategy, growing numbers of children have spent time understanding the conceptual foundations of multiplication and have also been shown conceptually based strategies for working out many of the 'harder' *tables* within the *tables* sequences. For example, children may be shown that 4 x n (or 4 x a number) can be worked out by doubling n, and then doubling the outcome again; and that 6 x n can be worked out by doubling 3 x n (or 3 x a number). While this is true, however, it is also true that most progressive approaches to maths teaching – and this includes the approach to the *tables* facts contained within the Numeracy Strategy Framework – expect that all children will, in time, come to know entire *tables* sequences *by heart* and it is usually a long-term requirement that they are able to recall *tables* facts very rapidly.

As Steve Chinn frequently points out, one result of stressing the importance of memorized instantly recalled *tables* facts is that it remains very common 'whole school policy' – or common practice by individual maths teachers – to insist that children learn the *tables* sequences in the familiar, chant-like ways. Indeed, informal research shows that a number of schools working within a broadly understanding-based framework, such as the Numeracy Strategy Framework, continue to emphasize rote-learned *tables* 'lists' from the very earliest stages of working on multiplication.

Some of the drawbacks of rote-learning the tables facts

It is important to understand that for all primary school children, rote *times tables* learning actually represents a very significant transition in maths learning terms. Over many years, serious concerns have been expressed about the impact of an overemphasis on rapid automatized responses to *tables* facts questions. Many writers have noted that the introduction of rote-learned multiplication *tables* catapults children into a new kind of mathematical world. In the 'pre-*tables*' world young primary school children generally begin by becoming familiar with addition and subtraction (and sometimes, multiplication) facts in quite a gradual way. In many instances, and sometimes for quite a long time, children are permitted to use their fingers or other simple counting-based strategies to work out the addition or subtraction (or multiplication) facts which they do not yet know. In contrast, a central assumption of *rote* approaches to learning the *tables* facts is that children will know the facts 'in one'.

When rote *tables* learning is introduced, it is generally a requirement that children will quickly give the answers from memory without engaging in active and logical thinking at all. This means that when *by heart* learning of the tables sequences are introduced, many children do not easily make the link between these 'special' and rather ritualized verbal associations and the knowledge which they already have about working with repeated groups. As Dehaene points out, some children manage this 'major upheaval' in the mental arithmetic system remarkably well. Children with good verbal memories for number fact associations manage to learn the *tables* facts *by heart* relatively easily. Although it would seem that many young children initially lose sight of what the *tables* sequence lists 'mean' when they are required to rote learn them, some children manage to reintegrate rote learned *tables* knowledge with what they have learned (and continue to learn) about multiplication in general, and therefore manage to regain and retain a *feel* for what the *tables* facts are really all 'about'.

For others, though, the transition is much more problematic. The new emphasis on rapidly recalled facts can mean that children do not acquire or regain any sense of what the *tables* 'associations' mean. As Dehaene (1997, p. 126) points out, an emphasis on memorized facts can mean that children 'lose their intuitions about arithmetic in the process'. National assessments of children's arithmetic abilities and numerous independent studies have found that a number of children who know their *times tables* nevertheless fail to arrive at correct answers to simple multiplication word problems and have difficulty applying their *tables* knowledge to figure out division questions and division word problems. In other words, many children do not recognize situations in which their *tables* knowledge applies. Studies also show that reliance on rote-learned associations can lead to a loss of flexible thinking. Thus children who have begun to 'lose their intuitions' often respond to quite simple and easily visualized questions such as 'What are three *fours*?' with answers such as 'But I haven't learned any *four times tables*' or even, and much more humiliatingly,

'But I've forgotten all of my *fours*.' It is not uncommon for children who have had difficulty learning the *tables* sequences to respond to a question such as 'What are three *fours*?' with the further question, 'Is that about the *times tables*?' and then decline to give a response.

'Refusals' to 'have a go' at answering multiplication and division questions are especially common among dyslexic and dyspraxic children. For example, in assessment situations it is particularly prevalent for dyslexic and dyspraxic children to make 'no attempt' to answer multiplication and division questions when it is apparent that *by heart* knowledge is required; but dyslexic and dyspraxic children also commonly fail to 'have a go' at answering multiplication and division questions when they are given time to figure them out. As Steve Chinn (1995) points out, many children with learning difficulties feel that they do not understand multiplication and division and prefer 'not to try than to fail'. Division questions, in particular, can make primary school children with specific learning difficulties anxious and even tearful; Steve Chinn affirms that division questions which are given in quite low-key assessment situations continue to 'upset' some secondary school aged (Year Seven) dyslexic pupils. It is this loss of an often quite hard-won *feel* for numbers and the discoveries that working with numbers involve which can lead to children experiencing their first serious and often worrying difficulties with maths. As most of the researcher-theorists who are concerned to explore how children learn about multiplicative reasoning point out, children quite frequently begin to fail in maths at the very point at which they are required to master multiplication and division. This observation very often applies to dyslexic and dyspraxic children.

A note on dyspraxia and the times tables

While much dyslexia-related maths literature has explored the dyslexic child's well-known problems learning the *times tables*, there is no comparable body of writing on how dyspraxic children fare in relation to *times tables* learning. Of course one aspect to bear in mind is the very important fact that dyslexia and dyspraxia are often cormorbid. Many dyspraxics have at least some 'dyslexic' processing difficulties, many dyspraxics have difficulties with verbally encoded maths facts and many dyspraxics consequently experience typically 'dyslexic' *tables* learning difficulties.

However while it is fair to say that the majority of dyslexic children have difficulty remembering rote-learned and verbally encoded facts, one cannot make such a general statement about dyspraxic children. In fact, as we have seen, a somewhat different pattern seems to apply to a small but significant number of dyspraxic children. While it is often the case that dyspraxic children have some difficulty with all kinds of rote-learning and that many dyspraxic children are therefore slower to rote-learn the *tables* facts than their peers, concerted overlearning practice can, in time, help some dyspraxic children achieve very good *tables* knowledge. On the other hand, the kinds of multiplicative weaknesses which are shown by many dyspraxic children very often relate to the subtler understanding-related aspect of rote *times tables* learning which were touched on, above. In general terms, the dyspraxic child's rote-learned knowledge of the *tables* often seems to be achieved at the cost of understanding. Thus dyspraxic children may be able to give 'rapidly recalled' answers to straightforward and familiar *tables* 'cues' such as $5 \times 4 = ?$ But many are unable to apply their *tables* skills to division calculations; many fail to work out the simplest multiplication puzzles ($\square \times 6 = 36$); many cannot solve word problems involving multiplication or division; and many struggle to make up word problems of their own to fit simple multiplication or division calculations. To sum up, then: while some dyspraxic children are able to rote-learn the *times tables*, the 'knowledge' that they gain in the process is often quite inflexible knowledge and is therefore of limited real benefit.

Understanding-based approaches to learning multiplication and division

A restatement of basic principles

Although there is a somewhat disheartening tendency in many otherwise progressive classrooms is to rush towards *rote* methods of learning the *tables*, there are also classrooms in which multiplication and division are taught in a predominantly or consistently understanding based way. As we saw in the introduction to this chapter, the starting point for 'non-traditional' and understanding-based approaches to teaching multiplication and division is that children should understand the rather new aspect of mathematical thinking that basic *multiplicative* reasoning (or reasoning about multiplication and division) involves. In simple terms, an understanding of *multiplicative* reasoning can be seen to involve three equally significant aspects:

1. an understanding of *multiplicative* relationships (the concepts of multiplication and division);

2. an ability to recognize and solve multiplication and division word problems;
3. an ability to quickly work out or know specific multiplication and division facts.

In fact, as we have also suggested, all three aspects are complexly interrelated in the learning process: understanding *multiplicative* relationships will be found to contribute towards, but also to develop through, practical problem-based and abstract number-based reasoning activities.

We have already seen that it is the third aspect, the 'facts' aspect, which traditional approaches consider to be the most important and hard part of learning about multiplication and it is certainly considered to be the aspect which needs most practice. Understanding, by contrast, is believed to be the easy part and it is thought that 'the understanding part' should be covered as rapidly as possible within the framework of the overall teaching programme. Thus, in what is essentially a *top-down* approach to the question of understanding multiplication, specific facts are illustrated, often pictorially, so that children can be given some access to what the facts 'mean'.

For example, $3 \times 4 = 3$ groups of $4 = $

A common premise of the traditional view on multiplication is that a limited experience of practical demonstrations or of pictorial illustrations will serve to render the meaning of multiplication and multiplication facts sufficiently transparent and that children will be able to apply this understanding to solving word problems, as well.

In recent years there has been a great deal of research which has challenged these widely held conventional assumptions. Important classroom-based studies show that the conceptual aspects of multiplication are not nearly as transparent or easy-to-understand as traditional approaches believe. In fact the reverse is found to be closer to the truth: on careful analysis, *multiplicative* reasoning is shown to be complex, many-faceted, difficult to grasp, and a form of reasoning which takes time for almost all children to make sense of. Classroom studies also show that mathematically less able children – and this includes dyslexic and dyspraxic children with maths learning difficulties – need considerable and quite lengthy support to acquire a reasonable grasp of multiplication and division. These findings have important implications. At the very least the findings mean that appropriate teaching needs to be better informed than it has tended to be in the past. As the very influential researcher and writer Judith Anghileri (1995c, p. 78) writes, 'Detailed analysis of some of the complexities inherent in the introduction of multiplication and division will help teachers to support and develop children's understanding.' Since dyslexic and dyspraxic children often have a particularly hard time trying to understand the concepts of multiplication and division, it is all the more necessary and urgent to set out to understand why *multiplicative* reasoning can be so hard for children .

For the sake of clarity, the difficulties which many primary school children experience in mastering multiplication and division have been brought together under two broad headings: conceptual difficulties, which include aspects 1 and 2 above; and execution difficulties which cover the broad range of difficulties which children often experience when they are required to produce multiplication and division answers.

Conceptual difficulties in making sense of multiplication

Multiplication as a difficult concept to grasp

The essential foundation and radically new aspect of *multiplicative* reasoning is that it is based on the idea of working with equal-sized groups or sets. This idea is usually introduced to children in its most accessible form as the repeated addition of equal-sized groups (the repeated addition of *repeated groups*). However, many six- to nine-year-old children have difficulty understanding and holding on to the new idea of working with groups as 'units' – that, for example, a *tables* sequence such as the *three times table* involves working, in a consistent way, with repeated units of *three*. A 'pre-group' mode of thinking in which groups are actually seen as *ones* often interferes with children's early thinking in multiplication. Many children struggle with the relatively simple task of interpreting a concrete arrangement of *threes* – their uncertainty seems to lie, in part, in an unresolved cognitive conflict between 'three *ones*' and 'one *three*'. At a slightly later stage, children will often add (or subtract) *one* in response to a group-based question such as, 'If three *threes* are nine, what are four *threes*?' and children who have had insufficient concrete experience of working with groups interpret abstract multiplication problems in a variety of *ones*-based ways. For example, some children draw individual dots and then count the dots individually in response to a question such as, 'What are four *threes*?' Others fail to apply the *repeated groups* idea to abstract multiplication questions or word-problem situations. In responding to questions such as, 'What is 4 *times* 3?' or 'I have 4 boxes and there are 3 sweets in each box,' such children struggle to hold on to the idea that one number in the multiplication question refers to the number of objects in each equal-sized set while the other number refers to the overall number of sets. Instead, they usually model or interpret multiplication situations as much simpler addition equations: thus 4×3, or 4 groups of 3, is interpreted as one group of 4 and one group of 3 and this is represented concretely as:

4 'add' 3:

The difficult language of multiplication, and its symbolic representation

The language of multiplication can also create difficulties. Much of Judith Anghileri's work focuses on what she describes as the 'scope and complexity' of the different forms of language used in early multiplication teaching (Anghileri, 1997, p. 43). First of all, Anghileri makes the important point that mathematically correct terms such as *multiply* and *multiplied by* and the more colloquial word *times* contain important 'translation' ambiguities. Strictly, 3 *multiplied by* 4 or three *times* 4 means 3 taken 4 *times* or $3 + 3 + 3 + 3$. On the other hand, because children are usually offered some very basic practical – or pictorial – *repeated group* experience, it is nowadays more common to interpret 3×4 as 3 *groups of* 4 or $4 + 4 + 4$. This way of interpreting 3 *multiplied by* 4 fits well with the other common and helpful translation of 3×4 as 3 *fours*. Although the different interpretations naturally make no difference to the final outcome, confusions can arise in the early and critical stages if adults unwittingly interpret *multiply* and *times* in a way which is different from the meanings that children are trying to give them.

Second of all, mathematically correct terms such as *multiply* and *divide* are particularly opaque terms which may require 'translating' for some time if children are to understand them. Children who have not fully grasped the *repeated groups* idea often fail to understand the abstract language of multiplication. Indeed, when mathematically correct language is used too early, children will often lose any growing *feel* for what difficult multiplication relationships are about.

Thirdly, when children do not understand the *repeated groups* basis of multiplication, the abstract multiplication sign, '×', can be difficult to interpret. As we have seen, children regularly interpret a multiplication sentence, such as 4 × 3, as the basic addition relationship, 4 + 3. Some children know as a rote-learned fact that 3 × 4 '*means*' 3 *times* 4 and that 3 *times* 4 equals 12 but still model an array of 3 objects plus 4 objects to illustrate the 'meaning' of 3 x 4, with concrete objects, or offer a word problem involving an additive relationship to 'match' the number sentence 3 × 4. Not infrequently, children who are asked to model or demonstrate what '3 × 4' (or 'three *times* four') means will ask for sufficient concrete materials to construct a physical '×' sign, and will produce the array:

$$3 \times 4 = \quad \begin{matrix} \circ \\ \circ \;\; \circ \end{matrix} \quad \begin{matrix} \circ \;\; \circ \\ \circ\circ \\ \circ\circ \\ \circ \;\;\;\; \circ \end{matrix} \quad \begin{matrix} \circ \; \circ \\ \circ \; \circ \end{matrix}$$

Word problems

Children's difficulties with basic *multiplicative* relationships are often evident in the difficulties they experience in trying to solve simple word problems which require multiplicative solutions. The most straightforward *multiplicative* word problems relate closely to the fundamental *repeated groups* structure of multiplication and division relationships. Problems such as the very simple multiplication problem, '3 bags of sweets; each bag contains 4 sweets; how many sweets altogether?' are called *equivalent group problems*; they involve, in a recognizable form, 3 groups of 4. As suggested above, however, children who have not mastered the 'groups of groups' relationship will believe that the problem situation refers to one set of 3 sweets and a further set of 4 sweets and will therefore add rather than multiply (or add, repeatedly). Children who sense that a basic additive relationship is not involved but who cannot clearly visualize the *repeated groups* of four will often ask for interpretative help. For example, 'Is it "timesing" or adding?' or 'What shall I do, use "*tables*" or add?' are the kinds of questions frequently asked by children with a fragile hold on *multiplicative* reasoning. (At this point it should be noted that other, more difficult *multiplicative* word-problem forms are covered later, on p. 373.)

Conceptual difficulties in making sense of division

Introducing division

Although many traditional maths approaches cover the topic of basic division as a further and distinct section of work, which is usually introduced after basic multiplication has been taught, it is now increasingly common for multiplication and division to be taught alongside each other. Since the teaching approach to basic multiplication and division which is described in this book rests on the premise that they are best understood together, it makes sense to outline children's conceptual difficulties with division alongside the description of their conceptual difficulties with multiplication.

It is widely accepted that children experience greater all-round difficulties with division than with multiplication. As we have noted, it is also quite commonly assumed that multiplication is the sole key to division and that children who can *multiply* can therefore *divide*. 'But you know this *times table*,' is a common response to a child baffled by a division question. While an understanding of multiplication is part of the key to division, division also has some of its own unique conceptual difficulties. It is consequently important to outline some of the more urgent problems which children often experience with many aspects of division work

In very basic conceptual terms, division, like multiplication, is based on the fundamental structure of equal-sized groups. As Anghileri (1999) explains, multiplication involves 'putting together equal groups' and division involves 'reversing the procedure and splitting the total back into groups'. In essence, multiplication involves putting groups together, to achieve a new outcome, and division involves taking numbers and splitting them apart into equal-sized groups. As we have seen, understanding the 'repeated addition of *repeated groups*' idea is hard enough for many children to come to terms with. Division, however, has an additional difficulty which is that the 'total', which is now the starting point, can be 'split' in one of two conceptually different ways. Making sense of division, in other words, involves making sense of *two* ideas of division:

1. According to one idea of division, an example like 12 ÷ 3 may be solved by *sharing* 12 into 3 groups. This is the most commonly demonstrated, frequently invoked concept of division and is called the *sharing* or 'partitive' concept of division. In *sharing* it is the size of the 3 equal-sized groups which has to be worked out.
2. In the other idea of division, the total 12 in 12 ÷ 3 is 'split' into 'prestructured' groups of 3. This is the '*grouping*' or 'quotitive' concept of division which until recently has been less widely understood by teachers and less frequently modelled by adults for children. In the *grouping* idea it is the number of equal-sized groups which has to be worked out; the size of the groups is already known.

A consideration of the two concepts of division

Although this is now changing – particularly under the influence of the Numeracy Strategy and other progressive approaches – the traditional approach to the concept of division has been to link it to one concept, that of *sharing*. In large part this is because *sharing* is a common and therefore meaningful 'everyday' experience. However, the *sharing* experience and concept is not, in fact, particularly easy for children to invoke in trying to solve division problems such as 12 ÷ 4, or even '12 sweets shared between 4 children; how many sweets does each child get?' – at least, not without using concrete materials. This is partly because the most intuitive, popular, and widely modelled understanding of sharing visualizes the 'splitting' process in a very basic 'direct counting' or 'dealing cards' form. To solve 12 ÷ 3, the total, or 12, is often understood to be shared one-by-one into the three different groups until all 12 have been distributed or 'fairly shared'. It is only at the end of the *sharing* process that the unknown quantity in each of the groups can be determined by mechanically counting the 'shares'. While this intuitive *sharing* model is pragmatic and provides an important very early experience of 'fair shares' and 'equal groups' it is also a very limiting idea of division. The reason for this is that this primitive *sharing* model, in which *ones* are distributed one-by-one, fails to help children develop a logical and groups-based (or *multiplicative*) idea of division – indeed, the very nature of the *ones*-based 'dealing' process tends to obscure the relationship between division and multiplication.

Sharing can, of course, be taught in more sophisticated *multiplicative* ways. For example, children can be encouraged to keep track of the number of shared 'rounds' which make up a basic 'dealing cards' *sharing* model: in 12 ÷ 4, 3 'rounds' or groups of 4 can be shared out between 4. Or teachers may help children understand and visualize the concept of *sharing* through the process of trying to 'guess' the likely size of 'fair shares' and then having children check the accuracy of the 'guess'. But the 'dealing in rounds' *sharing* model is still difficult for many children to visualize without concrete support; and although the guessing and checking model is (as we will see), one which children will need to develop, it is conceptually particularly challenging as a first model of division. This is because working out the size of an unknown 'fair share' (group or *table*) relies on quite a strong intuitive grasp of multiplication and places a large burden on working memory.

Nowadays, in contemporary understanding-based approaches to maths learning, it is much more common for teachers to teach both of the concepts of division. In fact, as Anghileri and many other researchers have found, most children find *grouping* related questions such as 'How many *fours* are there in 12?' rather easier to model or visualize, and therefore to solve, than the *sharing* concept of division. Introducing division work by exploring the *grouping* model of division can help children begin the process of making sense of division as the 'reverse' of multiplication and this can pave the way for an understanding of the more challenging process of *sharing*.

Nevertheless, the fact that there are two basic concepts of division is certainly one of the reasons that children find division very difficult to master. While concentrating on *sharing* alone does not help children build a flexible understanding of division and often makes the earliest division work unnecessarily difficult for children, making sense of two concepts of division, and keeping two concepts 'in mind' is quite a challenge for many primary school children. As Anghileri (1995c) argues, what makes the *two concepts* aspect of division particularly tricky to negotiate is that each different concept has its own unique structure. Each concept has its own starting point – on one hand 'empty' or unknown groups (*sharing*) and, on the other hand, an unknown number of groups (*grouping*). Each concept involves a different problem – how many in each group? (*sharing*) or how many groups? (*grouping*). And although the abstract answer to an analogous sharing division problem or grouping problem is always the same, each answer refers to an entirely different aspect of the problem and each answer is visualized very differently.

Judith Anghileri points out that some children try to avoid conceptual confusion by clinging to one model of division. In other words some children opt consistently for one or other of the two conceptual 'routes'. While such children may be able to solve most basic division questions by translating them in their preferred way they may experience problems solving division word problems which are based on the less preferred model. For instance, children who have got into the habit of visualizing division problems as *grouping* problems ('How many *threes* in 12?') may find a *sharing* problem difficult to understand ('12 sweets shared between 3 children. How many sweets does each child get?'). On the other hand, children who always mentally *share* can have difficulty with questions such as 'How many 20s are there in 100? Other children become confused about *multiplicative* relationships, in general. Children can feel so confused about the relationships and differences between multiplication and division that they may end up treating division questions as multiplication questions, and vice versa. Some children answer multiplication and division questions in an entirely arbitrary manner.

The language of division

The very complex ramifications of the language of division tend to add to children's difficulties with division. Anghileri (1995c) describes a number of ways in which the language of division can add to children's difficulties when they are trying to make sense of the division concepts and especially when they are trying to work out 'what to do' to solve abstract division examples. Of course, the abstract division sign, '÷', is classically translated into the formal term, *divided by*. 12 ÷ 3 can be 'translated' as '12 *divided by* 3'. However, the abstract term *divided by* is difficult to make sense of. In multiplication work, the terms *multiplied by* or *times* are helpfully translated as 'groups of', 'sets of' or 'lots of'. The first big problem in division work is that informal translations of *divided by* inevitably refer to either one or the other concept of division. For example, the common phrase, 'How many 3s in 12?' refers to the *grouping* model of division whereas the equally common 'translations', '3 *times* what is 12?' or, more obviously, '12 shared between 3', refer to the *sharing* model of division.

Of course, either one of the translations are helpful in solving most abstract division problems taken from within the framework of the ordinary *times tables*. However, language 'mismatches' are also common in division work. For example, as we have noted briefly, it is not helpful for a child to invoke *sharing* language in a division example such as 80 ÷ 20 or, indeed, in any mental *long division* problem or approximation. Thus, 187 ÷ 17 is hard to understand, and solve, as 187 shared between 17. In these instances, the *grouping* language, 'How many 20s in 80?' or 'How many 17s in 187?' are usually more helpful. Equally, it is not particularly helpful to translate 2000 ÷ 2 as 'How many 2s in 2000?' Rather, '2000 *shared* between 2', or '2 *times* what is 2000?' will more easily allow children to answer the question. Also, as Judith Anghileri suggests, language mismatch problems can be very subtle because they often emerge from a teacher's or a parent's interventions. In setting out to help children 'translate' specific division questions, many adults are not aware of the conceptual baggage associated with division phrases. Adults often mistakenly believe that division phrases are entirely interchangeable and they may consequently shift between one model of division and another without realizing the possible implications of doing this. For example, it is not uncommon for a child to say, 'So that means 12 shared between 3' and for an adult to respond with, 'Yes, how many 3s in 12?' The problem with this is that while some children may be flexible enough to select appropriate 'translations' and to find their way through confusing language usage, children who are already finding division hard may end up feeling even more confused when what is ultimately inappropriate 'help' with division work is offered.

The second big problem with colloquial division 'translations' is that the language order of the translations very often does not 'match' the way in which division questions are usually written or spoken: children have to reverse the linear order of a number sentence such as 12 ÷ 3 to translate the sentence into the easier-to-understand 'How many 3s in 12?' or '3 times what is 12?' Children who have little or no practical experience of finding out how many groups are contained in numbers and who are simply instructed to use any one of the colloquial translations (which 'help' by invoking *times tables* knowledge) have particular difficulty with the 'reordering' aspect of the translations. As Steve Chinn often argues, children who are vulnerable in maths, very often become 'stuck' when maths language does not map directly on to the most conventional linear arithmetic representations. In trying to figure out division questions, dyslexic and dyspraxic children often get as far as translating 12 ÷ 4 as '12 divided by 4' but then they fail to get any further because they cannot picture 'divided by' and they do not know, or cannot remember, how they are supposed to continue beyond this point.

Early execution difficulties

Multiplication

In the early conceptual stages of learning about multiplication, children in understanding-based classrooms are encouraged to work out specific multiplication questions such as 3 × 4 by *counting up* the repeated sets: 4 + 4 + 4 = 4, 8, 12. *Counting up* is closely related to 'counting in multiples' and is also known as *sequence counting* or *step-counting*. As we saw earlier when we discussed Miles's work on dyslexia and times tables knowledge, dyslexic and dyspraxic childen with verbal memory difficulties often continue to rely heavily on step-counting to generate *tables* answers. Although *step-counting* repeated sets is often quite easily mastered by children, there are a number of elements which can prove tricky for children to negotiate:

(a) At the most basic level, some children may have difficulty counting in groups and may insist on counting the sets by counting in *ones*. While direct counting is an important stage in very early multiplication work, children who do not progress on to *step-counting* may need to be offered additional work on very basic concepts such as the conservation of numbers and *adding on* in addition.

(b) A number of children have difficulty with *step-counting*, itself. This applies to dyslexic and dyspraxic children, in particular. For example, some children miss a step without noticing this (2, 4, 8, 10) or miss a *step* and move on to a different count without noticing this (5, 10, 20, 30). As we noted in Part IV, children who find it hard to remember patterned sequences or who find it hard to remember auditory sequences are forced to rely on addition to generate the next number in the sequence, e.g. 4, 8, ?. Children may make a mistake with the addition involved and because they cannot remember the auditory patterns in the way that ordinary children can, they will often fail to recognize anything strange about a 'wrong' number which they have generated. This is especially evident in larger *tables* sequences (e.g. 6, 12, 18, 23, 29). Many of the children with specific learning difficulties who chant *tables* sequences inaccurately, or who give a 'wrong' tables answer, are actually relying on faulty *step-counting* skills.

(c) Although some children find 'open-ended' *step-counting* difficult, it is actually much easier than *counting up* repeated sets to find a specific unknown fact. To work out the answer to 7 × 4, for example, at least 4 separate elements have to be held in working memory: first, the *tables* sequence which is involved, here the x 4 table; secondly, the sequence of the table involved, 4, 8, 12, and so on; thirdly, the tally of how many sets have been counted – in *step-counting*, '4, 8, 12, 16' only 4 sets have been counted; and finally, the specific *tables* fact which is needed – to work out 7 × 4 a child will need to tally 7 sets. In other words, the child will need to stop *step-counting* once the seventh set has been counted in. Common difficulties with using *step-counting* to work out specific facts include the following: a number of children lose track of how many sets they have counted and will often 'start over again'; some children forget which fact is needed and become confused. Some children simply 'count past' the needed fact and have to back-track or start from the beginning again. Although using fingers to keep track of the number of sets counted is a useful strategy, which helps many children, dyslexic and dyspraxic children with a poor basic *sense* of number (and poor subitizing skills) can become confused about the number of fingers they have used.

Division

In many traditional teaching approaches, as we have seen, division is introduced once multiplication has been covered and children have already learned the *tables* facts. Children are expected to use a known multiplication fact to solve a division question. In learning about division many children have no practical groups-based experience. The division 'rule' may be almost entirely abstractly taught. This may help explain why some children find division impossible to make sense of.

More recently, as we have seen, and again because of widespread curriculum changes, teachers have begun to introduce division alongside multiplication. In newer teaching guidelines, teachers are required to help children understand the link between multiplication and division. Many children are offered the practical experience of 'putting together' and 'splitting up' groups so that they can actually see that multiplication and division are inverse operations. In early division work children are also more likely to be encouraged to count sets to work out specific division questions. Since counting-based work in division has not been very widespread until recently, there is less information about how children succeed within the newer understanding-based frameworks.

A number of studies seem to show, however, that one important factor in helping children succeed in early division work has to do with the way children are encouraged to step-count the component groups in the process of solving division problems. Since division 'undoes' multiplication, division can be seen as *repeated subtraction* from the start-out total or dividend. When division is treated as *repeated subtraction*, children are encouraged to start with the total (the dividend) and then subtract the relevant set (the divisor) in a systematic way. With *grouping* division problems ('How many 3s in 12?') the subtraction process is fairly direct: children step-count backwards, '9, 6, 3, 0'. In mental solutions to *grouping* questions children have to keep a tally of how many sets have been subtracted: in *step-counting* '9, 6, 3, 0', 4 sets have been subtracted, so the answer to 'How many 3s in 12?' is 4. However in *sharing* problems (such as 12 shared between 3) children first have to guess what is 'in each set' to be subtracted; then they have to repeatedly subtract the chosen set, *step-counting*, '8, 4, 0'; finally they have to check that the procedure has legitimately ended with a '0'. In the *sharing* model, the subtraction back process simply ensures that the correct answer (here 4) has been selected.

While the *repeated subtraction back* model of division is the one which is most commonly presented by teachers to children as the division inverse of multiplication, there is research evidence to show that children who are given simple meaningful division problems to solve are much more likely to invent an alternative and much easier *step-counting up* strategy to figure out division answers than they are to invent the conventional *repeated subtraction* strategy (Kamii, 1989; Kouba, 1989; Mulligan and Mitchelmore,

1997). Mulligan and Mitchelmore's research also shows that the children who 'build up' repeated groups in division work achieve more consistently correct answers than the children who subtract back repeatedly. In the alternative *step-counting up* method of working out division examples, children build up to the dividend, *step-counting up* repeatedly, rather than *back* repeatedly. In a building up *grouping* example such as, 'How many 3s in 12?' Children step-count up until the dividend is reached, '3, 6, 9, 12'. The number of steps counted is tallied to find the answer. In a 'building up' *sharing* example, children have to guess the answer to the division question and then 'build up' the selected sequence, '4, 8, 12', to check that the guess is correct.

In important respects, of course, *repeated subtraction* and *repeated building up* division strategies are similar. However, children tend to have greater difficulties with *repeated subtraction* methods than with repeated addition methods. Such difficulties include the following:

1. Children find *repeated subtraction* difficult to execute and frequently make mistakes, especially where larger *tables* are involved.
2. Tallying at the same time as subtracting is very difficult.
3. Children with sequencing difficulties have especial difficulties with *repeated subtraction* in *grouping* because they tend to include the dividend in the count. For example, in 'How many 3s in 12?' such children often count 12, 9, 6, 3, 0, and believe that the answer to 12 ÷ 3 is 5, not 4.

On the basis of their research results, Mulligan and Mitchelmore firmly argue that 'repeated addition' in division work

> is a more advanced model than repeated subtraction because it allows the same model to be used for both division and multiplication problems. Such unification would be expected to reduce cognitive load and lead to greater efficiency and a more rapid adoption of a multiplicative operation model. (Mulligan and Mitchelmore, 1997)

An outline of typical understanding-based approaches to multiplicative reasoning

In very broad outline, the basic principles of newer and more consistently progressive understanding-based perspectives on teaching multiplication and division may be seen to reverse most of the traditional emphases and promote teaching from a 'bottom-up' perspective. Learning about *multiplicative* reasoning is conceived as taking place in three stages. In the first stage, children build or model *multiplicative* relationships and problems concretely. Children are encouraged to build and 'count up' materials in groups or multiples (*step-count*). In the second stage, children solve *multiplicative* problems and simple word problems through mental *step-counting* strategies. Through stages 1 and 2 children are expected to come to know a number of easy-to-visualize facts. They are also helped to develop an understanding of useful principles in multiplication such as the *commutativity* of multiplication facts. (In practical terms, 'commutativity' here means that 3×4 and 4×3 have the same outcome.) Finally, in the third stage, children are encouraged to think increasingly abstractly and economically. As much as possible, children are encouraged to figure out all *tables* answers without forming the entire sequence of multiples. To work out harder number facts and solve harder word problems children are helped to use the facts which they have come to know *by heart*, together with short sequences of 'top-up' *step-counting* or together with a practical understanding of multiplicative principles. For example, 7×3 can be worked out as $5 \times 3 = 15$, $15 + 3 = 18$, $18 + 3 = 21$; on the other hand, 8×3 can be worked out by *doubling* and *doubling again*, or as $(2 \times 3) \times 2 \times 2$. As children become more experienced at using strategies, they are expected to select an appropriate fact-derived strategy for a particular calculation from a broad range of possible fact-derived strategies. And finally it is expected that practise at using fact-derived strategies efficiently use will allow children to conquer the hardest table facts so that they simply 'know' them in a direct operational (or *automatized*) way. Research consistently finds that it is very important that children begin to see multiplication as a distinctive operation:

> In the operation model, the final term is extracted from the implicit sequence of multiples and treated as a single entity. In this respect, the operation model is based on the repeated addition model but is distinctly different from it. (Mulligan and Mitchelmore, 1997, p. 319)

An outline of the special cognitive needs of dyslexic and dyspraxic children

In essence, the teaching suggestions which follow in the very next section of this chapter are structured along very similar lines. However, to meet the special cognitive needs of children with learning difficulties a somewhat modified and more tightly structured approach is adopted in the latter part of the suggested multiplication and division 'programme'. There are three main reasons for this. First, for children to progress beyond basic *multiplicative* work and on to the next stage of multi-digit multiplication and division work – work for which they will have the necessary conceptual foundations – it is very important that children have 'quick' access to all of the *tables* facts, including the very hardest ones. While some visually able dyslexic children make good progress within the framework of a predominantly *conceptually* based teaching approach, most primary school children with specific learning difficulties need more explicit and structured reasoning guidelines than many of these approaches provide. Classroom-based studies show that it is 'above average' students who most easily make the transition from using counting strategies and reasoning strategies to knowing facts directly (Anghileri, 1989). Children with specific learning difficulties often do not. Secondly, as we have seen in the discussion of addition and subtraction work, many children with specific learning difficulties have difficulty remembering a large range of alternative strategies for working out calculations. Dyslexic and dyspraxic children who have been taught a number of fact-derived strategies for figuring out 'harder' *tables* facts tends to have difficulty selecting a particular and appropriate strategy for a specific *tables* fact. They often have difficulty 'seeing' appropriate and helpful patterns 'within' specific multiplication fact questions.

To figure out harder *tables* facts dyslexic and dyspraxic children tend to rely on – and become 'stuck' with – the much more basic, less efficient but familiar 'step-counting-from-the-beginning' strategy. A reliance on basic *step counting* means that children with specific learning difficulties are slow to figure out harder *tables* facts. Because of the working memory demands of long sequences of *step-counting*, dyslexic and dyspraxic children also lose concentration quite frequently. They frequently make calculation errors or lose their 'place' in the *step-counting* process ('Which table did you ask me?' is a frequent request in oral *tables* work). Thirdly, it is important to remember that many dyslexic and dyspraxic children have grave difficulty encoding and retrieving verbal fact associations. As we have seen, this is particularly pertinent to conventional rote-learning *tables* practices. However, inefficient *step-counting* procedures, which require large amounts of working memory capacity, make it difficult for harder *tables* facts associations to be made through *step-counting*. In Chapter 1 we saw that a large gap between *input* and *output* in ordinary *adding on* procedures helped explain why dyslexic and dyspraxic children rely on counting to work out harder addition and subtraction facts. The heavy working memory demands of long sequences of *step-counting* mean that dyslexic and dyspraxic children become 'trapped' at the stage of counting – or, more precisely, *step-counting* – in *tables* work, too.

CHAPTER 11

An understanding-based approach to multiplication and division for dyslexic and dyspraxic children

Introduction

In Parts II and IV we saw in some detail that dyslexic and dyspraxic children make the most assured progress in learning facts if they have access to *key* or *big value* strategies for working out the facts. In multiplication and division work, too, dyslexic and dyspraxic children are able to know the harder multiplication and division facts *by heart* – or at least they are enabled to work them out very quickly – if they learn and are helped to automatize a clearly understood reasoning route. For this reason most dyslexic and dyspraxic children succeed best within an understanding-based approach to *tables* fact learning which sets out to help them acquire the multiplication and division facts in a highly structured way.

In overall terms, the approach which follows can be characterized as a two-stage approach to teaching multiplication and division, although both stages need to be understood to contain a number of important developments within them. The first stage is intended to be a relatively informal stage. Children explore *multiplicative* patterns, relationships, concepts and principles through working with small and easily visualized groups. At first, number problems and word problems are modelled concretely. As soon as possible, children are encouraged to visualize problems rather than model them. As soon as possible, too, children are encouraged to solve the problems using *mental counting up* skills. Some children are able to progress through this first stage very quickly. Others need to spend time building a basic *feel* for multiplication and division.

The second stage is structured in a more formal way. Children work on specific *tables* sequences. Very broadly speaking, multiplication and division work proceeds in a sequence-by-sequence way. Children's understanding of patterns, relationships, concepts and principles is consolidated and

337

extended within the framework of studying the *tables* sequences. Children are taught a *key* or *big value* sequence-based strategy for working out 'harder' *tables* facts in each of the sequences. This simple *tables* strategy is used by children to derive the 'harder' *tables* facts in *all tables* sequences, except the x 10 and × 9 *tables* sequences. Children are given a great deal of practice at figuring out tables facts out of sequence. They are also given carefully orchestrated practice at figuring out facts from 'mixed' tables sequences.

Stage 1: Building a 'feel' for multiplication and division

Step-counting

We have seen that the ability to count in multiplies, or to *step-count*, is one of the key stages in the development of *multiplicative* reasoning. Many dyslexic and dyspraxic children, and especially children with aural memory and sequencing difficulties, need to practise *step-counting* as frequently as possible. Familiarity with *step-counting* patterns helps facilitate and speed up children's early ability to calculate multiplication and division answers. Confident *step-counting* also helps children to become better 'tuned in' to likely, and less likely, *tables* facts answers.

Some step-counting suggestions

1. It is best to start with 'easy' sequences, such as the *twos* and *fives*. *Step-counting* in *threes* and *fours* is also very useful. It is usually advisable to limit *step-counting* practice in *sixes*, *sevens*, *eights* and *nines* to counting shorter sequences of multiples. For example, 'Can you step-count in *sixes* from 30 to 60?'
2. To help children develop a *feel* for number sequences it is important to start by *step-counting* groups of objects. For example, children can be encouraged to count objects in *twos* rather than *ones*, making sure that each group of *two* is touched or moved along systematically. Small objects placed in groups of *three* or *four* can be step-counted. For example,

At a slightly more abstract level, children may be asked to count 2p coins and 5p coins. Cuisinaire rods, too, can be used in *step-counting* activities. It is very useful to build layers of *tens*, then *fives*, then *twos* on top of each other on the containing frame of an empty *100 square*. In this way, children will often suddenly make connections about how the different counting 'tracks' which make up sequences relate to each other. Dyslexic children who can manage 'fiddly' work can make further discoveries about more complex patterns of multiples through activities in which they are asked to 'count' rod *threes*, or *fours*, or *sixes*, on to the *100-square* frame. Counting groups of beads on an abacus frame can be a similarly useful activity.

3. It is worth practising oral *step-counting* frequently and in a number of different ways. Some younger children enjoy practising rhythmic *step-counting* while they are engaged in physical activities such as hopping, skipping or jumping. *Step-counting* can also be practised against the backdrop of rhythmic clapping or rhythmic percussive beats.

4. It is very helpful to begin ordinary oral *step-counting* from a range of different starting points within the sequence. In other words, step-counting should not always begin from the conventional '0'. For example, 'Can you count in 4s from 20 please? I'll tell you when to stop.' Again, this helps build foundations for flexible strategy use.

5. *Step-counting* backwards is very hard for children with sequencing difficulties but backwards *step-counting* helps children become flexible at counting and paves the way for subsequent confident strategy use. It is important to begin counting backwards from a modest starting point or to ask children to step-count a short way. For example, children could be asked to step-count backwards in *twos* from 10 or back in *threes* from 30 to 21. The *step-counting* demands made on children can then be extended in a gradual way.

6. It is extremely useful to extend the *step-counting* framework towards the beginning of *strategy-based* thinking. After *step-counting* in *threes* to 30, for example, children can be asked 'one-step' or 'two-step' sequence-based questions, such as, 'What is the *three* after 12?', 'What is one *three* more than 18?', 'What is one *three* less than 30?', 'What is two *threes* more than 15?' or 'What is two *threes* less than 30?' Such questions form a very helpful link between *step-counting* work and children's early thinking about individual *multiplicative* questions.

Pattern building

Since so many of the underlying structures and the methods for calculating answers are shared between multiplication and division, it makes sense for children to learn about the two concepts at the same time. Teaching the concepts and operations of multiplication and division alongside each other also has the advantage that children learn about division more gradually than they do in traditional teaching approaches and have a more extended period of practising solving division problems. Indeed, teaching experience shows that children with specific learning difficulties seem to understand division better if multiplication practice is not allowed to outstrip division competence too markedly.

To reinforce the fundamental 'groups' idea it is very helpful to start by working with groups as repeated patterns. Working with visually memorable quantity patterns, rather than with less memorable unstructured collections of things, gives children a great deal of strong visual support. Children can also understand and visualize the groups idea better by building small groups, or patterns, and by working with a relatively small overall number of groups, or patterns. For instance, it generally works best to have a rough upper limit of working with about 5 groups of 5 objects and with 2 or 3 groups of larger patterns, from patterns of 6 upwards. The language used at this stage should be kept as simple and as transparent as possible.

Groups as collections:

Groups as repeated patterns:

Introducing groups-based work can be very simple indeed. Since many children are fearful of multiplication and of division (and of the *tables*) it is often wise not to mention any of these 'labels' at all. Instead, it can be suggested that children are going to explore work with patterns and pattern-building in maths. It is not essential for children to build the *ones* into the 'standardized' dice-related *number patterns* which are introduced in early number-work but many children enjoy the familiarity of working with these patterns.

Activities

1. In very early multiplication activities children may be asked to respond to easy-to-follow instructions such as 'Take some of these counters and

build me 3 *fours*,' or 'Can you set out 3 groups of 4?' Once children have
made the groups of 4, they should be encouraged to calculate how
many counters have been used by *step-counting* the patterns, '4, 8, 12'.
Next, children could be asked to construct and then *step-count* a few
more repeated patterns, such as 4 *fives*, 3 *twos*, 2 *sixes* and so on. These
very basic repeated pattern-building exercises should be repeated in a
number of subsequent maths sessions.

three *fours*:

```
O O   O O   O O
O O   O O   O O
```

three *fives*:

```
O O   O O   O O
 O     O     O
O O   O O   O O
```

2. As we have seen, the *grouping* concept of division is easier to work with, in
   the beginning, than the *sharing* concept of division. *Grouping* is also more
   easily grasped as the 'inverse' of multiplication than *sharing*. In a very early
   grouping-based division activity, children can be asked to follow instructions such as, 'Take 9 of these counters, and let's see how many *threes* there
   are in 9', or 'How many groups of 3 would it take to build 9?' Children
   are encouraged to separate out, and build up groups of 3.

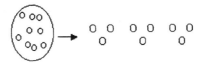

At the end of the splitting apart and building up process, children
should be asked to articulate the number of *threes* needed to 'build back
up to' the number 9. Again, this can be followed by further *splitting* and
rebuilding investigations, such as, 'How many *fours* are there in 8?' or 'If
you want to build 20 from *fives*, how many *fives* would you need?'
3. It generally works well to engage children in a number of fairly short
   bursts of 'putting together' and 'breaking apart' pattern-based work:
   working with repeated patterns builds up children's *feel* for multiplication and division in a fairly natural or osmosis-like way. For this reason,
   too, it is worth establishing children's basic *multiplicative sense* as early or
   on or as far ahead as possible. Thus, as children's addition, subtraction
   and *number system* work gets under way, it is useful to introduce a small

amount of *repeated pattern* work into maths sessions – or, indeed, into other non-maths classroom or everyday activities.

4. As children become confident about the *repeated groups* idea and are proficient at *step-counting* groups, they can be encouraged to remember that *two* groups also involve the well-known *doubles* facts and they can be nudged to *step-count* 'even more quickly' from 2 × n. For example:

$$4 \times 3 = 6, 9, 12.$$

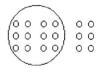

Likewise, in figuring out simple division problems, children can be encouraged to start from 2 x n. For example, to answer the question, 'How many fives do I need to build 20?' children could reason, '2 fives are ten, so three fives are 15 and 4 fives are 20.'

5. In a similar way, the doubles facts can be used to help children work out facts such as 3 × 6 or 4 × 8. It is hard for children to have a very immediate intuitive sense of numbers larger than about five, or so. Nevertheless, early multiplication work can once again capitalize and build on the fact that two groups of larger groups (2 × n) is also a well-internalized 'harder' doubles fact. In other words, 2 × 6 = 6 + 6. Working outwards from the doubles is a very practical way of beginning work with the larger tables facts. For instance, children could be asked to model 'two groups of six'. From this understanding it is a relatively simple step for children to see that '3 groups of six' or '3 sixes' is simply one group of six more than the well-known '2 sixes'.

2 SIXES + 1 SIX = 3 SIXES

Doubles knowledge can also be extended to cover 4 × n. '2 eights' is the well-known doubles fact, and is 16. 4 groups of 8 can be modelled as:

From the concrete model children can be helped to see that 4 eights or '4 groups of 8' is the same as '2 eights, or 16, plus 8, plus 8', or, even more economically, as '2 eights, or 16, plus another 2 eights, or 16, which is 32'.

Basic multiplicative problem-solving

Informal problem-solving

As suggested above, an important way in which children come to make sense of *multiplicative* reasoning is through solving simple, spoken word problems. As always, the earliest *multiplicative* problems should arise as informally and naturally as possible. In early problem-solving work it is a good idea to require children to solve the most straightforward *equivalent groups* types of problems. As far as division is concerned, the somewhat easier *grouping* problems should be presented to children first. However, an introduction to the *sharing* concept of division should not be too long delayed. Since *sharing* is best understood within the context of 'real-life' *sharing* situations it works best to introduce this concept of division through the framework of informal concrete *sharing* 'stories'.

Concrete materials should play a central part in early multiplicative problem-solving activities. As always, real items, replica objects, or classroom materials, such as glass nuggets (which represent real objects) may be used to help create word-problem situations. In Part I we noted that it is usually best to encourage children to figure out a solution to the problem *mentally*, first, and then permit them to construct the story situation to check (and hopefully confirm) the solution they have given.

Some informal word-problem examples: multiplication

1. A 'sweets' problem: 'The "gobstoppers" which we have here need to be packed in separate little bags. We're going to put 4 of the sweets in each little bag. We'll pack 3 bags of sweets. How many "gobstoppers" will we use?'

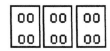

We will use 12 gobstoppers

2. A halma pawn problem: 'These pretend people are children exploring a dungeon. They decided to explore the dungeon in groups of 3. There

are 3 groups of 3 children in the dungeon. How many children are in the dungeon altogether?'

There are 9 children in the dungeon

The grouping concept of division

1. A halma pawn problem: 'These are 8 children who are exploring a wilderness together. Their teacher splits the children into groups of 2. How many groups of 2 are there?'

There are 4 groups of 2 children.

2. A 'food' problem: 'These chocolate cakes are to be packed in bags of 3 cakes each. There are 9 chocolate cakes. How many bags of 3 cakes can be made?'

There are 3 bags of 3 cakes.

The sharing concept of division

As we have seen, *sharing* problems are somewhat harder for children to figure out than *grouping* problems. Children who have developed a good *feel* for *repeated group* work are usually conceptually ready to try 'proper' *sharing* in groups. Instead of allowing children to 'deal out' the concrete materials in *ones* to find a solution to *sharing* problems, children should be encouraged to 'guess' or think hard about the number which each group may contain (the quantity which they have selected as the likely 'fair share'). They should then be helped to check or 'test' their proposed answer.

1. A food problem: 'Here are 10 little cakes which a mum has baked. She

wants to share the cakes out between 5 children. How many little cakes will each child get?'

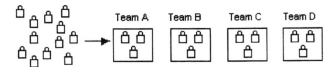

Each child can have 2 cakes.

2. A halma pawn problem: 'These pretend people are 12 children who have to solve a riddle. To solve the riddle, the children decide to split into 4 teams. How many children are there in each team?'

Each team has 3 children.

Formal problem-solving

As children are able to think more confidently about groups, multiplicative word problems should be gradually made more formal or 'school-like'. As we have seen, important steps in this direction include making the language and structure of the word problems increasingly formal-sounding and giving children written word problems to solve. Initially, though, and particularly where children have reading difficulties, formal-sounding problems should continue to be given in spoken form (or, at the very least, formal written word problems should at be read to, or with, children). Along the way, children may still need to model situations with concrete materials to confirm the solutions they have figured out.

A few formal problem examples:

1. James wanted to buy 4 bags of marbles. Inside each bag there were 5 marbles. How many marbles would he have altogether?
2. James had 20 model vintage cars. He put the cars into small groups of 4 cars. How many groups of cars did James make?
3. James's mum opened a packet of 12 biscuits. She shared the biscuits between her 3 children. How many biscuits did each child get?

Regular multiplicative arrays: introducing the area model of multiplication

As we will see, two-dimensional regular arrays (rectangles and squares) provide the most efficient model for demonstrating the helpful principle of *commutativity* ($3 \times 4 = 4 \times 3$) as well as the hard-to-describe abstract principle of *distributivity*. The distributive rule in multiplication is embodied in so-called *split-arrays*: for example, $7 \times 4 = 5 \times 4 + 2 \times 4$. Regular arrays also offer excellent ground for exploring the concepts of square numbers and prime numbers. It is thus worth introducing regular arrays as early as possible.

In working with repeated groups or repeated patterns, children often notice that they can organize *groups* into *rows*:

Even if they do not 'invent' regular arrays for themselves, most children enjoy the simple but instructive activity of reorganizing groups of *ones* into rows. Working with small, moveable objects makes the very ordered spatial organization of the area model particularly accessible.

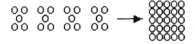

Once children have grasped the concrete regular array idea, other area model-based activities can quite rapidly follow. For example, children can draw dots or little diagrams, such as 'smiley faces', or they can stick brightly coloured gummed shapes in rows on to ordinary squared paper.

3 threes = 3 groups of 3, in which each row of 3 is a group or set of 3:

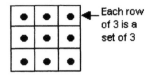

4 twos = 4 sets of 2 , in which each line of 2 is a group or 'lot' of 2:

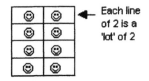

When children can readily identify regular rows as groups they are ready to be introduced to Cuisinaire rod array work. Again, it is usually best to make the links between rows and rods in an explicit way:

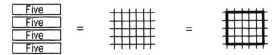

Following practical work with clearly identifiable concrete 'rows', children are often ready to understand rather more abstract area model arrays. When children are introduced to squared paper area model work, they should be clear that 'one row' is the same as 'one group' and they should be able to see the rows clearly.

4 fives = 4 rows of five:

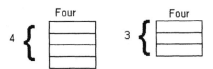

Regular array work provides particularly good access to ideas such as square numbers and rectangular numbers. For example, 4 rows of four, which is sixteen, clearly creates a square. 4×4 is a tables square and 16 is a square number. But 3 fours or 5 fours create rectangular arrays – their answers, 12 and 20 respectively, are called rectangular numbers.

The commutativity of multiplication can be very efficiently investigated through array work. With regard to commutativity the advantage of arrays over 'ordinary' *repeated groups* is that one aspect of a multiplication relationship, for example 2 *fours*, can be modelled, and then swivelled 180° to give the second aspect of the relationship, or 4 *twos*. Another way of demonstrating that 2 *fours* equals 4 *twos* is to place the equivalent, commutative Cuisinaire rod arrays on top of each other.

Children should also experience the fact that division is not commutative. 'How many *twos* in 8?' can be modelled and answered by exploring how many *twos* fit into a regular rectangle of 8.

How many twos in 8?

How many *eights* in 2 clearly does not make sense:

A rectangle of 2:

Becoming more abstract

As soon as children become more confident and proficient at working with *repeated groups*, multiplication and division work should become more abstract For example, instead of modelling questions concretely, children can be asked to try to visualize and mentally think about *multiplicative* relationships. In oral mental maths work, for example, children can be asked simple calculation questions such as, 'What are 5 *threes*?' or 'You have 12. How many *fours* in 12?' As long as numbers are kept small and easily visualized, most children will begin to move away from step-counting or relying on *additive composition* in order to give the answers to such questions. Instead, they will begin to respond in more sophisticated and efficient ways. At this stage a common response to simple multiplication questions, such as, 'What are 3 groups of *four*?', is 'That's easy!' often followed by an automatized correct answer. By now, simple word problems involving the 'easy' *tables* should also be given in written form and should be mentally figured out.

Once children's conceptual understanding is secure, their knowledge and understanding of the *language* of multiplication and division should be extended. They should be introduced to the abstract terms, *multiply, times, divide, divided by* and so on. Most dyslexic and dyspraxic children will need to be reminded for quite a long time that they can translate abstract, difficult *multiplicative* terms into language which makes sense to them. For example, 'three *multiplied by* five,' means 'three groups of five' or 'three *fives*'. Adults need to take care that *grouping* and *sharing* translations are used in appropriate contexts and that children are able to visualize both ways of decoding the more abstract division terms.

At this stage children should also be introduced to the abstract symbols, '×' and '÷'. The symbols will need to be carefully linked to all of the the different aspects or layers of multiplication and division which have been covered. In other words, the symbols need to be linked to the groups-based relationships, to the more basic and transparent *multiplicative* language describing the relationships, to the 'real-life' situations involving *multiplicative* relationships and to the abstract and formal language, *multiply*, *divide* and so on. One very valuable way of introducing work with the abstract 'x' symbol is to play a very simple game which contrasts the two (often confusing) signs, 'x' and '+'. The game helps provide enjoyable and safe opportunities for children to decode or translate the 'x' symbol into the informal multiplication terms which they prefer. Abstract language can be rehearsed, too. The **spinner multiplication game** is played with two 0–5 dice and a simple spinner base:

In each round, players take turns to throw both dice. For example, a player may throw a '2' and a '4'. He or she then spins to select the rule, 'x' or '+', works out the calculation and records the result. A winner may be determined for each round and rewarded with a point or token. Alternatively, scores may be recorded for a number of rounds, with the overall total determining the winner. It should be noted that there are two additional benefits of this very simple game. First, children refine their understanding of multiplication by contrasting it with what happens in addition relationships: $4 \times 3 = 12$, whereas $4 + 3 = 7$; $4 \times 0 = 0$, whereas $4 + 0 = 4$.

Secondly, work with dice tends to reinforce children's pragmatic understanding of commutativity: the dice '2' and '4' can be 'read' as $2 + 4$ or $4 + 2$, or likewise, as 2×4 or 4×2.

Area-based work can be consolidated by playing a game, too. Once children are managing to figure out multiplication calculations mentally, the advantages and discoveries of the regular arrays can be further explored and reinforced by employing half-sized, empty versions of a 10 x 10 multiplication square. Children can be shown that the final answer to any multiplication calculation can be recorded in the corner of the regular rectangle or square which it creates.

3 X 3 =

X	1	2	3	4	5
1					
2					
3			9		
4					
5					

2x4 =

X	1	2	3	4	5
1					
2				8	
3					
4					
5					

This understanding forms the basis for a scaled-down version of a fairly common 10 × 10 *tables* square game. In the 5 × 5 version of the game – the **5 × 5 multiplication game** – the numbers 1–5, only, are used. Each player requires his/her own 5 × 5 square base. In each round, players throw the two dice, the two numbers are multiplied and the product is recorded in the appropriate 1cm square position on the base. Play continues until one player has completed 3 squares in a row.

X	1	2	3	4	5	
1		2				(1 X 2)
2					10	(2 X 5)
3			9			(3 X 3)
4	8					(4 X 2)
5	5					(1 X 5)

It should be noted that children who struggle to locate the intersection of the two *tables* co-ordinates can use a simple right-angled shape made from paper or card to do so.

Stage 2: More formal multiplication work

Once children are able to reason multiplicatively and have a secure understanding of the 'easier' *tables* facts, they are ready for the next stage in multiplication and division work. As we have seen, this involves taking on the 'harder' multiplication and division facts. To do this, children are introduced to *tables* sequence work.. As we suggested earlier, dyslexic and dyspraxic children benefit from learning a *big value tables* strategy to master the 'harder' *tables* facts. In essence, once the second stage of multiplication and division work is reached:

1. Children work in a structured way on each of the *tables* sequences.
2. Children are taught one relatively simple and logical way to reason to work out the 'harder' tables facts. In other words, children learn one basic *key* or *big value* strategy for figuring out the harder *tables* in each of the *tables* sequences. The key *tables* strategy is a refinement of the simple step-counting strategy which many dyslexic and dyspraxic children intuitively rely on. It is also a strategy which children often 'spontaneously' devise in supportive understanding-based classrooms . A crucial feature of the strategy is that it reduces the number of 'steps' which need to be counted to work out 'harder' *tables* facts.
3. Children who are proficient at using the basic *tables* strategy are helped to understand further 'refinements' of the strategy. As we will see, the strategy

offers a very clear foundation for using an efficient 'partial products' approach to figuring out 'hard' *tables* facts. Children are also encouraged to use additional reasoning 'short-cuts'. In particular, *grasshopper* dyslexics are encouraged to devel vp and use alternative fact-derived strategies

It should be noted that however carefully *tables* sequence work is presented to children, some children are very fearful of learning the 'harder' tables facts. This is generally because they have had unfortunate *tables* learning experiences in the past. The fact that there are so many sequences ('twisted lists') to learn also represents an extremely large learning challenge for young children. We have seen that children should prefer-ably encounter the formal language of multiplication and division in the first pattern-building stage of learning about *multiplicative* reasoning. However, it is generally a very good idea to return to very transparent language 'translations' in early *tables* sequence work. In particular, returning to the very concrete 'building' language for division, helps children work out 'harder' sequence-based division facts with a far greater degree of understanding and confidence than if they are asked to answer formally worded questions such as 'What is 21 divided by 3?'

A note on the principle of commutativity

Many educationalists argue that the heavy 'learning load' of acquiring the *times tables* facts can be effectively halved if children are taught to apply the principle of *commutativity* in multiplication in a consistent way. In other words, it is argued that if children already know that 8 *sixes* are 48 ($8 \times 6 = 48$) then, if they apply the *commutative* principle, they will also know that 6 *eights* are 48 ($6 \times 8 = 48$). However, working with dyslexic and dyspraxic children has shown that it is advisable to be cautious about suggesting that young children with specific learning difficulties should use half-understood principles or 'rules' in a largely abstract way. An early purely 'rule-based' dependence on the principle of commutativity by primary school dyslexic and dyspraxic children can have serious negative consequences for multiplicative reasoning. There are a number of impor-tant reasons for this. First of all, the verbal memory of many dyslexic children is frequently so weak that it is often not possible for them to remember half of the 100 (or 144) *tables* facts *by heart*. This means that children have to derive most of the harder facts in each of the *tables* sequences from easier facts. Secondly, and related to this first problem, working memory weaknesses mean that inexperienced dyslexic and dyspraxic children, who rely on the commutative principle to work out a first step to figure out a harder *tables* fact, often become confused about the group or groups which require to be added in the next step. For example, in figuring out $8 \times 6 = ?$ a child may reason that $5 \times 8 = 40$, but he or she may then incorrectly add 6 to the 40, rather than 8. *Grasshopper* dyslexic children who make frequent 'near-miss' errors in figuring out *tables* are often confused in this way. Thirdly, dyslexic and dyspraxic children, who rely too early on the commutative principle to work out *tables* facts, often have difficulty figuring out the equivalent division facts. For example, 8 threes (8×3) is often easier to access as 3 eights (3×8), but the ability to know or quickly work out 3 eights may not help many children who have difficulty figuring out $24 \div 3 = ?$, or how many *threes* in 24? Again, *grasshopper* children who show some ability in *tables* work, but whose division work is extremely poor, may be relying heavily on the principle of commutativity to work out *tables* facts.

On the other hand, it should be noted that dyslexic and dyspraxic children who have internalized a consistent way to visualize and derive *tables* facts in all of the *tables* sequences are generally able to visualize the reasoning process fairly clearly and usually make considerably fewer reasoning errors. In general terms, children who have a clear grasp of the process of reasoning that they are choosing, become much more adept at using flexible reasoning paths. In addition to this, as children's confidence in their *tables* knowledge grows, and as they manage to autotamatize greater numbers of facts, the principle of commutativity is usually much more successfully applied.

Teaching the 'big value' tables strategy

Introducing the key facts

The two-stage approach to teaching multiplication and division, which is recommended in this book, means that when children are required to learn whole *tables* sequences, they will already be very familiar with the 'easier' *tables* in each sequence. In the x 3 *tables*, for example, children usually know, or are able to very quickly work out, the first half of the sequence.

1×3
2×3
3×3
4×3
5×3 * *key fact*
6×3
7×3

8×3
9×3
10×3 * *key fact*

It is the second half of the sequence – from about 5×3 – which children need further help with. As we have seen, dyslexic and dyspraxic children often rely on step-counting from 1×3 to work out a 'hard' fact, such as 8×3. The *big value* strategy rests on the very simple idea that children should be encouraged to step-count a much shorter way from *key facts* in the sequence – *key facts* which are learned *by heart* and consequently automatized. To work out the 'harder' tables, children are required to know just two 'easy' *key facts* in each sequence *by heart*. The *key facts* in any *tables* sequence are $10 \times n$ and $5 \times n$: in the $\times 3$ *tables* example, given above, the *key facts* which children are required to recall very quickly are 10×3 and 5×3.

10 x n and 5 x n: 'easy' facts to know

For reasons which will become clear very shortly, 10 x n (for example 10×3) is the truly pivotal key tables fact in any *tables* sequence. 10 × n (for example, 10×3) is generally not totally unfamiliar to children. Although early conceptually orientated *multiplicative* work focuses on small numbers of groups, children will nevertheless have had the experience of step-counting multiples all the way up to $10 \times n$. For example, in the $\times 3$ sequence, children will have step-counted 3, 6, 9, 12, 15, 18, 21, 24, 27, *30*. Children will also know the value of *n tens* from basic *place value* work. For example, most children know that 3 *tens* are 30. (A few children may, of course, need to review this aspect of place value work.) Some children intuitively extend their knowledge of n *tens* (3 *tens* = 30) to cover a knowledge of $10 \times n$ (10 *threes* = 30). In the context of thinking about *tens*, however, many children will need to be reminded of their early practical experiences of the commutativity of multiplication and will need to 'see' or experience (and then overlearn) that 10×3 or 10 *threes* is the same as, or has the same product as, 3×10 or 3 *tens*.

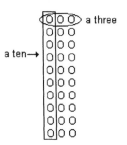

From similar concrete work, children will readily see that 10 *fours* equals 4 *tens*, which equals 40; 10 *fives* equals 5 *tens*, which equals 50, and so on. In this very practical way the 10 × n *key fact* can be established as a fact which can be very quickly worked out and which is also an easy fact to know.

5 × n (for example, 5 × 3) also needs to be quickly accessed if the tables strategy is to be successfully used. Some children are able to internalize many of the 5 × n facts in the first stage of pattern building work However, for children who don't know specific 5 × n facts *by heart, step-counting* to derive 5 × n is too laborious: it requires too much time and working memory space to be effective. A quick way to derive 5 × n is to understand that if 10 × n is known, then 5 × n is half of 10 × n and may be very quickly worked out. Thus, if 10 × 3 is 30, then 5 × 3 is half of 30, and half of 30 is 15.

Many children enjoy using chess pieces (or plastic figures) to create two 5 × n 'armies.'

```
                        000
                        000
                        000
                        000
                        000

                        000
                        000
                        000
                        000
                        000
```

A number of dyslexic children relate well to Cuisinaire rod use in multiplication work Cuisinaire rods show in a very economical way that, for example, 5 *threes* are half of 10 *threes:*

There are two advantages associated with the '5 × n is half of 10 × n' strategy: In essence, it means that the big value tables strategy rests on knowledge of *one key fact* only – an idea which many dyslexic and dyspraxic children find immensely heartening. Secondly, with practice, 5 × n can be derived from 10 × n very quickly indeed. Very quickly derived facts require small amounts of working memory and are more likely to be automatized than slowly derived facts.

The order in which to learn the tables sequences

There is no one binding or best order in which to cover the *tables* sequences. Generally speaking, and depending on the *tables* knowledge base which children may have already acquired, it makes sense to start with the easy-to-count and easy-to-visualize '× 5' or '× 2' *tables* sequences or with the fairly accessible × 3 and × 4 sequences. Some children make best progress if they work methodically through each 'harder' sequence in turn, leaving the slightly exceptional × 9 *tables* sequence until last. However, dyslexic and dyspraxic children often have additional school-related *tables* learning demands to meet: children are invariably required by their class teachers to learn and review *tables* sequences. For this reason, while it is usually best to introduce the *big value tables* strategy through fairly accessible *tables* sequences, it can help children feel more confident, overall, if they are allowed to select a particular sequence needed for school for *tables* sequence work. It also significantly boosts the confidence of some children to cover the 'very hard' and often feared '× 9' *tables* sequence, quite early on, and possibly immediately following the '× 3' and × '4' *tables* sequences. As we will see, the '× 9' *tables* sequence has a different logical starting point from the other *tables* sequences but there are so many in-built patterns for children to hold on to – and patterns which can be introduced in the process of learning the other sequences, anyway – that many children end up discovering that 'the *nines*' are not so difficult after all.

Two practical, detailed demonstrations of the basic tables strategy

The × 5 tables sequence

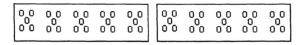

In early *tables* sequence work, the chosen *group* is best modelled as a repeated pattern or as repeated rows set out in a regular array formation. In the diagram above, patterns of 5 counters have been built into a linear arrangement. To begin with, children can be asked to lay out 5 patterns of *five*. If necessary, children should be gently reminded that they are very familiar with all of the *tables* facts to 5 × 5. After a small gap, 5 further sets of *five* are laid out until 10 *fives* are displayed. From the practical *commutativity* work described above, children will already know that 10 *fives* are 50. The patterned array of the two 'blocks' of 5 *fives* reinforces the understanding that 5 *fives* is half of 10 *fives*. It is explained to children that the two 'easy' *tables*, 10 × 5 and 5 × 5, will function as the *keys* to 'quickly unlock,' or help children figure out, all of the *tables* in the *fives* sequence which are 'harder' to know *by heart* and which also take time to step-count. (It can also be explained that the 10 × n facts and 5 × n facts act as the *keys* in nearly all of the *tables* sequences.)

From the concrete array of *fives*, children should be encouraged to see that they can use short sequences of *step-counting* forwards or backwards from the *key fact* to figure out quickly the facts in the sequence that they don't yet know *by heart*. In the '× 5' sequence, 6 *fives*, or 6 × 5, is one *five* more than the *key fact*, 5 × 5, and since 5 *fives* are 25, 6 *fives* are 30. Similarly, 7 *fives* are 2 *fives* more than 5 *fives*: 5 *fives* are 25, 6 *fives* are 30, and 7 *fives* are 35. 8 *fives* can be figured out in a similar way by *step-counting* 3 steps forwards from the *key* 5 × 5 facts: 5 *fives* are 25, 6 *fives* are 30, 7 *fives* are 35, and 8 *fives* are 40. The table 9 × 5, or 9 *fives*, is very close to the 10 × 5 key table. It is one *five* less than 50, and is thus 45. Likewise, if children prefer a slightly shorter sequence of backwards *step-counting*, 9 × 5 can be used to figure out the 'hard' 8 × 5 fact. If 10 *fives* are 50, 9 *fives* are 45, and 8 *fives* are 40.

It will be remembered that one aspect of tables-orientated counting work consisted of asking children to step-count one or two steps forwards or backwards from different multiples in a *tables* sequence. At this very early stage in *tables* sequence work it is helpful to build on this work and ask a range of questions such as 'What are two steps more than twenty-five?', 'If five *fives* are twenty-five, what are six *fives*?', and 'If ten *fives* are fifty, what are eight *fives*?' In this relatively 'safe' or contained way children begin to be able to reason about individual facts which are not presented in strict sequence. It is also always helpful to follow concrete work with 'thinking' mental work in which children are encouraged to visualize key elements of the concrete work that they have just engaged in. For example, 'Can you picture 5 groups of 5. What are 5 *fives*. If we have one more *five* – if we have 6 *fives* – how many would we have altogether? As always it is a good idea to cover the concrete model so that it is out of view while children are thinking – the covered model is still readily available should children have difficulty 'figuring out' any of the mental *tables* questions.

The *big value tables* strategy gives as much support in 'harder' division work as it does in *table sequence* work. To continue reinforcing the conceptual links between multiplication and division, sequence-based division work should be covered alongside 'ordinary' work to master the times tables sequences In other words, questions based on the operation of division should follow on from multiplication questions. The *key* facts are used to guide children towards appropriate division answers. *Key* facts can be rephrased in a division orientated way: for example, 'How many *fives* would you need to build 25?' Reinforcement of the *key* facts idea can be followed by questions such as 'If you have 30, how many *fives* could you "make" out of the 30?' and 'You start out with 45; how many fives could you build out of 45?' In answering such questions children may need to refer to the concrete model of the *fives* sequence at first. Soon, however, children should be asked to try and 'picture' the *fives* in order to answer *mental* division questions. For example, 'Can you picture 25? Now, can you picture 35? You want to make 35 out of *fives*. How many *fives* would you need?' To build the confidence of children who are very frightened of division it is often best to avoid referring to the operation by name, at least in early more 'advanced' division work of this kind. Also, before the abstract division sign, '÷' is reintroduced at this 'harder' division level, written division questions can be expressed in the easier 'mystery multiplication form: $\square \times 4 = 24$.

The × 4 tables sequence

```
0 0 0 0
0 0 0 0
0 0 0 0
0 0 0 0
0 0 0 0

0 0 0 0
0 0 0 0
0 0 0 0
0 0 0 0
0 0 0 0
```

In early *tables* sequence work, the *groups* under consideration should preferably be set out in a number of different ways. In the × 4 *tables* sequence example, illustrated above, groups of *four* have been set out in rows in a *split* rectangle or area formation. The rows of four can be built from concrete *ones*, such as glass nuggets, or from little coloured gummed 'dots' which are stuck into squares on squared paper. In both instances it is particularly useful to build the two-part array from two different colours – the first five *fives* from one colour, and the second set of *fives* – from six *fives* to ten *fives* – in a second colour. As always, children are trained to use the *key* 10×4 and 5×4 facts to work out the harder *tables* in the sequence. As children become familiar with the *big value tables* strategy, they can be encouraged to step-count forwards or backwards from the *key facts* in increasingly streamlined ways. For example, 7×4 is two steps more than the *key fact* $5 \times 4 = 20$ so it is 24, 28. 8×4 is three steps more than 20, and is 24, 28, 32. Alternatively, 8×4 is two steps less than 40, and is 36, 32.

As children become confident about working from the *key tables*, they can be introduced to additional patterns which help to ease the *tables* learning burden. First of all, for example, it is very helpful for children to know about the special features of $9 \times n$ (for example, 9×4). Children can be shown that the answers to any $9 \times n$ fact always add up to 9. In the 9×4 example, $9 \times 4 = 36$, the digits 3 plus 6 add up to 9. Likewise, in 9×2, the digits in the product, 18, add up to 9. 9×5 equals 45, and 4 plus 5 equals 9, and so on:

$$9 \times 1 = 9 \quad 9 \times 2 = 1\boxed{+}8 \quad 9 \times 3 = 2\boxed{+}7 \quad 9 \times 4 = 3\boxed{+}6 \quad 9 \times 5 = 4\boxed{+}5$$

By using this pattern in the *nines*, it is possible to figure out 9×4 from the *key fact* 10×4, without having to perform the subtraction, $40 - 4$. For instance, as Chinn and Ashcroft (1998, p. 78) show, one can reason, 'The *key fact* 10×4 equals 40; 9×4 is one *four* less than 40 so the answer to 9×4 must be in the 'thirties,' and is therefore 'thirty-something'. The digits in the $9 \times n$ facts always add up to 9, 3 *plus 6* equals 9, so 9 *times* 4 must be 36. It is true that the special features of the $9 \times n$ facts usually need quite a lot of reinforcement for children to master them, and that, at first, using them may feel laborious to children. However, as Chinn and Ashcroft (1998, p 78) point out,

> The child may think that this is a long process, but with regular practice it becomes quicker. Also, as the child becomes more adept, he starts to short-circuit the process and use it to top off a half-known answer.

Patterns which children may already be familiar with from pattern-building multiplicative work can also be reviewed and reinforced: for example children can be reminded that 4×4 is also $(2 \times 4) \times 2$.

The × 9 tables sequence: a somewhat exceptional sequence

The quickest and easiest reasoning-based way to work out all of the *nine times tables* facts is to reason from the very accessible *ten times tables*. While some children prefer to opt for the consistency of working from the *key facts* of 10 × 9 = 90 and 5 × 9 = 45, many children are happy to accept that the *nines* are most easily worked out from one key set of facts – the very easy *tens*. As we hinted above, experience at using the basic *tables* strategy gives children practice at an essential part of the reasoning needed for figuring out the facts in the × 9 sequence: '9 groups' of any number is so close to '10 groups' that we can use the '10 groups' fact to help us work out the '9 groups' answer. Thus, any number of *nines* (for example, 6 *nines*) is going to have a product which is so close to the product of the same number of *tens* (for example, 6 *tens*) that we can use the '*tens* fact' to help work out the '*nines* fact' that we need. To work out 6 × 9, we need to start from the fact that 6 *tens* are 60; each 9 is *one* less than each 10 so 6 *nines* will be six less than 6 *tens*.

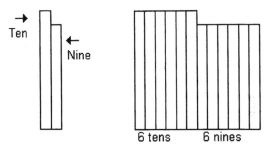

From this point on the reasoning is familiar. The fact that multiplication is commutative means that whichever way round the *tables* facts are expressed, any *tables* fact involving 'nine groups' or 'groups of nine' follows the same pattern and the same reasoning path: 6 × 9 is 6 less than 60. The answer to 6 × 9 will have to be in the 50s or '50-something'. The digits in any *nines tables* fact adds up to 9, 5 plus 4 equals 9, so the product of 6 × 9 is 54. It is worth noting that a number of children go on to discover related patterns 'in the digits' while they are reasoning from the *tens* to work out the *nines* and are able to derive digit-based reasoning shortcuts for themselves. For example, children often notice that every × 9 *tables* product begins with a *ten* less than the number of *nines* in question. Thus,

$$\underline{3} \times 9 = \underline{2}7 \qquad \underline{4} \times 9 = 36 \qquad \underline{5} \times 9 = \underline{4}5$$

And to add to the sense of the 'magic' of the × 9 facts, most children enjoy the patterns which emerge from the completed × 9 sequence. For example, most children enjoy the fact that the answers in the × 9 sequence contain the 0–9 digit sequence running forwards, then backwards.

$1 \times 9 = (0)9$
$2 \times 9 = 18$
$3 \times 9 = 27$
$4 \times 9 = 36$
$5 \times 9 = 45$
$6 \times 9 = 54$
$7 \times 9 = 63$
$8 \times 9 = 72$
$9 \times 9 = 81$
$10 \times 9 = 90$

In the process of learning the *tables sequences*, some children are shown the 'finger method' for working out the × 9 *tables*. Since the finger method can help make the × 9 *tables* feel particularly manageable, many adults and children passionately defend and support its use. In their book, *Mathematics for Dyslexics*, Chinn and Ashcroft (1998, p. 76) illustrate the finger method for devising the *tables* fact, 4 × 9. Whenever the finger method for the *nines* is to be used, Chinn and Ashcroft suggest that fingers should be placed hands-down on a flat surface such as a table. To work out 4 × 9, the *fourth* finger from the left should be tucked under. From right to left, the number of fingers *up to* the one which has been tucked under represents the number of *tens* in the answer, here *thirty*, and the number of fingers *beyond* the one which has been tucked under represents the number of *ones* in the answer, or in this instance, *six*. The fingers *show* the answer to 4 × 9 to be 36. If dyslexic and dyspraxic children are already using the finger method efficiently, it is usually wise to adopt the pragmatic approach suggested by Chinn and Ashcroft and allow children to continue doing so. However, although the finger method is quite simple, it is by no means foolproof. For example, some dyslexic and dyspraxic children find it hard to remember which finger to tuck under and some misinterpret the pattern of their fingers. Others become entirely dependent on using their fingers for the *nines* and begin to feel uncomfortable about this as they get older. In the end, as Chinn and Ashcroft point out, the most important arguments for resisting teaching the 'finger method' for the *nines* are really maths-based arguments. The reasoning-based method of deriving the *nines* from the *tens* is a very effective method, which involves a number of useful learning points and is not a one-off trick or gimmick which children may, in any case, forget. In fact, the majority of children manage to reason from the *tens* facts relatively easily and it is the experience of many teachers that the *tens*-based '9 *times tables*' patterns are often 'loved' by children almost as much as the *finger method* is.

Two useful methods of reinforcing tables sequence work

Some *grasshopper* dyslexics very quickly grasp the *key tables* way of reasoning and rapidly learn to apply it to all of the tables sequences. (After working on two or three sequences some dyslexic grasshoppers realize that they 'know' – or can figure out – all of the *tables* sequences and proudly announce their discovery.) However because the *tables* sequences make such complex sequential demands on learners, most dyslexic and dyspraxic children require fairly considerable amounts of overlearning practice in order to apply the *key tables* approach consistently and efficiently.

In early mental *times tables* work it is useful practice to help dyslexic and dyspraxic children figure out an entire sequence, out of sequence, and to record the process in the simplest linear and sequenced-based way. In this simple practice exercise, each tables question in the entire *tables* sequence is written down in its 'usual' position in the traditional 'list' format, but without any answers. At the beginning of the exercise children are asked to identify the key *tables* – in the '× 3' tables sequence, the key facts are 10 × 3 = 30 and 5 × 3 = 15. To indicate that correct answers have been given, the *key fact* questions are written down in their 'usual' location in the sequence and simply ticked (✓) or marked off in some way. The reason that the answers are not written down is that whenever the products are a recorded, in full, children usually exploit the written products to help them derive further unknown facts. *Ticking off* facts which have been answered, rather than recording the completed answer, ensures that each 'new' fact has to be recalled or derived 'from scratch' (for example, from a *key table*) in an appropriate and efficient way. Further *tables* questions are then asked from different parts of the sequence. Each time that a correct answer is given, the relevant *tables* fact is recorded in its 'place' in the sequence and *ticked*. To build children's confidence, it is usually best to begin by 'checking' the *tables* facts which are close to the *key facts* or which constitute easier and accessible *tables* facts. The 'very hard' 8 × n *tables* fact should be figured out once children are reasoning confidently. As an example, the 'X 3' *tables* could be figured out in the following order. (Of course, in the illustration which below, 1×3, 2×3 and 8×3 remain to be recalled or figured out.)

- $1 \times 3 =$
- $2 \times 3 =$
- $3 \times 3 =$ ✓ (2)
- $4 \times 3 =$ ✓ (4)
- $5 \times 3 =$ ✓ key table
- $6 \times 3 =$ ✓ (1)
- $7 \times 3 =$ ✓ (5)
- $8 \times 3 =$
- $9 \times 3 =$ ✓ (3)
- $10 \times 3 =$ ✓ key table

A second very effective way of practising the *big value tables* strategy is to play a simple **card lotto tables game** – a *tables* version of the versatile card lotto game, described on p. 429. This is a popular and particularly stress-free way of practising the *big value tables* strategy. In early sequence-based **tables lotto** the relevant *tables groups* should be concretely represented in some way. In essence, **tables lotto** proceeds according to the familiar card lotto rules. Each player has his or her own set of digit cards, here 1–10 or 1–12. The cards are placed, in sequence, face up on the table. A 1–10, or 1–12, die is required. Before play begins, players need to be clear about the *tables* sequence which is the focus of the game. In the early stages of working to consolidate knowledge of a *tables* sequence, the players should be asked to give the *key tables* facts in the relevant sequence, and the '5' card and '10' card can also be highlighted in some way:

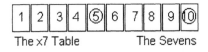

The x7 Table   The Sevens

In each round, players take turns to roll the dice. If the number '7' is rolled in a *seven times tables* game, this dice roll represents 7×7. The *big value* strategy is used to quickly work out 7×7 from the key table 5×7. Once a player has figured out the correct product (here, 49) the respective digit card (7) is turned over. Should the next player roll a dice 9, 9×7 is derived from the *key fact* 10×9 and the '9' digit card is turned over. Should a player roll a dice number which he or she has already rolled, and the card has therefore already been turned over, the player will 'miss a go.' As always, the first player to turn over 4 cards or 5 cards 'in a row' is the winner.

A **division** version of the **tables lotto game** can also be played. This is played using ordinary digit cards and a spinner. The multiples of a specific *tables* sequence are written on to a spinner base. Players take turns to generate a multiple in a specific sequence. For example, '28' could be generated in the *fours tables* sequence. Since 7 *fours* equal 28, the '7' card in the row of ordinary digit cards will be turned over.

Developing tables sequence work

Tables knowledge should not be practised for too long within the framework of a single sequence only. As soon as possible, *tables* sequence questions need to be 'mixed' with questions based on other *tables* sequences. Although children will be familiar with mixed multiplication questions from early conceptually orientated work, many children find 'harder' mixed *tables* work quite difficult.

There are a number of ways in which children's ability to derive tables facts from more than one *tables* sequence can be facilitated. At first it is best to cover two *tables* sequences only. As children's *tables* knowledge expands and consolidates, more and more sequences can be included in mixed *tables* 'quizzes'. At times, then, children will be studying one 'new' sequence; at other times, children will review their knowledge of the sequences which they have covered. In early mixed sequence work it is also helpful to 'cue children in' by checking their knowledge of the specific *key tables* facts in the sequences to be quizzed. For instance children can be asked, 'What are the *key* facts in the *threes* ... and in the *fives* ... and in the *twos*?' Indeed, since *key fact* knowledge is so pivotal to successful *tables* reasoning it is prudent to regularly check children's memory of the *key tables facts* from all of the *tables* sequences which they have studied. From very early on children should be encouraged to use the *big value tables strategy* as independently as possible. For example, in situations in which a child has 'forgotten' how to derive an individual fact, such as 8 × 5, early and quite directive prompts such as, 'What are the *key facts* in the *fives*?' should give way to more open questions such as, 'Where do you want to reason from?' Children with severe working memory difficulties are less efficient at reasoning and consequently often take longer to access tables facts. It is often helpful to create a special 'envelope' of cards containing the individual *tables* facts which children find particularly difficult: the *tables* 'question' can be written on the 'front' of the card and the answer, together with the 'reasoning route' on the back. These small numbers of cards can be 'shuffled' and reviewed for a few minutes every day, and individual cards can be removed from the envelope as soon as the child has autotamized the relevant *tables* fact or is able to figure out the fact very efficiently.

There are many *tables* games which require a broad knowledge of *tables* facts, and therefore require children to 'mix' sequences. Some games are designed on 'old-fashioned' bingo principles; pelmanism (pairs) games can also be organized to accommodate more than one *tables* sequence. (To reduce the number of 'pairs' in play, very 'easy' *tables* facts, such as 1 × 3 and 2 × 3, need not feature.) It should be noted that it is never helpful if adults simply provide the answers to tables facts which have been forgotten. The central emphasis in all *times tables* games should always be on helping children figure out *tables* answers as efficiently as possible. There are two contrasting 'mixed sequence' *tables* games which are particularly useful games to play. The first game is very simple but has the advantage that a small number of specific sequences can be targeted.

A simple spinner game

In this game, 2–4 *tables* sequences can be mixed. The spinner determines which *tables sequence* has been achieved, and a 4–10 die determines which particular *tables fact* needs to be figured out.

For example, if a player spins '3' and rolls '7', 7 × 3 will need to be figured out. Each player records his/her own scores, and after a certain number of rounds the winner – the player with the greatest overall score – can be declared.

A classic 100-square multiplication game

Many of the commercially available *times tables* games are versions of 10-by-10 *tables square* games. To play these games, all of the *tables* sequences need to have been studied. The classic *100-square* game is an expanded version of the multiplication game outlined on p. 350. To play the full game each player requires a 10 × 10 square base. Players take turns to roll two 1–10 dice and the product of the two dice scores is recorded in the appropriate square on the 100 square. (It will be remembered that rectangular numbers have two possible locations on the 100 square.) The player who first records 3 products in a row is the winner. Although it is valuable to spend some time exploring the patterns which emerge on the 10 × 10 square, the answers are clearly spread over quite a large frame and the full game is considerably slower than the 5 × 5 version. To maximize the benefits of the standard multiplication square game, it is often pragmatic to play a quicker and selective version of the game which targets the very hardest *tables* in the *tables* sequences. To play the 'harder' multiplication square game, two 5–10 dice, or spinners, should be used.

x	1	2	3	4	5	6	7	8	9	10
1										
2										
3										
4										
5										
6										
7										
8										
9										
10										

x	1	2	3	4	5	6	7	8	9	10
1										
2										
3										
4										
5										
6										
7										
8										
9										
10										

The full multiplication square game: The 'hard facts' multiplication square game:
two 1–10 dice   two 5–10 dice

Alternatively, a variation of the full *100-square* game can be played on just one full 10 × 10 base. In this version, 2–3 players play on the same base and each player requires a different colour pen/pencil to record his or her own products on the one base. The player to add the 'fourth' product to a row of three already-recorded products is the winner.

Once children are working to figure out mixed-sequence tables facts, they should be given mixed division questions to figure out, too. Mixed division games are relatively difficult to devise. The most successful mixed division games are bingo games or track games (see Appendix, p. 433) which use specially prepared division question cards.

Generally speaking, as children begin to use the *big value* strategy more confidently, work on the *tables* sequences can be further developed and refined. It should be noted that children who are very weak at reasoning in maths tend to do best if they focus on autotamatizing the *key tables strategy*. However able dyslexic and dyspraxic children who are confident that they can figure out 'any table' often begin to devise alternative strategies for themselves. They are also able to understand suggestions for alternative – and sometimes more economical – ways of reasoning. For example, children who enjoy *doubling* and who use the *doubling* route to figure out 4 × n will often quickly grasp that 8 × n is also double 4 × n:

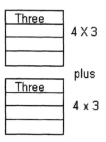

Many children are able to understand increasingly 'streamlined' *partial products* reasoning routes. Partial products thinking can be developed from the *big value* strategy. For instance, 8 × 7 can be seen as (5 × 7) + (3 × 7) rather than as (5 × 7) + 7 + 7 + 7, or, indeed, as (10 × 7) – (2 × 7).

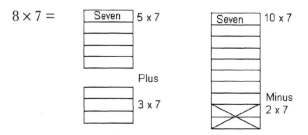

Another way to help children's thinking about the 'harder' tables to develop further is to highlight the *tables squares*. As we saw in the discussion of pattern building multiplicative work, early area model work explores the *tables square* relationships – together with rectangular numbers – up to about 5 × 5. The area model of multiplication makes clear that the *tables squares* really are squares, a fact which we have noted before, but a fact which surprises and delights many children.

$4 \times 4 =$ O O O O
          O O O O
          O O O O
          O O O O

Although the *tables squares* facts are, of course, also acquired within the individual *tables* sequences – for example 4 × 4 is covered in the × 4 *tables* sequence, and so on – it is very valuable to make a particular study of the whole 'special' set of *squares facts* to 100. Simply foregrounding the 'harder' *tables squares* often enables children to automatize the facts. Indeed, because the 6 × 6 and 9 × 9 facts are 'next door' to *key facts* they are generally automatized quite quickly. On the other hand, 7 × 7 and 8 × 8 are harder to know *by heart*. Although these quite difficult facts can, of course, be derived in the usual way, both of the facts can take quite a long time to figure out. It is sometimes helpful to teach children simple and memorable rhymes for just these two facts so that they can be generated quickly. We have stressed that dyslexic children and some dyspraxic children have poor memories for verbal associations and it can certainly be counterproductive to teach children with specific learning difficulties a large number of rhymes – but many children are able to remember the two rhymes for the two very distinctive *tables* facts. Children can be encouraged to make up their own rhymes to 'fit' the facts but many children are happy to use rhymes which are already in the public domain, such as

'Wakey, wakey, rise and shine, 7 × 7 is 49.'

and

'Wait a minute, there's a knock at the door, 8 × 8 is 64.'

For 8 × 8, some children prefer: 'I ate and I ate

Until I was sick on the floor, 8 × 8 is 64.'

Many children begin to use automatized *tables squares* facts as a quicker 'route' for deriving further facts. For example, 7 × 6 can be quickly figured out from 6 × 6 and the difficult 8 × 7 from 7 × 7. Many children find the *tables squares* facts particularly useful '*keys*' for figuring out division questions: for example, to figure out 56 ÷ 8, children often reason, '8 × 8 is 64, so 7 × 8 must be 56.

There are two ways in which *tables squares* work can be made very appealing to children. First of all, Cuisinaire rods are particularly good tools for exploring the *tables squares*. Most children enjoy constructing a 3-D rod pyramid of *tables squares* with 10 × 10 as the base, 9 × 9 placed on top, 8 × 8 on top of that, and so on, all the way to 1 × 1 at the very summit. Secondly, a special feature of *tables squares* which appeals to many children is that their recorded products can be made to create a diagonal line on an 'empty' 10 × 10 multiplication square. This particular feature creates the opportunity for playing **tables squares lotto** – a quick and fun way of practising the *tables squares* facts. Each player requires an 'empty' 10 × 10 *100 square* on which to record his or her answers. As usual, players take turns to roll a 1–10 die. In *tables squares lotto* the number rolled is 'squared' and the squared product is recorded in the correct square on the *100 square*. Thus, if a player rolls a 5, 5 × 5 is worked out and recorded in the appropriate position on the *100 square*.

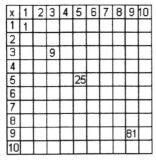

x	1	2	3	4	5	6	7	8	9	10
1	1									
2										
3			9							
4										
5					25					
6										
7										
8										
9									81	
10										

Player A

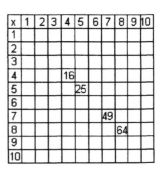

x	1	2	3	4	5	6	7	8	9	10
1										
2										
3										
4				16						
5					25					
6										
7							49			
8								64		
9										
10										

Player B

As usual, a player 'misses a go' if he or she has already been rolled a dice number and the relevant *tables* square fact has already been filled in. As usual, too, the first player to create a diagonal line of four facts in a row is the winner, and the game can be played again!

Some division issues

The difficult sharing concept of division

Sequence-based division work inevitably involves the *grouping* concept and language of division (for instance, How many sixes are there in 36?). The reason for this is that the tables sequence, or group, is obviously already declared in sequence-based multiplicative work. We saw earlier that *sharing* is harder than *grouping* because it is the group itself or the *tables* sequence which is involved which is the unknown, and it is this which has to be worked out. *Sharing* is much more open-ended than *grouping* and therefore requires larger amounts of working memory. Sharing based on 'harder' *tables* is more likely to be found difficult (and disliked) by dyslexic and dyspraxic children than *grouping* and is consequently best taught in a very structured way. For example, early practice at 'harder' *sharing* work is most successful if children know that a limited number of *tables* sequences are involved. Some examples of written questions include the following: These questions come from the 2 times tables and the 3 times tables

1. $8 \times \square = 24$
2. 7 *times* $\square = 14$
3. 18 sweets are shared between 6 children. How many sweets will each child get?

While children are learning to make sense of 'harder' *sharing* questions, teachers should ensure that concrete *sharing* activities are used to *check* 'trial-and-error' mental solutions. It is important to remember that a one-by-one 'dealing cards' solution does not foster division competence. However difficult the problem may feel to a child, teachers should guide the child towards a *mental* solution to *sharing* problems. For example, if a child is unable to solve the *sweets* example given above, a teacher may say, 'How many sweets do you *think* each child will get, and then let's check whether you are right.' If an incorrect answer is given, the child should be allowed to share 'incorrectly' and discover that a mistake has been made.

The concept of remainders in division

In traditional approaches to teaching maths, the idea of 'a remainder' is usually very abstractly presented to children, and it is often presented after children have worked through a lot of 'drill' at answering 'exact' divisions from the tables sequences. Children are often required to speed through abstract examples of divisions with remainders and dyslexic and dyspraxic children very often do not have a clear idea of what a 'remainder' means.

Understanding-based division work helps children to make sense of divisions-with-remainders in two important ways. First of all, children who have worked to build concrete groups to model division solutions, and who have spent time *sharing* concretely, do not have usually have difficulty with the concept of a remainder. For example, 'How many *fours* are there in 14?'

```
O O O O    3 x 4 = 12
O O O O
O O O O
           = 2 remaining
O O
```

It is very helpful to introduce divisions-with-remainders quite early on and, at first, it is certainly important to give children problems involving relatively small numbers to work with: this helps to ensure that children are able to focus on grasping the concept of the remainder without, at the same time, struggling to find a very difficult *tables* fact. Dyslexic and dyspraxic primary school children particularly enjoy mock serious discussions of what could, or 'should' happen to remainders in word-problem situations – for example, who is going to eat a 'remaining' chocolate bar (or 'remaining' bars). Such discussions help children make thoughtful sense of, and give correct answers to, notoriously 'tricky' division word problems, such as, '17 people want to go to the beach by car; 5 people will fit into each car. How many cars are needed?' As many maths researchers and educators point out, children who learn about remainders in purely formal, number-based ways, typically neglect the 'remaining' people who wish to get to the beach, and usually answer that 5 cars are needed, or conclude that the 'answer' to the 'cars' problem is 5 remainder 2! Although it is usually best to introduce children to 'remainders' through informal and fun problem-solving activities, dyslexic and dyspraxic children also need to be given practice at solving 'bare' division calculations: in some instances, dyspraxic children in particular, do not easily generalize from word-problem situations involving remainders, to number problems involving remainders, and may need access to concrete materials in early work in both contexts.

Children who have spent a great deal of their time rote-learning whole *tables* sequences (and who have not engaged in practical division work) try to use the overlearned verbal associations to help to them generate division answers. Dyslexic and dyspraxic children often find it almost impossible to find the appropriate associations in examples of 'divisions-with-remainders' because a multiple of the divisor is not involved. Searching for the correct *tables* association becomes particularly difficult when bigger numbers and bigger tables divisors (for example, 6, 7, 8 and 9) are involved. The *big value key fact* multiplication and division strategy helps to 'ground' and 'orientate' dyslexic and dyspraxic children in their search for a correct answer to divisions-with-remainders. In essence, they give children an approximate starting point in the search for a solution. For example: $40 \div 6 = \square$. Key table: $5 \times 6 = 30$; 30 is 'close enough' to 40; $6 \times 6 = 36$, $7 \times 6 =$ too big; $40 \div 6 = 6$ rem. 4.

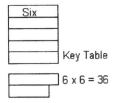

Children who have some proficiency at solving divisions-with-remainders enjoy learning to speed up in division work by playing a simple *mental division game*. A very basic version of the remainders game is described, here, but a harder version is described in Chapter 12. In the basic **remainders game** an ordinary 1–6 dice should be used. A simple numbered track which is suitable for children to move 'tokens' (counters) along is needed. The track should start from 7 and finish at 36. Each player should have his or her own token. Each player takes turns to roll the dice. If a player rolls 5, he or she divides the number his or her token currently occupies by 5. In the opening move, '7 *divided by* 5 equals 1 , with a remainder of 2.' In the **remainders game**, the player moves the number of spaces indicated by the remainder ('moves the remainder') which, in this example, is 2. However, if the number occupied on the track is a *multiple* of the die number rolled, no remainder can be generated, and the player cannot move in that round. For example, once the player described above has moved 2 to square number 9, should he or she roll '3' in his or her next 'go', he or she will be unable to move in that round. The winner is the first player to complete the track.

Less common and more complex multiplication and division word-problem forms

It will be remembered that all children solve *equivalent groups* multiplication problems most easily. For example, 'There are 6 eggs in a small carton of eggs. How many eggs does 7 cartons of eggs contain?' We have also seen that although *equivalent groups* multiplication problems are relatively straightforward, *equivalent groups* division problems are somewhat trickier for children to come to terms with. This is because some *equivalent groups* division problems are *grouping* problems and some basic division problems are *sharing* problems. An example of a *grouping* problem is '42 eggs are packed into cartons of 6 eggs. How many cartons of eggs are made?' An example of a *sharing* problem is '42 chocolate eggs are shared between 7 children. How many eggs will each child get?'

Although there is less research into multiplication and division word problems than there is into addition and subtraction word problems, many of the overall conclusions which commentators have reached are roughly the same in both areas. In general it is found that if children are to make sense of *multiplicative* word problems, they need to work in 'bottom-up' ways. In general, too, it is found that children are fed a limited diet of multiplication and division word problems to solve. Analyses of textbooks show that by far the greatest proportion of multiplication and division word problems are *equivalent groups* problems. This means that children tend to retain a rather limited and limiting concept of multiplication and division. Children are able to develop a deeper, more flexible understanding of multiplication if they are given a wider variety of problems to solve. For this reason, it is agreed that it is important that teachers have an understanding of a broader range of possible word-problem forms.

However, as Verschaffel and Corte suggest, the discussion of multiplication and division word problems is at an earlier stage of development than the discussion of addition and subtraction word-problem forms. As we have seen, it is possible to give a broadly 'standard' and widely accepted list of addition and subtraction word-problem types which teachers are able to use as a fairly comprehensive resource. The relative lack of research into multiplication and division word problems, and the fact that different researchers in the field have used very different ways of classifying the types of multiplication and division word problems, has meant that it is more difficult to present a comprehensive list of multiplication and division word-problem types. Nevertheless, as Verschaffel and Corte also acknowledge, there is some degree of consensus in the field. The very modest analysis of multiplication and division word-problem types, which is offered below, aims to represent this common ground. It draws primarily on the classifications of Vicky Kouba and Kathy Franklin, and on the classifications and examples described in Verschaffel and Corte's and Mulligan and Mitchelmore's work.

It would seem that most researchers agree that it is important to recognize that some *multiplicative* word problems are *psychologically commutative*, or *symmetrical*, while others are *psychologically non-commutative*, or *asymmetrical*. In discussions of multiplicative word-problem types it helps to know that a *multiplier* is a number which operates multiplicatively on another number, which is called the *multiplicand*. In *psychologically commutative* situations, as Kouba and

Franklin (1993) explain, 'factors have interchangeable roles. That is it doesn't matter within the context which factor is the multiplier.' On the other hand in psychologically non-commutative situations the multiplier and the multiplicand can be distinguished. *Psychologically commutative* situations include (1) *area* problems and (2) *Cartesian product* problems. Psychologically non-commutative situations, in which multiplier and multiplicand are not interchangeable, include: (1) *equivalent groups* problems, which involve groups comprised of *ones*; (2) the very similar *equal measures* problems, which involve continuous quantities, such as centimetres or litres, and so on; (3) *rate* problems; (4) *measure conversions*; and (5) *scalar* or *multiplicative comparison* problems. As Verschaffel and Corte (1997) point out, 'problems involving "Equal Groups" and "Equal Measures" are systematically found to be rather easy, while those involving "Cartesian product" and "Measure conversion" seem very difficult.' Not surprisingly, perhaps, the latter two types of *multiplicative* problems are usually particularly difficult for dyspraxic children to solve. Dyslexic children and dyspraxic children, who are still acquiring an understanding of *multiplicative* situations, can have difficulty with the suggestion that they could apply the principle of *commutativity* in multiplication word-problem situations which are *psychologically non-commutative*. In other words, when a dyslexic or dyspraxic child has to solve a problem, such as '8 tigers. How many eyes?' it can confuse the child if an adult suggests that he or she could see the problem as the easier-to-solve two *eights*.

Word-problem examples for all the main *multiplicative* word-problem types are given below so that they can be used as a quick reference by teachers. The harder problem forms should, of course, be introduced in the 'bottom-up' ways described earlier. It should be noted that problem types which necessarily involve parts-of-wholes (such as finding fractions of numbers) are not included here.

Psychologically non-commutative situations

Examples of *equivalent groups* problems have already been given on p. 326.

Equal measures problems

- 4 children each eat a liquorice strip. Each liquorice strip measures 9cm. How many centimetres of liquorice have the children eaten altogether?
- A mum bought a long liquorice strip of 36cm and cut it into equal-sized pieces for her 4 children. How long was each strip of liquorice which each of the 4 children got?

Rate problems

- Jane bought 4 balloons. Each balloon cost 5p. How much do the balloons cost altogether?
- Jane spent 20p on balloons. Each balloon cost 5p. How many balloons was Jane able to buy?

Scalar (or multiplicative comparison) problems

- Jack has three *times* as many computer games as his friend John. John has 4 computer games. How many computer games does Jack have?
- Jack has 12 computer games. He has three *times* as many computer games as his friend John. How many does John have?

Psychologically commutative word problems

Area (regular array) problems

- Jill put cards into rows. She put 4 cards in each row. She made 4 rows of cards. How many cards did Jill use?
- Jill put cards into rows. She used 16 cards in all. She put 4 cards into each row. How many rows did she make?

Cartesian product

- James has to choose what to wear. He has 3 different shirts to choose from, and 2 different types of pants. How many different combinations could he make?
- James can make 12 different combinations from shirts and pants. He has 3 very different types of shirts. How many types of pants does he have?

CHAPTER 12

More multiplication and division: working with larger numbers

The standard methods for short and long multiplication

From the very first stages of learning to multiply and divide beyond the domain of the *tables* sequences children have usually been taught the standard pencil-and-paper methods for completing *short* and *long multiplication* calculations and for completing *short* and *long division* calculations. Since the standard methods for long multiplication and division are particularly condensed and difficult to explain – for instance they are considerably more difficult than the standard procedures for addition – they are generally taught in a very procedural or recipe-like way.

The standard method for short multiplication: multiplying two digit numbers by a single-digit multiplier

In traditional classrooms, work on *short multiplication* calculations is introduced as soon as children are beginning to consolidate their knowledge of the *times tables* facts. Indeed *short multiplication* work often seems to be viewed by teachers as another more challenging way for children to practise the *tables*. The standard method for short multiplication requires children to set out the calculations in the traditional vertical column layout. As we have seen, most standard methods of calculation involve working from right to left, starting with any *units* numbers, first, then moving on to the *tens*, and so on. To complete *short multiplication* calculations, children follow this standard prescribed route. Thus children are required to multiply the *unit* digit first, 'carrying' any resulting *tens* into the *tens* position, if necessary, then multiply the *tens* digit and so on. The short multiplication procedure is usually taught as a set series of steps. Children are encouraged to memorize these steps in highly routinized language. For example, to complete the calculation 36 × 4, children are generally required to verbalize the short multiplication procedure as '4 times 6 is 24, put down the 4 and carry the 2; 4 times 3 is 12, plus the 2 is 14, so the answer is 145':

$$
\begin{array}{r}
3\ 6 \\
\times\ 4 \\
\hline
1\ 4\ 4 \\
2
\end{array}
$$

As we saw in Part IV, all standard procedures require that larger values are reduced to the status of the *ones* for the purposes of calculation. To manage the multiplication of 36 × 4 from the left to the right in one 'line' children are required to treat 30 as '3' but then accept that the *tens* outcome '14' in the answer makes the final product 144. As Thompson (1999c, p. 178) says, this means that 'the meaning and purpose of the actions are not really obvious, nor particularly easy to understand'. For primary school dyslexic and dyspraxic children, a number of problems typically arise in the traditional short multiplication work. These problems are similar in nature to the problems which arise in standard addition and subtraction calculation. Nevertheless the teaching issues are such significant ones that it is important to outline the difficulties which typically affect the process of acquiring the multiplication procedures.

First of all, it is widely reported that many children with specific learning difficulties find the *short multiplication* procedure very difficult to acquire. Many dyslexic and dyspraxic children make repeated errors in completing short multiplication work. A significant number of these mistakes are not due to 'mere' calculation carelessness. Like many of the mistakes which dyslexic and dyspraxic children make in standard addition and standard subtraction work, they are examples of well-known calculation 'bugs' and represent children's failed attempts to follow the rules which they have tried to learn and tried to remember.

The cognitive difficulties associated with specific learning difficulties contribute to the 'bug' errors. For instance, dyslexic and dyspraxic children with sequencing problems have difficulty grasping the sequence of steps which has to be followed, and consequently have difficulty with the early stages of learning the procedure. Children with sequencing difficulties typically 'forget' or misremember the exact sequence in which the steps have to be executed. Common execution errors include the following:

```
  3 6          3 6            3 6
  x 4           x 4            x 4
 1 2 2 4       1 6 2          1 2 4
                 4
```

Children with directional difficulties find the standard short multiplication procedures very confusing. For example, in the example of 36 × 4 given above, many children with directional difficulties find the action of starting with the '4', multiplying the '6' in 36 first and then returning back to the '4', before multiplying the ' 3' in 36, particularly difficult to grasp and remember:

```
        b a
   c 3 6
      x 4
    1 4 4
```

Finally, since it is hard for primary school dyslexic and dyspraxic children to understand the steps which they are taught to follow, they often execute the short multiplication procedure in an inflexible and uncomprehending way. Typically, dyslexic and dyspraxic children rigidly set out to follow the 'rules'. They are not able to offer a reasonable approximation for the calculation and have no sense of what the likely outcome of the calculation will be. Indeed many children feel compelled to 'start from the beginning' in order to give any form of answer at all – they cannot think about short multiplication calculations in any other way. This lack of a *feel* for short multiplication outcomes has important negative implications for children's ability to judge the appropriateness of word-problem solutions and for *short multiplication* 'puzzle solving'. It has very important implications for formal long division work, as well.

The procedural approach to long multiplication

Following considerable amounts of routine practice (or 'drill') at completing standard *short multiplication* algorithms, children in traditional classrooms are considered ready to acquire the next step in multiplication work. In other words, they are soon required to move on to learn the more complex and demanding standard method for working out 'true' *long multiplication* calculations. As we have just seen, *short multiplication* by a single-digit multiplier is often hard for dyslexic and dyspraxic children to master. 'True' *long multiplication* is very much more daunting to learn. The real cognitive complexities connected with multiplying two-digit numbers by *tens* (and later by *hundreds*) multipliers makes the standard long multiplication procedure particularly difficult to make sense of. For example, to complete a multiplication algorithm, such as 56 × 24, children have to be taught to make provision for the results of multiplying by a *multiple of ten* (here, 20 in 24). Teachers then have to ensure that children remember this procedural step in all further *long-multiplication* calculations.

In teaching the standard *long multiplication* procedure, the difficult 'problem' of the *tens* multiplier is usually dealt with by training children to put a 'place-holding' zero in the relevant tens calculation 'row':

$$
\begin{array}{r}
5\,6 \\
\times 2\,4 \\
\hline
0 \ (\times 20)
\end{array}
$$

In very 'old-fashioned' traditional maths teaching approaches, children are simply trained to place a 'zero' beneath the *units* number in the *multiplier* before they begin the step of multiplying by the *ten*. In this kind of approach, children are often required to remember the abstract 'rule' that ' when you multiply by the '2' you have to start writing numbers beneath the '2' so you need to place a '0' beneath the '4' first'. In less determinedly procedural approaches it is common practice to try and explain the *long multiplication* 'zero rule' to children. Typically, children are encouraged to understand and remember that a zero 'place-holder' has to be recorded to indicate that 'you are multiplying by a *ten* in this row'. However, there are two common difficulties with the usual 'place-holding zero' approaches in standard *long multiplication*. The first is that children are often taught a very abstract 'rule' that you 'add' a zero in this row to show that you are multiplying by 10 – a problematic 'rule' to which we will return shortly. On the other hand, if teachers try to explain the place-value holding role of the zero in genuine place value terms (the effects of multiplying by 20), this can cause children to become confused in the very next stage of the calculation. Once the actual standard process of multiplying 'in the *tens* row' begins, the *tens* digit is not treated as a *ten* at all. Instead, it is treated as a *units* number. In multiplying 36 by 24, the 20 in the 24 has to be treated as a '2' rather than as '20'. Children are required to articulate the 'tens multiplier' calculation row as, 'I'm multiplying by 20, so I have to put in a zero; *two* times 6 is 12, 'carry' the '1', *two* times 5 is 10, plus the 1 is 11.'

While most children with specific learning difficulties will attempt *short multiplication* calculations, once they have learned the procedure, a considerable number of children with specific learning difficulties routinely refuse to 'have a go' at completing *long multiplication* calculations. In assessment situations, for instance, dyslexic and dyspraxic children will often protect themselves from likely failure by claiming that they don't know how to 'do' long multiplication, that long multiplication is 'too difficult' or that they 'hate' long multiplication and can never remember how it 'goes'. Other dyslexic and dyspraxic children routinely and pragmatically ask for help in the crucial *tens* row. On the other hand, when primary school dyslexic and dyspraxic children attempt to complete formal long multiplication algorithms, they frequently make a range of quite common 'bug' errors. For example, dyslexic and dyspraxic children frequently omit the 'place holding zero' altogether. This 'bug' is particularly common in situations where a '0' results from the first stage multiplication. (For instance, in a calculation, such as 25×24.) Some dyslexic and dyspraxic routinely place a '0' in both rows regardless of the actual numbers involved. Children with directional weaknesses have great difficulty trying to keep track of the complex 'criss-crossing' directions in which they are required to work.

(a) $\times 4 =$ $\begin{array}{r} 5\,6 \\ \times 2\,4 \end{array}$ ↓↑   (b) $\times 20 =$ $\begin{array}{r} 5\,6 \\ \times 2\,4 \end{array}$ ↓↑↓

Children with writing difficulties and/or organizational difficulties often fail to align the layers of the columns correctly, or they sometimes become confused by the digits which they have recorded to represent the values which need to be 'carried'.

$$\begin{array}{r} 3\,6 \\ \times 2\,4 \\ \hline 1\,4\,4 \\ +\ 7\,2\,0 \\ \hline 2\,1\,2\,4 \end{array} \qquad \begin{array}{r} 3\,6 \\ \times 2\,4 \\ \hline 7\,2\,0 \\ +\,{}_{1}2\,4\,4 \\ \hline 9\,8\,4 \end{array}$$

Understanding-based approaches to short-multiplication

Overall, then, it is very common for children with specific learning difficulties to feel that the standard multiplication algorithms are devoid of meaning. As we have seen, the 'longer' multiplication procedures are very hard for dyslexic and dyspraxic children to understand, and to remember, and trying to learn them can contribute to a sense of incompetence in maths. The teaching implications of this are very familiar ones. Instead of insisting that children with specific learning difficulties learn the standard multiplication procedures, dyslexic and dyspraxic children generally benefit from being helped to develop more meaningful *mental* procedures for *short* and *long multiplication*. This approach usually helps them succeed in the short term, and also contributes towards ensuring that they continue to make progress in learning about numbers.

Thus far there has been less research into children's early understanding of multiplication than there has been into young children's understanding of addition and subtraction. There is also relatively little research into the methods which children devise or 'invent' for short and long multiplication. (There has been rather more research into the *mental* methods which children devise for *short and long division*). Broadly speaking, however, there would seem to be three different approaches which children commonly adopt in attempting to solve *short multiplication* problems:

1. A **'place value' partitioning** or **chunking** approach. In this approach, the two-digit number in a *short multiplication* question is broken down into its constituent values; each value is multiplied separately by the single-digit multiplier and then the partial values are combined. For example, $66 \times 3 = (60 + 6) \times 3 = 180 + 18 = 198$.

2. A **partitioning-into-multiples** approach. In this *partial products* approach, the two-digit number (the multiplicand) can be broken down into smaller component *multiples* to make calculation easier: for example, $16 \times 5 = (8 \times 5) + (8 \times 5)$. Alternatively, the single-digit multiplier can be 'split' so that the two-digit calculation is made easier: for example, $36 \times 4 = (36 \times 2) + (36 \times 2)$

3. A **rounding-and-adjusting or overshooting** approach. In rounding-and-adjusting types of solutions, children can simplify the calculation by modifying the two-digit number (the multiplicand) to figure out the *short multiplication* question. For example, 29×8 can be adjusted to 30×8 and then 8 has to be subtracted: $30 \times 8 = 240 - 8 = 232$. The single-digit multiplier can also be adjusted: for example 35×9 can be figured out as $(35 \times 10) - 35$: $35 \times 10 = 350$, $350 - 35 = 315$.

Teachers find that the place-value partitioning approach is the most popular and best understood *mental short multiplication* method. Generally speaking, dyslexic and dyspraxic primary school children also tend to devise the *partitioning* method for short multiplication (when they are given genuinely meaningful multiplication examples to solve and are given access to concrete materials). Although *grasshopper* dyslexics often devise and use a variety of the *mental* short multiplication methods described above, the cognitive weaknesses which characteristically make calculation difficult for many dyslexic or dyspraxic children mean that it is not advisable to teach them a range of different *mental* methods for *short multiplication*. As always, it is vital to remember that '*inchworm*' children with specific learning difficulties can become confused if they are asked to make sense of too many reasoning options. In particular, it can undermine children's confidence it they become confused very early on in *short* and *long* multiplication work. Once again, the majority of dyslexic and dyspraxic children do best in the early stages of *short multiplication* work if they learn one 'safe' *short multiplication* method which can be applied successfully to all *short multiplication* calculations and problems.

It seems to be very widely agreed in the literature on *short multiplication* that the *mental partitioning* method for *short multiplication* is a very good *mental* multiplication method for primary school children to learn. In fact, as educationalists, such as Ian Thompson and Judith Anghileri point out, there are many advantages associated with using the *mental partitioning* method for *short multiplication* (Anghileri, 1999; Thompson, 1999c). First of all, the *mental partitioning* method for *short multiplication* is relatively easy for children to grasp if they have a good understanding of *place value* (and of *place value* exchanges) and if they also have competent access to the *tables* facts. Secondly, the *partitioning* model builds on, and is fostered by, two highly significant previous aspects of understanding-based maths: the *chunking* or *partitioning* model in addition (for example, $36 + 36 = 60 + 12 = 72$); and the working knowledge gained from tables sequence work that the 'harder' *tables* facts can be built up from smaller components: for instance, $7 \times 8 = 5$ *eights* + 2 *eights*. Thirdly, the *mental partitioning* model has important advantages over the standard methods for *short multiplication*. For example, when the component parts of the numbers are multiplied, they always retain their real value; and, in a closely related advantage, the mental partitioning procedure involves no 'carrying', with all of its associated pitfalls. One longer term advantage of the *mental partitioning* method is that the *standard* method for short multiplication is essentially a column-based *partitioning* method. This means that many children with learning difficulties, who manage to master the *mental partitioning short multiplication* method, are able to adjust, relatively easily, to the compact standard method for *short multiplication*: indeed, teaching experience shows that many dyslexic and dyspraxic children who have learned both methods are able to 'switch' between the *mental* and the standard methods, depending on the form of presentation of the 'sum' and the difficulty of the required calculation .

An important pre-skill for short multiplication: multiplying tens etc.

Before children can progress from working with basic multiplication and *tables* facts to learning about *short multiplication* they will need to know how to multiply quantities of *tens, hundreds* and so on. In other words, children have to learn to multiply quantities of units of value which have a greater value than 'mere' *ones*. To give an example: working on *tables* sequences helps children multiply 7 by 8, whereas to use the *mental partitioning* method for *short multiplication* children need to be able to multiply 70, say, or 700, by 8. Fortunately, by this stage, learning to multiply large values is not usually a very difficult skill for children to acquire. There are three possible reasoning 'routes'; and one of these routes, in particular, is quite easily understood by the majority of children. First of all, it would seem that the majority of dyslexic and dyspraxic children prefer the *place value* 'same fact, different value' approach – an approach which is already very familiar from multi-digit addition work. In addition, 60 + 60 = 12 tens = 120, 600 + 600 = 12 hundreds, and so on. Likewise, large value multiplications can be understood in a very similar way: $3 \times 6 = 18$, so $3 \times 60 = 18$ *tens* = 180, and $3 \times 600 = 18$ *hundreds* = 1800. Alternatively, some children prefer an approach which 'chunks' larger decade values into multiples of 10: $3 \times 60 = 3 \times (6 \times 10) = 18 \times 10 = 180$. Finally, a very few dyslexic and dyspraxic children – generally those children who still rely on fact-derived strategies to work our harder tables facts – prefer to work out difficult calculations such as 6 x 70 using a two-stage *partial products* approach. For example, they may choose to figure out 6×70 from 5×70 because 5×7 is 'easy' ($5 \times 70 = 350 + 70 = 420$) or they may choose to double 3×70, because 3×7 is 'easy' too ($3 \times 70 = 210; 210 \times 2 = 420$). In this approach the component calculations are, of course, still understood in a 'same fact, different value' way: $5 \times 70 = 350$, since $5 \times 7 = 35$.

Teaching suggestions: 'same fact, different value'

When 'same fact different value' multiplication work is first introduced to children, it is best to select problems involving small quantities of the different values. This is to ensure that *place value* exchanges do not have to be made. Keeping the calculations simple means, in turn, that the patterned relationships can be easily grasped and visualized. A simple question such as 'what are 3 *thirties?*' can be made clear by setting '3 thirties' in relation to '3 *threes*'.

3 threes =   3 groups of 3 = 9 = 3 × 3 = 9

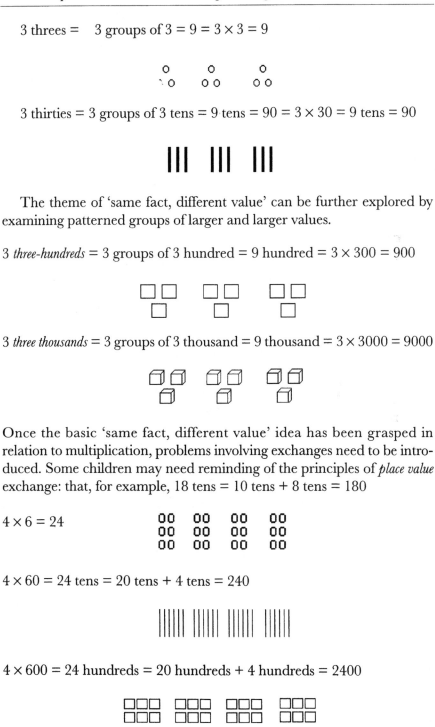

3 thirties = 3 groups of 3 tens = 9 tens = 90 = 3 × 30 = 9 tens = 90

The theme of 'same fact, different value' can be further explored by examining patterned groups of larger and larger values.

3 *three-hundreds* = 3 groups of 3 hundred = 9 hundred = 3 × 300 = 900

3 *three thousands* = 3 groups of 3 thousand = 9 thousand = 3 × 3000 = 9000

Once the basic 'same fact, different value' idea has been grasped in relation to multiplication, problems involving exchanges need to be introduced. Some children may need reminding of the principles of *place value* exchange: that, for example, 18 tens = 10 tens + 8 tens = 180

4 × 6 = 24

4 × 60 = 24 tens = 20 tens + 4 tens = 240

4 × 600 = 24 hundreds = 20 hundreds + 4 hundreds = 2400

The same understandings may be explored through encouraging children to lay out materials in the more structured area model formation. For example:

$4 \times 600 =$

A lively way of practising larger value multiplication – which allows children to have meaningful practice at negotiating the *place value* exchanges – is to play a simple spinner-based game in which children multiply radically different values. When the spinner multiplication games are introduced, it is useful to start with fewer, smaller quantities on the spinner base, for example, $\times 2, \times 20 \times 3, \times 30, \times 4, \times 40, \times 5$ and $\times 50$. In subsequent games, a greater range of larger quantities can be selected to work with, for example, $\times 7, \times 70, \times 8 \times 80$; or $\times 2, \times 20, \times 200; \times 3 \times 30, \times 300$ and so on. To play the **mixed value spinner game**, each player takes it in turn to throw a die (1–6 or 1–9) to secure a multiplier, then the player simply spins and multiplies! For example if a player rolls 6 and spins 500, he or she 'scores' 6×500 or 3000. If a second player rolls 4 and spins 40 he or she 'scores' 160 in this round. Points or tokens may be awarded to the 'winner' in each round; alternatively, scores may be added at the end to secure an overall winner.

Short multiplication; some general teaching recommendations and suggestions

Although many aspects of the *partitioning short multiplication* model build on earlier *partitioning* work in addition, multiplication is nevertheless harder than addition to understand and visualize. To ensure that dyslexic and dyspraxic children do not become overwhelmed by the conceptual and working memory demands of working with large repeated groups (and potentially very large quantities) it is helpful to structure and to sequence early short multiplication work quite carefully. From very early on it is important to ask children to explain in words what each short multiplication question 'means' and to give a verbal overview of what the 'figuring out process' will involve. It contributes greatly to children's immediate calculation success (and to their overall understanding) if they articulate that a calculation such as 13×5 (or 5×13) means '5 thirteens' (or '5 groups of thirteen' and that it is going to help to 'split' 13 into its component parts. It is usually best to begin structured *short multiplication* work by asking children to multiply the more manageable 'teen' numbers, such as the 13 × 5 example. The advantages of 'teen' numbers are that they are relatively small – just beyond the framework of the numbers within the *times tables* sequences – and they are therefore easy to represent concretely.

While children are still exploring the *partitioning* model (and adjusting to multiplying by more than 'one *ten*') it is helpful to monitor the number of exchanges which need to take place. For instance, the calculation 36 × 3 is much easier to manage than a calculation like 46 × 3, in which the 12 *tens* have to be interpreted as 120. Likewise, while children are learning to negotiate *place value* exchanges within the *short multiplication* framework, it is helpful to select 'easier tables' *multipliers*: multiplying a double-digit number by 2, 3, 4 or 5 is much more easily executed than multiplying the same number by 6, 7, 8 or 9. In other words, 76 × 3 is much easier to execute than 76 × 8.

As always, most dyslexic and dyspraxic children benefit from modelling the earlier stages of *short multiplication* work using concrete materials. Since the quantities involved are quite large, Cuisinaire rods and Base Ten materials are the most useful maths materials to use. In time, children can also be encouraged to draw multiplication arrays on squared paper. 'Concrete' work of this nature can significantly improve children's understanding of the way in which the components which comprise a completed multiplication calculation are built up and fit together. From the earliest concrete activities it is helpful to encourage children to lay out appropriate materials and solve examples of carefully selected problems as independently as possible. It should be noted that if primary school children are given a 'free hand' in the way that they model short multiplication calculations, the majority of them will tend to model the problems as rather loosely constructed repeated groups. From their very informal models children readily extract the *tens* and then combine and multiply the *ones*. 3 × 17 is very often modelled as:

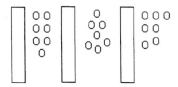

However, since working with the more tightly structured 'area model' way of representing *short* and *long multiplication* calculations can contribute greatly to children's understanding of the *partitioning* principle, teachers can also nudge or guide children towards organizing materials in an area-based way. Thus, 3 × 17 can also be represented as structured rows of 17. Likewise, a number of further calculations, such as 4 × 26, for instance, can be modelled more 'intuitively' and loosely, first, and then rebuilt into the more structured arrays:

TEN	TEN	SIX

Working with regularly arranged food items, such as large chocolate bars, large boxes of chocolates or a number of 'rolls' of sweets (such as wine gums) is a 'fun' way of consolidating the 'area' idea. Squared paper activities often allow children to make 'multiplicative' discoveries for themselves, as long as the principle that 'each row' represents one group or quantity is understood. (As we will see later, area model activities are not always understood by children.) Because 'bare' abstract rectangular areas can be visually difficult to make sense of, it is helpful to start out by having children construct 'concretized' versions of squared paper rectangular arrays.

'Stick 4 rows of 15 dot 'stickers' on the squares. Show that 15 is 10 + 5.'

4 × 15 =

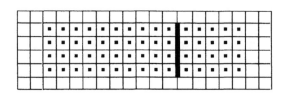

Many children also benefit from the simple step of shading the relevant groups – or rows – before drawing the outer edge of the rectangular array. For example, an area representation of 6 × 13 can be built up in this way, starting with 1 × 13.

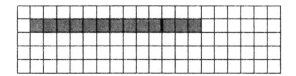

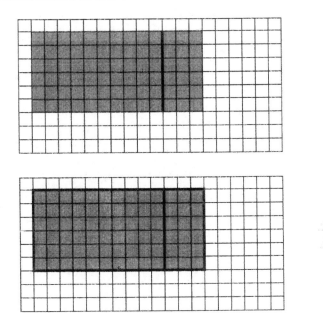

Dyslexic and dyspraxic children who are able to manage the working memory demands of performing *short multiplication* calculations entirely mentally ('in their heads') should be encouraged to do so. First, mental proficiency at completing *short multiplication* calculations is a useful 'real-life' skill. Secondly, the ability to complete *short multiplication* calculations in one step, or one line, makes *mental long multiplication* and *long division* very much quicker and easier to manage.

Recording the mental partitioning method

In the early stages of all *mental* calculation work, it is usual, as we have seen, to record calculations horizontally rather than vertically. For instance, 3 thirteens, or 13 multiplied by 3, is usually recorded as $13 \times 3 =$ or $3 \times 13 =$

TEN	THREE
TEN	THREE
TEN	THREE

(a) $13 \times 3 = 10 \times 3 + 3 \times 3 = 30 + 9 = 39$

(b) $13 \times 3 = 30 + 9 = 39$

In recording the *mental short multiplication* procedure it can be helpful to draw attention to the *place-value chunking* theme by recording the '10 + 4' components of, for instance, 3×14 or 3 fourteens, in the familiar triad form. This helps prepare the way for successful paper-and-pencil calculation. In the early stages of written number-work, dyslexic and dyspraxic children generally need to support their thinking processes and reduce their working memory load by recording the partial calculation steps. In very early work, many children benefit from indicating the reasoning 'path' which they are going to take.

Some written recording methods:

(a)

3 x   14

10   4
① ②

$= 30 + 12 = 42$

(b)

3 x 14

$= 30 + 12 = 42$

(c)

3 x 10

3 x 14

3 x 4

$= 30 + 12 = 42$

(d) 3×14 $= 30 + 12 = 42$

Non standard vertical short multiplication – 'stress-free' short multiplication

As we saw in Part IV, dyslexic and dyspraxic children are usually able to adapt to the standard algorithms for addition and subtraction. We also saw that many dyslexic and dyspraxic children benefit from an intermediate stage in which they use formal-looking horizontal layouts but employ informal, *mental* methods of calculating. The same general guidelines apply to *short multiplication*. Most dyslexic and dyspraxic children have little difficulty translating the *mental partitioning* multiplication method into a parallel, horizontal format:

(a) $14 \times 3 = 30 + 12 = 42$ →

$$
\begin{array}{r}
1\ 4 \\
\times\ \ \ 3 \\
\hline
3\ 0 \\
+\ 1\ 2 \\
\hline
4\ 2 \\
\hline
\end{array}
$$

(b) $363 \times 3 = 900 + 180 + 9$ →

$$
\begin{array}{r}
3\ \ 6\ \ 3 \\
\times\ \ \ \ \ \ \ \ 3 \\
\hline
9\ \ 0\ \ 0 \\
1\ \ 8\ \ 0 \\
+\ \ \ \ \ \ \ \ 9 \\
\hline
1\ \ 0\ \ 8\ \ 9 \\
\hline
\end{array}
$$

Dyslexic and dyspraxic children who work in traditional maths classrooms can be introduced to the vertical method of recording partial calculations quite early on. Later on, concrete materials can be used to show children that the standard *short multiplication* method is similar to the *mental partitioning* method: the difference between the standard method and the *mental* method is that standard multiplication begins, as always, with the smallest *units* position, rather than with the largest value position.

In this regard, diagrams also offer helpful cognitive support:

$14 \times 3 =$ $\ \|\ \ \ \|\ \ \ \|\ \longrightarrow\ \|\|\|\ \|\|\|$

Non-standard method

$$
\begin{array}{r}
1\ 4 \\
\times\ \ \ 3 \\
\hline
3\ 0 \\
+\ 1\ 2 \\
\hline
4\ 2 \\
\hline
\end{array}
$$

Standard method

$$
\begin{array}{r}
1\ 4 \\
\times\ \ \ 3 \\
\hline
4\ 2 \\
\hline
1\ \ \ \ \ \\
\end{array}
$$

It should be noted that dyslexic and dyspraxic children with very poor sequential memories, left–right operation difficulties and/or very weak working memories, might not adjust well to standard right-to-left multiplication and to the carrying difficulties which ensue. Such children perform best if they are permitted to continue using 'low-stress' non-standard algorithms.

Word problems: short multiplication

As a number of commentators argue, carefully designed word problems lend themselves to structured tens-based multiplicative thinking, and can considerably contribute to children's understanding of *short multiplication*. Children should be asked to solve carefully selected word problems alongside 'bare' calculation work, and teachers should always ensure that sufficient time is allocated to problem-solving work. In the early *short multiplication* problem-solving work children can use concrete materials to help support their thinking or they could be encouraged to use simplified diagrammatic representations of the problems to be solved. Children should certainly be asked to rephrase the word-problem situation and it is important to help children identify and articulate what the 'maths question' seems to be – what it is that children will have to figure out and what the 'maths question' in the word problem actually 'means': for example the felt-tip pens in the word problem below, involves the calculation, '3 fourteens'. Word problems which are readily visualized in a *tens-structured* way are the kinds of word problems which particularly lend themselves to area representations.

Area problems

(a) A very large box of felt-tip pens contains 3 rows of pens. Each row is made up of 14 pens. How many pens does the box contain altogether? Diagram:

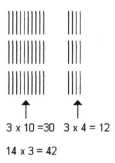

3 x 10 =30   3 x 4 = 12

14 x 3 = 42

(b) A long, thin box of chocolate balls contains 15 balls in a row. How many chocolate balls would there be in 4 boxes?
Diagram:

O = 1 Chocolate   ⊖⊖⊖⊖⊖⊖⊖⊖⊖⊖ ⊖⊖⊖⊖⊖
                    ⊖⊖⊖⊖⊖⊖⊖⊖⊖⊖ ⊖⊖⊖⊖⊖
                    ⊖⊖⊖⊖⊖⊖⊖⊖⊖⊖ ⊖⊖⊖⊖⊖
                    ⊖⊖⊖⊖⊖⊖⊖⊖⊖⊖ ⊖⊖⊖⊖⊖

(c) In one part of a football stadium, rows are made up of 26 seats, and there are 8 rows of seats. How many people can be seated in that part of the stadium?
Diagram:

        10   10   6

    8 x 20   +   8 x 6   = 160 + 48 = 208

Other word-problem examples

(a) Three children are on a family outing. Each child is given 15p to buy a sweet. How much money do the children have altogether?
Diagram:

      1 0   1 0   1 0   = 30 + 15 = 45
        5   5   5

(b) A 'tube' of marbles contains 24 marbles. A boy buys 4 'tubes' of marbles. How many new marbles does he have altogether?
Diagram:

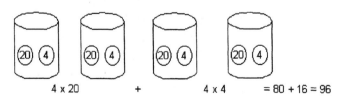

      4 x 20   +   4 x 4   = 80 + 16 = 96

A brief note on short multiplication word problems and commutativity

Some word problems are structured and worded in such a way that they require thinking about large quantities of small repeated groups, rather than smaller quantities of larger repeated groups. For example, '5 party poppers in a bag; 16 bags of party poppers; how many party poppers altogether?' is really 16×5 understood as 16 groups of *five*. Some children intuitively apply the principle of commutativity in multiplication, and happily solve problems involving sixteen fives as 5 '*sixteens*'. A few children will insist that they wish to visualize the problem as 16 *fives*. Accommodating such children, should they require help, requires building up repeated *fives*, rather than repeated *sixteens*. Many children are able to understand sixteen fives by visualizing them as containing 'even more groups' than the 10×5 key tables fact. In essence, large quantities of repeated small groups can be visualized through starting with the key $10 \times n$ fact.

A mental calculation approach to long multiplication

The quantities and processes involved in *long multiplication* – for example, 24×36 – are very difficult for children to visualize and hence it is difficult for children with specific learning difficulties to 'invent' calculation methods for them. In general, however, a good understanding of *short multiplication*, together with sufficient and varied practice at completing *short multiplication* calculations and word problems, helps prepare the way for competent mastery of the most accessible *mental partitioning* approach to long multiplication.

In essence, the *mental partitioning* approach to *long multiplication* is structured in a similar way to that of *short multiplication*. Children *partition* the numbers in the question into their *place value* components, multiply all the components or chunks, in turn, and then combine all of the partial products at the end. However, two aspects of the *mental long multiplication* make it significantly harder to execute than *mental short multiplication*. First of all, children have to learn how to multiply *tens* numbers by *tens* multipliers; for example, 50×20. Secondly, children have to understand how to figure out and keep track of a number of partial products. For example, if 56×24 is broken down into $(50 + 6) \times (20 + 4)$ there are four partial products – 1000, 120, 200 and 24 – to derive, and keep track of. Once again it is imperative that *long multiplication* is taught in a carefully structured way and once again it is helpful to continue asking children to explain *what* it is that they have to figure out ('56 twenty-fours; '24 groups of 56' and so on). Following this, they should be encouraged to give a broad outline of *how* they are going to approach the task of figuring the calculation out.

Multiplication on the 'place value grid'

Multiplying by 10 and 100

To know how to multiply *tens* numbers by *tens* multipliers (for example 50 × 20) or *hundreds* numbers by *tens* multipliers (for example, 500 × 20) children need to understand an important aspect of the number system. As Chinn and Ashcroft point out, a good grasp of *long multiplication* requires that children understand what happens in *place value* terms when numbers are multiplied by 10 and 100 – for example 50 × 10, or 10 × 20; and 56 × 10, or 56 × 100. Chinn and Ashcroft also point out that the clearest way for children to understand the *place value* implications of multiplying numbers by 10 and 100 is for them to experience what happens to number values on the *place value* 'grid'.

Most primary school dyslexic and dyspraxic children know, for example, that 10 × 3 = 30, and that 10 × 7 = 70. In the context of understanding what happens to all numbers when they are multiplied by 10, it is very helpful for children to experience 10 × 3 or 10 × 7 in a 'new' *place value* light.

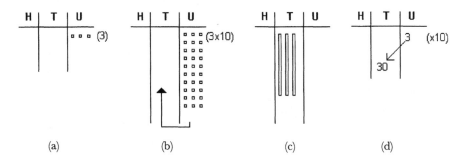

(a)   (b)   (c)   (d)

When 3 is multiplied by 10 what we see, in effect, on the place value grid, is that each *unit* becomes ten times bigger and consequently has to 'move up' on the grid. Each of the *3 tens* or *10 threes* have to be exchanged for a *ten*. The *tens* then have to 'move up' one position and are placed in the *tens* column. The *units* column is left empty as the 3 *ones* move up (or

move to the right) to become the three *tens*. In written recording, a zero
records the empty *units* place value position. The multiplication of the
two-digit (and later, three-digit) numbers by 10 can be explored in the
same way. Most children readily adjust to multiplying rounded *tens* (or
hundreds) by 10. For example, 30×10:

Multiplying 'ordinary' two-digit (and, later, three-digit) numbers by 10
is somewhat harder, however: for example, 35×10:

A mistake which dyslexic and dyspraxic children frequently make in
multiplication examples such as 10×35, is that they remember to 'move'
the '3' into the *hundreds* position, but they leave the '5' in the *units* position
and believe that $10 \times 35 = 305$. Concrete work should make clear that
when a two-digit numbers is multiplied by 10: (a) *each* value becomes
larger; (b) *each* value has to be exchanged; and (c) *each* value moves *up* on
the place value grid. It is helpful to reinforce children's understanding of
these general 'rules' by reiterating the simple expression, 'When you
multiply by 10 (or 100) all the numbers move up together, like a train.'

Multiplication by 100 is introduced in a similar way. Many primary
school dyslexic and dyspraxic children know, for example, that $100 \times 3 =$
300 and that $100 \times 7 = 700$. Again, it is useful for children to experience,
in concrete terms, what happens to quantities on a place value grid when
they are multiplied by 100 or become '100 times bigger'.

100×3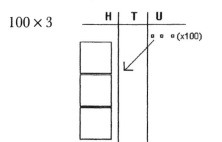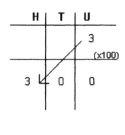

Concrete work on a place value grid helps children see that 'when we multiply a number by 100, we move the number two places up on the place value grid'.

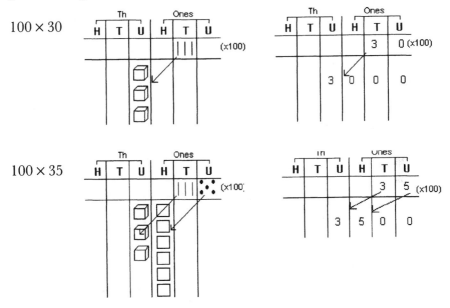

Division by 10, 100 and so on, is also an extremely useful *mental* skill for children to possess. Division by 10 and multiples of 10 comes into its own once children have been introduced to decimals and the decimal fraction idea. However, the ability to understand and visualize the division of rounded whole numbers by 10 and multiples of 10 in relation to 'what happens on the place value "grid"' helps pave the way for subsequent successful decimal fraction work. In essence, concrete work on a place value grid helps children see that when numbers are divided by 10 – or by 100 – they become smaller and therefore *move back* (or *down*) on the *place value* grid.

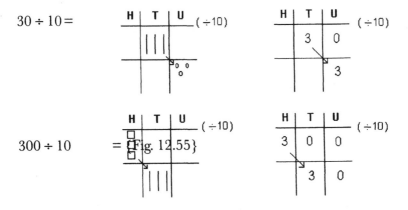

$360 \div 10 =$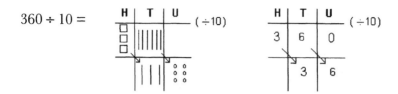

The mathematically correct *place value* rules for multiplying numbers by 10 and 100 are not very difficult for primary school children to understand, especially when they are modelled on the place value 'grid', but as Chinn and Ashcroft point out, teaching experience shows that 'this relatively basic operation needs frequent review' (Chinn and Ashcroft, 1998, p. 94). A largely painless way to build in sufficient practice and review of these 'operations' is to play one or two modified versions of the place value spinner game described on p. 197, Chapter 6. One of the aspects of the *place value* system which can confuse children when they learn to multiply numbers by 10 and 100 is trying to remember how to differentiate between the rules for adding 10 and 100 to numbers and the rules for *multiplying* numbers by 10 and 100. Contrasting the rules for *adding* 10 and 100 to numbers and *multiplying* numbers by 10 and 100 consolidates children's understanding – and makes for exciting games, as well.

In essence, two different types of *place value grid* multiplication games can be played. The first type includes simple games in which a new number is generated and operated on in each round. A dice (or two dice) is usually used to generate each new number so this can be called **a dice-and-spinner-game**. In this game the quantities do not become extremely large and it is therefore an appropriate game to play using concrete materials. The second type of game can be described as a **cumulative** multiplication game because one 'start-out' number is generated and is then operated on cumulatively. Most children particularly enjoy this game but the numbers on the 'grid' usually become large at quite a rapid rate. Because of this, the game cannot be played using Base Ten materials, although it can be played using digit cards. Most children particularly enjoy a pencil-and-paper version of the game. To play both games, each player requires his or her own empty *place value* grid which can drawn on squared paper.

(a) **The dice and spinner game**: The spinner base used should reflect the ability and needs of the child/children playing the game. For example:

(i)

x 10	+ 10
+ 100	+ 1

(ii)

x 10	+ 10
+ 100	x 100

In each round of the game players take turns to throw a 1–20 die (or two 0–9 dice). Each player records his or her die 'throw' on one line. Next, he or she spins the spinner, executes the required operation (concretely if necessary) and then records the result on the next line.
For example:

H	T	U
	1	7

H	T	U
	1	7
1	7	0

A winner – the player with the largest score in that round – is declared for each round. The overall winner of the game is the player who wins the greatest number of rounds.

A sample record of 3 rounds:

Th			Ones		
H	T	U	H	T	U
					8 (+10)
				1	8
				1	4 (x10)
			1	4	0
				1	8 (x100)
	1	8	0	0	

(b) **The cumulative place value multiplication game**: In this game, a 'start-out' number, which applies to all of the players, is simply given or may be obtained by a single dice 'throw'. Again, a spinner base should be designed which will appropriately challenge the child/children playing the game. The spinner base (ii) above is very popular with children who are becoming confident about working with very big numbers. In each round of the game, players take turns to spin the spinner. He or she then performs the designated operation on the most recent number to have been recorded on the grid. The winner is the player who has the largest recorded number after a certain number of rounds have been completed; alternatively, the winner may be the player who first reaches a target value of *units of millions, hundreds of millions* – or even *billions*! It is a curious fact that nearly all children seem to feel powerful when they work with extremely big numbers and most children volunteer that they 'love' this particular game.

A sample record of 4 rounds:

Th			Ones			
H	T	U	H	T	U	
				2	0	(+100)
			1	2	0	(+10)
			1	3	0	(×100)
	1	3	0	0	0	

A note on 'adding zeros' in multiplication

Many children are taught the pragmatic rule that 'to multiply a number by 10, you "add" one zero to the number' and 'to multiply a number by 100, you "add" two zeros to the number'. It is frequently pointed out that there are two potential dangers in promoting the 'adding zeros' rule. First of all, the language of 'adding zeros' is mathematically incorrect. If you add a zero to a number, the number remains the same – for example, if you 'add zero' to 3, the answer is still 3. Secondly, the 'adding zeros' rule can be very misleading when currency work and decimal work, in general, is encountered: For example, £4.20 × 10 is not £4.200, and 3.5 × 10 is not 3.50. However, as Chinn and Ashcroft note, children who find maths difficult will often continue to act pragmatically and many children cherish the 'easy' zeros rule. Secondly, some children discover the 'adding zeros' pattern for themselves. Teachers are generally able to give children who 'love' the 'adding zeros' rule the greatest amount of help by frequently reinforcing the *place-value*-holding basis for the 'zero patterns', and by making children aware of the multiplication situations in which they will need to be cautious. (Of course the same general points apply to the 'rule' that 'to divide a number by 10, you cross off a zero' and 'to divide a number by 100 you cross off two zeros'.)

Multiplying decade numbers: n x 20, X 30, X 40 and so on

As we have seen, long multiplication calculations, such as 24×36, require that children are able to multiply by rounded decade multipliers. To figure out these harder two-step calculations, primary school children generally adopt one of two fairly accessible reasoning routes. Both routes build on the basic understanding of the *place value* implications of multiplying by 10. Both routes can also be understood and modelled on the place value grid. For example, the calculation 20×30 can be understood as 'more than one group' of the more basic and well understood calculation, 10×30. In other words 20×30 can be seen as double 10×30, or $2 \times (10 \times 30)$.

H	T	U	
		¦ ¦ ¦	(x10)
▢▢ ▢			(x2)
▢▢▢ ▢▢▢			

H	T	U	
	3	0	(x10)
3	0	0	(x2)
6	0	0	

The calculation 30×32 can be understood in a similar way. 30×32 can be seen as 3 groups of the basic $\times 10$ calculation, 10×32. In other words 30×32 can be seen as $3 \times (10 \times 32)$.

H	T	U	
	¦ ¦ ¦	o o	(x10)
▢▢ ▢	¦ ¦		(x3)
▢▢▢ ▢▢▢ ▢▢▢	¦¦¦¦¦¦		

H	T	U	
	3	2	(x10)
3	2	0	(x3)
9	6	0	

On the other hand, some children prefer to start with the smaller calculation 2×30 (in 20×30) and then multiply by 10 in the second step. In other words, 20×30 can be seen as $(2 \times 30) \times 10$.

H	T	U	
	¦ ¦ ¦		(x2)
	¦¦¦¦¦¦		(x10)
▢▢▢ ▢▢▢			

H	T	U	
	3	0	(x2)
	6	0	(x10)
6	0	0	

Similarly, some children prefer to work out 30 x 32 by starting with '3 groups of 32' and then they multiply by 10 afterwards. In this way, 30 × 32 can be seen as (3 × 32) × 10.

The area model

Using a *place value grid* model helps many children figure out the component calculations in the mental *partitioning* approach to long multiplication. However, as we have noted, multiplication by two-digit multipliers is much harder to visualize than short multiplication and there are more component 'chunks' to keep track of. Many educationalists, including Chinn and Ashcroft, argue that an area representation of long multiplication can help children develop a better understanding and 'picture' of the *mental partitioning* long multiplication method. In very recent years, however, some doubts have been expressed about the value of complex conceptual models, including that of the area model for multiplication. Researchers, such as Outhred and Mitchelmore (2000), have found that many children who have completed area model work, do not seem to have understood the model. In general, it is true that those primary school dyslexic and dyspraxic children who have a significant degree of spatial difficulties often find quite basic area model work very difficult to understand. The area model for long multiplication is probably not a suitable learning tool for such children. However a number of dyslexic and dyspraxic children very much enjoy area model work. Area representations seem to help many dyslexic and dyspraxic children acquire a 'feel' for long multiplication and helps them to develop an overview of the part–whole relationships involved. One way to ensure that complex area model work makes sense to a large proportion of dyslexic and dyspraxic children is to see that they encounter area representations from the most basic levels of multiplication work and that the more advanced work continues to be covered in a carefully structured way.

The area model: 10 × n, 20 × n, 30 × n, and so on

In the early stages of 'advanced' area model work, children should be encouraged to build concrete area representations from Base Ten materials or from Cuisinaire rods. 10 × 10 arrays should be built from *tens* first. The *tens* can subsequently be exchanged for Base Ten 100 'flats.' Quite soon, most children are able to make sense of equivalent area work on squared paper and many children enjoy shading and drawing around the n × 10 chunks. It is useful to begin 'advanced' area model work by reviewing well-known basic facts, such as, 10 × 6, 10 × 10; children should then explore examples such as 10 × 20 and 10 × 40.

10 × 40, 'built' from *tens*:

TEN	TEN	TEN	TEN

Once children can confidently build, record and figure out 10 x n facts, they should begin working on constructing models of multiplication problems involving larger decade multipliers. For example:

10 × 12 =
10 rows of 10, plus 10 rows of 2
(10 × 10 = 100) + (10 × 2 = 20)

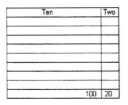

20 × 12 =
10 rows of 12 = 120, plus another 10 rows of 12; that equals 140 altogether.
(10 × 12 = 120) + (10 × 12 = 120) = 240

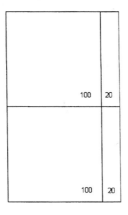

$30 \times 20 =$

10 rows of 20 equals 200, and 200 multiplied by 3 is 600.

$(10 \times 20 = 200) \times 3 = 600$

Note: If possible, the 600 should be built from *tens*.

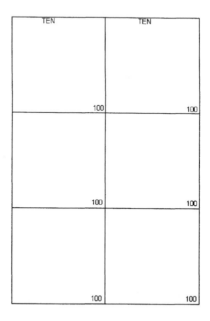

Mental methods for carrying out long multiplication calculations

As we have seen, *mental long multiplication* methods contain many component parts. It helps to facilitate the overall calculation process if teachers make sure that children are confident at figuring out all of the component parts, including the hardest component calculations. (This significantly reduces the working memory burden associated with using the *mental partitioning* method.) *Mental* practice at working out large rounded multiplication calculations, such as 30×50, should be built into the 'mental maths' slots of each maths session. Children can be asked to explain how they are reasoning and immediate verbal (or practical) feedback can be given. Structured written work can provide helpful support, and practice.

$6 \times 5 =$

$6 \times 50 =$

$60 \times 50 =$

A modified version of the *short multiplication* spinner game can be played using a *tens* dice and a similar spinner base. Some children may rapidly progress to multiplying numbers 'in the *hundreds*' by *tens* multipliers:

(a) 30 × 300; 30 groups of 300 =
    10 times 300 is 3 000, so 30 times 300 will be 3 times 3 000, which is 9 000.

	Th					
H	**T**	**U**	**H**	**T**	**U**	
			3	0	0	(x10)
		3	0	0	0	(x3)
		9	0	0	0	

(b) 60 × 600; 60 groups of 600
    6 groups of 600 is 36 hundred or 3 600; 60 groups will be 10 times larger, or 10 times 3 600, which is 36 000.

	Th					
H	**T**	**U**	**H**	**T**	**U**	
			6	0	0	(x6)
		3	6	0	0	(x10)
	3	6	0	0	0	

(c) Solving *area* problems can be helpful. For example: Some children were asked to set out chairs for a concert. They could fit 20 chairs in each row. They made a gap after they had set out 10 chairs in each row so that people could get to their chairs. The children set out 20 rows of 20 chairs. How many chairs did they set out altogether?

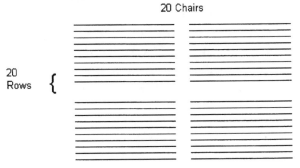

20 Chairs

20
Rows {

However, even when children are able to execute each of the component parts which make up *long multiplication* calculations with confidence, the calculations still present particular challenges. Because the multiplication of two-digit numbers by two-digit multipliers is hard to visualize, it is very hard for primary school children to remember all of the component calculations which have to be executed. In early mental long multiplication work, children can feel overwhelmed by the number of component parts which have to be dealt with and children frequently lose track of the steps which they need to follow.

The most common mistake which children make, is to treat *long multiplication* as a multiplication version of two-digit addition. In this mistake, children simply multiply the *tens* digits and the *units* digits together. In the *mental partitioning* addition procedure, 36 + 36 = 60 + 12 = 72. In completing the long multiplication calculation, 36 x 36, children will often proceed in a similar way

$$3\ 6 \times 3\ 6 \ : \ \ 30 \times 30 = 900, \ 6 \times 6 = 36 \text{ so } 900 + 36 = 936.$$

The omission of two component parts of the calculation is hard for children to detect since the difference between the answer which the child has obtained and the correct answer will not be particularly large – and checking by approximation will not highlight the quite subtle oversimplification of the *partitioning* calculation strategy which has taken place.

As we have seen, practical activities using the area model of multiplication allow many dyslexic and dyspraxic children to build up a *feel* for the different elements making up a *long multiplication* calculation. Rods or Base Ten materials can be used to model modest *long multiplication* calculations but working with huge amounts of concrete material can be cumbersome and can also end up distracting children. At this level of calculation, as Thompson notes, most primary school dyslexic and dyspraxic children find squared-paper area models somewhat easier to work with than large quantities of concrete materials. As always, children should be 'guided' through the process of modelling the selected *long multiplication* calculations. Children should be encouraged to talk through what they are doing and helped to record the various stages as they construct the model. Area model work should also be a carefully structured: dyslexic and dyspraxic children do best if they are allowed to progress in a contained way from easier calculations to more challenging calculations.

Multiplying 'teens' numbers by 'teens' multipliers (for example, 14×16) is easier to model, visualize and execute than multiplying larger two-digit numbers by much larger multipliers. Children should be encouraged to translate the abstract calculations into meaningful *groups-based* language. For example, 14×16 is also '14 groups of 16' or '14 rows of 16'. It is useful to analyse or clarify the rather opaque '14 groups of 16' even further: '14 groups of 16' is also '10 rows of 16 plus another 4 rows of 16'. As we saw in the discussion of *short multiplication* work it also helps to identify *one group* (or row) at the start of the modelling or drawing process. When squared paper is used, children often enjoy shading the different component parts using different coloured pencils. It is particularly effective if children use similar colour shades in sections which are *mentally* processed together: for example, two shades of blue could be used to colour the 10×16 section; and two shades of red to colour the 4×16 section.

$14 \times 16 = 14$ groups/rows of $16 = \underline{10 \times 16} + \underline{4 \times 16}$
$10 \times 16 = \underline{10 \times 10} + \underline{10 \times 6} = 100 \times 60 = 160$
$4 \times 16 = \underline{4 \times 10} + \underline{4 \times 6} = 40 + 24 = 64$
$14 \times 16 = 160 + 64 = 224$

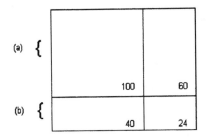

Calculations in which a two-digit number is multiplied by a 'teens' multiplier generally represent a good 'next step':
$15 \times 45 = 15$ groups of 45
$10 \times 45 = 450$
$5 \times 45 = 225$
$15 \times 45 = 420 + 225 = 675$

			400	50
			200	25

Finally, children can encounter multiplication questions in which ordinary two- digit numbers are multiplied by another two-digit number. Nevertheless it helps children maintain steady progress if numbers do not become too large too quickly, and if 'easier tables' are chosen in early *long multiplication* practice.

$23 \times 24 = 23$ groups/rows of $24 = 20$ groups of 20 and 20 groups of 4; plus 3 groups of 20 and 3 groups of 4.
$20 \times 20 = 400$
$20 \times 4 = 80$
$3 \times 20 = 60$
$3 \times 4 = 12$
$23 \times 24 = 400 + 80 + 60 + 12 = 552.$

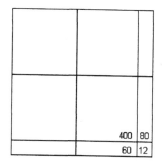

The box method of multiplication

Children who have drawn, enjoyed and developed a fairly good grasp of the area model of long multiplication calculations, can be introduced to the so-called *box method* for recording the component *long multiplication* calculations. In many ways, the increasingly popular *box model* can be viewed as a simplified 'record' of all of the area model components. To construct the *box model,* children simply sketch a 'box' (a square or rectangle) and then draw lines to make calculation compartments. The 'chunked' number components are represented at the side of the components. For example: $14 \times 16 =$

(a) Concrete model   (b) Box model

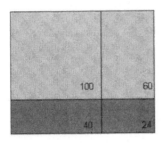

(c) Shaded area model   (d) Box recording

Once dyslexic and dyspraxic children are ready for pencil-and-paper multiplication work, the *box* format is an excellent non-standard written format to use to enable children to work out *long multiplication* calculations. Many children enjoy its seeming 'puzzle-like' structure. The box 'compartments' work extremely well to structure children's thinking and a number of children enjoy the sense of security which this affords them. This is especially true of children who have tried, but failed, to master the standard *long multiplication* algorithm: the fact that the components can be generated in a logical way can feel quite magical to children who have tried to memorize a routine which they simply fail to remember.

Pencil-and-paper mental long multiplication calculation

As *long multiplication* calculations become more complex, the choice of the methods which children use to record the partial products become increasingly important. When the *box method* is used, all of the partial products are already recorded. The final answer can be worked out by adding the partial products. The total can simply be recorded outside of the *box*.

15 × 35 =

X	30	+	5	
10	300		50	
+				
5	150		25	= 525

Long multiplication calculations can, of course, be recorded in a horizontal format. Children with severe spatial difficulties, who do not understand area representations (or the box model), usually prefer to record *long multi-plication* calculations in the typical *mental* horizontal format. To help children visualize the component calculations teachers could try designing 'meaningful' and vivid word problems; understanding can be supported by drawing simple sketches of the situation. Children should also be encour-aged to articulate the calculations in words: 15 × 35 = '35 lollipops in a bag,

15 bags of lollipops. How many lollipops altogether?' = 10 bags of 35 lollipops *plus* 5 bags of 35 lollipops = 350 + 150 + 25 = 625.

A more formal-looking horizontal layout may also be adopted. When dyslexic and dyspraxic children choose to work this way, they often need to 'chunk' calculations into the smallest component parts: $-23 \times 24 \rightarrow 23$ groups of 24 $\rightarrow$ 20 groups of 24 = 20 groups of 20 plus 20 groups of 4; 3 groups of 24 = 3 groups of 20 plus 3 groups of 4.

$$
\begin{array}{r}
2\,4 \\
\times\,2\,3 \\
\hline
4\,0\,0 \\
8\,0 \\
6\,0 \\
1\,2 \\
\hline
5\,5\,2 \\
\hline
\end{array}
$$

On the other hand, dyslexic and dyspraxic children with good *mental* multiplication skills can usually complete long multiplications in larger 'chunks'. In other words, they are able to work out fewer, larger, component calculations. $23 \times 24 \rightarrow 23$ groups of 24 = 20 groups of 24 *plus* 3 groups of 24.

$$
\begin{array}{r}
2\,4 \\
\times\,2\,3 \\
\hline
4\,8\,0 \quad (20 \times 24) \\
7\,2 \quad (3 \times 24) \\
\hline
5\,5\,2 \\
\hline
\end{array}
$$

Children who have been taught the column-based standard *long multiplication* algorithm in their classrooms, are often eager to conform to classroom practice, and frequently wish to learn how to write partial products in the standard two-tier vertical layout. The box method of working out *long multiplication* calculations can be transferred to the two-layer convention of the standard layout. For example: $46 \times 72 =$

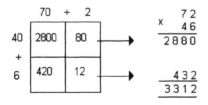

Children who are required to use the standard *long multiplication* format but who actually rely on the structure of the *box method* to complete the calculation can be shown how to use the *box format* as 'rough workings' in a right-hand 'margin' of their exercise book, or on a scrap piece of paper.

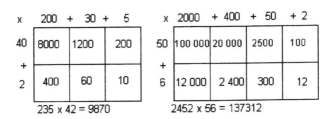

x	200	+ 30	+ 5
40	8000	1200	200
+			
2	400	60	10

235 x 42 = 9870

x	2000	+ 400	+ 50	+ 2
50	100 000	20 000	2500	100
+				
6	12 000	2 400	300	12

2452 x 56 = 137312

Teaching the standard multiplication algorithm

It has to be acknowledged that the standard *long multiplication* algorithm is generally much more efficient than the *mental* methods for *long multiplication*. Many understanding-based curricula, such as the Numeracy Strategy Framework, stipulate that children should ultimately learn the standard condensed method for *long multiplication* before they leave primary school. In fact, as we have just seen, the *mental partitioning* method, and particularly the vertical layout of the *mental partitioning* method, has much in common with the standard *long multiplication* method. For this reason, a number of dyslexic and dyspraxic children are able to adjust to learning the standard *long multiplication* method. It should be noted, however, that success in transferring to the standard method is more assured if the most difficult portion of the very condensed method is targeted for special consideration. As we saw in the brief discussion of standard *long multiplication* at the beginning of the chapter, it is the crucial *tens* multiplier 'line' which causes the greatest cognitive difficulty for many dyslexic and dyspraxic children. It will be remembered that children in traditional classrooms are taught to 'translate' the × 30 'line' of multiplication calculation, such as 36 × 45, into the *verbalizing patter*, 'Put in a zero to show that you are multiplying by 30; 3 times 5 is fifteen, 3 times 4 is 12, and so on.' Children who have learned to multiply two-digit numbers in the ways described earlier, will have already have encountered a model in *mental* multiplication work which is very similar to the standard × 30 calculation step. As we saw on p. 399, a calculation such as 30×45 can be modelled and understood as:

$(3 \times 45) \times 10 =$

H	T	U	H	T	U	
				4	5	(x3)
			1	3	5	(x10)
		1	3	5	0	

Dyslexic and dyspraxic children can be helped to see that the 'standard' way of doing things is similar to this *mental* method but starts with the $\times 10$ portion of the model, instead of with the '3×45' portion.

$30 \times 45 = 10 \times (3 \times 45) = 10 \times 135$ →

$$
\begin{array}{r}
4\ 5 \\
\times\ 3\ 0 \\
\hline
\end{array}
$$

$3 \times 45 \rightarrow \underline{(1\ 3\ 5)\ 0} \leftarrow 10 \times 45$

Nevertheless, while a good proportion of dyslexic and dyspraxic children adapt to the standard method, it also has to be acknowledged that the standard *long multiplication* algorithm is simply too difficult for some children with specific learning difficulties to manage. Many teachers confirm that they have worked with dyslexic and dyspraxic children who cannot cope with the spatial and sequencing demands of the traditional *long multiplication method*. Many teachers have also taught dyslexic and dyspraxic children who are so distressed at the thought of having to manage a procedure which has been consistently associated with painful failure that it is not worth pursuing formal *long multiplication* work with them, at all. Although the *mental* long multiplication methods are somewhat cumbersome when large numbers are involved, teachers can take heart from the fact that a considerable number of dyslexic and dyspraxic children learn *mental* methods, such as the *box method*, with huge (and sometimes tearful) relief. Indeed some dyslexic *grasshoppers* learn, absorb and become quite passionate about the *box method* in a very few lessons, indeed. Such children will continue to perform better and will remain more confident if they are allowed to continue using mental methods, such as the *box method*, throughout their primary school careers.

Division

Traditional short and long division

Short division: division by a single digit divisor

Like the standard *short multiplication* procedure, the standard procedure for *short division* is taught as a rigidly prescribed routine and *short division* is often introduced soon after basic division itself is taught. In traditional approaches to maths learning, children are taught to set out a calculation such as 52 ÷ 4 in the way shown below. The routine which children are taught to follow in order to work out '52 divided by 4' is usually verbalized as '4 into 5 goes 1 times, with a remainder of 1; carry the 1; 4 into 12 goes 3 times so the answer is 13'.

The traditional routine is recorded as:

$$4\overline{)5^12}\quad^{1\,3}$$

To ensure that children acquire the *short division* routine as soon as possible, many children are taught to work out answers to division calculations which are well within the *tables* range. For instance, many children are required to set out a basic division calculation such as 35 ÷ 5 in the more formal *short division* format and to proceed using the *short division* verbal routine: '5 into 3 doesn't go, carry the 3; 5 into 35 goes 7 times, so the answer is 7'.

$$5\overline{)3^35}\quad^{0\,7}\qquad 5\overline{)3\underset{\smile}{5}}\quad^{7}$$

The consequence of this is that children believe that division involves an entirely unique set of rules and routines and the relationship between division and multiplication is often lost very early on.

Dyslexic and dyspraxic children and the standard short division routine

Right from the outset, a great many dyslexic and dyspraxic children experience difficulties learning the prescribed steps for the standard division routines. Most importantly, directional weaknesses and directional confusions play a very big part in children's dislike of the division procedures. Chinn and Ashcroft make the important point that the spatial and organizational format and demands of the standard procedures upset many of the calculation 'rules' which children have learned up until now. For the first time in their primary school maths careers, children who are taught the standard division method are required to work from left to right rather than from right to left. They are also required to begin to work from the largest, rather than from the smallest, value position. In other words, children have to work 'down' to the smallest value rather than 'up' to the largest one and in the process they are required to 'carry down' numbers (the remainders) rather than 'carry up' numbers, as well. As Chinn and Ashcroft (1998, p. 106) say, 'These requirements are almost directly opposite to those for addition, subtraction and multiplication.'

Many children have especial difficulties with the 'carrying' convention in standard short division work. Although the traditional procedure is, in fact, structured in a *place value* column-based way – each value is worked with separately in turn – this is not usually explained to children. Instead, as we have seen, children are taught to think of each consecutive digit as a *unit* and not in terms of its real value within the number. This becomes confusing when the numbers involved require that 'remainders' are 'carried'. For instance, to divide 4 'into' 68, children are taught to think that they are dividing 4 into '6' rather than into '60' or '6 tens'. This means that the remainder of '2', which needs to be 'carried' (and recorded as a 'small 2' in front of the 8) is hard to understand as '20' in '28'.

$$68 \div 4 = \quad 4\overline{\smash{\big)}\,6^2 8}^{\;1}$$

The 'rule' which children have to internalize is that 'carry 2', or 'little 2', followed by 8 should be seen as '28' but primary school children with poor memories for procedural rules often fail to make sense of this key calculation step. Some children give up in this situation and copy from a neighbour or ask for help. Other children who are prepared to 'have a go' make procedural errors which demonstrate their confusion. For instance, some children record a remainder for each individual digit. In a similar error, children add 'remainders' at the end. Many children simply disregard all of the 'tricky' and 'bothersome' remainders generated in the middle stages of any short division calculation and work out remainders from the outcome of the division of the final digit of numbers, only.

$$4\overline{)6\ 9}^{\ 1^{r}2\ r1} \qquad 4\overline{)6\ 9}^{\ 1^{r}2\ r1} = 12\ r\ 3 \qquad 4\overline{)6\ 9\ 5}^{\ 1\ 2\ 1\ r1}$$

Because standard *short division* is not presented as a column-based procedure, many division steps can cause children to become confused. For example, to work out, 283 ÷ 7, children will often proceed, '7 'goes into' 28 four times; 7 into 3 doesn't 'go', so the answer is 4 remainder 3':

$$7\overline{)2\ 8\ 3} \qquad\qquad 7\overline{)2\ 8\ 3}^{\ 4\ r3}$$

In other words, the column-related rule that '0' has to be recorded as a 'placeholder' has not been understood and is therefore not remembered. This important gap in understanding affects larger calculations, such as 2835 ÷ 7:

$$7\overline{)2\ 8\ 3\ 5} \qquad\qquad 7\overline{)2\ 8\ 3\ 5}^{\ 4\ \ \ 7}$$

In traditional short division, children also often misinterpret zeros in division problems. To work out 609 ÷ 3, children often say '3 into 6 is 2, with no remainder, 3 into 9 is 3, so the answer is 23':

$$3\overline{)6\ 0\ 9} \qquad\qquad 3\overline{)6\ 0\ 9}^{\ 2\ \ \ 3}$$

Overall, it should be noted that a limited and rote-learned grasp of the *short division* procedures can mean that some children succeed in answering *short division* problems in which quite difficult 'internal' carrying is required but fail when technically 'easier' steps have to be interpreted in a more holistic way.

Traditional long division: division by double-digit divisors

In division operations with two-digit divisors, very large internal remainders often need to be 'carried' and the *short division* method generally becomes too unwieldy to operate efficiently.

Long division treated as short division:

$$1\ 7\overline{)8\ 4^{16}6}^{\ 4\ 9\ r13}$$

For this reason, a second, expanded and rather different *long division* standard procedure is traditionally taught to primary school children. It is often noted that the standard procedure for *long division* – usually the last whole-number calculation procedure to be learned by children – is the most consistently disliked and feared of all the formal procedures. It would seem that most children – including mathematically able children – have difficulty making sense of the stages which make up the *long division* routine. Trying to learn the seemingly arbitrary sequence of steps comprising standard *long division* calculations ends up making many children feel anxious and insecure. In fact, a surprising number of adults admit that they always disliked *long division* at school and (more to the point) that they cannot at present remember how to complete a typical *long division* 'sum'.

For children with specific learning difficulties, the convoluted sequence of steps which comprise the standard *long division* procedure is almost impossible to memorize and remember. To have some sense of how very complex the sequence of *long division* steps can feel to a pupil who is trying to master them, it is helpful to describe the first stage of the procedure, in detail. As Anghileri (1999, p. 192) points out, standard *long division* calculations start off in an unpromising and disheartening way 'with a guess or approximation that many pupils find difficult'. For instance, to divide 548 by 16, children have to decide, first, how many times 16 will 'go' into '54'. Once a child has established that '3 times 16' would seem to be the calculation which is required, 4 separate steps have to be executed to complete the '54' ÷ 16 part of the calculation. First, the '3', from the 3×16, has to be recorded above the '4' of '54'. Next, the answer to 3×16, or 48, has to be worked out exactly, or retrieved from memory. Then the 48 has to be subtracted from 54, to find the 'remainder', 6. And finally, the '8' from 548 has to 'brought down' to join the remainder, 6, and the two digits now have to be read together as '68'. Once children have reached this point (having completed the first stage in what is actually a very modest division problem) 68 remains to be divided, so the 4-step guessing, multiplying, and subtracting routine has to begin all over again.

```
            3 4  r4
        _____
    1 6 | 5 4 8
       - 4 8
        _____
            6 8
          - 6 4
        _____
              4
```

In all of this, too, as Judith Anghileri explains, 'The positioning of digits becomes vital as a way of keeping track of the stage reached in the calculation' (Anghileri, 1999, p. 192). Quite clearly, difficulties such as spatial difficulties, sequencing difficulties, orientation difficulties, organizational difficulties, hand-writing difficulties or difficulties remembering visual patterns – all of which, as we know, are typical dyslexic and dyspraxic difficulties – would compound the problems most children routinely experience in trying to learn the *long division* procedure. It is not surprising that *long division* problems are typically 'hated' and feared by dyslexic and dyspraxic children .

An informal method for working out short and long division calculations

While standard division procedures are generally experienced as much harder than standard multiplication procedures, the most widely devised and increasingly widely taught *mental* division strategy – the *chunking and subtracting* approach to division – is usually found to be considerably easier to learn than the equivalent *mental* multiplication procedures. Once basic division has been mastered, most children genuinely enjoy the *chunking* method of division.

A very big advantage of the *chunking* division method is that the same basic approach is used for both *short* and *long division* calculations. There is thus one 'method' or way of thinking to learn and making progress from division by single-digit divisors to division by double-digit divisors is relatively straightforward. A key difference between the standard division procedures and the *chunking* approach to 'longer division' calculations is that the latter does not emphasize *place value* positioning at all. As we have seen, standard long division proceeds by dividing numbers value by value. In contrast, the *chunking* approach to division teaches children to 'remove' chunks from numbers (dividends) which are viewed as wholes. In the *mental chunking* division strategy, the 'chunks' are easily visualized multiples of the divisor and the children themselves determine the size of the chunks they wish to 'remove'. While the *standard place value* model works hand in hand with a *sharing* model of division – in which the divisor indicates the number of groups the dividend is to be divided into – the *removing tens* method is really based on the readily visualized *grouping* model of division. In standard *long division* $14\overline{)168}$ is essentially understood as 168 divided into 14 groups; in contrast, the *chunking* way of thinking lends itself to the question, 'How many 14's are there in 68?' As we will see, however, the *removing tens* method of division works just as well to solve *sharing* word problems as it does to solve *grouping* word problems.

Mental short division

There are four teaching suggestions which help many dyslexic and dyspraxic children gain confidence in the crucial early stages of *short division* work. First of all (as always) it is best if *'longer' division* work is carefully structured. For example, it is a good idea to make sure that the first *short division* examples which children are given to solve involve division questions (or dividends) which are just large enough to be outside the relevant tables sequence. Secondly, as always, too, it is important to forge links with what children already know. It will be remembered that children were encouraged to develop a *counting up to* model of division in basic division work. For example, $15 \div 3$ is translated as, 'How many *threes* are needed to make 15?' and children were encouraged to build or visualize repeated groups of 3 until they reached the target of 15. Similarly, children benefit from concrete *building up* experience in *short division* work. To work out an answer to the division question $45 \div 3 =?$ children can be asked to *build up* the number of *threes* needed to 'make' or 'reach' 45. Thirdly, as many theorists point out, carefully devised and meaningful word problems tend to suggest the *chunking* model of division. Teaching experience confirms that an understanding of the *chunking* division procedure is certainly brought to life by asking children to solve examples of carefully selected division problems. Nevertheless, a balance should also be struck between problem-solving and figuring out 'bare' number problems. (Although some theorists seem to suggest that word-problem-solving offers the key to understanding *short division* and *long division* dyslexic and dyspraxic children whose division work has largely been limited to problem-solving, are not always able to apply their context-based understanding to 'pure' number calculations.) And, finally, the foundation skills which children require in order to be able to success-fully complete *short* and *long division* operations should be reviewed. For instance, children certainly need to have efficient access to the *tables* facts. Before *short division* is introduced, children should also review and practise their 'ordinary' division skills and the use of *key tables* to facilitate speedy division solutions. Children require good *mental* multiplication skills – especially multiplying by 10 and multiplies of 10. Children also require good subtraction skills: either standard subtraction procedures or *complementary addition* procedures can be used in the subtraction sub-components of chunking division algorithms.

Practical teaching suggestions: short division

Stage 1: Dividing numbers just outside the tables sequence

A division problem, such as 42 ÷ 3, is a very manageable introductory *short division* calculation. 42 ÷ 3 can be translated as 'How many *threes* are there in 42?' or 'How many *threes* would I need to be able to build 42?' In early concrete work at this level, children should be allowed to 'fold back' to the simplest strategy of building and step-counting single groups of *three* all the way up to 42 to establish how many *threes* are required. However, it is also important that children learn to work more efficiently in division. As soon as possible, children need to be steered towards the recognition that 42 is more than 10 *threes* or 10 × 3 – the largest fact in the basic × 3 tables sequence and an overlearned *key fact*. From the understanding that 10 *threes* or 30 constitute a part of 42 (or that 'building 30' is an important step towards building 42) children can rapidly work out how many more *threes* are needed to 'make' or 'build' 42. Practice at applying the tables strategy to work out harder basic division questions, means that most children are familiar with the idea of step-counting short distances to work out division answers.

Basic division strategy 21 ÷ 3 =   Short division problem 42 ÷ 3 =

```
        21 ÷ 3                         42 ÷ 3
        0 0 0                          0 0 0
        0 0 0                          0 0 0
        0 0 0                          0 0 0
        0 0 0                          0 0 0
        0 0 0   5 threes = 15          0 0 0
                                      _____
        0 0 0                          0 0 0
        0 0 0                          0 0 0
                                       0 0 0
                                       0 0 0
                                       0 0 0  10 threes are 30
                                      _____
                                       0 0 0
                                       0 0 0
                                       0 0 0
                                       0 0 0  14 threes are 42
```

However, children should also be encouraged towards the greatest reasoning efficiency. The second part of the *'building 42'* problem can be streamlined, too: once 30 has been reached, it is not hard to work out that a further 12 remain to be 'built'. Since 4 *threes* are 12, 4 more *threes* are required: 42 = 10 *threes* + 4 *threes* = 14 *threes*; *42 ÷ 3 = 14*

As we have suggested, children can also be asked to solve word problems. Problems involving play people (for example characters from a current film) are easily modelled using halma pawns. For example, '65 play people are put into packs of 5 people each. How many packs of play people are made?' At first, as we saw above, many children will choose to step-count in *fives* to establish the number of packs in question. Again, however, children should be prompted, if needs be, to find the answer a 'quicker' way. The quantity of 65 play people is more than 10 packs of 5 play people: if 10 packs of play people are made, 50 play people have been put into packs. This means that 15 play people remain to be put into packets. $10 \times 5 = 50$; 65 play people = 13 packs of 5 play people.

Sharing problems invite the use of simple diagrams to help chart the progress of the step-by-step division procedures. For example, '90 chocolate balls are shared between 5 children. How many chocolates will each child get?' 90 chocolate balls is greater than $\boxed{10} \times 5$ chocolate balls; each child can be given at least 10 chocolate balls. 50 balls have been shared; 40 balls are still left to share. 40 chocolates shared between 5 children gives each child 8 chocolate balls each.

Each child has 10 chocolates + 8 chocolates = 18 chocolates
Each child will get 18 chocolate balls

Stage 2: Dividing larger numbers

Once children have grasped the concept of dividing quantities which are larger than *ten times* the divisor, the numbers which are selected for problem-solving can be made more challenging. At the same time, it makes sense to introduce a specific format for recording the increasingly complex stages of thinking and calculation. A suitable *grouping* problem would be: '69 children want to learn magic tricks. The children have to be seated at small tables. Three children are seated at each table. How many tables will be needed?' 10 tables will seat 30 children, but 36 children are 'left'. 10 more tables will seat another 30 children but 9 children remain to be seated. 3 more tables are needed. To record these steps in more structured way, one of many slightly different recording variations may be used. For example,

```
3 | 6 9                    3 | 6 9
  - 3 0   (10)   (10 tables) - 3 0
    3 9                        3 9
  - 3 0   (10)   (10 tables) - 3 0
      9                          9
  -   9   (3)    (3 tables) -    9

  = 23 tables              = 23 tables
```

Sharing problems in which children are put into 'teams' are generally quite popular. For example: 208 children in a small school are put into 8 teams. How many children are there in each team?

Team 1	Team 2	Team 3	Team 4	Team 5	Team 6	Team 7	Team 8
10	10	10	10	10	10	10	10
10	10	10	10	10	10	10	10
6	6	6	6	6	6	6	6

10 children can be put in each team. This means that 80 children have been put into teams, leaving 128 children still to place in teams. Another 10 children can be placed in each team. This means 48 children are 'left over'. 48 divided by 8 is 6. Altogether there are 26 children in each of the eight teams.

```
8 | 2 0 8                      8 | 2 0 8
  -   8 0    10    10 Children  -   8 0
    1 2 8                         1 2 8
  -   8 0    10    10 Children  -   8 0
      4 8                           4 8
  -   4 8    6     6 Children   -   4 8
                                      0
  208 ÷ 8 = 26
```

As children become familiar with the idea that *short division* calculations may be seen as process involving repeated large chunks, the solution of division problems involving large dividends, relative to the divisor, can be speeded up and made more efficient. However, it is important to ensure that the process of working towards greater efficiency is taken at a pace which is appropriate to each individual child. *Grasshopper* dyslexics with relatively competent *tables* abilities may rapidly grasp and use the most efficient *chunking* solutions. Other children may need to increase the size of the 'chunks' that they are able to work with in a much more gradual way.

A short division calculation with a relatively large dividend , such as $245 \div 7$, can be figured out by employing a 'slow' *chunking* solution. Cuisinaire rods and Base Ten materials could be used as supports: for example, 245 could be set out in Base Ten materials. Using Cuisinaire rods, the successive stages of the division calculation could be built on top of the Base Ten materials.

```
7 |2 4 5|
  . 7 0| 10
   1 7 5|
  - 7 0| 10
   1 0 5|
     7 0| 10
     3 5|
     3 5| 5
```

$$245 \div 7 = 35$$

A more efficient solution to $245 \div 7$ could use squared paper and Base Ten materials as supports. For example, the area representing 245 could be drawn on squared paper. The *hundreds* should be clearly shown. Using Base Ten material, the successive stages of the division calculation can be built on top of the area.

```
7 |2 4 5|
   1 4 0| 20
   1 0 5|
     7 0| 10
     3 5|
     3 5| 5
```

$$245 \div 7 = 35$$

Solving word problems continues to be important. Topical *chunking* division problems are often enjoyed. For example, '252 firework rockets are packed into boxes of 6 rockets. How many boxes of 6 rockets are made?'

A slow chunking solution

```
6 |2 5 2|
   - 6 0| 10
    1 9 2|
   - 6 0| 10
    1 3 2|
   - 6 0| 10
      7 2|
   - 6 0| 10
      1 2|
   - 1 2| 2
```

= 42 boxes of fireworks

A more efficient solution

```
6 2 5 2
. 1 2 0  20
  1 3 2
. 1 2 0  20
    1 2
. _ 1 2  2
```

= 42 boxes of fireworks

An efficient chunking solution

```
6 2 5 2
- 2 4 0  40
    1 2
- _ 1 2  2
```

= 42 boxes of fireworks

Short division examples which require children to build up or remove chunks involving *hundreds* multiples or even *thousands* multiples of the single-digit divisor are not experienced as particularly difficult if children have a broad 'feel' for the relative sides of the numbers involved. ('Slower' *chunking* steps than the ones demonstrated below may, of course, be used by some children).

```
8 1 2 6 4                9 3 4 8 3
  8 0 0  100               2 7 0 0  300
  4 6 4                     7 8 3
- 4 0 0  50                 7 2 0  8 0
    6 4                       6 3
- _ 6 4  8               - _ 6 3  7
1264÷8 = 158             3483÷9 = 387
```

It is important to build children's *mental short division* proficiency. A harder version of **The Remainders Game**, described on p. 371, encourages children to practise *short division* and to speed up their *short division* skills. The harder game is played in the same way as the basic version. However, a 4–9 dice should be used and the track should begin at 11 (or 21) and finish at 100:

| 11 | 12 | 13 | 14 | ⋯ | 98 | 99 | 100 |

| 21 | 22 | 23 | 24 | ⋯ | 98 | 99 | 100 |

Mental long division

As we mentioned earlier, the *chunking and subtracting* method for solving *long division* problems and calculations works in exactly the same way as the *mental* method for division by single-digit divisors. For children with good *short multiplication* skills, the progression from *chunking and subtracting* in *short division* work to *chunking and subtracting* in *long division* work is generally experienced as an 'easy' next step. Nevertheless, although many children are able to make rapid progress through the stages of informal *long division* work, it is (as always) important to make sure that the difficulty of selected division problems is determined as sensitively as possible. Once again, many children need to be allowed to build up towards increasingly efficient *chunking* steps at a pace which feels manageable to them. Because it is hard to visualize complex *long division* calculations, it is always a good idea to encourage dyslexic and dyspraxic children to develop an 'approximation mindset' in long division work. (An 'approximating mindset' should, of course, be encouraged in all work involving larger numbers.) Although it can be very hard to convince dyslexic and dyspraxic children of the merits of working out approximate solutions, teachers can model the approximation ideal by 'musing' approximations 'out loud', or teachers can insist that children figure out 'rough ballpark' approximations of likely outcomes to *long division* problems. Children should be encouraged to 'round' numbers wherever appropriate. Useful formulations for approximating *long division* calculations such as $950 \div 37$ include, '$40 \times$ 'what' will come close to 950', or $40 \times \square = $ about 950? ($40 \times \pm = \quad 450$)

1. **Step 1:** division by a 'teens' divisor
   (a) $275 \div 19$
   Approximation: $20 \times \boxed{10} = 200$
   $20 \times \boxed{4} = \pm 75$
   ± 14

```
  19│2 7 5
     -1 9 0     10(x19)
        8 5     (left)
     -  7 6     4(x19)
          9
```

Answer = 14 remainder 9.

(b) 340 ÷ 16; a 'grouping' word problem.

340 children need to be driven by mini-bus to a theme park. 16 children can be seated in each mini-bus. How many buses are needed?

16 × 20 = ± 340

Approximation = ± 20 buses

```
16│3 4 0│
  │3 2 0│20
  │  2 0│
  │  1 6│1
  │─────│
  │  4  │
```

22 mini-buses are needed.

(c) 882 ÷ 14; a grouping word problem

A group of 14 children won £882 at a school fair. How much money did each child get?

Approximation: 10 × 86 = ± 882
                  14 × 60 = ± 882

```
14│8 8 2│
  │8 4 0│60 (£)
  │  4 2│
  │  4 2│3 (£)
```

Each child gets £63.

It should be noted that children who are working independently and who have not approximated at all, or have not approximated accurately enough can also 'chunk and subtract' more slowly, using easier mental multiplication skills. For example,

```
14│8 8 2│
  │4 2 0│× 30 (£)
  │4 6 2│
  │4 2 0│× 30 (£)
  │  4 2│
  │  4 2│× 3 (£)
```

2. **Step 2:** division by larger two-digit divisors
   (a) $978 \div 33$
   Approximation: $30 \times \boxed{30} = 900$
                         $33 \times \boxed{30} = 990$
   Approximation $= \pm\ 30$, but this time $\times\ 30$ itself is too large, as the second approximation makes clear.

```
  33 | 9 7 8 |
     - 6 6 0 | 20
       3 1 8 |
     - 2 9 7 | 9
         2 1 |
```

Answer = 29 remainder 21.

(b) $1597 \div 28$; a grouping word problem
   1597 hand-made chocolates were made in one day. They were packed into boxes of 28 chocolates. How many boxes of chocolates were made?
   Approximation: $30 \times \boxed{50} = 1500$
                         $28 \times \boxed{50} = \pm\ 1597$
   Approximation $= \pm\ 50$

```
  2 8 | 1 5 9 7 |
        1 4 0 0 | 50(boxes)
          1 9 7 | (left)
          1 9 6 | 7(boxes)
              1 | (left)
```

57 boxes of chocolates were made.

3. **Step 3:** division of very large numbers by larger two-digit divisors
   Once again the informal methods for completing long division problems can quite easily be adjusted to division problems with very large numbers. For example:
   (a) $3278 \div 27$
   Approximation: $30 \times \boxed{100} = 3000$
   Approximation $= (+)\ 100$

```
  2 7 | 3 2 7 8 |
        2 7 0 0 | (100)
          5 7 8 |
          5 4 0 | (20)
            3 8 |
            2 7 | (1)
            1 1 |
```

Answer = 121 remainder 11.

(b) $15900 \div 36$

    Approximation: $40 \times \boxed{400} = 16000$

    Approximation $= (+)\ 400$

```
3 6 | 1 5 9 0 0 |
      1 4 4 0 0 | (400)
      ---------
        1 5 0 0 |
        1 4 4 0 | (40)
        -------
            6 0 |
            3 6 | (1)
            ----
            2 4 |
```

Answer: 441 remainder 24.

Of course, some dyslexic and dyspraxic children should be permitted to 'build and subtract' much smaller chunks:

```
3 6 | 1 5 9 0 0 |
    -   7 2 0 0 | (x200)
      ---------
        8 7 0 0 |
    -   7 2 0 0 | (x200)
      ---------
        1 5 0 0 |
    -   1 4 4 0 | (x40)
      ---------
            6 0 |
    -       3 6 | (x1)
            ----
            2 4 |
```

Answer: 441 remainder 24

The standard division procedures

Short division

In time, many dyslexic and dyspraxic children are able to adjust to the compact standard *short division* procedures. There are three teaching and learning suggestions which help dyslexic and dyspraxic children make the transition to the standard procedure in a relatively smooth way: First, children benefit from understanding that the *sharing concept* of division will help them visualize the steps in the standard division procedure. Secondly, children should understand that standard division depends on a column-based or *place value* model of numbers, and not on a 'whole number' model; however, children should also understand that standard division is unusual because the division routine proceeds from left to right, from the largest value position to the smallest value position, and not in the usual right-to-left direction. Thirdly, children should be encouraged to work through a few standard division 'routines' using concrete materials, such as Base Ten materials.

Step 1

Step 2. '600 shared/split into 5 groups gives 100 in each group, with 100 left over; altogether, 175 is left to divide':

Step 3. '100 plus 7 *tens* equals 17 *tens*; 17 *tens* split into 5 groups gives 3 *tens* in each group with 2 *tens* left over; altogether, 25 is left to divide':

Step 4. '2 *tens* plus 5 equals 25; 25 split into 5 groups gives 5 in each group':

Standard long division

It will be remembered that the standard *long division* algorithm entails a second and rather different 'routine' from the standard *short division* procedure. In our teaching experience, very few primary school dyslexic and dyspraxic children learn to use the extremely complex standard *long division* routine confidently. Most primary school dyslexic and dyspraxic children quail at the prospect of having to remember how to generate the very confusing sequence of steps which the standard routine prescribes. Although structured concrete work – a 'large number of groups' equivalent of the work described above – seems to help some able primary school dyslexic and dyspraxic children understand 'what to do' to complete standard long division algorithms, the majority of children find it very confusing to work with such large numbers of groups. In contrast, as we have seen, most dyslexic and dyspraxic children are able to use the informal *chunking short* and *long division* method confidently, happily and competently. This means that, wherever this is possible, dyslexic and dyspraxic children should be allowed to use *mental* division methods for the duration of primary school years.

The Numeracy Strategy Framework, and the teaching guides which expand on aspects of it, illustrate the widely used *chunking and subtraction* method. Fortunately, too, a number of teaching schemes model and describe the *chunking mental* method of division. Secondly, compromise solutions should be found for those children whose teachers prefer them to avoid *mental* methods. For example, one compromise solution is to allow dyslexic and dyspraxic children to use the standard *short division* method for *long division* calculations. The difficult component calculations can be completed on rough paper or in a rough workings section created on the right-hand side of the page.

Two examples	Rough workings

(a)
$$19 \overline{\smash{)}\, 1\ 0\ 6\ ^{11}8} \quad \begin{array}{l} 5\ 6\ \text{R4} \end{array}$$

(a)
$$\begin{array}{cc} 19 & 19 \\ \underline{\times 5} & \underline{\times 6} \\ 95 & 114 \end{array}$$
$$106 - 95 = 11$$

(b)
$$36 \overline{\smash{)}\, 1\ 5\ 9\ ^{15}0\ ^{8}0} \quad \begin{array}{l} 4\ 4\ 1\ \text{r24} \end{array}$$

(a)
$$36 \times 4 = 144$$
$$159 - 144 = 15$$
$$36 \times 4 = 144$$

Appendix

Generic games tools

As I explained at the end of Part I, most of the concrete games which are described in this book require Cuisinaire rods, Base Ten material or plastic money. The 'digits' or 'numbers' which are needed as the basis for performing the specified operations in all of the games, are generated by rolling dice, spinning a spinner, using cards or by using combinations of two of these. As we will see, dice, spinners or cards are largely inter-changeable in many games. However games have a different 'feel' depending on how they are played: a **dice war** feels very different from a **card war**, for example. Some children have their favourite ways of playing games. For example some children 'love' **card wars** and prefer them to **dice wars**. Other children enjoy having as much variety as possible to be built into the selection of games that they play.

Spinners and cards are very flexible games tools. Spinner 'bases' can be drawn on to ordinary A4 paper. Digits, patterns or specific calculations can be written on to individual blank cards. Most games which require *playing cards* (usually, sets of digit cards or *number pattern* cards) require 4 sets of each card. (If more than 5 players are to play a card game, 5 sets of cards are usually required.) For example, a very basic addition card war game would have 4 sets of number cards, numbered 1–6. A slightly harder card war game would have 4 sets of digit cards, numbered 1–10. To play card lotto games, each player requires one set of the cards and each player has the same basic set of cards. For example, each player could have a set of *number pattern* cards. As suggested above, individual calculations, such as 9–5 or 16 ÷ 4, can also be written on individual cards. They can be used, for example, for playing **pelmanism** or for **track games**. Cards of this kind are particularly useful in designing subtraction games and division games, as we will see below.

Dice, too, are very versatile. A large range of dice are now available. To play many of the games which are described in the book, it is useful to have two 1–6 dice, two 0–9 dice, two 1–20 dice, two *tens dice* and two dice, numbered 4–9 or 5–10. Dice can be very easily 'modified' to suit the number requirements of a particular game. For example, the numbers 1–10 are required in a variety of games. Children readily accept that a '0' on a 0–9 dice is to be considered a '10' in that particular game. A 1–6 dice can be 'modified' to become a 1–5 dice by sticking a (temporary) gummed 'dot' over the '6': the '6' can become a 'joker', a '0' or another '4' or '5'. Most children enjoy playing games which include a 'joker' element. 'Jokers' represent any number of a player's choice. (Jokers can be represented very simply by drawing a star (*) or a question mark (?).) A 'joker' can be used to eliminate a 'too easy' calculation on a dice, for example +1 or x 1. Of course, blank dice are also very useful, flexible tools to have.

Generic games descriptions

As I said in the first chapter, a great many of the games which are referred to in this book, are examples of a relatively small number of 'generic games'. To avoid unnecessary repetition in the text, some of the games are described in some detail, here in the Appendix. Where detailed descriptions are given in the text, the games are listed here, and page references are given. It is also hoped that these descriptions will inspire teachers and parents to invent their own versions of the generic games – and, of course, to invent or 'high-jack' other games, as well!

Lotto – 4-in-a-row

Lotto-based games can be played on pre-prepared (possibly laminated) 'playing boards'. They can also be played using digit cards.

Card Lotto

In card lotto games each player has a set of individual *playing* cards. These are often digit cards, which are numbered 1–9 or 1–10. Sometimes they are *number pattern* cards. Each player's cards are laid out in a line, in sequence. When play begins, each player takes it in turn to generate a designated type of problem. One or two dice, a spinner, or a combination of a dice and spinner, are generally used to generate the problem. The *playing* cards relate to the generated problems in one of two ways. In some games the cards represent the *solution*. For example, in a **Facts of 10 game** (see p. 142) a dice roll of '7' requires '3' to make 10 and the '3' digit card is turned over. In other games, however, the cards relate to the *problem* rather than the solution – for example, in a simple but effective **doubles game**, a dice throw of '7' has to be doubled and the player gives the answer 14 but the '7' card in an ordinary row of 1-10 digit cards is turned over. In these particular lotto games, the cards quite intentionally do *not* represent the answers to the problems (for example 14). This is because representing the answers means that the lotto game becomes a game which 'tests' *recognition*, rather than a game which involves *reasoning* and/or *memory*. (Matching 7 + 7 to 14 is much easier than figuring out 14 from a known fact, or remembering it.)

The **times tables lotto game** (see p. 362) is a lotto game in which the cards relate to the tables *problem*. In all **card lotto** games, players take turns to generate a problem and (hopefully) turn over a card. Players 'miss a go' if they have already generated and solved a particular problem: for example, if the player in the doubles game mentioned above rolled another dice '7,' he or she could not roll the dice, again, but would simply miss that 'go'. It is this 'rule' which generates the necessary 'chance' element. It is usual to play that the winner is the player who first succeeds in turning over 4 consecutive cards in a row. One can play card lotto 'to the death' (until a player has managed to turn over a whole sequence of cards) but this can take a very long time, and children tend to become frustrated when they are consistently 'unlucky' at generating a required number.

Board lotto

Board lotto games generally proceed in the same way as the card lotto games, described above. In board lotto the sequence of individual digits, patterns or numbers are drawn on to individual 'playing boards' and each player has his or her own 'board'. (As we have seen, 'boards' can simply comprise photocopies of 'board' masters.) When a player generates an answer to a problem, the player covers the relevant 'number' on his or her 'board'. (The digit can be covered with a token or simply 'crossed out'.) Like card lotto games, board lotto games can be designed to test recognition rather than reasoning skill or memory. This can be useful when children are in the early stages of learning a new set of facts. For example, the 'board' in an early doubles game could represent the doubled outcomes, 2, 4, 6, 8, 10, 12, 14, 16, 18 and 20. In this game a dice roll of 7 would mean that 14 would be covered.

Card wars

Most children particularly enjoy card wars. Like the very versatile lotto games, described above, the card war idea can be adapted to a very wide variety of calculation situations: they are particularly valuable games for reinforcing addition and subtraction facts, and for practising so-called 'string' additions. They are also a very good vehicle for reinforcing work on the *place value* aspect of the written number system. (A **place value card war** is described on p. 203.) Many of the whole number card war games which are referred to in this book can be adapted to working with fractions and decimal numbers. In a card war game for 2–4 players, it is usual to begin play with a 'pack' of cards which comprises 4 or 5 sets of each card in play. The cards are usually individual digit cards. They could also be *number pattern* cards. In a **Bridging-through-ten addition card war**, for example, the pack of cards would contain 4 to 5 sets of the digits 5–9. In this game each player is dealt two cards. Card wars are played in short rounds. In each round, or 'battle', the winner takes all of the cards which have been 'in play' in that particular round, or 'battle.' In card wars the player with the largest number or outcome in each round is usually the winner of that particular battle, although it is also possible that the player with the smallest outcome will win each round. In a **through-ten-addition-war**, each player adds the numbers on the 2 cards which have been dealt to him or her. The player with the biggest *sum* or outcome is the winner of that particular round or 'battle'. If 3 players are playing the **through ten card war**, this will mean that the 'winner' of each 'battle' will take 6 cards. Players should place the cards which they have won into a separate pile. The overall winner is the player with the greatest number of cards at the end of the game (when all the cards have been played). He or she has won most 'battles' and has therefore won the 'war'.

Dice wars

Dice wars are similar to card wars, but players roll the same number of dice in each round. Dice wars work particularly well for addition and subtraction games. They can also be used to practise mixed *tables* knowledge. In a dice war, the winner of each round is awarded a token (for example, a glass nugget) or he or she could be awarded a certain specified number of points (for example, 1 point, 5 points or 10 points). Like card wars it is usual to play that the largest outcome in each round wins the round, but in subtraction games children often prefer an outcome in which the smallest *difference* wins.

In a dice war which is intended to encourage children to look for addition patterns (reinforcing the principle of associativity in addition) each player could roll 4 dice numbered 1–6, or 0–9. After each player has rolled the 4 dice, he or she looks for 'helpful' patterns and finds the total of the dice scores. After a certain number of rounds (for example, 10 rounds) the winner is the player who has earned the greatest number of tokens or the greatest number of points.

Pelmanism or pairs

Pelmanism is a classic 'matching' game which can be adapted to help children overlearn maths facts. To prepare a specific pelmanism game, teachers need to create a set of matching cards. One set of cards contains the *questions* and the other set of cards contains the matching *answers*. It is helpful to distinguish the *question* cards from the *answer* cards in some way – for instance, different colours can be used for the question and answer cards or a star (*) can be drawn on the back of the *answer* cards. The individual *questions* and *answers* are printed onto one side of individual cards. In a mixed *tables* sequence pelmanism game, tables questions from the *selected* tables are written on to *tables question* cards: for example:

$4 \times 4 =$
$6 \times 5 =$

The answers to the tables questions are printed on the *answer cards*. Before play begins, the *question cards* and the *answer cards* are shuffled and are placed face down in two separate clusters of cards. Each player takes it in turn to pick up a question card: for instance $4 \times 4 = $. He or she figures out the answer to the question and then tries to select and pick up the matching pair, in this instance, the '16' card. If the player manages to find the matching pair, the player takes both cards and has another go. If the player picks up a card which does not 'match' the question card, he or she puts both cards back, face down, in their original positions, and it is the turn of another player to have a go. The player who wins the most pairs in the game is the winner.

Although some children love pelmanism, severely dyspraxic children generally do not. This is because dyspraxic children frequently have difficulty remembering the location of the specific card which they require in order to make a 'pair'. If pelmanism is played with dyspraxic children, it is usually best to have a relatively limited number of pairs in play: for example, the most important facts which need to be learned can be targeted and written on just 6–8 pairs of cards.

Track games

Track games which involve moving tokens along a track

1. **'Empty space' track games**: In the most familiar basic track games, players take turns to generate a number and then move a token the relevant number of 'spaces' or 'squares' along a simple 'squared' track. Simple tracks can be 'borrowed' from commercial 'track' games (for example, a **snakes and ladders** board can be used) or they can be drawn on to A3 paper. The player who first reaches the end of the track is the winner. In **'maths' track games**, children have to complete an operation to generate a number. Tracks can be used as the basis for simple addition or *difference* games. The numbers for the operations can be generated by rolling dice, taking digit cards or taking specially prepared 'operation cards': for example, 7 – 4 = ; 3 + 5 = ; 12 ÷ 4 =. If the problem 7 – 4 is generated in this very basic game, the player figures out the outcome (here 3) and then moves 3 spaces along the track. Track games can have penalties or bonuses built into them; for example, instructions such as 'move back 2 spaces' or 'move forwards 5 spaces' can be printed on to some of the squares or on to some of the cards, if cards are being used. Some children enjoy devising simple track games. (Children usually have to be persuaded not to make track games too elaborate!)

2. **Specially prepared numbered tracks**: In these games, teachers take the full range of answers which could be generated in a specific game and write these outcomes three or four times in random order on to each of the squares on a track. For example the full range of outcomes in a basic (to 10) subtraction game would be the numbers 0 – 9. One possible first part of a track game representing these outcomes could be: 0, 6, 7, 3, 2, 6, 4 , 2, 9, 8, 1, 5, 3, 7, 8 ... Specially prepared tracks are a particularly useful way of practicing subtraction and division facts. Dice or digit cards can be used to generate addition or subtraction questions and answers. For example, in a basic subtraction each player could take turns to roll two 0–9 dice (0 = 10); if a player has first rolled '7' and '9', he or she would subtract 7 from 9 and would move his or her token to the first '2' on the track. In the next round, a dice roll of '10' and '6' would mean that the player would move his or

her token to the next '4' on the track. Specially prepared written 'operation' cards can be created to create a limited range of outcomes for all 4 operations. Division games require operation cards because appropriate division questions are hard to generate using 'chance' methods, such as rolling dice. Each player takes it in turns to generate a problem, for example, 36 ÷ 6. The player figures out the answer and moves his or her token to the first square on the track which has '6' written on it. In the next round, if the player generates the problem 54 ÷ 6, he or she will move to the next '9' square on the track. The winner is the player to reach the end of the track, first.

Track accumulation games

1. **Ones-based games**: In the simplest track accumulation games, *ones* are accumulated and placed on simple linear *tens-structured* tracks. For example, glass nuggets can be accumulated from left to right along a structured and squared 'emptier' track to 20 or 30. To make quantity comparisons possible, individual tracks should be drawn directly beneath each other. Simple ones-based track accumulation games help foster *number-sense*. The quantities which each player 'earns' and places along the track can be generated by throwing a dice, taking a digit card or taking a *number pattern* card. A simple track accumulation game is described on p. 94.

2. **Cuisinaire rod track games**: In Cuisinaire rod track games, the values which are generated by the players represent individual rod values which have to be added (or subtracted). Players place rods on to 'emptier', but structured, rod tracks. Rod accumulation games are designed to practise tens-structured calculation; in the book this is also described as *bridging* or *bridging-through-ten* calculation. In **rod accumulation games**, individual rods are not allowed to cross *tens* boundaries. Instead, rods have to be 'broken down' in all through-ten calculation situations. The **basic bridging track accumulation game** is described in detail on p. 220. In **subtraction rod track** games, each player starts out with the same value of rod *tens* which 'cover' a tens structured track; For instance, players may start with rod tracks of 40. Each player takes it in turns to generate a number and a matching value is removed from the track. The player to 'clear' his or her track, first, is the winner. Subtraction track games are described on page 231. Larger through-ten calculations can be played on longer tracks (for example to 50) or on a *100 square*.

3. **Pencil-and-paper track games**: The basic 'quantity accumulation' and 'quantity subtraction' idea can be transferred to 'abstract' or pencil-and-paper versions. A basic pencil-and-paper track game is described on p. 241.
4. **Number-line games**: Pencil-and-paper *cumulative* or *running total* addition and subtraction practice can also take place in the form of *emptier* or *empty number-line* games. **Empty number-line** games are described on p. 297.

Bingo games

Each individual Bingo game has to be specially prepared. In Bingo games each player has a Bingo 'board', usually with 9 or 12 answers written on it. Each player has a largely unique set of outcomes (numbers) which he or she covers with tokens or 'crosses out' when the problem which matches it is generated but a few outcomes should be duplicated on the playing boards of another player. 'Operation cards' are a particularly good way to generate problems in Bingo. For this reason, Bingo games are very well suited to reinforcing children's knowledge of subtraction and division facts. Bingo games can be played according to the 'rule' that all outcomes have to be 'covered' to win; alternatively, a 'row' of 'covered' outcomes may win.

Teaching materials

The addresses of suppliers are provided below. Most suppliers will allow goods to be purchased by credit card or by cheque, and suppliers will usually post them to the purchaser. Most suppliers will sell materials to 'ordinary' customers, as well as to schools and they are usually happy to send a catalogue to prospective purchasers. A supplier is specified if the material is not widely available. Crossbow Educational, Galt and Taskmaster sell maths games.

Crossbow Educational, 8 Causeway Road, Cinderford, Glos. GL14 2BY (spinners)
The Cuisinaire Company, Educational Solutions (UK) Ltd, 11 Crown Street, Reading RG1 2TQ
Galt Materials, UK: James Galt & Co. Ltd, Ruthin Road, Wrexham, Clwyd LL13 7TQ
LDA (Learning Development Aids), Duke Street, Wisbech, Cambs, PE 13 2AE
NES Arnold, Ludlow Hill Road, West Bridgeford, Notts, NG2 6HD
Philip and Tacey, North Way, Andover, Hampshire, SP 10 5BA
Taskmaster Ltd, Morris Street. Leicester. LE2 6BR (100 bead string)

The London Science Museum Shop sells very attractive 1–6, 1–9 and 1–20 dice. Blank cards can also be bought from some 'gift shops' and large newsagents. They are sometimes called 'Calling cards'. Glass nuggets are often labelled 'Decor nuggets'. They are widely used in flower displays and in 'interior design'. They can be purchased in some florists, some toy shops, interior design shops or departments and in many 'gift shops'.

Maths assessment tests

Basic Number Screening Test. For pupils from 7 to 12 years. Hodder & Stoughton.

Graded Arithmetic-Mathematic Test. For pupils from 5 to 12 years. Hodder & Stoughton.

The Informal Assessment of Numeracy Skills. Mark College. For pupils from 8 years old upwards.

Numeracy Impact. NFER-Nelson. For pupils from 8 to 14 years. Available to schools, Education Authorities, etc; not available to members of the general public.

Numeracy Progress Tests. Stage One: for children from 5 to 8 years. Stage Two: for pupils from 7 to 12 years. Hodder & Stoughton.

Profile of Mathematical Skills. NFER Nelson. Stage One for children from 9 to 11 years; see above.

Wide Range Achievement Test (WRAT 3). For pupils from 5 years old upwards. Dyslexia Institute.

Purchasing details of assessment tests

The Dyslexia Institute. 133 Gresham Road, Staines, Middlesex, TW18 2AJ

Hodder & Stoughton. Bookpoint Ltd. 130 Milton Park, Abington. Oxon OX 14 4SB

Mark College. Mark, Highbridge, Somerset, TA9 4NP

NFER-Nelson. Darville House, 2 Oxford Road East, Windsor Berkshire,SL4 1DF

References

Adams JW, Hitch G (1998) Children's mental arithmetic and working memory. In C Donlan (ed.) The Development of Mathematical Skills. Hove, East Sussex: Psychology Press.

Anghileri J (1989) An investigation of young children's understanding of multiplication. Journal for Research in Mathematics Education 20: 367–85

Anghileri J (ed.) (1995a) Children's Mathematical Thinking in the Primary Years. London and New York: Cassell.

Anghileri J (1995b) Focus on thinking. In J. Anghileri (ed.) Children's Maths Thinking in the Primary Years. London and New York: Cassell.

Anghileri J (1995c) Making sense of symbols. In J Anghileri (ed.) Children's Mathematical Thinking in the Primary Years. London and New York: Cassell.

Anghilheri J (1997) Uses of counting in multiplication in multiplication and division. In I Thompson (ed.) Teaching and Learning Early Number. Buckingham: Open University Press.

Anghileri J (1999) Issues in teaching multiplication and division. In I Thompson (ed.) Issues in Teaching Numeracy in Primary Schools. Buckingham: Open University Press.

Ashcraft MH, Kirk EP, Hopko D (1998) On the cognitive consequences of mathematics anxiety in C Donlan (ed.) The Development of Mathematical Skills. Hove, East Sussex: Psychology Press.

Ashlock R (1982) Error Patterns in Computation. Columbus OH : Merrill.

Ashlock R, Johnson M, Jones W (1983) Guiding Each Child's Learning of Mathematics. Columbus OH : Merrill.

Askew M (1999) It ain't (just) what you do: effective teachers of numeracy. In I Thompson (ed.) Issues in Teaching Numeracy in Primary Schools. Buckingham. Open University Press.

Askew M, William D (1995) Recent Research in Mathematics Education 5–16. HMSO.

Aubrey C (1993) An investigation of the mathematical knowledge and competencies which young children bring into school. British Educational Research Journal 19(1): 27–41.

Aubrey C (1997) Children's early learning of number in school and out. In I Thompson (ed.) Teaching and Learning Early Number. Buckingham : Oxford University Press.

Baddeley A (1990) Human Memory: Theory and Practice. Hove, UK and Hillsdale NJ: Erlbaum.

Baroody AJ (1984) Children's difficulties in subtraction: some causes and questions. Journal for Research in Mathematics Education 15(3): 203–13.

Baroody AJ (1990) How and when should place-value concepts and skills be taught? Journal for Research in Mathematcs Education, 4, 281–6.

437

Baroody, AJ (1992) The development of preschooler's counting skills and principles. In J. Bideaud, C. Meljac, J-P Fischer (eds) Pathways to Number: Children's Developing Numerical Abilities. Hillsdale, NJ : Erlbaum.

Baroody AJ, Standifer DJ (1993) Addition and Subtraction in the primary grades. In RJ Jensen (ed) Research Ideas for The Classroom: Early Childhood Mathematics. New York: Simon & Schuster Macmillan.

Bath JB, Knox DE (1984) Two styles of performing mathematics. In JB Bath, SJ Chinn, DE Knox (eds) Dyslexia Research and its Application to the Adolescent. Bath: Better Books.

Bierhoff H (1996) Laying the Foundations of Numeracy: A Comparison of Primary School Textbooks in Britain, Germany and Switzerland. London: The National Institute of Economic and Social Research.

Beishuizen M (1993) Mental strategies and materials or models for addition and subtraction up to 100 in Dutch second grades. Journal for Research in Mathematics Education 24: 294–323.

Beishuizen M (1997) Mental Arithmetic: mental recall or mental strategies? Mathematics Teaching, September: 16-19.

Beishuizen M (1999) The empty number line as a new model. In I Thompson (ed.) Issues in Teaching Numeracy in Primary Classrooms. Buckingham: Open University Press.

Beishuizen M, Anghileri J (1998) Which mental strategies in the early number curriculum? a comparison of British ideas and Dutch views. British Educational Research Journal 24: 518–38.

Bryant P (1997) Mathematical Understanding in the Nursery Years. In T Nunes, P Bryant (eds) Learning and Teaching Mathematics. Hove, East Sussex: Psychology Press.

Bryant P (1999) Sharing and dividing. Paper presented at the Language, Reasoning and Early Mathematical Development at University College London.

Butterworth B (1999) The Mathematical Brain. London: Macmillan.

Cakir T, Saxon M (1999) Tens and ones: children's knowledge of the Base Ten system. Paper presented at the Language, Reasoning and Early Mathematical Development Conference, University College London.

Cannobi KH, Reeve RA, Pattison PE (1998) The role of conceptual understanding in children's addition problem solving. Developmental Psychology 34(5): 882–91.

Carpenter TP, Moser JM (1982) The development of addition and subtraction problem-solving skills. In TP Carpenter, JM Moser, TA Romberg (eds) Addition and Subtraction: a Cognitive Perspective. Hillsdale NJ: Erlbaum.

Carpenter TP, Moser JM (1984) The acquisition of addition and subtraction concepts in Grades 1 through 3. Journal for Research in Mathematics Education 15(3): 179–202.

Carpenter TP, Fennema, Franke ML (1993) Cognitive Guided Instruction: Multiplication and Division. Wisconsin Center for Educational Research, University of Wisconsin Maddison.

Carpenter TP, Franke ML, Jacobs VR et al. (1997) A longitudinal study of intervention and understanding in children's multidigit addition and subtraction. Journal for Research in Mathematics Education 29(1): 3–20.

Carter C, Crawley R, Lewis C (1999a) Children's working memory and achievement in arithmetic. Poster presented at the Language, Reasoning and Early Mathematical Development Conference at University College London.

Carter C, Crawley R, Lewis C (1999b) Children's working memory and achievement in arithmetic (2). A poster presented at the Psy PAG Conference, Lancaster University, July 1999.

Chinn SJ (1991) Factors to consider when designing a test protocol in mathematics for dyslexics. In M Snowling, M Thompson (eds) Dyslexia: Integrating Theory and Practice. London: Whurr.

Chinn SJ (1992) Individual diagnosis and cognitive style. In TR Miles, E Miles (eds) Dyslexia and Mathematics. London: Routledge.

Chinn SJ (1994) A study of the basic number fact skills of children from specialist dyslexic and normal schools. Dyslexia Review 2: 4–6.

Chinn SJ (1995) A Pilot Study to Compare Aspects of Arithmetic Skills. Dyslexia Review 7(1): 4–7.

Chinn SJ (1996) What To Do When You Can't Learn the Times Tables. Baldock: Egon.

Chinn SJ (1999) What To Do When You Can't Do Addition and Subtraction. Baldock: Egon.

Chinn SJ (2000) Dyslexic pupils learning in the Numeracy Strategy. In The Dyslexia Handbook 2000. Reading: The British Dyslexia Association.

Chinn SJ (2002) Numbers and the Numeracy Strategy in secondary schools. In The Dyslexia Handbook 2002. Reading: The British Dyslexia Association.

Chinn SJ, Ashcroft JR (1992) The use of patterns. In TR Miles, E. Miles (eds) Dyslexia and Mathematics. London: Routledge.

Chinn SJ, Ashcroft JR (1998) Mathematics for Dyslexics: A Teaching Handbook. 2nd edn. London: Whurr.

Chinn S, McDonagh D, van Elswijk R et al. (2001) Classroom studies into cognitive style in mathematics for pupils with dyslexia in special education in the Netherlands, Ireland and the UK. British Journal of Special Education 28(2): 80–5.

Clemson D, Clemson W (1994) Mathematics in the Early Years. London: Routledge.

Cobb P, Wood T, Yackel E (1991) Learning through problem -solving: a constructivist approach to second grade mathematics. In E von Glaserfeld (ed) Radical Constructivism in Mathematics Educaation. Dordrecht, The Netherlands: Kluwer. 157–76.

Cobb P, Yackel E, Wood T (1992) Interaction and learning in mathematics classroom situations. Educational Studies in Mathematics Education 2: 99–122.

Cockburn A (1999) Teaching Mathematics with Insight: The Identification, Diagnosis and Remediation of Young Children's Mathematical Errors. London: Falmer Press.

Corte E de, Verschaffel, L (1987) The effect of semantic structure of first-grader's solution strategies of elementary addition and subtraction word problems. Journal for Research in Mathematics Education 18: 363–86.

Corte E de and Verschaffel L (1991) Some factors influencing the solution of addition and subtraction word problems. In K. Durkin, B. Shire (eds) Language in Mathematical Education. Milton Keynes UK and Philadelphia: Open University Press.

Cowan R, Foster CM, Al-Zubaidi AS (1993) Encouraging children to count. British Journal of Developmental Psychology 11: 411–20.

Deboys M, Pitt E (1988) Lines of Development in Primary Mathematics. 3rd edn. Belfast: Blackstaff Press.

Dehaene S (ed) (1993a) Numerical Cognition. Cambridge, MA and Oxford, UK: Blackwell.

Dehaene S (1993b) Varieties of numerical abilities. In S Dehaene (ed) Numerical Cognition. Cambridge, MA and Oxford, UK: Blackwell.

Dehaene S (1997) The Number Sense. London: Penguin Books.

Dehaene S, Spelke E, Pinet R et al. (1999) Sources of mathematical thinking: behavioural and brain-imaging evidence. Science 284: 970–3.

DfEE (Department for Education and Employment) (1998a) The Implementation of the National Numeracy Strategy: The Final Report of the Numeracy Task Force. London: DfEE.

DfEE (Department for Education and Employment) (1998b) Numeracy Matters: The Preliminary Report of the Numeracy Task Force. London: DfEE.

DfEE (Department for Education and Employment) (1999) The National Numeracy Strategy Framework for Teaching Mathematics from Reception to Year 6. London: DfEE.

Donaldson M (1978) Children's Minds. Glasgow: Fontana/Collins.

Donlan C (ed) (1998a) The Development of Mathematical Skills. Hove, East Sussex: Psycholology Press Ltd.

Donlan C (1998b) Number without language? studies of children with specific language impairments. In C. Donlan (ed) The Development of Mathematical Skills. Hove, East Sussex: Psychology Press.

Dowker AD (1995) Children with specific calculation difficulties. Links 2: 7–12.

Dowker AD (1997) Young children's addition estimates. Mathematical Cognition 3: 141–54.

Dowker AD (1998) Individual differences in normal arithmetical development. In C Donlan (ed) The Development of Mathematical Skills. Hove, East Sussex: Psychology Press.

Doyle J (1996) Dyslexia: An Introductory Guide. London: Whurr.

El-Naggar O (1996) Specific Leaning Difficulties in Mathematics: A Classroom Approach. Staffs: NASEN.

Ernest P (ed) (1989) Mathematics Teaching: The State of the Art. Lewes; Falmer Press.

Fawcett A (ed) (2001) Dyslexia and Good Practice. London: Whurr.

Flegg G (1983) Numbers, Their History and Meaning. London: André Deutsch.

Fuson KC (1982) An analysis of the counting on procedure. In T Carpenter, J Moser, T Romberg (eds) Addition and Subtraction: A Cognitive Perspective. Hillsdale NJ: Erlbaum.

Fuson KC (1984) More complexities in subtraction. Journal for Research in Mathematics Education 15(3): 203–13.

Fuson KC (1988) Children's Counting and Concept of Number. New York: Springer Verlag.

Fuson KC (1991) Children's early counting: saying the number-word sequence, counting objects, and understanding cardinality. In K Durkin, B Shire (eds) Language in Mathematical Education. Milton Keynes, UK and Philadelphia: Open University Press.

Fuson KC (1992) Research on learning and teaching addition and subtraction of whole numbers. In G Leinhardt, R Putman, RA Hattrup (eds) Analysis of Arithmetic for Mathematics Teaching. Hillsdale, NJ: Erlbaum.

Fuson KC, Hall JW (1983) The acquisition of early number word meaning: a conceptual analysis and review. In Ginsberg HP (ed) The Development of Mathematical Thinking. London and New York: Academic Press.

Fuson KC, Willis GB (1988) Subtracting by counting up: more evidence. Journal for Research in Mathematics Education 19(5): 402–20.

Fuson KC, Briars D (1990) Using a base-ten blocks learning/teaching approach for first and second-grade place-value and multi-digit addition and subtraction. Journal for Research in Mathematics Education 21: 180–206.

Fuson KC, Kwon Y (1991) Chinese-based regular and European irregular systems of number words: the disadvantages for English speaking children. In K Durkin, B Shire (eds) Language in Mathematical Education. Milton Keynes, UK and Philadelphia: Open University Press.

Fuson KC, Fuson C (1992) Instruction supporting children's counting on for addition and counting up for subtraction. Journal for Research in Mathematics Education 23: 72–8.

Fuson KC, Richards J, Briars DJ (1982) The acquisition and elaboration of the number word sequence. In CJ Brainerd (ed) Children's Logical and Mathematical Cognition: Progress in Cognitive Development Research .New York: Springer Verlag.

Fuson KC, Smith ST, LoCicero AM (1997) Supporting Latino first-graders' ten structures thinking in urban classrooms. Journal of Research in Mathematics Education 28: 738–66.

Fuson KC, Wearne D, Hiebert JC et al. (1997) Children's conceptual structures for multidigit numbers and methods of multidigit addition and subtraction. Journal for Research in Mathematics Education 28(2): 136–62.

Freudenthal H (1973) Mathematics as an Educational Task. Dordecht: Reidel.

Gelman R, Gallistel CR (1978) The Child's Understanding of Number. Cambridge MA: Harvard University Press.

Gelman R, Meck E (1986) The notion of principle: the case of counting. In J Hiebert (ed) Conceptual Knowledge and Procedural Knowledge: The Case of Mathematics. Hillsdale, NJ: Lawrence Erlbaum Associates.

Ginsberg HP (1981) Learning difficulties. In A. Floyd (ed) Developing Mathematical Thinking. Wokingham: Addison Wesley Publishers in association with The Open University.

Ginsburg HP (ed) (1983) The Development of Mathematical Thinking. London and New York: Academic Press.

Ginsberg HP, Baron J (1993) Cognition: Young Children's Construction of Mathematics. In RJ Jensen (ed) Research Ideas for the Classroom. New York: Simon & Schuster Macmillan.

Grauberg E (1998) Elementary Mathematics and Language Difficulties: London. Whurr.

Gravemeijer K (1994) Educational development and development research in mathematics education. Journal for Research in Mathematics Education 25(5): 443–71.

Gravemeijer K (1997) Mediating between concrete and abstract. In T Nunes, P Bryant (eds) Learning and Teaching Mathematics: An International Perspective. Hove, East Sussex: Psychology Press.

Gray E (1991) An analysis of diverging approaches to simple arithmetic preference and its consequences. Educational Studies in Mathematics 22(6): 551–74.

Gray E (1997) Compressing the counting process: developing a flexible interpretation of symbols. In I Thompson (ed) Teaching and Early Number. Buckingham: Open University Press.

Gray E, Tall DO (1993) Success and failure in mathematics: the flexible meaning of symbols as process and concept. Mathematics Teaching 142: 6–10.

Gray E, Tall DO (1994) Duality, ambiguity and flexibility: a proceptual view of simple arithmetic. Journal for Research in Mathematics Education 25(2): 116–40.

Greer B (1992) Multiplication and division as models of situations. In DA Grouws (ed) Handbook of Research on Mathematics Teaching and Learning. New York: Macmillan.

Harries T, Sutherland R (1999) Primary school mathematics textbooks: an international comparison. In I Thompson (ed) Issues in Teaching Numeracy in Primary Schools. Buckingham: Open University Press.

Hart K (1978) Children's Understanding of Mathematics. London: John Murray.

Hart K (1989) There is little connection. In P Ernest (ed) Mathematics Teaching: The State of the Art. Lewes: Falmer Press.

Haylock D (1991) Teaching Mathematics to Low Attainers. London: Paul Chapman

Haylock D (1995) Mathematics Explained for Primary Teachers. London : Paul Chapman

Haylock D, Cockburn A (1989) Understanding Early Years Mathematics. London: Paul Chapman.

Heaton P, Winterson P (eds) (1996) Dealing with Dyslexia. London: Whurr.

Henderson A (1989) Maths and Dyslexics. Llandudno: St David's College.

Henderson A (1998) Maths for the Dyslexic: A Practical Guide. London: David Fulton.

Henderson A, Miles E (2001) Basic Topics in Mathematics for Dyslexics. London: Whurr.

Hiebert J (ed) (1986) Conceptual Knowledge and Procedural Knowledge: The Case of Mathematics. Hilsdale NJ: Lawrence Erlbaum Associates.

Hiebert J, Carpenter TP, Fennema E et al. (1997) Making Sense: Teaching and Learning Mathematics with Understanding. Portsmouth: Heinemann.

Hopkins C, Gifford S, Pepperell S (1996) Mathematics in the Primary School: A Sense of Progression. London: David Fulton.

Hughes M (1986) Children and Number. Oxford and New York: Blackwell.

Hughes M, Desforges C, Mitchell C (1999) Using and applying mathematics at Key Stage 1. In I Thompson (ed) Issues in Teaching Numeracy in Primary Schools Buckingham: Open University Press.

Hughes M, Desforges C, Mitchell C (2000) Numeracy and Beyond: Applying Mathematics in the Primary School. Buckingham: Open University Press.

Jaworski B (1994) Investigating Mathematics Teaching: A Constructivist Enquiry. London. Falmer Press.

Jensen RJ (ed) (1993) Research Ideas for the Classroom: Early Mathematics. New York: Simon & Schuster Macmillan.

Joffe L (1983a) Dyslexia and attainment in school mathematics: Part 2, Error types and remediation. Dyslexia Review 3(2): 12–18.

Joffe L (1983b) School mathematics and dyslexia ... a matter of verbal labelling, generalisation, horses and carts. Cambridge Journal of Education 13(3): 22–7.

Johnson M, Peer L (eds) (2002) The Dyslexia Handbook, 2002. Reading: The British Dyslexia Association.

Kamii CK (1985) Young Children Reinvent Arithmetic. New York: Teachers College Press.

Kamii CK (1989) Young Children Continue to Re-invent Arithmetic. Second Grade. New York: Teachers College Press.

Klein AS, Beishuizen M, Treffers A (1998) The empty number line in Dutch second grades: realistic versus gradual program design. Journal for Research in Mathematics Education 29: 443–64.

Koshy V (1999) Effective Teaching of Numeracy; For the National Mathematics Framework. Oxford: Hodder & Stoughton.

Kouba VL (1989) Children's solution strategies for equivalent set multiplication and division word problems. Journal for Research in Mathematics Education 20(2): 147–58.

Kouba VL, Franklin K (1993) Multiplication and Division: Sense Making and Meaning. In RJ Jensen (ed) Research Ideas for the Classroom: Early Childhood Mathematics. New York: Simon & Schuster Macmillan.

Lampert M (1990) When the problem is not the question and the solution is not the answer: mathematical knowing and teaching. American Education Research Journal 27: 29–63.

Liebeck P (1984) How Children Learn Mathematics. London: Penguin Books.

Macaruso P, Sokol SM (1998) Cognitive neuropsychology and developmental dyscalculia. In C Donlan (ed) The Development of Mathematical Skills. Hove, East Sussex: Psychology Press.

McIntosh A (1981) Learning their tables: a suggested reorientation. In A Floyd (ed) Developing Mathematical Thinking. Wokingham: Addison-Wesley Publishers in association with the Open University Press.

Mackay D (1995) Investigational starting points and children's thinking. In J Anghileri (ed) Children's Maths Thinking in the Primary Years. London and New York: Cassell.

Maclellan E (1997) The importance of counting. In I Thompson (ed) Teaching and Early Number. Buckingham: Open University Press.

Miles E (1983) Dyslexia :The Pattern of Difficulties. Oxford: Blackwell.

Miles T (1993) The Pattern of Difficulties, 2nd edn. London: Whurr.

Miles T, Miles E (eds) (1992) Dyslexia and Mathematics. London: Routledge.

Mulligan JT, Mitchelmore MC (1997) Young Children's Intuitive Models of Multiplication and Division. Journal for Research in Mathematics Education 28(3): 309–30.

Munn P (1997a) Children's beliefs about counting. In I Thompson (ed) Teaching and Early Number. Buckingham: Open University Press.

Munn P (1997b) Symbolic Function in Pre-schoolers. In C Donlan (ed) The Development of Mathematical Skills. Hove: Psychology Press.

Munn P (1997c) Writing and Number. In I Thompson (ed) Teaching and Early Number: Buckingham: Open University Press.

Nickson M (2000) Teaching and Learning Mathematics: A Teacher's Guide to Recent Research and its Application. London and New York: Cassell.

Nunes T, Schliemann AD, Carraher DW (1993) Street Mathematics and School Mathematics. Cambridge: Cambridge University Press.

Nunes T, Bryant P (1996) Children Doing Mathematics. Oxford: Blackwell.

Nunes T, Bryant P (eds) (1997) Learning and Teaching Mathematics: An International Perspective. Hove: Psychology Press.

Nunes T, Moreno C (1998) Is hearing impairment a cause of difficulties in learning mathematics? In C Donlan (ed) The Development of Mathematical Skills. Hove: Psychology Press.

Ott P (1997) How to Manage and Detect Dyslexia: A Reference and Resource Manual. London: Heinemann.

Outhred LN, Mitchelmore MC (2000) Young children's intuitive understanding of rectangular measurement. Journal for Research in Mathematics Education 31(2): 144–67.

Payne JN, Huinker DM (1993) Early Number and Numeration. In RJ Jensen (ed) Research Ideas for the Classroom. New York: Simon & Schuster Macmillan.

Plunkett S (1979) Decomposition and all that rot. Mathematics in School 8(3): 2–5.

Polya G (1990) How To Solve It. London: Penguin Books.

Portwood M (1996) Developmental Dyspraxia, Identification and Intervention: A Manual for Parents and Professionals. London: David Fulton.

Portwood M (2000) Understanding Developmental Dyspraxia: A Textbook for Students and Professionals. London: David Fulton.

Poustie J (2001) Mathematics Solutions: An Introduction to Dyscalculia. Taunton: Next Generation.

Pritchard RA, Miles TR, Chinn SJ, Taggart AT (1989) Dyslexia and knowledge of the number facts. Links 14(3).

Resnick L (1983) A developmental theory of number understanding. In H Ginsberg (ed) The Development of Mathematical Thinking. London: Academic Press, 109–57.

Reynolds D, Muijs D (1999) Numeracy matters: contemporary policy issues in the teaching of mathematics. In I Thompson (ed) Issues in Teaching Numeracy in Primary Classrooms. Buckingham: Open University Press.

Riley M, Greeno JG, Heller JI (1983) Development of children's problem solving ability in arithmetic. In Ginsberg HP (ed) The Development of Mathematical Thinking. New York and London: Academic Press.

Rittle-Johnson B, Siegler RS (1998) The relationship between conceptual and procedural knowledge in learning mathematics. In C Donlan (ed) The Development of Mathematical Skills. Hove: Psychology Press.

Rowland T (1995) Between the lines: the language of mathematics. In J Anghileri (ed) Children's Thinking in the Primary Years. London and New York: Cassell.

Schaeffer B, Eggleston VH, Scott JL (1974) Number development in young children. Cognitive Psychology 6: 357–79.

Schmidt WH, McKnight CC, Valverde GA et al. (1997) Many Visions, Many Aims, Vol. 1: A Cross-National Investigation of Curricular Intentions in School Mathematics. London: Kluwer Academic Press.

Sharma MC (1981a) Pattern recognition and its applications to mathematics. Math Notebook 2(8 & 9).

Sharma MC (1981b) Visual clustering and number conceptualisation. Math Notebook 2(10).

Sharma MC (1985) Reversal problems in maths and their remediation. Math Notebook 6: 1–20.

Sharma MC (1986) Dyscalculia and other learning problems in arithmetic: a historical perspective. Focus on Learning Problems in Mathematics 8 (3 & 4): 7–45.

Sharma MC (1987) Reversal problems in mathematics and their remediation. Math Notebook 5(6 & 7).

Sharma MC (1987) How to take a child from concrete to abstract. Math Notebook 5(8, 9 & 10).

Sharma MC (1988a) Division: how to teach it? Math Notebook 6(3 & 4).

Sharma MC (1988b) Ontogeny takes over phylogeny: how do we learn arithmetic? Math Notebook 6(7 & 8).

Sharma MC (1988c) Levels of knowing mathematics. Math Notebook 6: 1–2

Sharma MC (1989a) Mathematics Learning Personality. Math Notebook 7: 1–2.

Sharma MC (1989b) Games and their uses in mathematics learning. Math Notebook 7(3 & 4).

Sharma MC (1990a) Basic skills: development of number concepts 2. Math Notebook 8(3 & 4).

Sharma MC (1990b) Concept of number. Math Notebook 8(1 & 2).

Sharma MC (1990c) Dyslexia, dyscalculia, and some remedial perspectives for mathematics learning problems. Math Notebook 8(7, 8, 9 & 10).

Sharma MC (1993a) Cuisinaire rods and mathematics teaching. Math Notebook 10(3 & 4).

Sharma MC (1993b) Place value concept: how children learn it and how to teach it. Math Notebook 10(1 & 2).

Silver EA (1992) Referential mappings and the solution of division story problems involving remainders. Focus on Learning Problems in Mathematics 14(3): 29–39.

Skemp R (1971) Mathematics in the Primary School. London: Penguin

Skemp R (1989) Mathematics in the Primary School. London: Routledge

Smythe I (ed) (2000) The Dyslexia Handbook, 2000. Reading: The British Dyslexia Association.

Snowling M, Thompson M (eds) (1991) Dyslexia: Integrating Theory and practice. London: Whurr.

Sophian C (1996) Children's Numbers. Oxford: Westview Press.

Sophian C (1997) A developmental perspective on children's counting. In C Donlan (ed) The Development of Mathematical Skills. Hove: Psychology Press.

Squire S, Correa J, Bryant P (1999) Young children's understanding of division. Paper presented at the Language, Reasoning and Early Mathematics Development Conference, UCL.

Steeves, KJ (1983) Memory as a factor in the computational efficiency of dyslexic children with high abstract reasoning ability. Annals of Dyslexia 33: 141–52.

Sugarman I (1997) Teaching for strategies. In I Thompson (ed) Teaching and Learning Early Number. Buckingham: Open University Press.

Straker A (1999) The National Numeracy Project: 1996–1999. In I Thompson (ed) Issues in Teaching Numeracy in Primary School Classrooms. Buckingham: Open University Press.

Thompson I (1994) Young children's idiosyncratic written algorithms for addition. Educational Studies in Mathematics 26(4): 323–25.

Thompson I (1997a) Developing young children's counting skills. In I Thompson (ed) Teaching and Learning Early Number. Buckingham: Open University Press.

Thompson I (1997b) Mental and written algorithms: can the gap be bridged? In I Thompson (ed) Teaching and Learning Early Number. Buckingham: Open University Press.

Thompson I (1997c) The role of counting in fact derived strategies. In I Thompson (ed) Teaching and Learning Early Number. Buckingham: Open University Press.

Thompson I (ed) (1997d) Teaching and Learning Early Number. Buckingham: Open University Press.

Thompson I (1999a) Getting your head around mental calculation in I. Thompson (ed) Issues in Teaching Numeracy in Primary Schools. Buckingham: Open University Press.

Thompson I (ed) (1999b) Issues in Teaching Numeracy in Primary Schools. Buckingham: Open University Press.

Thompson I (1999c) Written methods of calculation. In I. Thompson (ed) Issues in Teaching Numeracy in Primary Schools. Buckingham: Open University Press.

Thompson I, Smith F (1999) Mental Calculation Strategies for the Addition and Subtraction of 2-digit Numbers. Final Report, Funded by the Nuffield Foundation. Department of Education, University of Newcastle.

Tirosh D, Graeber AO (1990) Inconsistencies in preservice elementaty teachers' beliefs about multiplication and division. Focus on Learning Problems in Mathematics 12(3 & 4): 65–74.

Towse J, Saxton M (1998) Mathematics across national boundaries: cultural and linguistic perspectives on numerical competence. In C. Donlan (ed) The Development of Mathematical Skills. Hove: Psychology Press.

Treffers A, Beishuizen M (1999) Realistic mathematics education in the Netherlands. In I Thompson (ed) Issues in Teaching Numeracy in Primary Schools. Buckingham: Open University Press.

Turner M (1997) Psychological Assessment of Dyslexia. London: Whurr.

Van den Heuvel-Panhuizen, M (1999) Context problems and assessment: ideas from the Netherlands. In I Thompson (ed) Issues in Teaching Numeracy in Primary Schools. Buckingham: Open University Press.

Van de Walle J, Bowman Watkins K (1993) Early development of number sense. In JP Jensen (ed) Research Ideas for the Classroom: Early Childhood Mathematics. New York: Simon & Schuster Macmillan.

Verschaffel L, Corte E de (1997) Word problems: a vehicle for promoting authentic mathematical understanding and problem solving in the primary school? In T Nunes, P Bryant (eds) Learning and Teaching Mathematics: An International Perspective. Hove: Psychology Press.

Von Glaserfeld E (ed) (1991) Radical Constructivism in Mathematics Education. Dordrecht: Kluwer Academic Press.

Whitebread D (1995) Emergent mathematics or how to help young children become confident mathematicians. In J Anghileri (ed) Children's Maths Thinking in the Primary Years. London and New York: Cassell.

Wigley A (1997) Approaching number through language. In I Thompson (ed) Teaching and Learning Number. Buckingham: Open University Press.

Wynn K (1992) Addition and subtraction in human infants. Nature 358: 749–50.

Wynn K (1998) Numerical competence in infants. In C Donlan (ed) The Development of Mathematical Skills. Hove: Psychology Press.

Yeo D (2002) Newer approaches to teaching maths to primary children. In M. Johnson, L Peer (eds) The Dyslexia Handbook 2002. Reading: The British Dyslexia Association.

Note: papers by Mahesh Sharma (and teaching videos, details of short training courses etc.) are available through Berkshire Mathematics, tel: 0118 9483476. fax: 0118 9461574.

Index